MW00652828

RACE, REMOVAL, AND THE RIGHT TO REMAIN

RACE, REMOVAL, AND THE RIGHT TO REMAIN

Migration and the Making of the United States

SAMANTHA SEELEY

Published by the
OMOHUNDRO INSTITUTE OF
EARLY AMERICAN HISTORY AND CULTURE,
Williamsburg, Virginia,
and the
UNIVERSITY OF NORTH CAROLINA PRESS,
Chapel Hill

The Omohundro Institute of
Early American History and Culture (OI)
is sponsored by William & Mary.
On November 15, 1996, the OI adopted the present name
in honor of a bequest from Malvern H. Omohundro, Jr.,
and Elizabeth Omohundro

© 2021 The Omohundro Institute of Early American History and Culture
All rights reserved
Manufactured in the United States of America

Cover illustration: Details from Mathew Carey, "The Middle States and Western Territories of the United States Including the Seat of the Western War," 1812. From Carey, *A General Atlas, Being a Collection of Maps of the World and Quarters . . .* (Philadelphia, 1814), Plate 6. Edward E. Ayer Collection, Special Collections, the Newberry, Chicago.

Library of Congress Cataloging-in-Publication Data
Names: Seeley, Samantha, author. | Omohundro Institute of Early American History & Culture, issuing body.
Title: Race, removal, and the right to remain : migration and the making of the United States / Samantha Seeley.
Description: Williamsburg, Virginia : Omohundro Institute of Early American History and Culture ; Chapel Hill : University of North Carolina Press, [2021] | Includes bibliographical references and index.
Identifiers: LCCN 2021007915 | ISBN 9781469664811 (cloth) | ISBN 9781469664828 (ebook)
Subjects: LCSH: Forced migration—United States—History. | Migration, Internal—United States—History. | Indians of North America—Relocation—United States. | African Americans—Relocation. | United States—Race relations—History.
Classification: LCC HB1965 .S64 2021 | DDC 304.80973/09033—dc23
LC record available at https://lccn.loc.gov/2021007915

The University of North Carolina Press has been a
member of the Green Press Initiative since 2003.

For Susan and George

and for Geoff

CONTENTS

ILLUSTRATIONS

FIGURES

MAPS

ABBREVIATIONS

ASCP — Arthur St. Clair Papers, Ohio History Connection Archives and Library, Columbus (microfilm edition)

ASPIA — *American State Papers; Class II, Indian Affairs,* I–II (1832; rpt., Buffalo, N.Y., 1997–1998)

AWP — Anthony Wayne Papers, Historical Society of Pennsylvania, Philadelphia

BHC — Burton Historical Collection, Detroit Public Library, Michigan

BL — British Library, London

CJGS — E. A. Cruikshank, ed., *The Correspondence of Lieut. Governor John Graves Simcoe, with Allied Documents relating to His Administration of the Government of Upper Canada,* 5 vols. (Toronto, 1923–1931)

CL — William L. Clements Library, University of Michigan, Ann Arbor

DHS — Delaware Historical Society, Wilmington

DPA — Delaware Public Archives, Dover

EAID — Alden T. Vaughan, ed., *Early American Indian Documents: Treaties and Laws, 1607–1789,* 20 vols. (Washington, D.C., 1979–2004)

ECQA — Friends Collection and College Archives, Earlham College, Earlham, Indiana

FHL — Friends Historical Library, Swarthmore College, Swarthmore, Pennsylvania

HL — Huntington Library, San Marino, California

HQC — Quaker and Special Collections, Haverford College Libraries, Haverford, Pennsylvania

HSP — Historical Society of Pennsylvania, Philadelphia

IHS — Indiana Historical Society, Indianapolis

ISL — Indiana State Library, Indianapolis

JCC — Worthington Chauncey Ford et al., eds., *Journals of the Continental Congress, 1774–1789,* 34 vols. (Washington, D.C., 1904–1937)

JHP — Josiah Harmar Papers, William L. Clements Library, Ann Arbor, Michigan

LOC — Library of Congress, Washington, D.C.

LVA	Library of Virginia, Richmond
MHS	Massachusetts Historical Society, Boston
MPHC	*Collections and Researches Made by the Pioneer and Historical Society of the State of Michigan*
NARA	National Archives and Records Administration, Washington D.C.
NL	Newberry Library, Chicago
NYPL	New York Public Library, New York, New York
OHC	Ohio History Connection Archives and Library, Columbus
OSEC	Office of the Speaker, Executive Communications, Library of Virginia, Richmond
PGW	*The Papers of George Washington*
TNA	The National Archives, Kew, U.K.
TPP	Timothy Pickering Papers, Massachusetts Historical Society, Boston (microfilm edition)
TPUS	Clarence Edwin Carter, ed., *The Territorial Papers of the United States,* 28 vols. (Washington, D.C.—)
VLP	Legislative Petitions of the General Assembly, 1776–1865, Library of Virginia, Richmond
VMHC	Virginia Museum of History and Culture, Richmond
WHH	William Henry Harrison Papers, Newberry Library, Chicago (microfilm edition; originals at Indiana Historical Society, Indianapolis, Indiana)
WRHS	Western Reserve Historical Society, Cleveland, Ohio
YUA	Manuscripts and Archives, Yale University Library, New Haven, Connecticut

RACE, REMOVAL, AND THE RIGHT TO REMAIN

INTRODUCTION

Free movement looms large as the defining story of the early national United States. Thousands of people took to the roads after the American Revolution to claim North American lands as their own or to seek out new opportunities in the nation's growing cities and towns. The story of migrants and immigrants on the move is part of the fabric of U.S. history. The idea of free movement has informed national myths and national policy. Yet many eastern North Americans experienced the early national period, not as one of free movement, but of removal.

This was true for Shawnee leader Kekewepellethe, who in 1786 summarized Shawnee opposition to U.S. demands for Native land, telling federal representatives that "God gave us this country, we do not understand measuring out the lands, it is all ours." Federal and state governments pursued removal against Native people across the new nation, but they made a concerted effort to dispossess Indigenous people north of the Ohio River. In 1791, George Washington told Miami emissaries that if they did not agree to land cessions, "Your doom must be sealed forever."[1]

While Kekewepellethe negotiated with federal agents, the Free African Union Society of Providence, Rhode Island—an African American mutual aid society—followed news of Sierra Leone, a West African colony for emancipated refugees of the American Revolution organized by British abolitionists in 1787. Society members hoped that Sierra Leone might give them "a portion of Land and the right of Citizenship," both of which were "denied them in America." Even after members of the society lost interest in Sierra Leone in the 1790s, some white Americans continued to pursue colonization as a scheme to whiten the nation. By the turn of the nineteenth century, Virginia governor John Page pressed his state's legislature to sponsor a colonization plan or to give free African Americans "some inducement to

1. "Gen. Butler's Journal, Continued," Jan. 30, [1786], in Neville B. Craig, ed., *The Olden Time, a Monthly Publication . . .*, II (Pittsburgh, Pa., 1848), 522 ("God"); "The Message of the President of the United States to the Miami Indians," Mar. 11, 1791, TPP, LX, 41 ("Your").

leave the country." State legislatures across the South and the mid-Atlantic followed suit by making it difficult for free African Americans to live, work, or travel within and across state borders.[2]

Removal was one of the most enduring answers to social challenges in the Anglo-Atlantic world. It accompanied U.S. nation building. It took different forms—violent expulsion, voluntary departure, or coerced relocation. Legislators, reformers, intellectuals, and ordinary people proposed removal as a solution to the major debates of the post-Revolutionary period—debates over political disaffection, land hunger, war debts, and the limits of slavery, emancipation, and citizenship. Amid the upheavals of the late eighteenth century, eastern North America's diverse inhabitants were united in their determination to control territory and belonging by managing people and their movements. For the United States, that determination was particularly important. This book shows how, in the years after the American Revolution, the states and the federal government tried to exclude groups of people from the nation. Interrogating the roots of removal in the early United States recasts the story of the early Republic. Removal, as much as free migration, made the United States, by defining who should be part of it.[3]

The term *removal* is usually applied to the antebellum period. During Georgia's campaign to dispossess the Cherokees, the 1830 Indian Removal Act made the expulsion of eastern Native people beyond the Mississippi River federal policy. A little more than a decade earlier, southern slaveholders and northern reformers founded the American Colonization Society (ACS) to raise funds to send free Black men and women to a colony on the west coast of Africa called Liberia. More than ten thousand African Americans went to Liberia under the auspices of the ACS by force or by choice between 1820 and 1860. Eighty thousand Native Americans were displaced from their homelands east of the Mississippi River in the same

2. Zachary Macaulay to the Honorable the Chairman and Directors of the Sierra Leone Company, Jan. 31, 1795, CO 268/5/16, TNA ("portion"); John Page to the Speaker of the House of Delegates, Dec. 10, 1805, OSEC, box 9, folder 34 ("some inducement").

3. For the entire early national era as one of removal, see James H. Merrell, "American Nations, Old and New: Reflections on Indians and the Early Republic," in Frederick E. Hoxie, Ronald Hoffman, and Peter J. Albert, eds., *Native Americans and the Early Republic* (Charlottesville, Va., 1999), 350–353; Stuart Banner, *How the Indians Lost Their Land: Law and Power on the Frontier* (Cambridge, Mass., 2007), 191–192; Nicholas Guyatt, *Bind Us Apart: How Enlightened Americans Invented Racial Segregation* (New York, 2016); John P. Bowes, *Land Too Good for Indians: Northern Indian Removal* (Norman, Okla., 2016), 4, 8–9, 17.

period. These familiar experiences of expulsion did not emerge suddenly in the 1820s and 1830s. Such projects proceeded rapidly and with devastating effects because they had been tried in more diffuse ways for decades beforehand. Different plans had long urged the removal of both Native Americans and African Americans from the states and the nation. Those plans were important to the formation of the United States from its inception.[4]

This book follows early national removal policies outside the walls of the council house, the offices of the War Department, and the doors of the state legislatures into the communities and homes of everyday people. It presents the experiences of Native Americans and African Americans in parallel to show how white Americans used exclusion to shape the racial geography of the nation. Connecting Native American and African American history also reveals that Indigenous and Black people were decisive participants in determining what kind of nation the United States would become. They shifted policy with their actions—by petitioning, going to court, cultivating new alliances and patrons, or waging war. Even individual choices to move or remain underscored the tenuousness of federal and state efforts to remove people from their homes or homelands. Free African Americans and Native Americans were "founding critics" of the nation who pushed back against removal as an idea and as policy. Most important, they pressed for the right to remain in place, arguing that a permanent home lay at the crux of freedom or sovereignty. Their responses helped to define both removal policy and the membership and borders of the nation itself.[5]

In 1785, a white migrant named John Emerson crossed north of the Ohio River and pinned a manifesto to a tree declaring that "all mankind agreeable to every constitution formed in America have an undoubted right to pass into any vacant country." Emerson celebrated his ability to go into "vacant country" and to take it for himself. He called on a "right to pass," invoking a long-standing Anglo-American tradition celebrated by seventeenth- and eighteenth-century writers of proclaiming one's rights in order to protect them. In the decades after the Revolution, migrants like Emerson believed

4. Eric Burin, *Slavery and the Peculiar Solution: A History of the American Colonization Society* (Gainesville, Fla., 2005), 170; Sean Wilentz, *The Rise of American Democracy: Jefferson to Lincoln* (New York, 2006), 425; Claudio Saunt, *Unworthy Republic: The Dispossession of Native Americans and the Road to Indian Territory* (New York, 2020), 42, 81.

5. For "founding critics," see Manisha Sinha, *The Slave's Cause: A History of Abolition* (New Haven, Conn., 2016), 131.

that free movement and access to Native lands were just rewards for a long and difficult war.[6]

Roads filled with people who turned their backs on the Atlantic and headed for the Appalachian Mountains were the wonder and pride of early national writers. Both foreign and domestic observers saw American migration as exceptional, likening it to "a species of mania" and a force of nature. Migrants were "Kentucky mad," wrote Baptist minister Morgan John Rhees. In 1782, French-born New Yorker J. Hector St. John de Crèvecoeur marveled at the extraordinary movement of Americans and "the boldness the undiffidence with which these new settlers scatter themselves, here and there in the bosom of such an extensive country, without even a previous path to direct their steps." Fifty years later, Alexis de Tocqueville could still wonder at "the avidity with which the American" moved west. "Ahead of him lies a continent virtually without limit, yet he seems already afraid that room may run out, and makes haste lest he arrive too late." The "spirit of emigration" that drove population growth seemed vital to U.S. nationalism.[7]

Migration is essential to understanding the early United States, though not in the way that Crèvecoeur or Tocqueville imagined it. Over the past fifty years, historians have asked readers to look east from the interior of North America to understand Euro-American migration as an invasion of Native homelands. They have reinterpreted the colonial period from the perspective of the enslaved, highlighting the experience of the Middle Passage for African captives and the scale of Native American bondage. They have shown how coverture limited women's property rights and thus also their ability to control where and when they moved. Forced migrants con-

6. John Emerson, "Advertisement," Mar. 12, 1785, JHP, II (quotations). For a discussion of popular rights traditions, see Hannah Weiss Muller, *Subjects and Sovereign: Bonds of Belonging in the Eighteenth-Century British Empire* (New York, 2017), 46–79.

7. John T. Griffith, *Rev. Morgan John Rhys, "The Welsh Baptist Hero of Civil and Religious Liberty of the 18th Century"* (Lansford, Pa., 1899), 115 ("species"); Morgan John Rhees, "Diary of Tour of United States," "Original Diary," Aug. 4, 1795, Morgan J. Rhees Papers, box 1, Rare Book and Manuscript Library, Columbia University, New York ("Kentucky mad"); J. Hector St. John de Crèvecoeur, *Letters from an American Farmer and Other Essays,* ed. Dennis D. Moore (Cambridge, Mass., 2013), 262 ("boldness"); Alexis de Tocqueville, *Democracy in America,* trans. Arthur Goldhammer (New York, 2004), 326 ("avidity"); Arthur St. Clair to John Jay, Dec. 13, 1788, ASCP, box 2, folder 6 ("spirit"). Scholars who have also emphasized the restlessness of Americans include Daniel J. Boorstin, *The Americans: The National Experience* (New York, 1965), 49–112; Robert H. Wiebe, *The Opening of American Society: From the Adoption of the Constitution to the Eve of Disunion* (New York, 1984), 147, 324–327, 330; Bernard Bailyn, *Voyagers to the West: A Passage in the Peopling of America on the Eve of the Revolution* (New York, 1986).

nected the Atlantic world, planted the North American colonies, and built the United States. Whether historians have interpreted movement as free or forced, it has always been at the center of U.S. history.[8]

Migration was not spontaneous. The federal government and the states shaped and encouraged it. Veterans of the American Revolution saw unchecked movement as the spoils of war because the states recruited them into military service by promising enlistment bounties paid in land. Northern legislatures limited free African American migration by threatening to arrest and exile those who crossed state lines. Speculators became rich buying up lands in the trans-Appalachian West because they kept company with powerful men in government who speculated themselves.

Men and women who moved tore the bonds of family to threads and pulled at the fabric of the communities they left behind. They transformed the map of the nation with every road traveled. Within seven years of the ratification of the Constitution, thousands of enslaved and free people had laid out three new states—Vermont, Kentucky, and Tennessee—on Abenaki, Shawnee, Cherokee, and Chickasaw homelands. By the 1830s, the number of "slave" and "free" states in the union had doubled from thirteen to twenty-six. That doubling was the result of choices made by individuals

8. For "facing east," see Daniel K. Richter, *Facing East from Indian Country: A Native History of Early America* (Cambridge, Mass., 2003). For invasion, see, for example, Jean M. O'Brien, *Dispossession by Degrees: Indian Land and Identity in Natick, Massachusetts, 1650–1790* (Lincoln, Neb., 2003); Alan Taylor, *The Divided Ground: Indians, Settlers, and the Northern Borderland of the American Revolution* (New York, 2006); Banner, *How the Indians Lost Their Land;* Susan Sleeper-Smith, *Indigenous Prosperity and American Conquest: Indian Women of the Ohio River Valley, 1690–1792* (Williamsburg, Va., and Chapel Hill, N.C., 2018). For the Middle Passage, see, for example, Alexander X. Byrd, *Captives and Voyagers: Black Migrants across the Eighteenth-Century British Atlantic World* (Baton Rouge, La., 2008); Marcus Rediker, *The Slave Ship: A Human History* (New York, 2007); Stephanie E. Smallwood, *Saltwater Slavery: A Middle Passage from Africa to American Diaspora* (Cambridge, Mass., 2008); Sowande' M. Mustakeem, *Slavery at Sea: Terror, Sex, and Sickness in the Middle Passage* (Urbana, Ill., 2016). For Native slavery, see, for example, James F. Brooks, *Captives and Cousins: Slavery, Kinship, and Community in the Southwest Borderlands* (Williamsburg, Va., and Chapel Hill, N.C., 2002); Alan Gallay, *The Indian Slave Trade: The Rise of the English Empire in the American South, 1670–1717* (New Haven, Conn., 2003); Christina Snyder, *Slavery in Indian Country: The Changing Face of Captivity in Early America* (Cambridge, Mass., 2010); Brett Rushforth, *Bonds of Alliance: Indigenous and Atlantic Slaveries in New France* (Williamsburg, Va., and Chapel Hill, N.C., 2014); Andrés Reséndez, *The Other Slavery; The Uncovered Story of Indian Enslavement in America* (New York, 2016). For coverture, see, for example, Marylynn Salmon, *Women and the Law of Property in Early America* (Chapel Hill, N.C., 1989); Linda K. Kerber, *No Constitutional Right to Be Ladies: Women and the Obligations of Citizenship* (New York, 1998), 3–46.

and early national governments to promote the free migration of some over others. Movement was not a given but a problem at the root of heated late-eighteenth-century debates about what kind of nation the United States might become.[9]

Removal was the foundation for the spirit of enterprise that laid out these new states and that was celebrated by eighteenth-century observers. It was rooted in early modern debates over the management of people. All sovereign people used their power to move others in order to assert their claims to territory or jurisdiction. The seventeenth-century Powhatan Confederacy, for example, dispersed people to identify insiders and outsiders, as did the Iroquois Confederacy. In the British Empire, managing people through removal was the king's prerogative. Seventeenth-century English monarchs and their ministers believed that the transportation of large groups of people to new places would reform convicts, suppress rebellion, support claims to territory, and ameliorate poverty. The king deported those who were convicted of crimes to the North American colonies and banished people who were potential enemies of the state. At the local level, Elizabethan poor laws gave localities the power to warn out indigent people and send them back to the place of their birth for poor support. These British precedents became the foundation for removal projects in the early United States.[10]

After the American Revolution, removal informed critical conversations about the formation of the United States at the highest levels of government and in the halls of local town councils and courts. When state statutes, local committees, and individual citizens legally banished or compelled the departure of sixty thousand loyalists during the war, citizens of the Republic were claiming what had been the king's prerogative—the power to remove people. White Americans turned to removal as a tool of postwar reconstruction as well. Because republican political power was derived from

9. Merrell, "American Nations, Old and New," in Hoxie, Hoffman, and Albert, eds., *Native Americans and the Early Republic*, 350.

10. Gwenda Morgan and Peter Rushton, *Eighteenth-Century Criminal Transportation: The Formation of the Criminal Atlantic* (New York, 2004); Christopher Tomlins, *Freedom Bound: Law, Labor, and Civic Identity in Colonizing English America, 1580–1865* (New York, 2010), 21–92. On the poor laws, see Ruth Wallis Herndon, *Unwelcome Americans: Living on the Margin in Early New England* (Philadelphia, 2001); Cornelia H. Dayton and Sharon V. Salinger, *Robert Love's Warnings: Searching for Strangers in Colonial Boston* (Philadelphia, 2017); Hidetaka Hirota, *Expelling the Poor: Atlantic Seaboard States and the Nineteenth-Century Origins of American Immigration Policy* (New York, 2017); Kristin O'Brassill-Kulfan, *Vagrants and Vagabonds: Poverty and Mobility in the Early American Republic* (New York, 2019).

the people, population formed the basis for representation, statehood, and political power. At the center of early national politics, then, was the question of who *the people* actually were. The departure of loyalists fostered the sense that those who remained supported the union. But the stories that white Americans used to garner support for the Revolution between 1776 and 1783—tales of Native violence and slave revolt—lingered and tested that notion of unanimity. Many early national writers saw removal as necessary to the republic based on whiteness that they wished to create. Removal could redraw belonging, excluding some people from their homelands or preempting claims to a permanent home based on race. These proposals were a means of working out who could be a member of the new nation.[11]

In the early national period, *removal* was a capacious term. People used it to refer to freely chosen movement from one town or county to another—as in, "I removed from Baltimore to New York." By the 1830s, removal was a gloss. In some cases, it meant deportation or expulsion. In others, it described what we might now call elimination or genocide. Removal as "self-deportation" was ubiquitous, too. Poor laws or restrictive settlement statutes did not always specify the mechanisms by which persons should leave. Rather, such legislation presumed they would remove themselves from territories or states through coercion. Many people—Irish immigrants, political dissidents prosecuted under the Alien and Sedition Acts, white squatters on federal lands, and Mormons—experienced some kind of forced relocation in the early Republic. All the same, state and federal officials most often directed removal toward free African Americans and Native Americans. They used it to draw the limits of belonging based on race. In the case of African Americans and Native Americans, removal's multiple meanings were intentional. As much as state or federal officials pursued removal, they also papered over its violence by calling it a benevolent project to protect free African Americans and Indigenous people from white Americans. Re-

11. Maya Jasanoff, *Liberty's Exiles: American Loyalists in the Revolutionary World* (New York, 2011), 357. For the myth of unanimity, see Douglas Bradburn, *The Citizenship Revolution: Politics and the Creation of the American Union, 1774–1804* (Charlottesville, Va., 2009), 58. For race and testing that myth, see Peter Silver, *Our Savage Neighbors: How Indian War Transformed Early America* (New York, 2009); Alan Taylor, *The Internal Enemy: Slavery and War in Virginia, 1772–1832* (New York, 2014); Robert G. Parkinson, *The Common Cause: Creating Race and Nation in the American Revolution* (Williamsburg, Va., and Chapel Hill, N.C., 2016). For race making, see Nancy Shoemaker, "How Indians Got to Be Red," *American Historical Review*, CII (1997), 625–644; James Sidbury, *Becoming African in America: Race and Nation in the Early Black Atlantic* (New York, 2007); John Wood Sweet, *Bodies Politic: Negotiating Race in the American North, 1730–1830* (Philadelphia, 2006).

moval's broad tent hid its devastation. The purposeful occlusions and multiple meanings of the term are the subject of this book.[12]

Early national federal and state officials who debated the strength of Native nations had removal in mind. When the Revolution ended, U.S. officials reimagined Native lands in the West as a fund to pay the new nation's war debts. Along with speculators, migrants, and geographers, they hoped to replace eastern Native people with white families. To settle the new territories they claimed after independence, white Americans also had to "unsettle" them. The men at the helm of early federal Indian policy declared that removal was inevitable. But what they called unavoidable was the product of their own policies. In their reports, they scratched out plans—military campaigns, "civilization" plans, broken treaties—that made removal a fait accompli. Decades before Andrew Jackson's Indian Removal Act, Thomas Jefferson and then James Monroe pressured Native Americans east of the Mississippi River to exchange their lands for those west of it while state and territorial governments worked assiduously to do the same.[13]

Beginning in the 1770s, writers from New England to Virginia intertwined removal with debates about gradual emancipation and Black citizenship. Enslavers in the upper South hoped to exile a growing number of free African Americans whom they feared would challenge slavery. Mid-Atlantic Quakers embraced colonization because they thought it might bring about

12. On "self-deportation," see K-Sue Park, "Self-Deportation Nation," *Harvard Law Review,* CXXXII (2019), 1878–1941. I occasionally lean on terms such as *banishment* or *exile* or *expulsion* to illuminate the meaning of *removal* in its diverse contexts. On the inadequacy of the term *removal,* see Scott Richard Lyons, *X-Marks: Native Signatures of Assent* (Minneapolis, Minn., 2010), 8; Saunt, *Unworthy Republic,* xii–xiv. On genocide and elimination, see Patrick Wolfe, "Settler Colonialism and the Elimination of the Native," *Journal of Genocide Research,* VIII (2006), 387–409; Benjamin Madley, *An American Genocide: The United States and the California Indian Catastrophe* (New Haven, Conn., 2017); Jeffrey Ostler, *Surviving Genocide: Native Nations and the United States from the American Revolution to Bleeding Kansas* (New Haven, Conn., 2019). For benevolence, see Nicholas Guyatt, "'The Outskirts of Our Happiness': Race and the Lure of Colonization in the Early Republic," *Journal of American History,* XCV (2009), esp. 987–988; Susan M. Ryan, *The Grammar of Good Intentions: Race and the Antebellum Culture of Benevolence* (Ithaca, N.Y., 2003), 14–16; Bruce Dorsey, *Reforming Men and Women: Gender in the Antebellum City* (Ithaca, N.Y., 2002), 76–79.

13. Rob Harper, *Unsettling the West: Violence and State Building in the Ohio Valley* (Philadelphia, 2018); Andrew Lipman, *The Saltwater Frontier: Indians and the Contest for the American Coast* (New Haven, Conn., 2018), 5; James P. Ronda, "'We Have a Country': Race, Geography, and the Invention of Indian Territory," *Journal of the Early Republic,* XIX (1999), 739–755. For an overview of early national Indian policy, see David Andrew Nichols, *Red Gentlemen and White Savages: Indians, Federalists, and the Search for Order on the American Frontier* (Charlottesville, Va., 2008).

gradual emancipation. Meanwhile, African American emigrationists believed that a venture they controlled themselves could deliver independence and economic prosperity at a moment when both were uncertain. They partnered with white ministers in New England who saw colonization as a missionary movement aimed at West Africans. Depending on who controlled the venture, removal could symbolize exclusion or political autonomy.[14]

There were substantive differences between Native American and African American experiences of removal. North Americans understood the circumstances of free Black and Native peoples to be distinct from one another. Consequently, the underpinnings of exclusion varied for both. Federal and state officials used removal to expropriate Native territory. By contrast, colonizationists planned to remove free African Americans to preserve slavery and limit Black citizenship rights. Nevertheless, the plans echoed one another. For example, reformers and legislators hoped to send all removed people out of the nation with farm implements and spinning wheels, and Quakers sometimes worked in both fields simultaneously. Both efforts began from the presumption that Black and Indigenous people needed moral improvement and could not achieve it within the United States.[15]

When white Americans embraced removal, they were also debating the legal rights of free African Americans and chipping away at Native sovereignty. Removal was symptomatic of how, as Barbara Young Welke has written, "Legal exclusions marked borders of belonging within the territorial boundaries of the nation." Citizenship was ill-defined in the early national

14. For work on early colonization and emigration ideas in the United States before the ACS and its connections to Sierra Leone, see Peter S. Onuf, *Jefferson's Empire: The Language of American Nationhood* (Charlottesville, Va., 2000), 174–188; David Kazanjian, *The Colonizing Trick: National Culture and Imperial Citizenship in Early America* (Minneapolis, Minn., 2003), 89–138; Cassandra Pybus, *Epic Journeys of Freedom: Runaway Slaves of the American Revolution and Their Global Quest for Liberty* (Boston, 2006); Sidbury, *Becoming African in America*, 17–155; Byrd, *Captives and Voyagers*, 125–244; Christopher Cameron, *To Plead Our Own Cause: African Americans in Massachusetts and the Making of the Antislavery Movement* (Kent, Ohio, 2014), 100–113; Christa Dierksheide, *Amelioration and Empire: Progress and Slavery in the Plantation Americas* (Charlottesville, Va., 2014), 25–66; Guyatt, *Bind Us Apart*.

15. Patrick Wolfe, "Land, Labor, and Difference: Elementary Structures of Race," *American Historical Review*, CVI (2001), 866–905. These substantive differences include the inherent sovereignty of Native people; see Kevin Bruyneel, *The Third Space of Sovereignty: The Postcolonial Politics of U.S.-Indigenous Relations* (Minneapolis, Minn., 2007). For two scholars who have examined the overlap between African American colonization and Indian removal, see Guyatt, *Bind Us Apart;* Ikuko Asaka, *Tropical Freedom: Climate, Settler Colonialism, and Black Exclusion in the Age of Emancipation* (Durham, N.C., 2017).

period. Voting rights, property rights, and naturalization were controlled by the states and varied between them. When colonization's proponents argued that free African Americans should leave because they would never find equality within the union, they brought into sharp relief the limited set of rights available to free Black men and women at the state level in many places. Removal similarly revealed state and federal aspirations to dismantle Native sovereignty within the borders of the United States. When federal officials demanded that Native Americans dissolve tribal governments in return for citizenship, they held out dispossession as the alternative. States struggling to solidify their own jurisdiction similarly resisted overlapping and "tenacious pluaralities." As judges and legislators tried to redefine the status of tribal nations from sovereign powers to "domestic dependent nations" over the course of the early national period, removal made plain the stakes of the discussion. White Americans chose removal as one tool among many to cope with the precariousness of the new nation. They created a new racial geography in which Native Americans and African Americans only had rights in certain spaces.[16]

Removal projects appear totalizing when viewed from the desks of their most passionate advocates. As intellectuals and legislators observed the nation's rapid growth in the late eighteenth century, they hoped to manipulate the movements of abstract populations to strengthen the military and economic power of the states and territories. They wielded census data and maps to bring the nation into being from their offices and counting rooms. It was heady arithmetic.[17]

The view from the planner's desk is partial, however, and the arithmetic is deceiving. White Americans clamored for the idea of removal even though many of the proposals they put forward were impossible to enforce and

16. Barbara Young Welke, *Law and the Borders of Belonging in the Long Nineteenth Century United States* (New York, 2010), 181 ("Legal"); Lisa Ford, *Settler Sovereignty: Jurisdiction and Indigenous People in America and Australia, 1788–1836* (Cambridge, Mass., 2011), 3 ("tenacious"); Cherokee Nation vs. the State of Georgia, 30 U.S. (5 Pet.) 1 (1831) ("domestic"); Deborah A. Rosen, *American Indians and State Law: Sovereignty, Race, and Citizenship, 1790–1880* (Lincoln, Neb., 2009). For racial geography, see Marilyn Lake and Henry Reynolds, *Drawing the Global Colour Line: White Men's Countries and the International Challenge of Racial Equality* (Cambridge, 2008); Welke, *Law and the Borders of Belonging,* 26.

17. On population, state making, and ordering people, see James C. Scott, *Seeing Like a State: How Certain Schemes to Improve the Human Condition Have Failed* (New Haven, Conn., 1998); Ford, *Settler Sovereignty,* 1; Caroline Winterer, *American Enlightenments: Pursuing Happiness in the Age of Reason* (New Haven, Conn., 2016), 110–141.

often contradictory. State power was limited in the early national period. By the late nineteenth century, the growth of the federal government—with its powers of surveillance, immigration control, licensing, passports, and border agents—allowed American officials to impose removal at the federal level with a degree of efficiency that was unimaginable in the early national period. After the American Revolution, the new United States struggled to make its people legible. In practice, early American governments could not control what the English jurist William Blackstone in his 1765 *Commentaries on the Laws of England* had called "the power of loco-motion." Migrants crossed borders and squatted on lands without regard for laws intended to keep them out. Locomotion was "power" and thus a problem to be managed. Early Americans treated it as such.[18]

Nonetheless, state power was not nonexistent. It simply operated in ways we might not recognize today. It was "out of sight," carried out by federal officials and everday people who had no official role in government. This was particularly true in the trans-Appalachian region, where federal officials relied on white migrants to wage war on Native settlements or tasked individual go-betweens with brokering peace agreements. The example of the extraordinary efforts taken by the federal government to expel Indigenous people might have led eastern colonizationists to believe that their projects were also realistic. Early American governments already protected property (including property in enslaved people), and they had an exclusive right to coercive force. Could they not also regulate mobility and settlement?[19]

It would be easy to see Native Americans and African Americans as casualties of these visions, but that is only part of the story. They were not just can-

18. William Blackstone, *Commentaries on the Laws of England: A Facsimile of the First Edition of 1765–1769*, I, *Of the Rights of Persons* (Chicago, 1979), 130–133 (quotation, 130). For works that link Revolutionary-era removal and later histories of immigration, see Daniel Kanstroom, *Deportation Nation: Outsiders in American History* (Cambridge, Mass., 2007), ix–x; Kunal M. Parker, *Making Foreigners: Immigration and Citizenship Law in America, 1600–2000* (New York, 2015); Hirota, *Expelling the Poor;* Park, "Self-Deportation Nation," *Harvard Law Review*, CXXXII (2019), 1878–1941.

19. For work bringing the state back into the history of the early Republic, see, for example, Brian Balogh, *A Government Out of Sight: The Mystery of National Authority in Nineteenth-Century America* (New York, 2009); William J. Novak, "The Myth of the 'Weak' American State," *American Historical Review*, CXIII (2008), 752–772; Max M. Edling, *A Hercules in the Cradle: War, Money, and the American State, 1783–1867* (Chicago, 2014). A cohort of Ohio Valley historians have debated the extent to which the federal government exercised power and was responsible for violence there. See Eric Hinderaker, *Elusive Empires: Constructing Colonialism in the Ohio Valley, 1673–1800* (New York, 1999); Patrick Griffin, *American Leviathan: Empire, Nation, and Revolutionary Frontier* (New York, 2008); Harper, *Unsettling the West.*

didates for removal. They also sought to control movement themselves. Free Black men and women championed emigration movements that led thousands of people to Sierra Leone, Haiti, and Canada to escape racism in the United States. Native nations had a clear conception of their territorial sovereignty, and they routinely forced intruders out of their lands. When Wyandot speakers or Odawa messengers pressed American officials to move white migrants back across the Ohio River, they were demanding the removal of white Americans. Facing west from the federal capital, U.S. military campaigns in Indian country look like removal efforts; facing east from Indian country, the same battles look like Native efforts to push out white interlopers.[20]

Borders were also both malleable and indistinct, Black and white Americans ignored state laws against migration, and Native Americans thwarted land dispossession. Free African Americans from the upper South traveled west in the early nineteenth century despite restrictive statutes that limited their movements. They settled alongside former neighbors, recreating their old neighborhoods in Ohio or Indiana. Native people forged paths away from dispossession that were outside the control of state and federal legislators. In the 1770s, some Shawnees and Delawares chose to move beyond the claims of the United States by crossing the Mississippi River at the invitation of the Quapaws and Spanish. White, Black, and Native migrants also had alternative understandings of geography that had little to do with the United States. Native nations retained power over their homelands even though the United States did not recognize their sovereignty. Enslaved people developed what Stephanie M. H. Camp has called a "rival geography"—an understanding of the space of the plantation, town, or swamp where they could find a modicum of freedom in a nation underpinned by slavery.[21]

20. For emigration, see Nikki M. Taylor, *Frontiers of Freedom: Cincinnati's Black Community, 1802–1868* (Athens, Ohio, 2005), 58–79; Pybus, *Epic Journeys of Freedom;* Sidbury, *Becoming African in America,* 17–155; Byrd, *Captives and Voyagers,* 125–244; Ada Ferrer, "Haiti, Free Soil, and Antislavery in the Revolutionary Atlantic," *American Historical Review,* CXVII (2012), 40–66; Sara Fanning, *Caribbean Crossing: African Americans and the Haitian Emigration Movement* (New York, 2015). For Native people removing others from their lands, see Sami Lakomäki, *Gathering Together: The Shawnee People through Diaspora and Nationhood, 1600–1870* (New Haven, Conn., 2014), 102–131, 143–152; Colin G. Calloway, *The Victory with No Name: The Native American Defeat of the First American Army* (New York, 2015).

21. For "rival geography," see Stephanie M. H. Camp, *Closer to Freedom: Enslaved Women and Everyday Resistance in the Plantation South* (Chapel Hill, N.C., 2004), 7 (quotation); Katherine McKittrick, *Demonic Grounds: Black Women and the Cartographies of Struggle* (Minneapolis, Minn., 2006), xxviii; Anthony E. Kaye, *Joining Places: Slave Neighborhoods in the Old South* (Chapel Hill, N.C., 2009); Sylviane A. Diouf, *Slavery's Exiles: The Story of the American Maroons* (New York, 2014); Marisa J.

The heady arithmetic of early American planners notwithstanding, states were made by ordinary people. Individual choices to move transformed territories into states. They produced new understandings of space. With their decisions to move or to remain, people altered the political landscape of Indian country and of the United States as well as categories like "free state" and "slave state" on the ground. White migrants who went west also did the work of settler colonialism. Miamis who invited other Native people to live on their lands clarified their own borders in the process. By foregrounding the movements of everyday people, this book bridges the gap between political history and the rich social history of migration, crafting a history of state making from both above and below.[22]

Putting removal at the center of the story of the founding of the United States reveals another underexamined intellectual current in American life. Because removal was so common in the early Republic, African American

---

Fuentes, *Dispossessed Lives: Enslaved Women, Violence, and the Archive* (Philadelphia, 2016), 13–45. For African American western migration, see Stephen A. Vincent, *Southern Seed, Northern Soil: African-American Farm Communities in the Midwest, 1765–1900* (Bloomington, Ind., 1999); Cheryl Janifer LaRoche, *Free Black Communities and the Underground Railroad: The Geography of Resistance* (Urbana, Ill., 2014). For Shawnees and Delawares, see Kathleen DuVal, *The Native Ground: Indians and Colonists in the Heart of the Continent* (Philadelphia, 2007), 162–163, 175; John P. Bowes, *Exiles and Pioneers: Eastern Indians in the Trans-Mississippi West* (New York, 2007), 19–52. Rashauna Johnson argues for the "confined cosmopolitanism" of enslaved people in the city of New Orleans. See Johnson, *Slavery's Metropolis: Unfree Labor in New Orleans during the Age of Revolutions* (New York, 2016), 6.

22. For scholarship on African American and Native American travel, see, for example, Camp, *Closer to Freedom;* Bowes, *Exiles and Pioneers;* Edlie L. Wong, *Neither Fugitive nor Free: Atlantic Slavery, Freedom Suits, and the Legal Culture of Travel* (New York, 2009); Elizabeth Stordeur Pryor, *Colored Travelers: Mobility and the Fight for Citizenship before the Civil War* (Chapel Hill, N.C., 2016). For works that explore the transatlantic movement of Indigenous people, see Coll Thrush, *Indigenous London: Native Travelers at the Heart of Empire* (New Haven, Conn., 2016); Nancy Shoemaker, *Native American Whalemen and the World: Indigenous Encounters and the Contingency of Race* (Chapel Hill, N.C., 2017); Jace Weaver, *The Red Atlantic: American Indigenes and the Making of the Modern World, 1000–1927* (Chapel Hill, N.C., 2017). For white migrants, see Bethel Saler, *The Settlers' Empire: Colonialism and State Formation in America's Old Northwest* (Philadelphia, 2015); Laurel Clark Shire, *The Threshold of Manifest Destiny: Gender and National Expansion in Florida* (Philadelphia, 2016), 1, 4–5. For Native borders, see Taylor, *Divided Ground;* Juliana Barr, "Geographies of Power: Mapping Indian Borders in the 'Borderlands' of the Early Southwest," *William and Mary Quarterly,* 3d Ser., LXVIII (2011), 5–46; Sami Lakomäki, "'Our Line': The Shawnees, the United States, and Competing Borders on the Great Lakes 'Borderlands,' 1795–1832," *Journal of the Early Republic,* XXXIV (2014), 597–624.

and Indigenous communities staunchly protected their right to remain in their homes and homelands. In a period when the dislocations of revolution, state making, and expansion accelerated movement both forced and free, the pursuit of a permanent home mattered deeply to many people. History and the bonds of affection tied people to particular places. Most people in the early national period did not want unfettered migration—they hoped to remain in place.

In 1773, an enslaved man named Felix attested to the importance of the right to remain when he submitted an abolitionist petition to the Massachusetts House of Representatives. "We have no Property! We have no Wives! No Children! We have no City! No Country!" Felix cried. To be enslaved was to be deprived of land, possessions, family, and a permanent home. Within a decade of Felix's petition, a series of court cases brought by two enslaved people, Quock Walker and Elizabeth Freeman, helped to undermine slavery in Massachusetts. If he survived the war, Felix presumably claimed his freedom, too. And yet, some of Felix's laments also seemed pertinent to the experience of freedom. Between 1780 and 1804, thousands of enslaved people across the new nation became free as a result of gradual emancipation acts and the liberalization of manumission laws in individual states. As they did, states passed new laws restricting Black residency and travel. In 1811, Black sailmaker and Philadelphia leader James Forten echoed Felix's protest when he wondered of free African Americans, "Where shall he go? Shut every state against him . . . . Is there no spot on earth that will protect him!" Newly freed people pursued the right to remain by petitioning state governments and going to court. In the fifty years after the Revolution, the right to remain became central to African American activism.[23]

Similarly, Native Americans waged effective campaigns for the right to remain long before Indian removal gained national attention in eastern re-

23. Felix, Petition to Thomas Hutchinson, Jan. 6, 1773, reprinted in Gary B. Nash, *Race and Revolution* (Lanham, Md., 2001), 172 ("We have"); [James Forten], *Letters from a Man of Colour, on a Late Bill before the Senate of Pennsylvania* (n.p. [Pa., 1813]), 10–11 ("Where"). For Quok Walker and Elizabeth Freeman, see Arthur Zilversmit, "Quok Walker, Mumbet, and the Abolition of Slavery in Massachusetts," *William and Mary Quarterly*, 3d Ser., XXV (1968), 614–624; Joanne Pope Melish, *Disowning Slavery: Gradual Emancipation and "Race" in New England, 1780–1860* (Ithaca, N.Y., 1998), 64–65. For the right to remain, see Adrienne Monteith Petty, *Standing Their Ground: Small Farmers in North Carolina since the Civil War* (New York, 2013); Sydney Nathans, *A Mind to Stay: White Plantation, Black Homeland* (Cambridge, Mass., 2017); Martha S. Jones, *Birthright Citizens: A History of Race and Rights in Antebellum America* (New York, 2018), 4, 90; Christopher James Bonner, *Remaking the Republic: Black Politics and the Creation of American Citizenship* (Philadelphia, 2020), 13, 40.

form circles in the late 1820s. Seneca, Mohawk, Shawnee, and Miami chiefs traveled to the federal capital to press for U.S. recognition of their borders. Indigenous people from the Ohio Valley and lower Great Lakes met with British officials in Canada, they traveled across the Mississippi River to strengthen their ties to the Spanish, and they went south to Creek country. They also confederated to rival the United States, even as they struggled to speak with a unified message. In 1793, at the height of their resistance to the United States, confederated leaders met with U.S. commissioners in Detroit, where they demanded that white Americans remove from their lands north of the Ohio River. "We can retreat no further," they declared, insisting "we have therefore resolved, to leave our bones in this small space, to which we are now confined."[24]

United in their desire to remain, Native Americans and African Americans nonetheless pursued that goal differently. All used alliance building to their advantage, whether they sought out the patronage of powerful individuals or connections with neighboring towns, nations, and empires. As sovereign nations, Native people cemented these ties by acting collectively. A landscape of alliances with traders and British forts helped them determine their own futures amid colonialism. Free Black men and women fostered personal relationships with white and Black patrons to win customary rights that they did not enjoy under state law. Personal connections were important to people whose rights were only narrowly protected by the law because local jurisdiction ultimately mattered most. Removal for free Black people could mean losing intermediaries who formed communities of protection when early national state governments did not formally defend their rights. Increasingly in the early Republic, free Black men and women acted collectively as well. They formed independent churches, societies, and towns to secure their right to remain.[25]

24. "Message from the Western Indians to the Commissioners of the United States," Aug. 13, 1793, in *CJGS,* II, 20 (quotations). For confederation, see Gregory Evans Dowd, *A Spirited Resistance: The North American Indian Struggle for Unity, 1745–1815* (Baltimore, Md., 1993); Colin G. Calloway, *The Shawnees and the War for America* (New York, 2007); Lisa Brooks, *The Common Pot: The Recovery of Native Space in the Northeast* (Minneapolis, Minn., 2008), 106–162; Nichols, *Red Gentlemen and White Savages;* Stephen Warren, *The Shawnees and Their Neighbors, 1795–1870* (Urbanna, Ill., 2008), 13–42; Adam Jortner, *The Gods of Prophetstown: The Battle of Tippecanoe and the Holy War for the American Frontier* (New York, 2012); Calloway, *Victory with No Name;* Lakomäki, *Gathering Together,* 102–131, 143–152; Sleeper-Smith, *Indigenous Prosperity and American Conquest,* 218–320.

25. For collaboration and alliance building, see Richard White, *The Middle Ground: Indians, Empires, and Republics in the Great Lakes Region, 1650–1815* (1991; rpt.

Comparisons allow the terms of one field to illuminate those of another. Although remaining is at the center of Native American and Indigenous Studies, focusing on the right to remain in African American history of the early national period illuminates how often Black Americans also called for the same thing. Antoinette Burton writes that Native peoples who lived amid European and American empires in the nineteenth century "exhibited a keen sense of how history was being made at their expense." When African Americans argued against state policies that limited their rights and freedoms, they armed themselves with the same historical sensibility and "anticipatory posture" as Indigenous people. The public arguments for the right to remain that they disseminated influenced quieter moments of dissent that never reached beyond a few neighbors or correspondents. Together, these documents and speeches constitute an archive of Black and Indigenous efforts to secure the right to remain, although historians have seldom thought of it as one. Living in the midst of settler colonialism or in the shadow of slavery, those who dissented did not always ask to be part of the new United States. Oftentimes, they simply asked to be left alone.[26]

This book is national in scope, but it centers on the upper South, mid-Atlantic, and the Ohio Valley, where removal played a key role in U.S. state making. In an 1814 atlas, Pennsylvania publisher Mathew Carey pictured Virginia, Maryland, Delaware, Pennsylvania, New Jersey, Kentucky, Ohio, and the territories of Indiana and Illinois together on a map that he labeled *The Middle States and Western Territories of the United States.* The designation "middle states" was not common in the early nineteenth century. Nonetheless, early Americans would have understood Carey's map as depicting

New York, 2011); Colin G. Calloway, *Crown and Calumet: British-Indian Relations, 1783–1815* (Norman, Okla., 1987); Robert Michael Morrissey, *Empire by Collaboration: Indians, Colonists, and Governments in Colonial Illinois Country* (Philadelphia, 2015). For patronage, see Melvin Patrick Ely, *Israel on the Appomattox: A Southern Experiment in Black Freedom from the 1790s through the Civil War* (New York, 2005); Laura F. Edwards, *The People and Their Peace: Legal Culture and the Transformation of Inequality in the Post-Revolutionary South* (Chapel Hill, N.C., 2009), 100–132; Kirt von Daacke, *Freedom Has a Face: Race, Identity, and Community in Jefferson's Virginia* (Charlottesville, Va., 2012), 41–112; Kimberly M. Welch, *Black Litigants in the Antebellum American South* (Chapel Hill, N.C., 2018), 60–81. For collective action and institutions, see, for example, Leslie M. Harris, *In the Shadow of Slavery: African Americans in New York City, 1626–1863* (Chicago, 2004), 72–95; Erica Armstrong Dunbar, *A Fragile Freedom: African American Women and Emancipation in the Antebellum City* (New Haven, Conn., 2008), 48–69; Sinha, *Slave's Cause,* 130–144.

26. Antoinette Burton, "Introduction: Travelling Criticism? On the Dynamic Histories of Indigenous Modernity," *Cultural and Social History,* IX (2012), 492.

a coherent region, linked by migration from East to West. Long before the United States existed on any map, Native people also likely saw the area as connected. By the early eighteenth century, Delaware, Shawnee, and Haudenosaunee migrants pulled west by the Ohio River went to the Ohio Valley as refugees of eastern dispossession in the mid-Atlantic colonies. Anglo-Americans quickly followed. They also thought of the region as a corridor, perched on the edges of the Ohio River, which carried people and goods from West to East and back.[27]

Scholarship on removal has typically focused on the South or New England, but nowhere was early national removal more important than in Carey's middle states. Federal officials believed the division and sale of Native lands in the fertile region of the Ohio Valley was vital to the financial, political, and moral foundations of the nation. Many Native people who controlled the Ohio Valley had already experienced Anglo-American removal once, so they were even more resolute in their efforts to remain. By the post-Revolutionary period, the middle states shared common borders, but they pursued very different paths when it came to slavery. Virginia and Maryland held fast to the institution, Delaware's slaveholding elite reduced but did not eliminate their reliance on enslaved labor, and Pennsylvania gradually abolished bondage altogether. In the Ohio Valley, slavery was the foundation of Kentucky's prosperity, while north of the Ohio River, it was banned. The middle states were linked by migration, and the differences between them when it came to slavery and freedom led to a persistent debate about colonization and migration restriction.[28]

Carey's map is useful for showing how North Americans imagined the middle states as interconnected. It is also, in itself, a marker of the transformations that removal wrought in the upper South, mid-Atlantic, and Ohio Valley. North American consumers were discerning map readers. They knew that maps were as much expressions of the world their authors wished

27. Mathew Carey, *A General Atlas, Being a Collection of Maps of the World and Quarters . . .* (Philadelphia, 1814), Edward E. Ayer Collection, Special Collections, NL; Stephen Warren, *The Worlds the Shawnees Made: Migration and Violence in Early America* (Chapel Hill, N.C., 2014), 27–56.

28. For connections across the broader region around the Ohio River Valley, see, for example, Hinderaker, *Elusive Empires;* Lakomäki, *Gathering Together;* Warren, *Worlds the Shawnees Made;* Amy C. Schutt, *Peoples of the River Valleys: The Odyssey of the Delaware Indians* (Philadelphia, 2007). For slavery's borderland in the middle states, see Richard S. Newman, "'Lucky to Be Born in Pennsylvania': Free Soil, Fugitive Slaves, and the Making of Pennsylvania's Anti-Slavery Borderland," *Slavery and Abolition,* XXXII (2011), 413–430; Matthew Salafia, *Slavery's Borderland: Freedom and Bondage along the Ohio River* (Philadelphia, 2013).

FIGURE 1. *Mathew Carey, "The Middle States and Western Territories of the United States Including the Seat of the Western War," 1812. From Carey,* A General Atlas, Being a Collection of Maps of the World and Quarters . . . *(Philadelphia, 1814). Plate 6. Edward E. Ayer Collection, Special Collections. Courtesy Newberry Library, Chicago*

to create as reflections of the world as it was. As they perused the map of the middle states, Carey's subscribers might have noticed that it was a political project. The map envisioned the region as a blank canvas divided neatly into states awaiting incorporation into the union. Carey reproduced the rivers, mountain ranges, and towns of the middle states from earlier colonial maps, but he purposefully omitted Native place-names from his rendering of the region. Shawnees, Delawares, Wyandots, Odawas, Senecas, Miamis, Ojibwes, and Potawatomis had long controlled the middle states, though one would never know it from Carey's map. It made migration from East to West easy to imagine. This book shows how the broad region surrounding the Ohio Valley was linked by migration and rapidly carved into a set of states by removal. Carey's choices also facilitated that transformation.[29]

Although removal was uniquely important in the middle states, it was also a national project. Southern colonizationists corresponded with northeasterners about their plans. Black intellectuals and leaders in Massachusetts and Rhode Island led inquiries into the founding of a West African colony. Conversely, removal had its geographic limits. For much of the nineteenth century, most of North America was controlled by Native nations and empires for whom U.S. policy mattered little. North of the middle states in what would become Michigan and Wisconsin—both within Anishinaabewaki, or the territory of the Anishinaabeg—U.S. officials had no choice but to acknowledge Anishinaabe borders and customary law, and they depended on mixed-race families to prop up their claims to statehood. Removal proceeded very differently to the south, in Ohio, Indiana, and Illinois.[30]

29. For maps as tools of empire, see J. B. Harley, "Maps, Knowledge, and Power," in Denis Cosgrove and Stephen Daniels, eds., *The Iconography of Landscape: Essays on the Symbolic Representation, Design, and Use of Past Environments* (1988; rpt. Cambridge, 1989), 277–312; Harley, "Rereading the Maps of the Columbian Encounter," *Annals of the Association of American Geographers*, LXXXII (1992), 522–536; Gregory H. Nobles, "Straight Lines and Stability: Mapping the Political Order of the Anglo-American Frontier," *Journal of American History*, LXXX (1993), 9–35; Michael Witgen, "The Rituals of Possession: Native Identity and the Invention of Empire in Seventeenth-Century Western North America," *Ethnohistory*, LIV (2007), 639–668; Barr, "Geographies of Power," *William and Mary Quarterly*, 3d Ser., LXVIII (2011), 5–46.

30. Michael Witgen, "Seeing Red: Race, Citizenship, and Indigeneity in the Old Northwest," *Journal of the Early Republic*, XXXVIII (2018), 581–611. Witgen writes that "there are too few histories of nineteenth-century North America that tell the story of the numerically significant and politically independent Native peoples who controlled the majority of continent's territory, and who helped to shape the historical development of the modern American, Canadian, and Mexican nations." See Witgen, *An Infinity of Nations: How the Native New World Shaped Early North America* (Philadel-

Before the 1830s, very few people compared Native American and African American struggles for the right to remain. When they did, they set the broad sins of the new nation next to each other on a global stage. A writer using the pseudonym Othello compared the immorality of American slavery and Native dispossession to the captivity of American sailors by the Barbary states, concluding that "the Algerines are no greater pirates than the Americans." Mohican diplomat Hendrick Aupaumut reported that Delawares and Shawnees in the Ohio Valley celebrated news of the Haitian Revolution in 1792. They cautioned that U.S. policy would reduce them to bondage, too. A speaker for the United Indian Nations claimed that "if we have peace with [Americans], they would make slaves of us." Fear of bondage was a consistent refrain of Indigenous orators in the Ohio country from the mid-eighteenth century onward, and for good reason. The enslavement of Native people had been important to colonial economies and politics.[31]

White reformers and ministers writing in the 1790s compared the experiences of Native Americans and African Americans to critique U.S. history. In a defense of the Haitian Revolution, Connecticut Republican Abraham Bishop denounced the United States, where Black men and women were enslaved, Natives were pushed from their lands, "and we glory in the equal rights of men, provided that *we white men can enjoy the whole of them.*" Bishop's Yale classmate Zephaniah Swift similarly suggested that Native peoples and those of African descent "have long mourned the day, when Columbus sailed from Europe." Baptist minister Rhees warned his white countrymen that "Indians and Negroes will rise up in judgment against you, if you do not exert your influence to emancipate the one and send messengers of peace to the other."[32]

---

phia, 2012), 16. For scholarship that does address Native control over the continent, see DuVal, *Native Ground;* Pekka Hämäläinen, *The Comanche Empire* (New Haven, Conn., 2008); Anne F. Hyde, *Empires, Nations, and Families: A History of the North American West, 1800–1860* (Lincoln, Neb., 2011); Michael A. McDonnell, *Masters of Empire: Great Lakes Indians and the Making of America* (New York, 2015).

31. Othello, "Essay on Negro Slavery," *American Museum; or, Repository of Ancient and Modern Fugitive Pieces, etc.; Prose and Poetical* (Philadelphia), December 1788, 510 ("Algerines"); "A Narrative of an Embassy to the Western Indians, from the Original Manuscript of Hendrick Aupaumut, with Prefatory Remarks by Dr. B. H. Coates," *Memoirs of the Historical Society of Pennsylvania,* II (Philadelphia, 1827), 128 ("if we have"); Gregory Evans Dowd, *Groundless: Rumors, Legends, and Hoaxes on the Early American Frontier* (Baltimore, Md., 2015), 77–78, 116, 125–143.

32. Abraham Bishop, "Rights of Black Men," in Tim Matthewson, "Abraham Bishop, 'The Rights of Black Men,' and the American Reaction to the Haitian Revolution," *Journal of Negro History,* LXVII (1982), 151 ("we glory"); Zephaniah Swift, *An Oration on Domestic Slavery; Delivered at the North Meeting-House in Hartford, on the*

Nods to these solidarities, however, were rare. They were not always easy for contemporaries to see because Native American and African American histories themselves entailed unequal power relationships. Native people had experienced slavery, but they also enslaved and trafficked people of African descent. By the early nineteenth century, free African Americans forced out of southern states carved out autonomous towns on Native homelands in Ohio, Indiana, and Illinois alongside their white neighbors. They participated in the settler-colonial project of creating "free states" but not under terms of their own making, nor with the same rights and investments as white migrants. The disjuncture between these histories shows the limits of the dichotomy between terms like *settler* and *Indigenous.*[33]

Some readers may wonder why these two stories that are so fundamentally connected by the end of the book are told separately at its beginning. After all, the similarities between colonization and Indian removal are easy to see when the letters, reports, and pamphlets scratched out by the men at the helm of removal policy are set side by side. In the local and regional contexts where Black and Indigenous people waged struggles for self-determination, however, these stories often played out separately. Even when these histories do clearly overlap, as in Ohio, Indiana, and Illinois by the War of 1812, the differences between them invite sustained attention to each on its own terms as well as together.

By the 1830s, the prevalence of early national removal projects did inspire some Native Americans and African Americans to see their histories as linked. Removal reached a fever pitch by the antebellum period, and

---

12th Day of May, A.D. 1791; at the Meeting of the Connecticut Society for the Promotion of Freedom, and the Relief of Persons Unlawfully Holden in Bondage (Hartford, Conn., 1791), 9 ("have long mourned"); Morgan John Rhees, "To the Ministers of Religion in the United States of America," in Griffith, *Rev. Morgan John Rhys,* 52 ("Indians"). For further context, see Sinha, *Slave's Cause,* 10, 60; François Furstenberg, "Beyond Freedom and Slavery: Autonomy, Virtue, and Resistance in Early American Political Discourse," *Journal of American History,* LXXXIX (2003), 1320–1321.

33. For Native slaveholders, see Tiya Miles, *Ties That Bind: The Story of an Afro-Cherokee Family in Slavery and Freedom* (Berkeley, Calif., 2005); Claudio Saunt, *Black, White, and Indian: Race and the Unmaking of an American Family* (New York, 2006); Barbara Krauthamer, *Black Slaves, Indian Masters: Slavery, Emancipation, and Citizenship in the Native American South* (Chapel Hill, N.C., 2015). For African Americans and the "settler-Native" divide, see Miles, "Beyond a Boundary: Black Lives and the Settler-Native Divide," *William and Mary Quarterly,* 3d Ser., LXXVI (2019), 417–426; Jodi A. Byrd, *The Transit of Empire: Indigenous Critiques of Colonialism* (Minneapolis, Minn., 2011), xix. For these entanglements in the 1830s, see Natalie Joy, "The Indian's Cause: Abolitionists and Native American Rights," *Journal of the Civil War Era,* VIII (2018), 215–242.

persistent proposals for exclusion transformed interracial dissent against such measures. Radicals and reformers began to view removal as unique to American politics because of the near simultaneous rise of the ACS and the passage of the 1830 Indian Removal Act. Many free Black men and women protested the ACS shortly after its establishment. Within a little more than a decade, their protest inspired the Black convention movement and spurred the activism of Black and white leaders from Richard Allen to William Watkins to William Lloyd Garrison.[34]

Meanwhile, with the passage of the Indian Removal Act in 1830, President Andrew Jackson solidified federal power over the removal of Native nations and declared his intention to expel them beyond the Mississippi River. The passage of the act came at a time when eastern Native Americans were under mounting pressure to leave their homelands. Many people resisted dispossession, but the Cherokees made their battle visible on a national stage by lobbying the federal government and forming a constitutional government. Although the Cherokee struggle became a cause célèbre among northeastern reformers, Native nations across both the North and South also sought to thwart removal.[35]

Increasingly, activists identified removal as a national project. At a New York convention called in 1831, Black attendees denounced the state's auxiliary colonization society and demanded that "those who have so eloquently pleaded the cause of the Indian, will at least endeavor to preserve consistency in their conduct" and reject the ACS as well. When Black Baltimorean activists Watkins and Jacob Greener urged Garrison to abandon the ACS, Garrison also called on white Americans in his 1832 volume *Thoughts on Colonization* to withdraw their support from colonization and Indian removal.[36]

34. For the ACS, see Claude A. Clegg, III, *The Price of Liberty: African Americans and the Making of Liberia* (Chapel Hill, N.C., 2004); Burin, *Slavery and the Peculiar Solution;* Marie Tyler-McGraw, *An African Republic: Black and White Virginians in the Making of Liberia* (Chapel Hill, N.C., 2007); Beverly C. Tomek, *Colonization and Its Discontents: Emancipation, Emigration, and Antislavery in Antebellum Pennsylvania* (New York, 2011); Ousmane K. Power-Greene, *Against Wind and Tide: The African American Struggle against the Colonization Movement* (New York, 2014); Tomek and Matthew J. Hetrick, eds., *New Directions in the Study of African American Recolonization* (Gainesville, Fla., 2017).

35. William G. McLoughlin, *Cherokee Renascence in the New Republic* (Princeton, N.J., 1986); Theda Perdue and Michael D. Green, *The Cherokee Nation and the Trail of Tears* (New York, 2008).

36. *Resolutions of the People of Color, at a Meeting Held on the 25th of January, 1831; with an Address to the Citizens of New York, in Answer to Those of the New York Coloniza-*

Removal moved so rapidly and with such devastation by the 1830s because its foundations had been prepared over the proceeding decades. The antebellum expulsions of Indigenous people and African Americans were anomalous in their scale, destruction, speed, and organization. They rested, however, on a firm foundation of exclusion with roots in the waning years of the American Revolution. In *Thoughts on Colonization,* Garrison considered the power of "FIGURING" in this new political landscape. Garrison asked his readers to picture the "philanthropic arithmeticians" with their slates and pencils. "In fifteen minutes they will clear the continent of every black skin; and, if desired, throw in the Indians to boot." This was "the surpassing utility of the arithmetic," he wrote wryly. Garrison's arithmetician might as well have been Thomas Jefferson, who imagined the neat exchange of eastern Native lands for those west of the Mississippi River as early as 1803, or his fellow Virginian, jurist St. George Tucker, who proposed Black colonization to the state legislature in the 1790s. Both laid the groundwork for the age of removal in the 1830s.[37]

The philanthropic arithmetician was a powerful symbol of the period. In the post-Revolutionary era, many people envisioned a republic in which the expansion of white freedom of movement and security of property would be assured through the banishment of African Americans and Native Americans. By the 1830s, the Black convention movement and writers like Garrison pointed out what many people had known and experienced for decades—removal was already woven into the fabric of the nation itself.

---

tion Society (New York, 1831), in Dorothy Porter, ed., *Early Negro Writing: 1760–1837* (Boston, 1971), 285 (quotation); W[illia]m Lloyd Garrison, *Thoughts on African Colonization: or, An Impartial Exhibition of the Doctrines, Principles, and Purposes of the American Colonization Society; Together with the Resolutions, Addresses, and Remonstrances of the Free People of Color* (Boston, 1832).

37. Garrison, *Thoughts on African Colonization,* 155 (quotations); Thomas Jefferson to Pierre Samuel Du Pont de Nemours, Nov. 1, 1803, in Julian P. Boyd et al., eds., *The Papers of Thomas Jefferson,* 43 vols. (Princeton, N.J., 1950–), XLI, 647–648; St. George Tucker, *A Dissertation on Slavery: With a Proposal for the Gradual Abolition of It, in the State of Virginia* (Philadelphia, 1796).

CHAPTER 1
REMOVAL AND THE BRITISH EMPIRE

The seventeenth-century English Atlantic world was a world of motion, as colonial projects sent people toward the Americas. Atlantic crossings were largely made by those who were bound to labor for someone else. Demands for labor in the Caribbean and North America brought three hundred thousand English, upward of twenty thousand Irish, and seven thousand Scottish migrants to the English colonies over the course of the century. Half of them were indentured servants with contracts that obligated them to remain in service for a set number of years, while a much smaller number were convicted prisoners from England and Scotland also subject to terms of indenture. By the eighteenth century, the great majority were forced African migrants. Enslaved Africans taken to the English colonies far outnumbered indentured servants.[1]

Removal and seventeenth-century English colonization went hand in hand. Migration was calculated, something to be managed by the monarch toward the ends of empire. In vagrancy statutes, Elizabethan poor laws, and criminal transportation, expulsion was the punishment and solution for a variety of social ills. English monarchs, their counselors, and colonial promoters believed that the transportation of large groups of people to new colonies would reform those convicted of crimes, suppress rebellion, support claims to territory, and mitigate poverty while funneling laboring men and women to North America. English traders took thousands of Africans into bondage in the English colonies, in part by defining them as removable. In the colonies themselves, English migrants used removal once again as they attempted to dispossess Native people.

Whether forced, coerced, or free, transatlantic migrants entered a Native world that had also been in motion long before Europeans appeared. In the early thirteenth century, Mississippian societies—characterized by

1. Aaron S. Fogleman, "From Slaves, Convicts, and Servants to Free Passengers: The Transformation of Immigration in the Era of the American Revolution," *Journal of American History*, LXXXV (1998), 43–76; Alison Games, "Migration," in David Armitage and Michael J. Braddick, eds., *The British Atlantic World, 1500–1800* (Basingstoke, U.K., 2002), 36–43; Alexander X. Byrd, *Captives and Voyagers: Black Migrants across the Eighteenth-Century British Atlantic World* (Baton Rouge, La., 2008), 2, 4, 9.

concentrated towns surrounded by villages and centered on maize agriculture—had predominated across the Eastern Woodlands for centuries. On the eve of European arrival in the Americas, those centralized communities had begun to disperse and form new confederacies that would dominate the eastern half of the continent by the seventeenth century. Those polities already sought to expel outsiders to their benefit. When the English set foot in what is now Virginia, the Powhatan Confederacy was in the process of replacing rival chiefdoms along the Chesapeake Bay's coastal plain with those they had subjugated. Haudenosaunees would similarly displace outsiders, broadening the boundaries of Iroqouia in what is now New York. Up and down the Atlantic seaboard, seventeenth-century Native people fought English colonization and defended their borders by keeping colonial settlements to the coasts. For Indigenous people, as for transatlantic migrants, who moved and where had enormous consequences.[2]

Before the United States appeared on any map, removal had an extensive history in North America. British imperial officials relied on it as an instrument of colonization. Fueled by removal, the British Empire expanded dramatically by the eighteenth century. Removal made population serve the growing empire. Later, it would come to inform early national debates about population and who constituted *the people* in the new United States. British precedents lay the groundwork for those early national debates.

Early modern English thinkers vaunted removal as a crucial tool of governance—a way to harness population to the ends of state building. Accounting for population, however, had not always been important to how the English made sense of the world. Before the seventeenth century, European writers debated whether counting people was desirable or even useful. The first censuses taken in Europe were accounts made after the plagues of the Middle Ages, as societies sought to comprehend the devastation of epidemic disease. More routine curiosity in population only emerged later, in the seventeenth century. Colonization drove an interest in demography—a field for which European writers had no name. In an era of Atlantic connection and migration, counting people suddenly seemed important. What

2. Neal Salisbury, "The Indians' Old World: Native Americans and the Coming of Europeans," *William and Mary Quarterly*, 3d Ser., LIII (1996), 439–449; Robbie Ethridge, "Introduction: Mapping the Mississippian Shatter Zone," in Ethridge and Sheri M. Shuck-Hall, *Mapping the Mississippian Shatter Zone: The Colonial Indian Slave Trade and Regional Instability in the American South* (Lincoln, Nebr., 2009), 1–62; Jon Parmenter, *The Edge of the Woods: Iroquoia, 1534–1701* (East Lansing, Mich., 2010), xxvii–xlv.

Molly Farrell has called "human accounting" lay at the center of English ventures in North America. As Native people grappled with the arrival of Europeans on their shores, they also used population counts to make sense of the changes the outsiders brought with them. Counting people provided a way to comprehend the vast new epidemiological, political, and cultural worlds that Europeans, Africans, and Natives had created by the seventeenth century.[3]

Sixteenth-century English colonial promoters took advantage of this newfound preoccupation with counting people to propose North American ventures as solutions for the social ills they associated with high population density. Between 1560 and 1600, England's population increased from three to four million people. Enclosures, poor harvests, and declining wages prompted the long-distance migration of people from rural areas to towns. English thinkers argued that these changes caused poverty and criminality, two mounting social ills that needed to be managed. Most dangerous in their eyes were those they called vagrants, the able-bodied poor who traveled looking for work and opportunity beyond their home counties. Vagrancy had been categorized as a criminal offense in the fourteenth century, but vagrancy statutes proliferated as long-distance migration became more prominent. From the late sixteenth to the seventeenth centuries, a series of thirteen poor laws defined the poverty of the able bodied as lawlessness.[4]

Colonial promoters promised to reform the able-bodied poor through removal. They made a case for their projects at court by suggesting that colonization would transport undesirable people out of England. Excess populations at home, they argued, would become the building blocks for successful colonization. People were key to what the early English lawyer Richard Hakluyt the elder believed was necessary to "man," "plant," and "keepe" the new North American colonies. Coerced and forced migration solved two interrelated problems of early modern statecraft—how to reduce the population of the metropole and how to "man" North American colonial ventures.[5]

3. Molly Farrell, *Counting Bodies: Population in Colonial American Writing* (New York, 2016), 2–32 (quotation, 8).

4. A. L. Beier, *Masterless Men: The Vagrancy Problem in England, 1560–1640* (New York, 1985), 9, 16.

5. Richard Hakluyt (the elder), "Pamphlet for the Virginia Enterprise," (1585), in E. G. R. Taylor, ed., *The Original Writings and Correspondence of the Two Richard Hakluyts,* II (London, 1935), 333 (quotations); Christopher Tomlins, *Freedom Bound: Law, Labor, and Civic Identity in Colonizing English America, 1580–1865* (New York, 2010), 21; Marilyn C. Baseler, *"Asylum for Mankind": America, 1607–1800* (Ithaca, N.Y., 1998), 26. For colonies as safety valves, see Beier, *Masterless Men,* 150; Tomlins, *Freedom*

Control over the movements of English subjects had long been the king's prerogative. A 1381 act had allowed the king to restrain the emigration of subjects whose services he required. Elizabeth I and James I both assumed that monarchs enjoyed complete control over the movement of their subjects within and beyond England when they limited the mobility of Catholics. Proprietors were granted permission in colonial charters to transport people to new realms in the name of the monarch. The Georgia Charter of 1732, for example, authorized colonial proprietors "at all times hereafter, to transport and convey" people to the colony by permission of the king. People were, as Christopher Tomlins writes, "A resource of the Crown, to be rendered mobile or immobile *propter communem utilitatem,* that is, according to the best interests of the state." Mobile subjects, however, never lost their allegiance. Sir Edward Coke's 1603 interpretation of *Calvin's Case* cemented a theory of subjecthood that was underpinned by feudal ideas about perpetual allegiance. Even traveling subjects could never renounce their responsibilities to the monarch.[6]

English monarchs could also transport undesirable subjects to new colonial spaces, where they would help to establish colonies on behalf of the crown. In the sixteenth century during the reign of Elizabeth I, the English began to punish vagrancy and transiency with transportation. A 1598 act threatened vagrants with whipping, removal to their place of birth, imprisonment, or banishment. In 1603, under James I, the Privy Council specified that "dangerous Rogues" could be sent to Newfoundland, the East and West Indies, France, Germany, Spain, or the Low Countries. Local officials also had the ability to move people domestically to address the problem of poverty. The Elizabethan poor law of 1601 made parish officials responsible for raising taxes to provide basic poor support for those who could not work and for building almshouses and arranging apprenticeships for those who could. As English men and women traveled longer distances to find work in the seventeenth century, the poor laws changed to address this new reality. To avoid overburdening the relief rolls of populous towns, a 1572 act

---

Bound, 5, 21; William A. Pettigrew, *Freedom's Debt: The Royal African Company and the Politics of the Atlantic Slave Trade, 1672–1752* (Williamsburg, Va., and Chapel Hill, N.C., 2013), 29; Farrell, *Counting Bodies,* 2–32.

6. Charter of Georgia (1732), in Francis Newton Thorpe, ed., *The Federal and State Constitutions: Colonial Charters, and Other Organic Laws of the States, Territories, and Colonies Now or Heretofore Forming the United States of America,* II, *Florida—Kansas* (Washington, D.C., 1909), 773 ("at all times"); Tomlins, *Freedom Bound,* 70–78 ("resource," 71); Baseler, *"Asylum for Mankind,"* 28; James H. Kettner, *The Development of American Citizenship, 1608–1870* (Williamsburg, Va., and Chapel Hill, N.C., 1984), 7–8.

gave people a settlement where they were born or where they had lived for three years or more, which made them eligible for poor support. The time it took to gain a settlement was reduced to forty days in 1662. Parish officers could remove those who did not have a settlement before they could apply for poor support. They decided who could make a claim on the community and who could not, determining its membership and policing its boundaries.[7]

English colonists in North America adopted poor laws wholesale, modeling colonial poor relief on English precedents. In Virginia, counties administered poor relief locally through the mechanisms of settlement and removal even before the colonial legislature passed a poor relief statute of its own. The vestrymen of Virginia parishes assessed the needs of impoverished people and determined the appropriate poll tax to levy on residents of their parish. In New England, it was town leaders who administered poor relief. To gain a settlement in a colonial town or parish, one had to be born or purchase land there. Children inherited settlements from their fathers. Women could obtain a settlement in their husband's town or parish through marriage—a result of coverture, in which women's legal rights were suspended and represented by her husband. Poor laws led to removal in some colonies but not others. In eighteenth-century Rhode Island, transients were often warned out, or told to leave, and sent back to the town where they had a settlement. In Vermont and Massachusetts, actual removal was infrequent, even when colonists were warned out. Boston overseers used warning out as a preliminary step to strip the transient poor from the city's rolls and shift them onto the colony's poor rolls. It was less a means of social exclusion than a clever accounting trick that kept Bostonians from having to assume financial responsibility for mobile people.[8]

Undesirable people subject to removal to the colonies also included

7. By the King, "A Proclamation for the Due and Speedy Execution of the Statute against Rogues, Vagabonds, Idle, and Dissolute Persons," Sept. 17, 1603, in Clarence S. Brigham, ed., *British Royal Proclamations relating to America, 1603–1783* (New York, 1911), 2 ("dangerous"), also cited in Baseler, *"Asylum for Mankind,"* 29, 32–38; Beier, *Masterless Men,* 158–162; Bernard Bailyn, *The Peopling of British North America: An Introduction* (1986; rpt. New York, 1988), 20–25; Keith Wrightson, *Earthly Necessities: Economic Lives in Early Modern Britain* (New Haven, Conn., 2000), 215–221; Ruth Wallis Herndon, *Unwelcome Americans: Living on the Margin in Early New England* (Philadelphia, 2001), 4; Elna C. Green, *This Business of Relief: Confronting Poverty in a Southern City, 1740–1940* (Athens, Ga., 2003), 12; Tomlins, *Freedom Bound,* 76.

8. Herndon, *Unwelcome Americans,* 5, 10; Green, *This Business of Relief,* 10–11, 14; Cornelia H. Dayton and Sharon V. Salinger, *Robert Love's Warnings: Searching for Strangers in Colonial Boston* (Philadelphia, 2014), 4–5, 8–9, 15, 20–21.

those convicted of a wide range of crimes as well as indigent children, political radicals, and religious dissenters. In 1615, an act of James I's Privy Council allowed banishment as a punishment for pardoned felons who had been found guilty of certain capital crimes. They could choose banishment, usually but not always accompanied by a fixed term of servitude. Criminal transportation in the seventeenth century was carried out in an ad hoc manner. Sometimes those convicted of crimes were allowed to arrange their own transportation while others were consigned to merchants who transported them alongside other unfree laborers. When a new Transportation Act made exile a statutory punishment for many noncapital as well as capital crimes in 1718, rather than as a conditional requirement for a pardon, the convict transportation business expanded to meet the needs of the new law. After its passage, transportation became the most common punishment for noncapital crimes. Thirty thousand English convicts were exiled to North America between 1718 and 1775, and at least fifty thousand English, Irish, and Scottish convicts were transported over the course of the eighteenth century as a whole. Convict transportation was a lucrative business for English merchants, who carried people from London and Bristol to Virginia, Maryland, Pennsylvania, and colonies in the West Indies. From the perspective of English ministers and colonial promoters, transportation made those convicted of crimes useful to the state by sending them to the colonies where they would serve colonial labor needs. In the cases of vagrancy and criminal transportation, removal and colonization were bound together.[9]

In the colonies themselves, the success of English imperial projects depended on the removal and replacement of people who already lived there. Ireland, where the English sought greater control beginning in the sixteenth century, provided a model for colonizers in North America. During the Elizabethan era, the English feared Irish Catholics as internal enemies who might assist a Spanish army to invade Protestant England. Military campaigns targeted rebels who defended Ireland's autonomy, confiscated their lands, and removed them to make way for English migrants. As punishment for threatening the security of the realm, Irish dissidents were expelled after rebellions in the 1570s, 1598, 1606, and 1641. English colonizers hoped that transplanted English migrants would have a civilizing effect on local communities, turning those they called savages into subjects by reforming Irish

9. A. Roger Ekirch, *Bound for America: The Transportation of British Convicts to the Colonies, 1718–1775* (Oxford, 1987), 1, 21–23, 70–71, 112; Bailyn, *Peopling of British North America,* 61; Baseler, *"Asylum for Mankind,"* 74–75. For convict transportation as a broader European colonial practice, see Lauren Benton, *A Search for Sovereignty: Law and Geography in European Empires, 1400–1900* (New York, 2010), 162–187.

religion, language, modes of dress, and farming. By placing their own bureaucrats in charge, English officials believed they could diminish the power of clan leaders. They put this agenda into practice in Munster in southern Ireland in the late sixteenth century, where they sent thousands of English settlers to create a model colony on land taken from Irish rebels. They did the same in Ulster in the early seventeenth century, attracting one hundred thousand Scottish, Welsh, and English migrants there by 1641.[10]

The English brought the example of Ireland with them to colonial projects across the Atlantic. Indeed, the same colonial promoters were sometimes involved in ventures in both places. They also looked to Spanish colonization and the tributary relationship the Spanish had imposed on Indigenous people as a model for their own colonies. English state builders believed that moving English subjects to North America, as they had done in Ireland, would similarly transform Native agriculture, dress, religion, and politics. When the English landed in 1607 in what is now Virginia, it was with these assumptions and expectations that they first approached the Algonquian, Iroquoian, and Siouan people who controlled the region.[11]

The coastal plain where the English established Jamestown was the territory of the Powhatan Confederacy, a paramount chiefdom of more than thirty Algonquian polities ruled by the paramount chief Powhatan. The confederacy's chiefdoms stretched across Tsenacommacah, the coastal territory from the James River to the Potomac River, and they all paid tribute to Powhatan, who had the power to allocate use rights to lands held in common to particular communities. Powhatan had the same idea as the English. He planned to fold them into a tributary relationship that would allow him to augment his own power and dominate English trade networks.[12]

When conflict ruled out the subordinate relationships that both the English and the Powhatans imagined, they turned to war—the English to dispossess the Powhatans and the Powhatans to conquer the English. Powhatan had already successfully subjugated and relocated other Indigenous people along the coastal plain. By the early seventeenth century, he was engaged in a campaign to incorporate Algonquians around the Chesapeake Bay to add to the chiefdoms he had inherited along the James and York

10. Nicholas P. Canny, *Making Ireland British, 1580–1650* (New York, 2001), 121–164, 187–242; Baseler, *"Asylum for Mankind,"* 25; Karen Ordahl Kupperman, *The Jamestown Project* (Cambridge, Mass., 2007), 34, 194–198.

11. Kupperman, *Jamestown Project,* 198–209; April Lee Hatfield, *Atlantic Virginia: Intercolonial Relations in the Seventeenth Century* (Philadelphia, 2004), 7, 9.

12. Karen Ordahl Kupperman, *Indians and English Facing Off in Early America* (Ithaca, N.Y., 2000), 174–176; Hatfield, *Atlantic Virginia,* 12, 18.

Rivers. Those who resisted were subject to reprisals. In 1608, Powhatan sent a party to attack and disperse the Piankatanks after they skirted him by sending their own diplomatic mission to the English. He settled the Kecoughtans and more loyal followers in Piankatank territory in their place. He treated the English in the same way, confining them to the coast and containing their ability to trade with his enemies. In 1622, after Powhatan's brother and successor Opechancanough and the Powhatan Confederacy determined that the English had not properly fulfilled their tributary relationship, they orchestrated a military campaign to destroy English settlements, killing one-third of the colonists. Still, English migrants kept moving further inland. Opechancanough attacked colonial settlements again in 1644. When the war ended two years later, the Virginia colonists began a concerted campaign to remove the Powhatans and replace them with their own colonial population along the coastal plain.[13]

In most places in eastern North America and for much of the seventeenth century, however, the English had little power to carry out their plans to dispossess Indigenous people. From the Carolinas to New York, Native people controlled regional geopolitics, and Europeans engaged in trade and diplomacy on Indigenous terms. Indeed, in much of northeastern North America, for example, it was the Haudenosaunees who had the power to disperse outsiders. Reeling from population losses caused by epidemics, Haudenosaunees went to war in the mid-seventeenth century across the Great Lakes and the Ohio Valley to cement their position in the fur trade and to replace kin who had died of disease by adopting captives. Between 1650 and 1689, Haudenosaunee campaigns reached as far south as Cherokee country, west to the Quapaws and Iowas, and north to the Wendats. Even though it was not their primary aim, Haudenosaunee campaigns caused dispersal. Wendats left their territory in 1649 after Haudenosaunee attacks. Fort Ancient villagers abandoned what is now Ohio, Kentucky, and West Virginia from 1630 to 1680 because of war and the spread of epidemic diseases. As a result of these campaigns, Iroquoia expanded well beyond upstate New York.[14]

13. Helen C. Rountree, *The Powhatan Indians of Virginia: Their Traditional Culture* (Norman, Okla., 1989), 119, 140–141, 146; Rountree, *Powhatan Foreign Relations, 1500–1722* (Charlottesville, Va., 1993), 1–13; Hatfield, *Atlantic Virginia*, 19, 24–25; James D. Rice, "War and Politics: Powhatan Expansionism and the Problem of Native American Warfare," *William and Mary Quarterly*, 3d Ser., LXXVII (2020), 25–28.

14. Michael Guasco, "To 'Doe Some Good upon Their Countrymen': The Paradox of Indian Slavery in Early Anglo-America," *Journal of Social History*, XLI (2007), 389–411; Margaret Ellen Newell, *Brethren by Nature: New England Indians, Colonists, and the Origins of American Slavery* (Ithaca, N.Y. 2015).

Nevertheless, English colonists did not hesitate to use removal to secure the North American colonies when and where they could, just as other Englishmen had attempted in Ireland. After the Pequot War in 1636–1637 and King Philip's War in 1675–1676, for example, Puritans explained that the expulsion of Natives from their homelands as well as their execution, banishment, or sale into slavery was punishment for their going to war with the colonies. Seventeen Pequot men and women were sent out of Massachusetts and into bondage on Providence Island off the coast of Nicaragua in 1637 after the Pequot War—an act that Puritans believed was justified because they were prisoners of war. As colonists enslaved hundreds of Pequots after the conflict, and in the aftermath of later wars, they called on classical ideas from political theorists about who was enslaveable. Legal writing by Hugo Grotius, John Locke, and Emer de Vattel explained that enemies could be enslaved during the course of a just war.[15]

The English justified their participation in the Atlantic slave trade and the removal of Africans from their homelands along the same lines. In addition to leaning on emerging racial categories of whiteness and blackness, they also argued that they had a right to enslave Africans because they were captives of war from legitimate conflicts between African polities. Africans were movable according to European writing on international law. Enslavement in West Africa derived from outsider status, too, though it differed from chattel slavery. Africans enslaved debtors, criminals, and war captives who might then be incorporated into kingdoms and societies in a dependent relationship. Outsiders—those without kin or local connections or those from different polities or lineages—were also at risk of enslavement. In the eighteenth century, the expansion of European demand for slaves increased social stratification and cycles of war across West Africa, drawing more and more people into the slave trade. Justifications for who was enslaveable shifted to meet the demands of the coastal trade in enslaved people.[16]

15. Daniel K. Richter, *The Ordeal of the Longhouse: The Peoples of the Iroquois League in the Era of European Colonization* (Williamsburg, Va., and Chapel Hill, N.C., 1992), 62, 74; Parmenter, *Edge of the Woods,* 60, 80–81, 128; Stephen Warren, *The Worlds the Shawnees Made: Migration and Violence in Early America* (Chapel Hill, N.C., 2014), 13; Kathryn Magee Labelle, *Dispersed but Not Destroyed: A History of the Seventeenth-Century Wendat People* (Vancouver, B.C., 2013), 3–4.

16. Kim F. Hall, *Things of Darkness: Economies of Race and Gender in Early Modern England* (Ithaca, N.Y., 1995); Jennifer L. Morgan, "'Some Could Suckle over Their Shoulder': Male Travelers, Female Bodies, and the Gendering of Racial Ideology, 1500–1700," *William and Mary Quarterly,* 3d Ser., LIV (1997), 167–192; Jeffrey Glover, "Witnessing African War: Slavery, the Laws of War, and Anglo-American Abolitionism," *William and Mary Quarterly,* 3d Ser., LXXIV (2017), 503–532; Toby Green, *A Fistful*

Regardless, English slave traders felt little need to expend much effort in explaining their participation in the Atlantic slave trade. By the time they began to trade for captives on the West African coast in large numbers in the early seventeenth century, Portuguese and Spanish slave traders had already carried more than six hundred thousand people across the Atlantic into bondage in Mexico, Peru, Brazil, and the Caribbean. The English were late to enter into the slave trade. When English migrants arrived in North America, they were expecting that Africans would labor there as slaves.[17]

English writers embraced the slave trade at the exact moment that they also rethought England's own populousness. English ideas about population shifted as both population growth and the numbers of indentured servants seeking to cross the Atlantic slowed in the 1660s. After 1680, members of the Privy Council and Lords of Trade attempted to collect accurate data about English subjects through censuses and customs registers. Population counts allowed ministers to observe changes in population and to put numbers to work in policy making. Mercantilists believed that a growing population and a favorable balance of trade were good measures of one country's position in relation to another. Conversely, England's shrinking population could be a marker of decline. Colonization had once seemed like a boon to writers who hoped to reform vagrants and convicts by sending them across the Atlantic. By the late seventeenth century, intellectuals, councillors, and monarchs were beginning to flip conventional thinking about colonization and population on its head. Writers William Petyt and Roger Coke suddenly imagined the colonies as drains on the metropole's prosperity rather than guarantors of its stability. The colonies stole away white migrants to the detriment of England. As population growth slowed, the movement of Englishmen across the Atlantic no longer seemed so fortuitous.[18]

English thinkers believed that African bondage provided the solution to the problem of migration and depopulation. Enslaved Africans would fulfill colonial labor needs without impacting labor needs at home. These were convenient justifications, since the English embraced the slave trade

of Shells: West Africa from the Rise of the Slave Trade to the Age of Revolution (Chicago, 2019), 4–5, 216–217, 267–270.

17. Hatfield, *Atlantic Virginia,* 137–138; Michael Guasco, *Slaves and Englishmen: Human Bondage in the Early Modern Atlantic World* (Philadelphia, 2014), 195–226; John C. Coombs, "'Others Not Christians in the Service of the English': Interpreting the Status of Africans and African Americans in Early Virginia," *Virginia Magazine of History and Biography,* CXXVII (2019), 212–238.

18. Patricia Cline Cohen, *A Calculating People: The Spread of Numeracy in Early America* (New York, 1999), 77; Games, "Migration," in Armitage and Braddick, eds., *British Atlantic World,* 38–39; Pettigrew, *Freedom's Debt,* 29.

with a persistence and ruthlessness that, by the late seventeenth century, made them the leading carriers of enslaved Africans in the Atlantic world, surpassing the Dutch and the French. In 1698, Parliament opened up the slave trade beyond the monopoly of the Royal African Company, flooding the market with traders eager to meet colonial demand for enslaved people. The English government and metropolitan and colonial elites encouraged the slave trade at every turn with devastating effects. Between 1662 and 1749, slave traders transformed the British colonies by forcing 1.4 million people into the holds of slave ships and into bondage in North America. British Atlantic trade solidified around slave-grown commodities, and even colonists who did not participate directly in the slave trade profited from the ancillary businesses—rum distilleries, ropewalks, and farms—that supported it. As British policymakers began to reconceptualize the relationship between population and colonization, enslavement bound the British Empire's many parts together and powered its expansion.[19]

The Atlantic slave trade, free migration to North America, and natural reproduction augmented colonial populations in the eighteenth century, shifting imperial debate away from orchestrating removal to controlling migration. In his *Commentaries on the Laws of England,* the jurist William Blackstone listed the power of movement and "loco-motion" next to personal security and property as essential rights preserved by English common law. The power "of changing situation" offered protection from imprisonment without "due course of law." Nevertheless, the power of locomotion could be rescinded as well as directed by the crown. British officials, for example, took measures to retain skilled workers and prohibit them from leaving England in 1718, 1750, and 1765. As European immigration to the mainland North American colonies tripled by the mid-eighteenth century with the arrival of thousands of German, Irish, Scottish, and Welsh migrants, British reformers began to address movement as an imperial problem.[20]

19. Wrightson, *Earthly Necessities,* 238; Stephanie E. Smallwood, *Saltwater Slavery: A Middle Passage from Africa to American Diaspora* (Cambridge, Mass., 2007), 71; Byrd, *Captives and Voyagers,* 2, 4, 9; Pettigrew, *Freedom's Debt,* 29; Abigail L. Swingen, *Competing Visions of Empire: Labor, Slavery, and the Origins of the British Atlantic Empire* (New Haven, Conn., 2015), 1–9.

20. William Blackstone, *Commentaries on the Laws of England: A Facsimile of the First Edition of 1765–1769,* I, *Of the Rights of Persons* (Chicago, 1979), 130 (quotations); Bernard Bailyn, *Voyagers to the West: A Passage in the Peopling of America on the Eve of the Revolution* (New York, 1986), 26; Baseler, *"Asylum for Mankind,"* 124–127; Andrea A. Rusnock, *Vital Accounts: Quantifying Health and Population in Eighteenth-Century England and France* (New York, 2002), 4; Tomlins, *Freedom Bound,* 74; Colin G. Callo-

Population was power, but who benefitted from that power concerned writers, ministers, and reformers across the empire. From the colonial perspective, population growth was a source of pride. In 1751, Pennsylvanian Benjamin Franklin reflected with pleasure on the increasing population of Britain's North American colonies, whose inhabitants at the time numbered at more than one million people. He suggested that, at the going rate of population growth in the colonies, Englishmen in North America would outnumber Englishmen in England within a century. "What an Accession of Power to the British Empire by Sea as well as Land!" he exclaimed. Franklin's work circulated widely across the Anglo-Atlantic. It was reprinted in England throughout the 1750s and 1760s. He found common ground with men like Ezra Stiles, Adam Smith, David Hume, and the Abbe Raynal, for whom population was a signifier of social and political power and an indicator of the health of imperial economies. In his 1748 *Esprit de Lois,* Montesquieu wrote that despotism led to depopulation. Political philosophers like Montesquieu saw fertility as a political question rather than a household concern. In North America, population was a marker of the well-being of British colonial society, economy, and government. Franklin's calculations praised free women in the colonies as more productive child bearers than their English counterparts, who married later and had fewer children. Like Franklin, colonial North Americans celebrated population as proof of the colonies' mounting importance.[21]

Back in Britain, imperial administrators believed that the increase of colonial populations would make them ungovernable. William Knox, a former colonial official in Georgia, began a 1763 proposal for colonial reform, "Hints respecting the Settlement of Our American Provinces," with a reflection on the dangers of population growth. He wrote that "His Majesties possessions in North America, are so many times more extensive than the Island of Great Britain, that if they were equally well inhabited, Great Britain could no longer maintain her dominion over them." Knox projected forward in time to when the population of the colonies might one day make

---

way, *The Scratch of a Pen: 1763 and the Transformation of North America* (New York, 2006), 24.

21. "Observations concerning the Increase of Mankind," 1751, in Leonard W. Labaree, ed., *Papers of Benjamin Franklin,* IV, *July 1, 1750, through June 30, 1753* (New Haven, Conn., 1961), 233 (quotation); James H. Cassedy, *Demography in Early America: Beginnings of the Statistical Mind, 1600–1800* (Cambridge, Mass., 1969), 158–179. For eighteenth-century fertility and population, see Susan E. Klepp, *Revolutionary Conceptions: Women, Fertility, and Family Limitation in America, 1760–1820* (Williamsburg, Va., and Chapel Hill, N.C., 2009).

the empire irrelevant. Colonists, too, marshaled these same arguments to different ends. The expanding population of the North American colonies gave them a new sense of their own importance. In 1765, during the debate over the Stamp Act, Franklin went before the House of Commons and lobbied for its repeal on the grounds of North America's strength within the empire. He argued that the loss of the colonies' increasing purchasing power would harm the English more than North Americans. Fears of colonial population growth led the Privy Council to prohibit royal governors from granting large tracts of land to speculators in 1773, to keep them from tempting thousands of migrants to British North America with the promise of cheap land for rent or sale.[22]

For eastern Indigenous people, population as power looked very different. In 1763, the Peace of Paris that ended the Seven Years' War left Native peoples without their French allies while also granting France's North American claims—a vast expanse of Native lands—east of the Mississippi River to Britain and those west of it to Spain. Although Britain's title to much of that land was on paper only, the peace nevertheless emboldened speculators and migrants. The war left a legacy of racial enmity and Indian hating along the frontier that justified colonial land grabs. Increases in the colonial population intensified struggles over land, making it difficult for Native and colonial communities to resolve their conflicts through diplomatic rituals. Colonial migrants squatted on Native lands protected by treaty, and speculators made claims to those territories by petition and patent. When Native peoples in western Pennsylvania and the Ohio country looked to the British garrisons that proliferated across their country after 1763, they found little reassurance. British troops made no moves to vacate western posts as British officials had earlier promised. Despite that gift giving had been a vital part of diplomatic rituals that had sustained Native alliances with the French, British commander-in-chief Jeffrey Amherst sought to eliminate extraneous expenditures in the aftermath of the Seven Years' War and strictly control trade. As the French administration exited North America, Amherst simultaneously cut back on customary gift giving at British posts.

22. Thomas C. Barrow, "A Project for Imperial Reform: 'Hints respecting the Settlement for Our American Provinces,' 1763," *William and Mary Quarterly,* 3d Ser., XXIV (1967), 113 (quotation); William Cobbett, ed., *The Parliamentary History of England, from the Earliest Period to the Year 1803 . . . ,* XVI, *A. D. 1765–1771* (London, 1813), 141; Cassedy, *Demography in Early America,* 164, 174, 178–182; Bailyn, *Peopling of British North America,* 72–74; Baseler, *"Asylum for Mankind,"* 127–130; Rusnock, *Vital Accounts,* 181; Nicole Eustace, *1812: War and the Passions of Patriotism* (Philadelphia, 2012), 6.

By the mid-eighteenth century, the growth of the North American colonies had come to put unbearable pressure on many eastern Indigenous people.[23]

To protest British policy, Native people in the Great Lakes region went to war to defend their borders. Delaware prophet Neolin preached that the only way to solve the crises of land loss, famine, and disease in western towns was to cast off Euro-American culture and trade. Odawa war chief Pontiac took the Delaware message to the Odawas, Ojibwes, Potawatomis, and Wyandots. In the spring of 1763, a new confederation waged war on British forts across the Great Lakes, capturing the majority of them within months. Pontiac's War was a successful and coordinated effort to push the British military out of Indigenous lands. Native power made British administrators rethink the relationship between population and sovereignty in the colonies.[24]

After the Seven Years' War and Pontiac's War, British administrators quickly took up Native demands for a firm border that would keep colonists on the coasts. They had already begun to focus on restricting the settlement of western lands in 1761. In May 1763, Charles Wyndham, second earl of Egremont, secretary of state for the Southern Department in charge of overseeing the North American colonies, asked the Board of Trade, a committee of the Privy Council that advised on colonial matters, to formulate a plan for governing Britain's western land claims. The royal Proclamation of October 7, 1763, made the Appalachian Mountains the boundary of British settlement. Promising to protect Native lands west of the line, the proclamation restricted governors from granting warrants to survey beyond it. Those east of the line had to be purchased by the colonies rather than private individuals.[25]

By restricting western land settlement, British administrators hoped to make their North American subjects useful to the empire. Knox, the former colonial governor of Georgia, and his contemporaries in the ministry and the Board of Trade, wanted to encourage coastal settlements to keep British colonists focused on their Atlantic connections. Knox believed that it was

23. Eric Hinderaker, *Elusive Empires: Constructing Colonialism in the Ohio Valley, 1673–1800* (New York, 1999), 134–175.

24. Gregory Evans Dowd, *War under Heaven: Pontiac, the Indian Nations, and the British Empire* (Baltimore, Md., 2002); Jon William Parmenter, "Pontiac's War: Forging New Links in the Anglo-Iroquois Covenant Chain, 1758–1766," *Ethnohistory*, XLIV (1997), 617–654.

25. "By the King; A Proclamation," Oct. 7, 1763, in Adam Shortt and Arthur G. Doughty, eds., *Documents relating to the Constitutional History of Canada, 1759–1791*, Part 1 (Ottawa, 1918), 163–168; Hinderaker, *Elusive Empires*, 164–165.

important to limit "the Increment of People" and "the extent of the Settlements" in North America. Egremont agreed. Tasked with managing colonial policy, he argued that an extended frontier would foment expensive wars with Native peoples. Egremont told the Board of Trade that restricting settlements west of the Appalachian Mountains would funnel new migrants to coastal areas in the south or Nova Scotia, where "they would be usefull to their Mother Country," rather than "out of the reach of Government." Limiting western settlement would keep the peace while binding colonists to the metropole.[26]

Native people who had pressed for a boundary surely hoped the line established by the Proclamation of 1763 would be permanent. British administers were more circumspect. President of the Board of Trade, Lord Hillsborough, imagined a permanent line that would serve the metropole by keeping colonists to the coast, while Egremont thought that speculation would one day resume. It would not be long before Egremont's prediction came to fruition. Although intended to prevent warfare, encourage settlement in Nova Scotia and the Floridas, and reduce the administrative cost of empire, the boundary line would quickly prove ineffective.[27]

The idea of protecting Native land rights was anathema to speculators, who saw access to the West as one of the prizes of the Seven Years' War. They protested that British ministers had abandoned their interests and turned removal against colonists. The proclamation line did little to stop the settlement of ordinary migrants west of the Appalachians either. They simply continued to pour into the Ohio Valley and the southern backcountry with the expectation that the line would eventually be abandoned and their claims confirmed. At the treaties of Fort Augusta with Cherokee, Creek, Catawba, Chickasaw, and Choctaw delegates in 1763 and at Hard

26. Barrow, "Project for Imperial Reform," *William and Mary Quarterly,* 3d Ser., XXIV (1967), 113 ("Increment"), 115; Verner W. Crane, "Notes and Documents: Hints Relative to the Division and Government of the Conquered and Newly Acquired Countries in America," *Mississippi Valley Historical Review,* VIII (1922), 371 ("they would be usefull"); Richard White, *The Middle Ground: Indians, Empires, and Republics in the Great Lakes Region, 1650–1815* (1991; rpt. New York, 2011), 308; Colin G. Calloway, *The Indian World of George Washington: The First President, the First Americans, and the Birth of the Nation* (New York, 2018), 180.

27. [R. A. Humphreys], "Lord Shelburne and the Proclamation of 1763," *English Historical Review,* XLIX (1934), 241–264; Jack M. Sosin, *Whitehall and the Wilderness: The Middle West in British Colonial Policy, 1760–1775* ([Lincoln, Nebr.], 1961), 52–78; Hinderaker, *Elusive Empires,* 164–165; Stuart Banner, *How the Indians Lost Their Land: Law and Power on the Frontier* (Cambridge, Mass., 2007), 92–95; Calloway, *Scratch of a Pen,* 92–96.

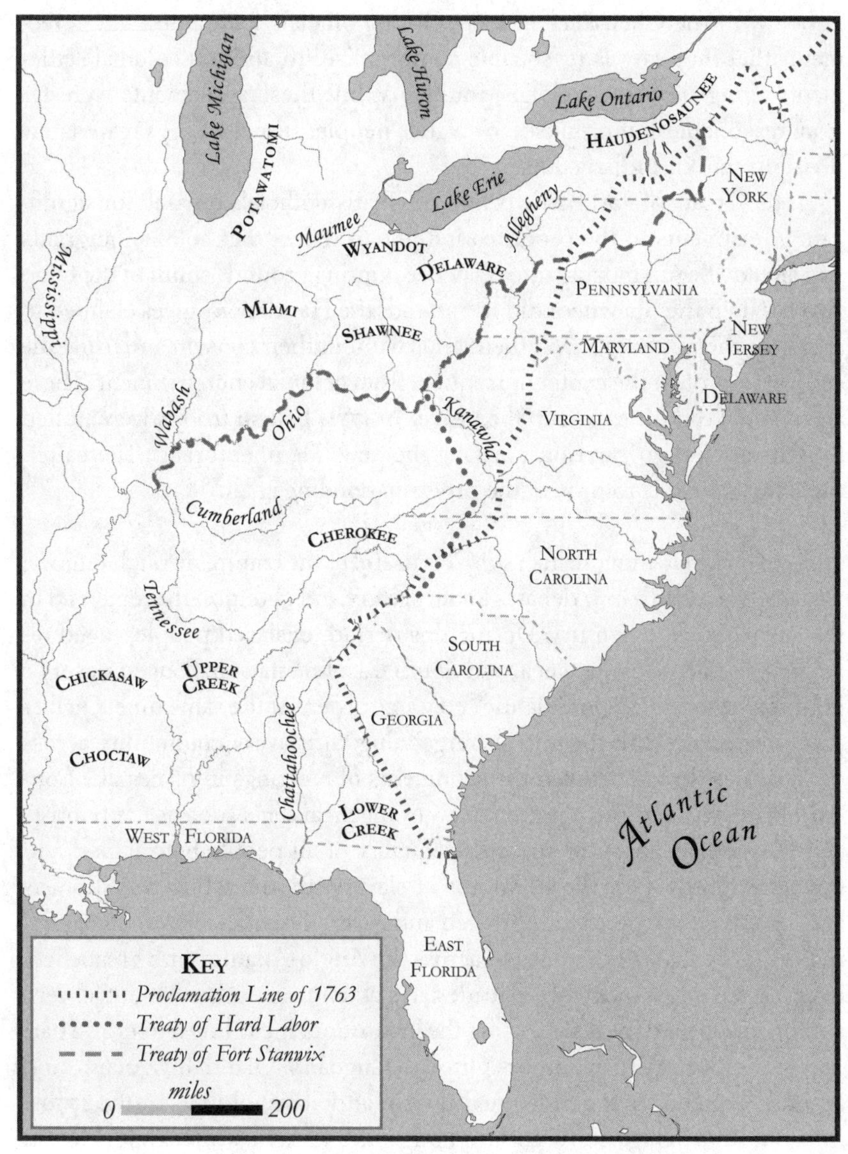

MAP 1. *Proclamation Line of 1763. Drawn by Rebecca Wrenn*

Labor with the Cherokees in 1768, British officials hammered out agreements that they saw as reasonable compromises to address colonial settlements along the Appalachian Mountains, but these agreements were far from reasonable compromises for Native people. Instead, they created new divisions within Indian country.[28]

At the Treaty of Fort Stanwix in 1768, British officials pressed for significant adjustments to the proclamation line to reflect that colonial migrants had already begun moving into Shawnee hunting grounds south of the Ohio River. When the Shawnees did not attend, the Haudenosaunees claimed to speak for them, trading away their lands without their consent and using the cession to protect the center of Iroquoia from colonial encroachment. These agreements did little to keep the peace. In 1771, British troops were pulled back from western garrisons, leaving the new line unenforced. Thereafter, there was no effort to protect the proclamation line at all.[29]

Plans to make far-flung British subjects useful to the empire through removal also resonated with new debates about slavery and abolition that emerged in the late eighteenth century. During this period, enslaved people waged rebellions in Barbados, Jamaica, and South Carolina that challenged slavery's importance to the Anglo-Atlantic economic order. At the same time, Quaker peace testimony knit together a burgeoning antislavery community across the colonies. Friends linked the sentiments of meetings in places like London, Pennsylvania, and Virginia. New evangelical sects such as the Baptists and Methodists began to stress the equality of all people before God and divine retribution for the sinfulness of slavery. By the 1760s, abolitionists had already developed a full-throated antislavery discourse based on natural rights theory that they circulated across the Anglo-Atlantic with great effectiveness. Over the next two decades, Black and white British antislavery authors published pieces attacking the institution, including letters and narratives by Black British authors Ottobah Cugoano, Olaudah Equiano, and Ignatius Sancho, that condemned racism and slaveholding. In the 1770s, freedom suits instigated by enslaved litigants and their white lawyers tested the limits of natural rights in England and in the colonies. Black petitioners derided the yawning gap between American cries for liberty and the prac-

28. Banner, *How the Indians Lost Their Land,* 93, 95–104; Calloway, *Scratch of a Pen,* 98–100; Daniel K. Richter, *Before the Revolution: America's Ancient Pasts* (Cambridge, Mass., 2011), 408–412; Calloway, *Indian World of George Washington,* 180–184.

29. Hinderaker, *Elusive Empires,* 168–170; Daniel K. Richter, *Facing East from Indian Country: A Native History of Early America* (Cambridge, Mass., 2001), 210–211; Banner, *How the Indians Lost Their Land,* 97.

tice of slavery. On the eve of the American Revolution, antislavery writers moved from critiques of slaveholding to plans for dismantling the institution itself. From the outset, some of them argued that newly freed people should be removed from slave societies to free colonies.[30]

Colonization was one of the most enduring answers to social challenges in the eighteenth-century Anglo-Atlantic world. It gained adherents in the moment of imperial reorganization after the Seven Years' War, as British imperial officials sought to bring order to the new territories Britain had gained during the conflict. Maurice Morgann, private secretary to William Fitzmaurice Petty, second earl of Shelburne, recommended in 1772 that freed slaves in the North American colonies be transported to the newly acquired British West Florida. Shelburne held posts in the 1760s as the president of the Board of Trade and as secretary of state for the Southern Department. Morgann's job was to retain and order new imperial possessions by populating them with migrants who would rival Native inhabitants and French or Spanish competitors. British Quaker physician John Fothergill penned his own 1772 plan for colonizing free people on Tobago and Saint Vincent, which had both been ceded to Britain by the French in 1763. Morgann and Fothergill imagined that freed people could be useful to the empire by populating new colonial spaces. Removal and abolition were linked from the beginning.[31]

Early colonizationists believed that removal might transform people who were property under the law into owners of property instead. Private property was essential to late-eighteenth-century ideas about self-sufficiency and virtue, so it is not surprising that antislavery writers perceived landownership as a crucial component of freedom. Some white antislavery writers saw

30. James D. Essig, *The Bonds of Wickedness: American Evangelicals against Slavery, 1770–1808* (Philadelphia, 1982); Gary B. Nash and Jean R. Soderlund, *Freedom by Degrees: Emancipation in Pennsylvania and Its Aftermath* (New York, 1991), 41–73; Brycchan Carey, *From Peace to Freedom: Quaker Rhetoric and the Birth of American Antislavery, 1657–1761* (New Haven, Conn., 2012); Manisha Sinha, *The Slave's Cause: A History of Abolition* (New Haven, Conn., 2016), 9–33. On Cugoano, Sancho, and Equiano, see Vincent Carretta and Philip Gould, eds., *Genius in Bondage: Literature of the Early Black Atlantic* (Lexington, Ky., 2001). For early freedom suits, see, for example, David Waldstreicher, *Slavery's Constitution: From Revolution to Ratification* (New York, 2009), 39–42; Kirsten Sword, "Remembering Dinah Nevil: Strategic Deceptions in Eighteenth-Century Antislavery," *Journal of American History,* XCVII (2010), 315–343.

31. [Morgann], *A Plan for the Abolition of Slavery in the West Indies* (London, 1772); Christopher Leslie Brown, *Moral Capital: Foundations of British Abolitionism* (Williamsburg, Va., and Chapel Hill, N.C., 2006), 209–258, esp. 231, 259 (for Fothergill), 214–221, 230 (for Morgan); Sosin, *Whitehall and the Wilderness,* 151–152, 157–158.

opportunity for landownership in territories that were newly won in 1763. In 1771, Quaker abolitionist Anthony Benezet proposed that freed families should be given twenty acres west of the southern colonies, presumably in the midst of Indian country. British abolitionist Granville Sharp joined Benezet in suggesting in 1775 that enslaved people in the North American colonies should be freed and placed on "*compact little Farms.*" Landownership would give freed people "a natural interest in the welfare and safety of the Community," he wrote.[32]

Colonists of African descent, too, considered creating independent settlements beyond North America. In 1773, four Black Bostonians petitioned the town asking for abolition, explaining that they intended to depart the province "as we can from our joynt labours procure money to transport ourselves to some part of the coast of Africa, where we propose a settlement." Their emigration plan was part of a series of petitions calling for the abolition of slavery in Massachusetts submitted to the colony's General Court on the eve of revolution. Most early colonization plans did not circulate very far, but the Massachusetts petition was reprinted in a popular antislavery tract the following year, apparently at the request of the petitioners, making it one of the first widely received emigration plans in the American colonies.[33]

The Boston petitioners were not alone in proposing free communities beyond the control of their enslavers. Fugitives from bondage had formed maroon communities—autonomous settlements at the edges of slave societies—long before the 1770s. In Jamaica, maroon communities defended separatism so successfully that British colonizers recognized their independence with a military alliance against future slave revolts in 1739. Maroon communities were organized across eastern North America in landscapes that had been deemed uninhabitable by white migrants and speculators. They occupied swamps and borderlands where they could avoid slave catchers. Enslaved men and women fled bondage in South Carolina to

32. Granville Sharp to Benjamin Rush, July 18, 1775, in John A. Woods, "The Correspondence of Benjamin Rush and Granville Sharp, 1773–1809," *Journal of American Studies,* I (1967), 15 (quotations); [Anthony Benezet], *A Short Account of That Part of Africa, Inhabited by the Negroes . . . ,* 2d ed. (Philadelphia, 1762), 69–72; Nicholas Guyatt, *Bind Us Apart: How Enlightened Americans Invented Racial Segregation* (New York, 2016), 220–222.

33. "Petition of Peter Bestes, Sambo Freeman, Felix Holbrook, and Chester Joie, Boston," Apr. 20, 1773, in Dorothy Porter, ed., *Early Negro Writing: 1760–1837* (Boston, 1971), 254–255 (quotation, 255); Christopher Cameron, *To Plead Our Own Cause: African Americans in Massachusetts and the Making of the Antislavery Movement* (Kent, Ohio, 2014), 59–61; Sinha, *Slave's Cause,* 42.

form independent settlements away from slaveholders beginning in the mid-seventeenth century. On the Virginia-North Carolina border, enslaved fugitives formed a maroon community in the Great Dismal Swamp. During the American Revolution, escaped slaves in Georgia organized a maroon community that led attacks against Georgia troops in the name of the king.[34]

Meanwhile, white antislavery ministers promoted parallel plans for formerly enslaved people to serve as Christian missionaries in West Africa. Antislavery ministers believed that conversion could repay the sin of slavery by bringing on the millennium—the establishment by Christ of a one-thousand-year reign of the saints on earth. Some Black British writers also espoused the idea that the conversion of Africans would encourage Christ's return. Both Equiano and Cugoano were interested in Christian missions to West Africa. Such plans were equally appealing in the North American colonies. Black and white ministers and lay people in Newport, Rhode Island, supported the idea of African missions. New Light Congregationalist minister Samuel Hopkins took up colonization as a missionary enterprise on the suggestion of two of his congregants, Bristol Yamma and John Quamine. Hopkins had graduated from Yale in 1741 and studied with the New Light minister Jonathan Edwards in Northampton, Massachusetts. Edwards was a slaveholder who yet critized the slave trade, and many of the New Divinity men whom he taught—Nathaniel Niles, Levi Hart, Ebenezer Baldwin, Jonathan Edwards Jr., and Hopkins—became strong opponents of slavery. For Hopkins, his move to Newport in 1769 pushed his antislavery convictions beyond his teacher. Newport was the center of the slave trade in British North America, and the numbers of enslaved people brought by slave ships to the port city reached its peak in the early 1770s. There, the lay religious leader Sarah Osborne connected Hopkins and the more conservative Ezra Stiles, minister of the First Congregational Church, to the Ethiopian Society, a free Black prayer group of which Yamma and Quamine were a part. The two men had purchased their freedom with lottery winnings. Afterward, they sought to become missionaries through the British Society for the Propagation of the Gospel in Foreign Parts. By 1773, Stiles and Hopkins had drafted a circular to raise money to educate Yamma and Quamine at the College of New Jersey in Princeton and to pay for their passage to West Africa on a mission of conversion.[35]

34. Sylviane A. Diouf, *Slavery's Exiles: The Story of the American Maroons* (New York, 2014).

35. Jon Butler, *Awash in a Sea of Faith: Christianizing the American People* (Cambridge, Mass., 1990), 216; Charles E. Hambrick-Stowe, "The Spiritual Pilgrimage of Sarah Osborn (1714–1796)," *Church History*, LXI (1992), 408–421; Jonathan D. Sassi,

If Stiles and Hopkins were fairly clear about their aims, Yamma's and Quamine's intentions are more difficult to parse. On the one hand, Yamma and Quamine might have believed the conversion of Africans would bring on the millennium. On the other, the scheme also presented them with opportunities that had little to do with Christian missions. Yamma, for one, was fifty dollars in debt for the purchase of his freedom, a debt which Stiles and Hopkins promised to pay. Both Yamma and Quamine had also been born in West Africa. Quamine was sent by his father from Anomabo, the center of the British slave trade on the Gold Coast, to the North American colonies in 1760. He was sold into slavery on arrival in Rhode Island. The Society for the Propagation of the Gospel in Foreign Parts had already connected Quamine to family members in West Africa eager for his return. The concept of a "return" to West Africa likely felt quite literal for him.[36]

The American Revolution interrupted Yamma, Quamine, Stiles, and Hopkins's plans. Princeton was occupied by British troops in 1776, and the College of New Jersey's central Nassau Hall became a barracks. Quamine died during the war while serving on a privateer in 1779, trying to win prize money to free his wife from slavery. After the war, Hopkins picked up the missionary project again in 1784, but Yamma never traveled to West Africa. Although the Revolution temporarily disrupted plans for colonization and emigration, these ideas reemerged after the war as an integral part of conversations about emancipation, race, and rights in the Anglo-Atlantic world.[37]

As the American Revolution transformed the political arithmetic of population and power by giving *the people* new meaning, removal was again used as a tool to determine the bounds of the new nation's body politic. The emerging Republic forged a different relationship to population than the

---

"'This Whole Country Have Their Hands Full of Blood This Day': Transcription and Introduction of an Antislavery Sermon Manuscript Attributed to the Reverend Samuel Hopkins," American Antiquarian Society, *Proceedings*, CXII (2002), 42–43; James Sidbury, *Becoming African in America: Race and Nation in the Early Black Atlantic* (New York, 2007), 77–78; John Wood Sweet, *Bodies Politic: Negotiating Race in the American North, 1730–1830* (Philadelphia, 2006), 115, 123; Guyatt, *Bind Us Apart*, 210–211; Sinha, *Slave's Cause*, 37–38. For the circular, see Sewall Harding, ed., *The Works of Samuel Hopkins, D. D., First Pastor of the Church in Great Barrington, Mass., afterwards Pastor of the First Congregational Church in Newport, R.I.; with a Memoir of His Life and Character*, I (Boston, 1854), 131–132.

36. Sweet, *Bodies Politic*, 331.

37. George E. Brooks, Jr., "The Providence African Society's Sierra Leone Emigration Scheme, 1794–1795: Prologue to the African Colonization Movement," *International Journal of African Historical Studies*, VII (1974), 186; Sinha, *Slave's Cause*, 38.

one that marked the British Empire. The thirteen colonies that declared independence in 1776 made *the people*—a broad and undefined political community—the foundation of government. Republican political power was derived from *the people* both in theory and in practice. Population served as the basis for representation, statehood, and political power. The question of who *the people* actually were thus lay at the center of national politics.[38]

Before the war, the idea of "volitional allegiance"—in which people chose their own political community—was unique to the colonies. There, perpetual subjecthood did not sit easily with emerging notions of the consent of the governed, particularly so because of immigration. In 1740, an act of Parliament allowed individual colonies to naturalize foreigners, but North American colonists had already begun to do so even before the passage of the act. The experience of local control over naturalization led them to think about allegiance differently from their counterparts in Britain. Colonists, as James H. Kettner has written, "slowly came to see the allegiance of the naturalized subject as reflecting the attributes of the process by which it was acquired; that is, it was volitional and contractual," rather than natural and perpetual. Because everyone ended up with the same status in the colonies, they might also all claim volitional allegiance, whether they were naturalized subjects or not. The practical experience of bringing outsiders into the political community raised an important question for colonists: If foreigners could elect to be subjects, did natural-born subjects also have the power to choose their allegiance?[39]

The Revolution put this theoretical question into practice. Revolutionaries began to think differently about allegiance because of their experience forming a new political community during the war. Even before there was a new political community, they forced their neighbors to take sides early in the imperial crisis, more than a decade before they declared independence. Radicals first put pressure on nonconformers beginning in 1765–1766, when they encouraged nonimportation of British goods on a limited scale to compel the repeal of the Stamp Act. This local pressure on nonconformers culminated in 1774, when the First Continental Congress announced a new nonimportation and nonconsumption agreement. Communities were responsible for enforcing these agreements through the in-

38. Douglas Bradburn, *The Citizenship Revolution: Politics and the Creation of the American Union, 1774–1804* (Charlottesville, Va., 2009), 60.

39. James H. Kettner, "The Development of American Citizenship in the Revolutionary Era: The Idea of Volitional Allegiance," *American Journal of Legal History,* XVIII (1974), 210 (quotation); Kettner, *Development of American Citizenship,* 65–78, 105–107.

timidation and public exposure of those who refused to support them. By 1774, the Continental Association instituted local committees that set prices for particular goods and organized boycotts of nonconformers. Thousands of men who were elected to serve on the committees interviewed potential offenders, punished them publicly, listed their offenses in newspapers, and boycotted their businesses. The committees forced dissenters to publicly seek forgiveness before they were welcomed back into the community. The experience of making public declarations of one's politics before the war cemented Revolutionary unity. Identifying those who remained loyal to the king on the eve of the Revolution, as much as consumer boycotts or mob action, brought the Republic into being.[40]

After the war began, the Second Continental Congress did not wait long to decide who had forfeited political allegiance in the new republic by siding with the king. In June 1776, just before signing the Declaration of Independence, Congress defined treason and urged the states to take independent measures to root out loyalists. Beginning in 1776, the states punished loyalists by confiscating their estates. The harshest of these measures committed recalcitrant loyalists to jail or banished them on pain of death. A raft of new laws required loyalists to take loyalty oaths to participate in the political life of the states. By 1777, most states required adult men to take loyalty oaths that were qualifications for voting, gun ownership, office holding, jury service, transferring land, and using the courts. In the midst of war, the states sorted out loyalists from the great body of *the people.*[41]

40. Janice Potter, *The Liberty We Seek: Loyalist Ideology in Colonial New York and Massachusetts* (Cambridge, Mass., 1983), 155–156; Robert M. Calhoon, "The Reintegration of the Loyalists and the Disaffected," in Calhoon, *The Loyalist Perception and Other Essays* (Columbia, S.C., 1989), 196; David H. Villers, "'King Mob' and the Rule of Law: Revolutionary Justice and the Suppression of Loyalism in Connecticut, 1774–1783," in Calhoon, Timothy M. Barnes, and George A. Rawlyk, eds., *Loyalists and Community in North America* (Westport, Conn., 1994), 18; T. H. Breen, *The Marketplace of Revolution: How Consumer Politics Shaped American Independence* (New York, 2004), 222–293; Bradburn, *Citizenship Revolution,* 57. For consumer boycotts, see Breen, *Marketplace of Revolution.* For popular collective action, see Gary B. Nash, *The Urban Crucible: Social Change, Political Consciousness, and the Origins of the American Revolution* (Cambridge, Mass., 1979); Paul A. Gilje, *The Road to Mobocracy: Popular Disorder in New York City, 1763–1834* (Williamsburg, Va., and Chapel Hill, N.C., 1987); Alfred F. Young, *Liberty Tree: Ordinary People and the American Revolution* (New York, 2006).

41. Baseler, *"Asylum for Mankind,"* 143; Kettner, *Development of American Citizenship,* 179–180; Bradburn, *Citizenship Revolution,* 57. For an appendix of the measures passed by the new states, see Claude Halstead Van Tyne, *The Loyalists in the American Revolution* (New York, 1902), 318–341.

State laws defined treason, but deciding who would be removed was a local process. Ordinary people waged campaigns of intimidation and harassment against their neighbors. In 1774, Revolutionaries in Windham and Norwich, Connecticut, conducted a loyalist out of the colony and afterward informed the governor that this was a "private Quarrel" beyond his jurisdiction. The outbreak of war spurred local committees to target those who had not yet declared a side. Revolutionary leaders used mobs, threats, and imprisonment to pressure loyalists to join the anticolonial struggle or emigrate. When Virginia physician Alexander Gordon broke the Continental Association's ban on trade with Britain by importing medicines, for example, he was forced to move to England in early 1775. Virginian Adam Bell was imprisoned for loyalism in 1779, and his wife and four children left for England without him. Bell eventually escaped and joined the British army but died before he could be reunited with his family. Philadelphia writer Elizabeth Graeme Ferguson recouped her loyalist husband's confiscated property and stayed in Pennsylvania after he decamped for England. They never saw each other again. The choices that loyalists made broke apart their homes and families.[42]

During the Revolution, removal was a common tool of war that neighbors used against neighbors. This was true in the case of loyalist Joseph Hooper, whose public shaming resulted in his self-exile from Marblehead, Massachusetts, where he was a wealthy merchant. In June 1774, the embattled royal governor of Massachusetts, Thomas Hutchinson, left for England in the wake of the Boston Tea Party. On the governor's departure, Joseph and his father, Robert Hooper, joined a group of other Boston-area merchants in signing a flattering address to Hutchinson asking him to advocate on their behalf in England. Protest mounted against the signers until May 1775, when the men were publicly castigated in the press. Robert Hooper eventually recanted before the Boston Committee of Safety, but Joseph refused to do the same, and he was threatened in the streets. At Marblehead's town meeting that month, Joseph's neighbors issued a resolution requiring him

42. Caleb Scott et al. to Jonathan Trumbell, Aug. 5, 1774, Trumbull Papers, Connecticut State Library, Hartford ("private"), quoted in Villers, "'King Mob' and the Rule of Law," in Calhoon, Barnes, and Rawlyk, eds., *Loyalists and Community in North America,* 17; Lorenzo Sabine, *Biographical Sketches of Loyalists of the American Revolution with an Historical Essay,* I (Boston, 1864), 483; Mary Beth Norton, *The British-Americans: The Loyalist Exiles in England, 1774–1789* (Boston, 1972), 25–28; Ruma Chopra, *Unnatural Rebellion: Loyalists in New York City during the Revolution* (Charlottesville, Va., 2011), 13.

to sign an oath, on pain of death, to the Revolutionary cause. He chose exile in England instead.[43]

Such measures extended to those who attempted to stay neutral and were consequently targeted as suspected loyalists. Quaker peace testimony, for example, prohibited Friends from serving in the army, and they were forbade from taking oaths. When Virginia Quakers refused to hire substitutes in their place to perform military service, local officials confiscated their property to pay the associated fines. Pennsylvania Quakers publicly renounced Revolutionary violence, and their Yearly Meeting prohibited Friends from serving in local militias or paying taxes to support the war. Like one Philadelphia Friend, they feared that the young were particularly vulnerable to becoming "ensnar'd" by demands from Revolutionaries to give up their religious principles and bear arms in the conflict. In September 1777, when the British invasion of Philadelphia seemed imminent, Congress directed Pennsylvania's Supreme Council to arrest specific Friends they had identified as disloyal as well as those "who have, in their general conduct and conversation, evidenced a disposition inimical to the cause of America." Forty Friends were arrested and eighteen were exiled to Winchester, Virginia, until April 1778, despite a string of memorials they sent to Congress protesting their removal.[44]

There was precedent for the use of removal to suppress dissent in the colonies. The largest group to be portrayed as removeable enemies within British North America were the Acadians. In the early seventeenth century, the French colonized Acadia on the northern shore of Nova Scotia. By the mid-eighteenth century, their French and Mi'kmaq descendants lived in settlements scattered around the Bay of Fundy. Between 1604 and 1710, Acadia

43. Claims of Losses Reported by the Loyalist Commissioners, 1783–1784, by John Wilmot et. al., Lincoln's Inn Fields, container 2, I, 56–59, LOC; James H. Stark, *The Loyalists of Massachusetts and the Other Side of the American Revolution* (Boston, 1910), 221–224; William Huntting Howell, "Entering the Lists: The Politics of Ephemera in Eastern Massachusetts, 1774," *Early American Studies: An Interdisciplinary Journal*, IX (2011), 187–217.

44. Israel Pemberton to Robert Pleasants, Jan. 13, 1777, Pleasants Family Papers, HL ("ensnar'd"); *JCC*, VIII, 695 ("who have"); John Pemberton to John Parrish, Oct. 16, 1777, Cox-Parrish-Wharton Papers, box 1, folder 7, HSP, "Copy of the Petition to Congress Now Sitting at York Town," 1778. See also Sally Schwartz, *"A Mixed Multitude": The Struggle for Toleration in Colonial Pennsylvania* (New York, 1987), 173–284, 284; A. Glenn Crothers, "Northern Virginia's Quakers and the War for Independence: Negotiating a Path of Virtue in a Revolutionary World," in Joseph S. Tiedemann, Eugene R. Fingerhut, and Robert W. Venables, eds., *The Other Loyalists: Ordinary People, Royalism, and the Revolution in the Middle Colonies, 1763–1787* (Albany, N.Y., 2009), 113–121.

was transferred between Britain and France ten times. Through periods of war and imperial change, the Acadians managed to preserve their settlements because they professed neutrality in every conflict. By the beginning of the Seven Years' War, however, British officials, who eyed the Acadian settlements with envy and believed them to be internal enemies, rejected their claims to neutrality. One newspaper labeled the Acadians "The neutral French . . . who have always been secret Enemies, and have encouraged our Savages to cut our Throats." Soldiers from Massachusetts acting under the authority of the colonial governments of Massachusetts and Nova Scotia systematically expelled the Acadians from their homes. Thousands of Acadians were packed onto British transports and sent in small groups to Georgia, South Carolina, Virginia, Maryland, Pennsylvania, Massachusetts, New York, and Connecticut. Seven thousand Acadians were banished, while ten to twelve thousand managed to escape and live as refugees across the North American colonies.[45]

During the American Revolution, loyalists were also forced out or chose to leave. They fled to British-held cities for safety. New York, occupied from 1776 until the end of the war, became a primary place of refuge. When British troops first arrived, five thousand people remained in the city. By 1783, the population of New York had increased to thirty-three thousand people and ten thousand British soldiers. Along with New York, loyalists used British-occupied cities like Charleston or Philadelphia as departure points throughout the war, and they left with transport ships for Nova Scotia or the West Indies or England through 1783. In all, sixty thousand loyalists preferred exile to declaring loyalty to the new states.[46]

The exile of loyalists created a sense of unanimous allegiance to the United States. Those who were left behind had supposedly chosen membership in the new nation, although historians have shown that this was not so. Plenty of new citizens of the United States were disaffected, deeply uncertain about the course of the war, or strove to preserve their neutrality in the conflict. But it was Native and enslaved people—both painted as "internal enemies" and agents of the British—for whom the label stuck.[47]

45. *New York Gazette,* Aug. 25, 1755, *Pennsylvania Gazette,* Sept. 4, 1755, and *Maryland Gazette,* Sept. 18, 1755, quoted in John Mack Faragher, *A Great and Noble Scheme: The Tragic Story of the Expulsion of the French Acadians from Their American Homeland* (New York, 2005), 333 ("neutral"); Faraghar, *Great and Noble Scheme,* esp. xvii–xix, 325–351; Christopher Hodson, *The Acadian Diaspora: An Eighteenth-Century History* (New York, 2012).

46. Norton, *British-Americans,* 31–36; Maya Jasanoff, *Liberty's Exiles: American Loyalists in the Revolutionary World* (New York, 2011), 6.

47. Alan Taylor, *The Internal Enemy: Slavery and War in Virginia, 1772–1832* (New

Most eastern Native nations tried to stay out of a conflict that they did not see as their own, but the war nonetheless came to them. This was the case for Delaware leader White Eyes, who negotiated the 1778 Treaty of Fort Pitt, which gave the Continental Army the right of passage through Delaware lands. The treaty recognized Delaware sovereignty and suggested that they might eventually form a fourteenth state in the new union. After White Eyes was murdered by white militiamen, the Delaware alliance fell apart, and many Delawares were pushed toward the British. War forced Native nations to ally with one side or the other. Most fought for the British without being entirely certain that they would protect their interests.[48]

Enslaved people turned the American Revolution into a war for emancipation when and where they could. In the North, they served in the Continental Army, exchanging military service for the promise of emancipation. As commander of the army, George Washington barred enslaved men from serving in 1775, but the extraordinary demands of a long war for independence forced him to reverse course. By 1777, all of the states except South Carolina and Georgia allowed enslaved people to enlist. Enslaved individuals served in the Continental Army in greater numbers, proportionately, than did white men. In the South, thousands of enslaved people ran for British lines to secure their freedom. In Virginia, the royal governor John Murray, fourth earl of Dunmore, issued a proclamation in November 1775 freeing any enslaved person who fought for the British army. Men, women, and children joined refugee communities across British lines on Gwynn's Island in Virginia and Sullivan's and Tybee Islands in South Carolina as well as occupied Savannah, Charleston, Philadelphia, and New York.[49]

Stories of Native violence and slave rebellion mobilized white men for

---

York, 2013). For unanimity of allegiance, see Bradburn, *Citizenship Revolution*, 8–10, 58. For the disaffected, see Sung Bok Kim, "The Limits of Politicization in the American Revolution: The Experience of Westchester County, New York," *Journal of American History*, LXXX (1993), 868–889; Aaron Sullivan, *The Disaffected: Britain's Occupation of Philadelphia during the American Revolution* (Philadelphia, 2019).

48. Rob Harper, *Unsettling the West: Violence and State Building in the Ohio Valley* (Philadelphia, 2018), 111–113.

49. Sylvia R. Frey, *Water from the Rock: Black Resistance in a Revolutionary Age* (Princeton, N.J., 1991), 45–80; Cassandra Pybus, *Epic Journeys of Freedom: Runaway Slaves of the American Revolution and Their Global Quest for Liberty* (Boston, 2006), 28–29; Christopher Leslie Brown, "The Problems of Slavery," in Edward G. Gray and Jane Kamensky, eds., *The Oxford Handbook of the American Revolution* (New York, 2013), 429–430; Byrd, *Captives and Voyagers*, 125–243; Judith L. Van Buskirk, *Standing in Their Own Light: African American Patriots in the American Revolution* (Norman, Okla., 2017).

war and unified the new states. The specter of both Indigenous and Black people as "internal enemies" who fought with the British spurred war service. The "common cause" of the American Revolution was built on the creation of a common enemy. After the war, white Americans forgot the war service of American-allied Native people and Black soldiers, but they remembered Lord Dunmore's effort to undermine the Revolutionary cause in Virginia with his proclamation and British-allied Cherokee campaigns in the South. The promise of individual liberty, natural rights, and volitional allegiance were legacies of the war, but so were, as Eric Hinderaker writes, "decentralized, atomized political authority and deeper, sharper lines of racial separation and hatred."[50]

Loyalists and the disaffected, meanwhile, were not burdened with the label "internal enemy" for long. After the British defeat at Yorktown in 1782, the states passed harsh penalties against loyalists to make their victory decisive. The laws aimed at reintegration—bringing the hesitant back into the United States while expelling those who would not declare allegiance to the new states. North and South Carolina, Georgia, New York, and Pennsylvania all passed laws targeting loyalists in the final years of the war. The Treaty of Paris, which ended the war in 1783, recommended that the states return confiscated property to loyalists and restore their rights. But antiloyalist sentiment and the passage of punitive laws in the states meant the recommendations of the treaty went unfulfilled. After eight long years of war, the state governments were not willing to restore loyalists to their former positions so easily. Loyalists who stayed or returned to recoup their losses earned no sympathy from the state legislatures in 1783. Within just a few years, however, many states quickly invited loyalists back into the political community.[51]

All of the states confiscated loyalist property during and after the war, but, by 1785–1786, many of them also laid out a pathway for the reintegration of loyalists by permitting them to pay reparations to the state or to individual claimants. At the local level, white Virginians actively used the courts to demand reparations from loyalists as a first step toward allowing them to

50. Robert G. Parkinson, *Common Cause: Creating Race and Nation in the American Revolution* (Williamsburg, Va., and Chapel Hill, N.C., 2016), 23–24; Hinderaker, *Elusive Empires,* 186 ("decentralized"); Peter Silver, *Our Savage Neighbors: How Indian War Transformed Early America* (New York, 2008); Peter S. Onuf, *Jefferson's Empire: The Language of American Nationhood* (Charlottesville, Va., 2000), 14.

51. Calhoon, "Reintegration of the Loyalists and the Disaffected," in Calhoon, *Loyalist Perception and Other Essays,* 206; Rebecca Brannon, *From Revolution to Reunion: The Reintegration of the South Carolina Loyalists* (Columbia, S.C., 2016), 36.

remain in their former towns and counties. In Massachusetts, the public sale and private plunder of loyalist property made their return more palatable to their neighbors. In South Carolina, the scene of a vicious civil war that pitted neighbor against neighbor in some of the most violent confrontations of the Revolution, the legislature appropriated the property of 232 prominent loyalists in 1782. Just two years later, 70 percent of all South Carolina loyalists subject to confiscation and banishment were granted clemency. In nearly all of the states, confiscation appeased anger against loyalists, and their rights were restored quickly thereafter. Connecticut extended amnesty to loyalists in 1783, Massachusetts in 1787, and Delaware in 1789. During the American Revolution, Revolutionaries used removal to punish disloyalty. After the war ended, white Americans would similarly use removal as they made calculations about who belonged in the Republic.[52]

Population symbolized the promise of equality at the heart of new republican institutions—it made people commensurable. Over the first several decades of the Republic, the population of the United States grew exponentially. Geographers and intellectuals in the early Republic calculated the growth of the nation's population over time, inserting their projections into newspapers, geographies, and histories. In his popular tract on the new state of Kentucky, speculator Gilbert Imlay repeated Franklin's 1751 assertion that the population of the United States doubled every twenty-five years. Within a hundred years, he suggested, the nation's inhabitants would grow from four million to sixty-four million—surely a sign that Kentucky would quickly grow in wealth and stature, too. Philadelphian Mathew Carey ran these numbers on the pages of his popular magazine *American Museum.* In their correspondence and behind the closed doors of the American Philosophical Society, intellectuals like Benjamin Rush, Franklin, and Thomas Jefferson made similar suggestions.[53]

52. Harold B. Hancock, *The Loyalists of Revolutionary Delaware* (Newark, N.J., 1977), 43; Kettner, *Development of American Citizenship,* 180, 204–209; Calhoon, "Reintegration of Loyalists and the Disaffected," in Calhoon, *Loyalist Perception and Other Essays,* 206; Villers, "'King Mob' and the Rule of Law," in Calhoon, Barnes, and Rawlyk, eds., *Loyalists and Community in North America,* 27, David E. Maas, "The Massachusetts Loyalists and the Problem of Amnesty, 1775–1790," 69–73; Brannon, *From Revolution to Reunion,* 9, 35, 57.

53. G[ilbert] Imlay, *A Topographical Description of the Western Territory of North America . . . to Which Is Annexed, a Delineation of the Laws and Government of the State of Kentucky; Tending to Shew the Probable Rise and Grandeur of the American Empire; in a Series of Letters to a Friend in England* (London, 1792), ix–x; Cassedy, *Demography in*

The increasing popularity of statistics and arithmetic supported public interest in population, but so did the structure of republican institutions. Population was vital to early national governance. The 1787 Northwest Ordinance required that western territories reach a population threshold before they could apply for statehood. New technologies made population growth apparent. A regular census was embedded in the U.S. Constitution by the apportionment clause that determined representation in the House of Representatives. The first federal census in 1790 took eighteen months to collect, and the returns were printed in newspapers and publicly posted. On the one hand, the process of counting people and grouping them together as a population suggested a rough kind of equality. On the other hand, that was only true within groups. From the beginning, the census separated people into categories by age, gender, race, and free or enslaved status.[54]

Like population, the term *the people* also seemed to hold within it the rough promise of equality. It was a flexible and broad political community. White Revolutionaries, however, clearly did not believe that *the people* encompassed everyone who lived within the national boundaries claimed by the new United States. For one thing, who *the people* were mattered to republican institutions. The integrity of the Republic depended on individual virtue and independent will, qualities that eighteenth-century intellectuals believed were only available to white men who owned property. Many white Revolutionaries believed that republics required homogeneity in terms of race, language, or national origins.

White Americans began debating limits on *the people* shortly after the Revolution, and they used removal to define its bounds. Removal projects had long been aimed at the precarious in British colonial society—paupers, vagrants, criminals, slaves. In the early Republic, removal ideas cemented strict hierarchies of race, particularly targeting African Americans and Native people. Those who embraced removal leaned on British precedents. English poor laws provided the legal architecture for state statutes restricting movement. Colonizationists modeled their plans on those developed in the 1770s. Policymakers took their cues for Indian removal from the history of British colonial dispossession. Long a panacea for problems of state formation, removal was proposed often in the decades after 1783 by people

---

Early America, 206–242, esp. 236; Cohen, *Calculating People,* 116–157. For population as symbolic of "radical equality," see Rusnock, *Vital Accounts,* 217.

54. Cassedy, *Demography in Early America,* 211–222, esp. 216–217; Cohen, *Calculating People,* 158–164.

who hoped to monopolize Native land and to control Black labor. The new Republic's decentralized political authority meant that removal was a tool of state making that belonged to many people. White Americans would use it to define belonging, identifying who was and was not of *the people.*[55]

55. Hinderaker, *Elusive Empires,* 175, 186; Patrick Wolfe, "Land, Labor, and Difference: Elementary Structures of Race," *American Historical Review,* CVI (2001), 866–905. For the carryover of colonial legal precedents into the early Republic, see Christopher L. Tomlins and Bruce H. Mann, eds., *The Many Legalities of Early America* (Williamsburg, Va., and Chapel Hill, N.C., 2001), 8, 19; Laura F. Edwards, "Sarah Allingham's Sheet and Other Lessons from Legal History," *Journal of the Early Republic,* XXXVIII (2018), 128.

Part 1

For Native people, the American Revolution was a continuation of a war of removal that began before 1776 and ended well after the signing of the Treaty of Paris in 1783. As tens of thousands of speculators and migrants moved across the Appalachian Mountains in the late eighteenth century, they fomented a struggle over Native land. North of the Ohio River, conflict began in 1774, when the royal governor of Virginia, John Murray, fourth earl of Dunmore, marched on Shawnee towns on the Muskingum River in what is now eastern Ohio, routing their forces and compelling Shawnees to give up their Kentucky territory to secure peace. Some Shawnees protested the cession and continued to fight it. South of the Ohio River, Cherokee leader Dragging Canoe led resistance to white migration into Cherokee homelands from a new town on the Tennessee River between Chickamauga and Muscle Shoals while his father Attakullakulla sought to avoid conflict by agreeing to land cessions on the headwaters of the Tennessee River. By the beginning of the Revolution, Native leaders split, with young militants in the trans-Appalachian region planning for war and traditional chiefs struggling to keep the peace.

As the Revolution spilled into Indigenous homelands, however, neutrality became increasingly difficult to maintain. Native leaders who had hoped to avoid commitments to fight were forced to take sides. Both Britain and the United States sought assistance from Native communities. Soldiers also brought the conflict to Indian Country. In response to Cherokee and Shawnee campaigns against white settlements in the Carolinas, Georgia, Tennessee, and Virginia, white militias burned Native towns and crops to the ground. When Senecas, Cayugas, Onondagas, and Mohawks assisted the British in their campaigns in the Wyoming Valley in eastern Pennsylvania and the Cherry Valley in New York, General John Sullivan led the Continental Army on a retaliatory campaign that devastated Iroqouia.

Removal had always been at the center of the colonial project, but the pace of dispossession accelerated in the decades after the American Revolution. In 1783, federal officials named nearly all Native homelands east of the Mississippi River conquered territory. White migrants who had experienced Native attacks on their homes and fortifications had already begun to identify all Indigenous people as enemies, no matter their politics. They entered the post-Revolutionary period with the expectation that the new government would serve their interests. Meanwhile, Natives in the trans-Appalachian region who suddenly found white settlements at their borders revived efforts to confederate against the United States. Long after the war's formal conclusion, the experience and memory of violence continued to encourage new solidarities.

Writing in 1795, Philadelphia printer John M'Culloch tried to account for the sprawling conflict between Native people and the United States west of the Appalachians. He saw the ongoing struggle clearly as "a remnant of the revolutionary war." The Revolution had created a nation dependent on Native land for its own future. It had made removal a founding project.[1]

1. John M'Culloch, *A Concise History of the United States: From the Discovery of America till 1795; with a Correct Map of the United States* (Philadelphia, 1795), 174.

CHAPTER 2

"THE WHOLE DEBT OF THE NATION"

Removal in Indian Country

In September 1783, John Adams, Benjamin Franklin, and John Jay huddled around a table at the Hotel d'York in Paris. They were members of the U.S. peace commission sent to France on the orders of Congress to negotiate an end to the American Revolution. By their side was British envoy David Hartley, a member of the House of Commons. When the four men put pen to paper, they agreed that Britain would give up "all claims to the Government, Propriety, and Territorial Rights" of its former thirteen colonies. They also agreed to double the size of the confederation of states that had entered the war against Britain. The new boundaries of the union stretched from British Nova Scotia, south to the Floridas, and west past the Appalachian Mountains to the Mississippi River. George III found the loss difficult to bear. He did not send along jewelry and portraits to the U.S. delegation as was customary, and he balked at the idea of receiving an ambassador from "a Revolted State." The artist Benjamin West was unable to complete a 1784 painting commemorating the event for want of the likenesses of the British negotiators, who did not sit for him. Their absence seemed symbolic. For the U.S. delegation, the negotiations were a triumph. Looking back on the Treaty of Paris thirty years later, Adams would declare it "one of the most important political events, that ever happened on this globe."[1]

Native North Americans would have disputed Adams's bravado. Thousands of eastern Native people fought in the American Revolution, largely—

1. Treaty of Paris, 1783, International Treaties and Related Records, 1778–1974, General Records of the United States Government, Record Group 11, NARA ("all claims"); George III to [Charles] Fox, Aug. 7, 1783, in John Fortescue, *The Correspondence of King George the Third from 1760 to December 1783 . . . ,* VI (London, 1928), 430 ("Revolted"), also cited in Andrew Jackson O'Shaughnessy, *The Men Who Lost America: British Leadership, the American Revolution, and the Fate of the Empire* (New Haven, Conn., 2013), 43; John Adams, "To the Boston Patriot," Apr. 6, 1811, *Founders Online,* NARA, http://founders.archives.gov ("one of the most"); Richard B. Morris, "The Great Peace of 1783," MHS, *Proceedings,* XCV (1983), 29–51; Ronald Hoffman and Peter J. Albert, eds., *Peace and the Peacemakers: The Treaty of 1783* (Charlottesville, Va., 1986); Kathleen DuVal, *Independence Lost: Lives on the Edge of the American Revolution* (New York, 2015), 229–236.

FIGURE 2. *Benjamin West,* American Commissioners of the Preliminary Peace Negotiations with Great Britain. *1783–1819. Oil on canvas. Gift of Henry Francis du Pont, 1957.0586, 1964.2107. Courtesy Winterthur Museum, Winterthur, Del.*

but not all—as allies of the British. They did not appear in West's unfinished painting either—not because they refused to sit for it, but because they were never invited to the Paris negotiations to begin with. In 1783, British commissioners had traded away Native lands to the United States without their consent. The United States claimed the right of conquest over Indigenous homelands from the Appalachians to the Mississippi. That July, trader and veteran Ephraim Douglass traveled on orders from Congress to inform Natives of the lower Great Lakes that they "must no longer look to the King beyond the Water, but they must now look to the great Council, the C[ongress] of the United States at Philadelphia." At Delaware Captain Pipe's town at Upper Sandusky in what is now northern Ohio, Douglass was "frustrated in every attempt to obtain a public audience of the Indians." Native leaders had already left for Detroit to meet with British officials. Nonetheless, Douglass found a welcoming host in Captain Pipe, who was eager for peace and helped him convey his message to eleven Native nations at Detroit. Everywhere he traveled, Douglass found that Native peoples would never agree to peace if it meant losing their territory. At Niagara, he was intercepted by Mohawk leader Joseph Brant, or Thayendanegea, and the British commandant of the post, who likewise told him that the Haudenosaunees would resist any efforts to claim their lands.[2]

As Adams, Franklin, Jay, and Douglass completed their journeys that summer and fall, Dunquat, the Half-King of the Sandusky Wyandots, traveled to Lower Sandusky with a delegation of three hundred. There, they joined British Indian agents and hundreds of Shawnees, Haudenosaunees, Wyandots, Delawares, Odawas, Ojibwes, Potawatomis, Creeks, and Cherokees, who pressed for the restoration of the old border agreed on at the Treaty of Fort Stanwix in 1768, which had halted white settlement at the Ohio River. Southern Shawnee and Cherokee speakers opened the council by returning a large war belt that the Haudenosaunees had sent them during the Revolution to unite Indigenous people against the United States. Federal officials "made no secret of their designs upon their country declaring pretentions to it by conquest," the speakers warned. With the return of the war belt to the northern nations, the southern Shawnees and Cherokees reaffirmed their commitment to defend their homelands. British agents tried to soften the meaning of the Paris negotiations, but even Dunquat, who had repeatedly made peace overtures to the United States throughout the war, argued that U.S. independence was dependent on removal. He called on the council to "be strong" and to resist white Americans, who were already pushing into Indian country.[3]

These parallel negotiations in 1783 show how Native sovereignty was undermined at the very moment the new United States gained international recognition. The two went hand in hand. Anxious to repay European and domestic creditors after the war's conclusion, eastern legislators presumed

2. Clarence M. Burton, ed., "Ephraim Douglass and His Times a Fragment of History with the Journal of George McCully (Hitherto Unpublished) and Various Letters of the Period," *Magazine of History with Notes and Queries,* extra no. 10 (New York, 1910), 221, 247 ("must"), 264–272, 274 ("frustrated"); David Andrew Nichols, *Red Gentlemen and White Savages: Indians, Federalists, and the Search for Order on the American Frontier* (Charlottesville, Va., 2008), 25; Rob Harper, *Unsettling the West: Violence and State Building in the Ohio Valley* (Philadelphia, 2018), 146–149.

3. "Transactions with Indians at Sandusky," Aug. 26–Sept. 8, 1783, *MPHC,* XX, 175 ("made"), 182 ("strong"); Helen Hornbeck Tanner, ed., *Atlas of Great Lakes Indian History* (Norman, Okla., 1987), 84; Nichols, *Red Gentlemen and White Savages,* 26–27; Sami Lakomäki, *Gathering Together: The Shawnee People through Diaspora and Nationhood, 1600–1870* (New Haven, Conn., 2014), 116–117; Harper, *Unsettling the West,* 148.

that the source of the nation's wealth lay in Indian land—what they called a great "fund" to pay off "the whole debt of the nation." In surveys and reports, in ordinances and federal statutes, officials, speculators, and geographers made Native homelands legible as homelands for white Americans. Federal planners described removal as a bloodless process of peopling land in which Native Americans would either take on Anglo-American cultural norms or leave and white migrants would transform into settlers. They imagined the replacement of Indigenous people with white migrants. Although federal officials professed peaceful intentions, they also planned violent wars of dispossession to realize these visions. Removal contained both the promise of so-called benevolence and the threat of "extirpation" for those who resisted.[4]

All the same, removal was a contest rather than an inevitability. North of the Ohio River, federal officials planned dispossession. In the South, they competed with state governors and speculators, who grasped at Native homelands. Both federal and state officials needed but also complained about the extraordinary movement of white migrants who rushed to the trans-Appalachian West, carrying out removal on the ground as they went. Removal was not a single, concerted effort from the vantage point of the federal capital. Native Americans in the North and South resisted dispossession, too, building powerful confederacies to evict interlopers from their lands. South of the Ohio River, Creeks led some Cherokees, Choctaws, and Chickasaws in a "general defense against all invaders of Indian rights."

4. *JCC,* XXVII, 626 ("fund"); "The Fount," *Columbian Centinel* (Boston), Jan. 7, 1792, 172 [4] ("whole debt"). For "extirpation," see Jeffrey Ostler, *Surviving Genocide: Native Nations and the United States from the American Revolution to Bleeding Kansas* (New Haven, Conn., 2019). For legibility, see James C. Scott, *Seeing Like a State: How Certain Schemes to Improve the Human Condition Have Failed* (New Haven, Conn., 1998), 2. For replacement, see Patrick Wolfe, "Settler Colonialism and the Elimination of the Native," *Journal of Genocide Research,* VIII (2006), 387–409. For competing interpretations of early national Indian policy at the federal level, see Richard White, *The Middle Ground: Indians, Empires, and Republics in the Great Lakes Region, 1650–1815* (1991; rpt. New York, 2011), 413–517; Francis Paul Prucha, *The Great Father: The United States Government and the American Indians,* abridged ed. (Lincoln, Nebr., 1984), 13–47; Eric Hinderaker, *Elusive Empires: Constructing Colonialism in the Ohio Valley, 1673–1800* (New York, 1999), 226–270; Stuart Banner, *How the Indians Lost Their Land: Law and Power on the Frontier* (Cambridge, Mass., 2007), 112–190; Patrick Griffin, *American Leviathan: Empire, Nation, and Revolutionary Frontier* (New York, 2008); Nichols, *Red Gentlemen and White Savages;* Colin G. Calloway, *The Victory with No Name: The Native American Defeat of the First American Army* (New York, 2015); Bethel Saler, *The Settlers' Empire: Colonialism and State Formation in America's Old Northwest* (Philadelphia, 2015), 13–82; Harper, *Unsettling the West,* 145–172.

In the Ohio Valley, Native federationists formed a military and diplomatic alliance they called the United Indian Nations to stymy surveyors and militias. Native diplomats allied with the British and Spanish empires on their borders. Yet, like the union of states, federationists did not always agree on the best course of action. Ultimately, removal was a process rather than a single act. In the Ohio country, where federal officials focused their attention first, imagining the region without Indigenous peoples became an expensive fiction to pursue. Instead of providing a fund for the confederation, the expropriation of Native land became a drain on federal finances and a problem for the new nation.[5]

Native peoples west of the Appalachians might have guessed that removal would be instrumental to U.S. plans for postwar prosperity. They only had to look east to the middle states to understand the intentions of federal officials. In Virginia, for example, the colony's seventeenth-century campaign to remove and replace the Powhatans gradually diminished the livelihoods of Virginia's coastal plains peoples. After 1646, the Virginia colony forced them into a tributary agreement under which they paid to access English protection and trade. They contended with land purchases and encroachment by individual colonists, roaming livestock, and a 1705 law that cut most remaining Algonquian reserves in half. By 1705, the Pamunkey, Mattaponi, Chickahominy, Wicocomico, Nansemond, and Gingaskin peoples found themselves on shrinking reservations working as farmers, traders, laborers, and indentured servants. In Maryland, the colonial assembly began to take control over the affairs of the Piscataways, Nanticokes,

5. Alexander McGillivray to Esteban Miró, June 20, 1787, "Papers from the Spanish Archives relating to Tennessee and the Old Southwest," 11, 82–84 ("general"), quoted in DuVal, *Independence Lost,* 302. For the Republic's dependence on dispossession, see Patrick Griffin, "Reconsidering the Ideological Origins of Indian Removal: The Case of the Big Bottom 'Massacre,'" in Andrew R. L. Cayton and Stuart D. Hobbs, eds., *The Center of a Great Empire: The Ohio Country in the Early American Republic* (Athens, Ohio, 2005), 13; Michael Witgen, *An Infinity of Nations: How the Native New World Shaped Early North America* (Philadelphia, 2012), 322–323. For the relationship between white migrants and frontier violence, see Griffin, *American Leviathan;* Saler, *Settlers' Empire;* Laurel Clark Shire, *The Threshold of Manifest Destiny: Gender and National Expansion in Florida* (Philadelphia, 2016); Harper, *Unsettling the West.* For confederacies, see White, *Middle Ground,* 413–468; Gregory Evans Dowd, *A Spirited Resistance: The North American Indian Struggle for Unity, 1745–1815* (Baltimore, Md., 1993); Lakomäki, *Gathering Together,* 120–131; DuVal, *Independence Lost,* 238, 292–339, 302. For the West as both a source of wealth and a threat, see Saler, *Settlers' Empire,* 17; Woody Holton, *Unruly Americans and the Origins of the Constitution* (New York, 2007), 268–269.

Choptanks, and Mattawomans. Further north in Pennsylvania, Delawares, who had already relocated once from New Jersey and Delaware, were compelled to move once again. The 1737 Walking Purchase made by Pennsylvania alienated twelve thousand acres from the Delawares in a fraudulent land grab that displaced them from the eastern part of the colony. Delawares who were forced from the Susquehanna River valley relocated to the western reaches of the colony and across the Ohio River. They eventually left Pennsylvania in the 1750s for refuge in what is now eastern Ohio.[6]

Although the Ohio Valley was a region in transition, however, Delaware refugees did not arrive in an empty land. In the mid-seventeenth century, the people of the lower Great Lakes were set in motion by disease, war, and trade. In response to a catastrophic epidemic, Haudenosaunees embarked on raids on their Indigenous neighbors, wreaking havoc on Huron, Petun, Neutral, and Erie communities by dispersing some and taking others captive. By the time Haudenosaunees invaded the Ohio Valley in the late seventeenth century, Shawnees along the upper Ohio River had already largely been driven from their towns in the region by epidemic disease. Shawnees relocated to the Savannah River and to what is now Alabama to join with communities that would later consolidate into the Creek Confederacy. They joined the Miami and Illinois Confederacies to their northwest. Other Shawnees eventually went east to live with the Delawares in Pennsylvania. When the Delawares moved west in the early eighteenth century, Shawnees went with them, making new towns first on the Allegheny and Ohio Rivers, and then on the Scioto River in what is now Ohio. By the end of the Seven Years' War, most Pennsylvania Shawnees had returned to the Ohio country.[7]

6. Helen C. Rountree, *Pocahontas's People: The Powhatan Indians of Virginia through Four Centuries* (Norman, Okla., 1990), 89–186, esp. 91, 105, 128–129; Rountree and E. Randolph Turner, III, *Before and after Jamestown: Virginia's Powhatans and Their Predecessors* (Gainesville, Fla., 2002), 177–202; Stephen Warren, *The Worlds the Shawnees Made: Migration and Violence in Early America* (Chapel Hill, N.C., 2014), 134–153; Kristalyn Marie Shefveland, *Anglo-Native Virginia: Trade, Conversion, and Indian Slavery in the Old Dominion, 1646–1722* (Athens, Ga., 2016), 8–9. For Delaware migration, see Jane T. Merritt, *At the Crossroads: Indians and Empires on a Mid-Atlantic Frontier, 1700–1763* (Williamsburg, Va., and Chapel Hill, N.C., 2003), 41–49; Amy C. Schutt, *Peoples of the River Valleys: The Odyssey of the Delaware Indians* (Philadelphia, 2007), 62–123.

7. Scholars have revised their assessments of displacement in the Ohio Valley to emphasize trade as an inducement for relocation in the region rather than Haudenosaunee violence. See Kathryn Magee Labelle, *Dispersed but Not Destroyed: A History of the Seventeenth-Century Wendat People* (Vancouver, B.C., 2013), 120–140; Lakomäki, *Gathering Together,* 26–29; Warren, *Worlds the Shawnees Made,* 61–63, 73–74, 90–92,

Other Natives departed the Ohio Valley and lower Great Lakes in the 1670s and 1680s to follow trading opportunities. Miamis, Potawatomis, Mascoutens, and Kickapoos went to Green Bay, which had become a thriving center of the fur trade for Assiniboines, Crees, Ho-Chunks, Odawas, Ojibwes, Menominees, Mesquakies, and Sauks. When the French decided to move their fur-trading operations to Detroit in 1696, French and British competition over pelts from Native hunters concentrated people in new ways. Wyandots, Potawatomis, and Odawas relocated near French traders in Detroit. In 1736, Wyandots established a settlement closer to French and British traders in Sandusky Bay in what is now Ohio. The Miami Confederacy inhabited the area between the Mississippi and Ohio Rivers in the early seventeenth century. Miamis eventually moved to the Maumee and Wabash River valleys to participate more effectively in the fur trade. Mascoutens and Kickapoos joined the Miamis on their Wabash River lands in what is now Indiana at their invitation, settling across the river from the Weas in 1735.[8]

Native people created a world of multiethnic communities in the early eighteenth century by inviting eastern refugees of dispossession to move closer for their mutual safety and protection. For example, when eastern Delaware and Shawnee refugees moved into the Ohio country, they did so at the invitation of westerners like the Wyandots. By 1775, there were twenty-five hundred to three thousand Delawares living on tributaries of the Ohio River. A few hundred of these migrants were Moravian converts who formed mission towns with Moravian ministers at Gekelemukpechunk in the 1760s, and at Schoenbrunn, Gnadenhutten, and Lichtenau in the 1770s. Shawnees made towns in southeastern Ohio on the Scioto River. New migrants created buffer settlements against Anglo-Americans to the east. These settlements also allowed Delawares, Haudenosaunees, Miamis, Shawnees, Wyandots and others to build alliances that led them away from the bitter violence of the seventeenth century. By the 1780s, Native politics in the Ohio Valley were centered on individual towns, which occasionally aligned with the phratries and clans of particular nations but had increasingly become composite villages made up of many different peoples. These migrants were drawn to the Ohio Valley because it was a rich agricultural region. They managed horses and cattle, and Native women tended abun-

---

98–99, 101, 113–114, 131–132, 146–150, 157–179; Susan Sleeper-Smith, *Indigenous Prosperity and American Conquest: Indian Women of the Ohio River Valley, 1690–1792* (Williamsburg, Va., and Chapel Hill, N.C., 2018), 71–72; Ostler, *Surviving Genocide,* 23.

8. Hinderaker, *Elusive Empires,* 10–17; Tanner, ed., *Atlas of Great Lakes Indian History,* 39–47; Sleeper-Smith, *Indigenous Prosperity and American Conquest,* 73–81; Ostler, *Surviving Genocide,* 23–28.

dant fields and orchards. When one speculator predicted in the 1780s that the Ohio Valley would soon be "the garden of the world, the seat of wealth, and the centre of a great empire," he overlooked that, for Native people, it already was.[9]

By the 1770s, the pattern of dispossession in the east began to repeat west of the Appalachians. The end of the Seven Years' War opened a startling wave of migration from the British colonies. Small numbers of white migrants had moved west through the Cumberland Gap and along the Ohio River, sometimes forcing enslaved people to move with them. They went in spite of the Proclamation Line of 1763 that prohibited settlement and speculation beyond the Appalachian Mountains. The end of the American Revolution in 1783 accelerated migration and with it the competition for land along the New York, Pennsylvania, Virginia, North Carolina, South Carolina, and Georgia frontiers. Indigenous people had made alliances during the Seven Years' War, Pontiac's War, Lord Dunmore's War, and the Revolution to contest removal. They revived alliance building in 1782 and 1783 as news of the Treaty of Paris trickled into Indian country. The insistence of federal commissioners that eastern Native Americans were a conquered people galvanized confederacies in the North and South. So did the long history of removal to the east. In 1776, a Shawnee speaker had warned a Cherokee council that the United States would "extirpate" them if they won the American Revolution. As they contemplated the end of the war in 1783, centuries of experience made federationists believe this might be true.[10]

Federal officials pursued Indian removal from the Republic's founding. On Douglass's return from Upper Sandusky, Detroit, and Niagara, he reported his findings to the Committee on Indian Affairs, the congressional committee in charge of Indian policy. Members of Congress were distracted that summer. In June 1783, mutinous soldiers had surrounded the Philadelphia statehouse to protest the lengthy demobilization of the Continental Army.

9. [Manasseh Cutler], *An Explanation of the Map Which Delineates That Part of the Federal Lands; Comprehended between Pennsylvania West Line, the Rivers Ohio and Sioto, and Lake Erie; Confirmed to the United States by Sundry Tribes of Indians, in the Treaties of 1784 and 1786, and Now Ready for Settlement* (Salem, [Mass.], 1787), 14 (quotation). For migration into the Ohio Valley, see Tanner, ed., *Atlas of Great Lakes Indian History,* 42–45; Hinderaker, *Elusive Empires,* 27–32; Lakomäki, *Gathering Together,* 44–49; Harper, *Unsettling the West,* 10–11.

10. Henry Stuart to John Stuart, Aug. 25, 1776, in K. G. Davies, ed., *Documents of the American Revolution, 1770–1783,* XII (Dublin, 1976), 202 ("extirpate"), quoted in Dowd, *Spirited Resistance,* 47; Dowd, *Spirited Resistance,* 47–52; Nichols, *Red Gentlemen and White Savages,* 51; DuVal, *Independence Lost,* 236.

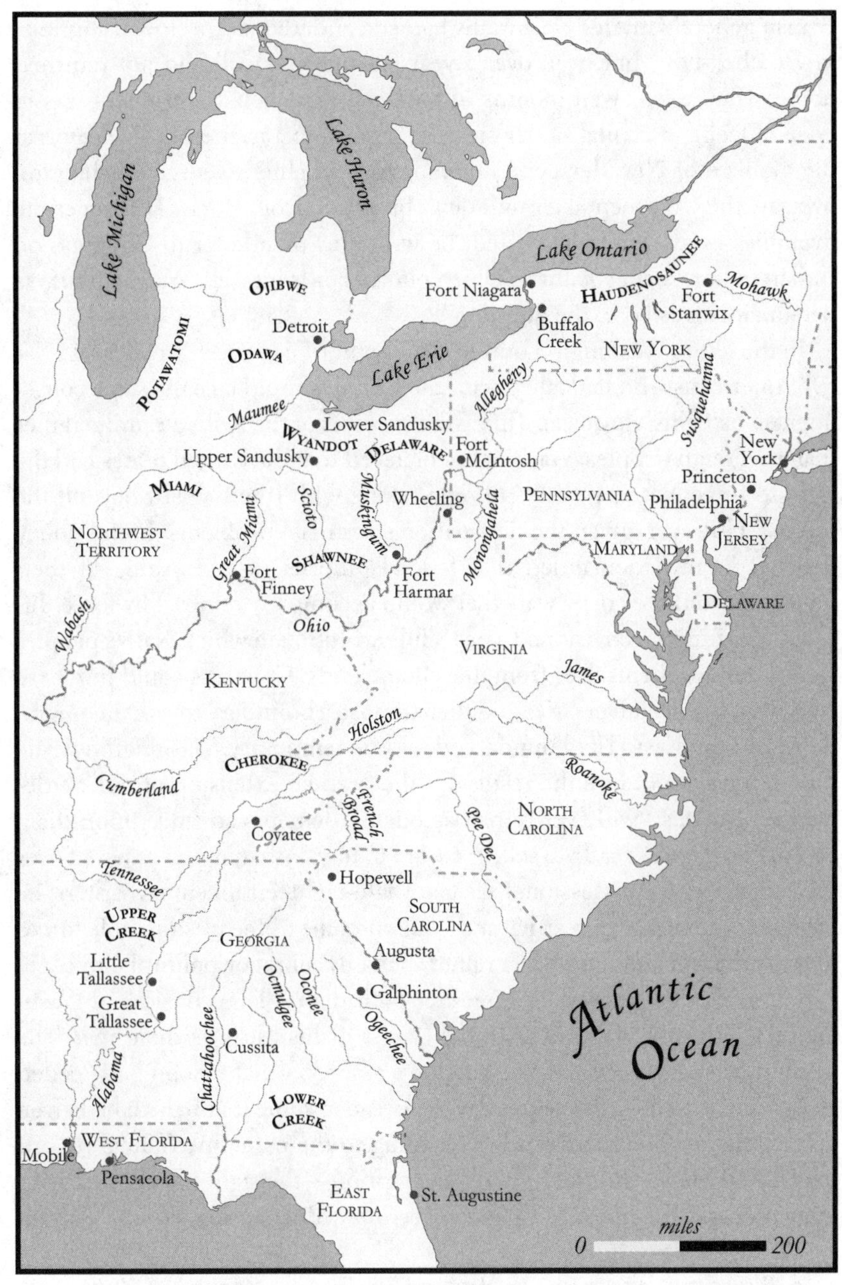

MAP 2. *Trans-Appalachian Region, 1780s. Drawn by Rebecca Wrenn*

British general Charles Cornwallis had surrendered at Yorktown, Virginia, in October 1781, but, well over a year later, troops still had not returned home. They were owed months of back pay. The new government was in crisis. Fleeing a capital under siege, Congress reconvened in Princeton at the College of New Jersey. As commander in chief, George Washington oversaw the Continental Army's demobilization from Rocky Hill, an estate five miles away. While he waited, he wrote his own letter to Congress on Indian policy. A speculator in Ohio country lands himself, Washington was personally invested in the question.[11]

In the letter, Washington outlined the right of conquest. In his eyes, Native Americans who had allied with the British should face the same consequences as British loyalists. They were subjects of the British Empire rather than sovereign peoples. Washington believed that the United States had the right to force Native people "to retire along with [the British] beyond the Lakes." However, given the new nation's financial problems, both "policy and oeconomy" demanded that federal officials do everything in their power to avoid the costly wars that would accompany removal by force. Instead, Washington envisioned a peaceful revolution in which Native peoples would remove themselves from their homelands. Congress could purchase land from former adversaries and then impose a boundary to contain migration from the East. The boundary would be temporary. Washington wrote that removal would be the result of "the gradual extension of our Settlements." Natives "will ever retreat as our Settlements advance upon them and they will be as ready to sell, as we are to buy." Washington papered over the violence of dispossession. Like many late-eighteenth-century writers, he promoted dispossession as natural—an outcome of the unstoppable forces of reproduction and migration rather than any moral or political choice.[12]

When the congressional Committee on Indian Affairs considered Washington's letter that fall, they adopted most of his ideas as their own. The committee slightly revised Washington's assertion that Britain had "ceded all the lands" to the Mississippi River, instead arguing that Britain had given up "all claim" to western land. According to the committee's final report, the United States had the right of preemption—the right of purchase over other European empires—to Native territory. Preemption assumed future

11. Burton, ed., "Ephraim Douglass and His Times," *Magazine of History with Notes and Queries,* extra no. 10 (New York, 1910), 264–275; *JCC,* XXV, 681–695; Alan Taylor, *American Revolutions: A Continental History, 1750–1804* (New York, 2016), 319.

12. George Washington to James Duane, Sept. 7, 1783, George Washington Papers, Ser. 3, Varick Transcripts, 1775–1785, Subser. 3A, Continental and State Military Personnel, 1775–1783, Letter book 7, Manuscript Division, LOC (quotations).

purchases before Natives had agreed to sell. Congress would seek land cessions on the grounds that Native nations had been "the aggressors in the war." According to the report, Native people were obligated to "make atonement for the enormities which they have perpetrated." The committee called on war stories blaming Native people for wartime violence that had previously been used to muster white support for the Revolution, only this time they used them to justify removal.[13]

Legislators insisted on the right of preemption because they saw Native lands as a fund to pay the confederation's war debts. They expected land to solve a series of problems that arose out of the American Revolution, chief among them the need for revenue. Under the Articles of Confederation, the federal government had no power to tax directly or to compel the states to pay their bills. During the war, the Continental Congress had opened Continental loan offices and used bonds to pay for war expenses. IOUs to soldiers, domestic lenders, and army contractors distributed during the war were also converted into bonds. Meanwhile, loans from Spanish, French, and Dutch investors also supported the U.S. war effort. By the end of the American Revolution, the confederation owed outsize debts—fifty-four million dollars—to foreign and domestic creditors. The government struggled to pay the interest on these bonds and debts. In most states, the majority of taxes went to pay the interest on government bonds issued to creditors. Burdened by their own financial crises, the states failed to send requisitions to Congress to pay federal debts and expenses. Congress was not being hyperbolic when they wrote that "this inattention in the States has almost endangered our very existence as a People." In dire straits, the confederation's leaders looked to land sales to fund the debt.[14]

Throughout the war, recruiters coaxed soldiers into service with the promise of Native lands as payment. Those who fought in western cam-

13. *JCC,* XXV, 683–684 ("ceded," 684, "aggressors," 683); Washington to Duane, Sept. 7, 1783, George Washington Papers; Nichols, *Red Gentlemen and White Savages,* 21–22; Leonard J. Sadosky, *Revolutionary Negotiations: Indians, Empires, and Diplomats in the Founding of America* (Charlottesville, Va., 2010), 130. For preemption, see Banner, *How the Indians Lost Their Land,* 8. For war stories, see Robert G. Parkinson, *The Common Cause: Creating Race and Nation in the American Revolution* (Williamsburg, Va., and Chapel Hill, N.C., 2016); Gregory Ablavsky, "The Savage Constitution," *Duke Law Journal,* LXIII (2014), 1015.

14. *JCC,* XXII, 132–135 (quotation, 134); Nichols, *Red Gentlemen and White Savages,* 20. For war debt, see Holton, *Unruly Americans;* Stephen Mihm, "Funding the Revolution: Monetary and Fiscal Policy in Eighteenth-Century America," in Edward G. Gray and Jane Kamensky, eds., *The Oxford Handbook of the American Revolution* (New York, 2013), 327–354.

paigns took advantage of their travels to claim what they saw as the spoils of war. One military official observed that Virginia militiamen who had participated in General George Rogers Clark's campaign to take several British posts in the Illinois country in 1778–1779 "had cast their eyes on choice lands, and I am informed had made what they called tomahawk rights" in the area, settling there without proper title. Recruiters for the Continental Army also used land bounties to encourage soldiers to sign up for three-year terms of service. Native homelands were currency for soldiers, or, in Washington's words, a "reward of their past dangers and toils."[15]

At the conclusion of the war, however, many veterans could not afford to wait for bounty lands to be surveyed and sited. Inflation made government bonds and continental currency nearly worthless. When months of back pay finally arrived for soldiers, it was paid out in government certificates redeemable for cash plus interest at a future date. Veterans who could not afford to hold on to government scrip sold it at a fraction of its value to wealthy bondholders. By 1787, Secretary of War Henry Knox despaired that he was inundated with "incessant enquiries" about locating bounty lands from veterans who had sold their scrip. "These unfortunate men now consider the lands promised them, as their only resource against poverty, in old age," he wrote. Washington, too, hoped to hasten the purchase and survey of Native lands for the benefit of veterans before other migrants claimed "the Cream of the Country at the expence of many suffering officers and Soldiers who have fought and bled to obtain it."[16]

The states had their own plans for Native homelands. Many claimed land running all the way to the Mississippi River under the terms of their colonial charters (which often conflicted with each other). One of the first tasks of the confederation government was to convince the individual states to give up those claims. When the states finally began to do so, they negotiated to secure small reserves of Native homelands for themselves. Virginia's claims, for example, stretched west to the Mississippi River and north to Lake Michigan. Virginia officials only ceded the state's claims on the condi-

15. Brigadier-General Harmar to the Secretary of War, Aug. 7, 1787, in William Henry Smith, *The St. Clair Papers: The Life and Public Services of Arthur St. Clair Soldier of the Revolutionary War; President of the Continental Congress; and Governor of the North-Western Territory with His Correspondenc and Other Papers Arranged and Annotated,* II (Cincinnati, Ohio, 1882), 27–29 ("had cast," 29); Washington to Duane, Sept. 7, 1783, George Washington Papers, 131 ("reward").

16. Henry Knox to the President of Congress, Apr. 26, 1787, in *TPUS,* II, 27–28 ("incessant," 27, "unfortunate," 28); Washington to Duane, Sept. 7, 1783, George Washington Papers, 131 ("Cream"); *JCC,* XXV, 682; Andrew R. L. Cayton, *The Frontier Republic: Ideology and Politics in the Ohio Country, 1780–1825* (Kent, Ohio, 1986), 53.

tion that they would be able to secure bounty lands for their veterans north of the Ohio River. By the 1790s, Virginia's veterans could locate land in the 150 million acres of the Virginia Military District in what is now Ohio and register it at a state land office.[17]

Under the terms of its cession, Connecticut reserved a tract of land just below Lake Erie in what is now northern Ohio to pay war veterans and those who had lost property during the war. In 1787, a group of Connecticut petitioners asked the state legislature to compensate them for property that had been destroyed in nine towns during British raids. The assembly agreed to make restitution to the petitioners for their burned homes, stores, and barns. Between 1790 and 1792, the state created a commission to tally the wartime losses of 1,870 Connecticut residents, and they repaid them with land claims in a tract of the Ohio country that came to be known as "the Firelands." Connecticut's promises were speculative investments in preemption rights. The Firelands were Delaware, Shawnee, and Wyandot lands. Native people held on to the Firelands despite Connecticut's plans until they ceded the tract alongside Odawa, Ojibwe, and Potawatomi delegations in 1805 at the Treaty of Fort Industry.[18]

Public creditors also expected that Ohio lands would be "speedily improved" and converted into cash to repay war debts. Speculators were instrumental in this quick conversion because they surveyed and marketed the land themselves. The federal government sold millions of Ohio lands to three major land companies: the Ohio Company of Associates, the Scioto Company, and the associates of John Cleves Symmes. At the state and federal level, land policy and land sales favored wealthy buyers. In 1785, Congress set the minimum purchase for a tract of western land at 640 acres, far too large for an ordinary farmer to afford.[19]

Land speculation attracted men like Manasseh Cutler, a Massachusetts veteran and a founder of the Ohio Company of Associates, and Gilbert Imlay, an author and speculator. Both men wrote geographies of the lands they acquired to promote them to potential buyers. They described Native lands as empty Edens. In 1788, Cutler published a tract to advertise the

17. *JCC,* XXIV, 406–409, esp. 409; Nichols, *Red Gentlemen and White Savages,* 20–21.

18. Clarence D. Laylin, "The Firelands Grant," *Ohio Archaeological and Historical Quarterly,* X (1902), 435–451; Charles C. Royce, "Schedule of Indian Land Cessions," U.S. Serial Set, no. 4015, 56th Congress, 1st Sess., 666–677.

19. *JCC,* XXIII, 551, 604–606, XXV, 682–683 (quotation); Joseph W. Ernst, *With Compass and Chain: Federal Land Surveyors in the Old Northwest, 1785–1816* (New York, 1979), 91–99; Nichols, *Red Gentlemen and White Savages,* 59–60.

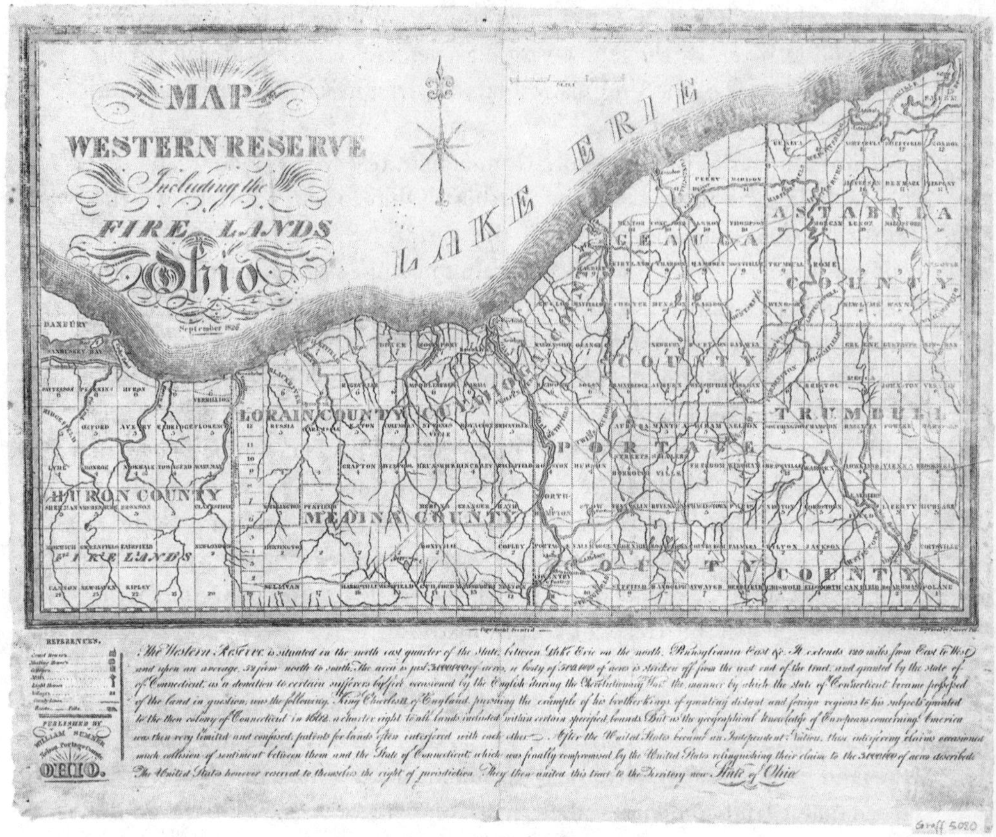

FIGURE 3. *William Sumner,* Map of Western Reserve Including the Fire Lands in Ohio. *1826. Everett D. Graff Collection of Western America, Special Collections. Courtesy Newberry Library, Chicago*

lands purchased by the Ohio Company. He celebrated the unique opportunity that arose from creating a new society from scratch—"in order to begin *right,* there will be no *wrong* habits to combat, and no inveterate systems to overturn—there is no rubbish to remove, before you can lay the foundation." In his appended "Map of the Federal Territory," Cutler projected neat parcels of land onto the Ohio Valley's natural features that could be easily distributed to white migrants. Imlay similarly pitched his geography as a celebration of U.S. empire and Kentucky's ascension to statehood.[20]

20. [Cutler], *Explanation of the Map,* 20 ("in order"); G[ilbert] Imlay, *A Topographical Description of the Western Territory of North America . . . to Which Is Annexed, a Delineation of the Laws and Government of the State of Kentucky . . .* (London, 1792).

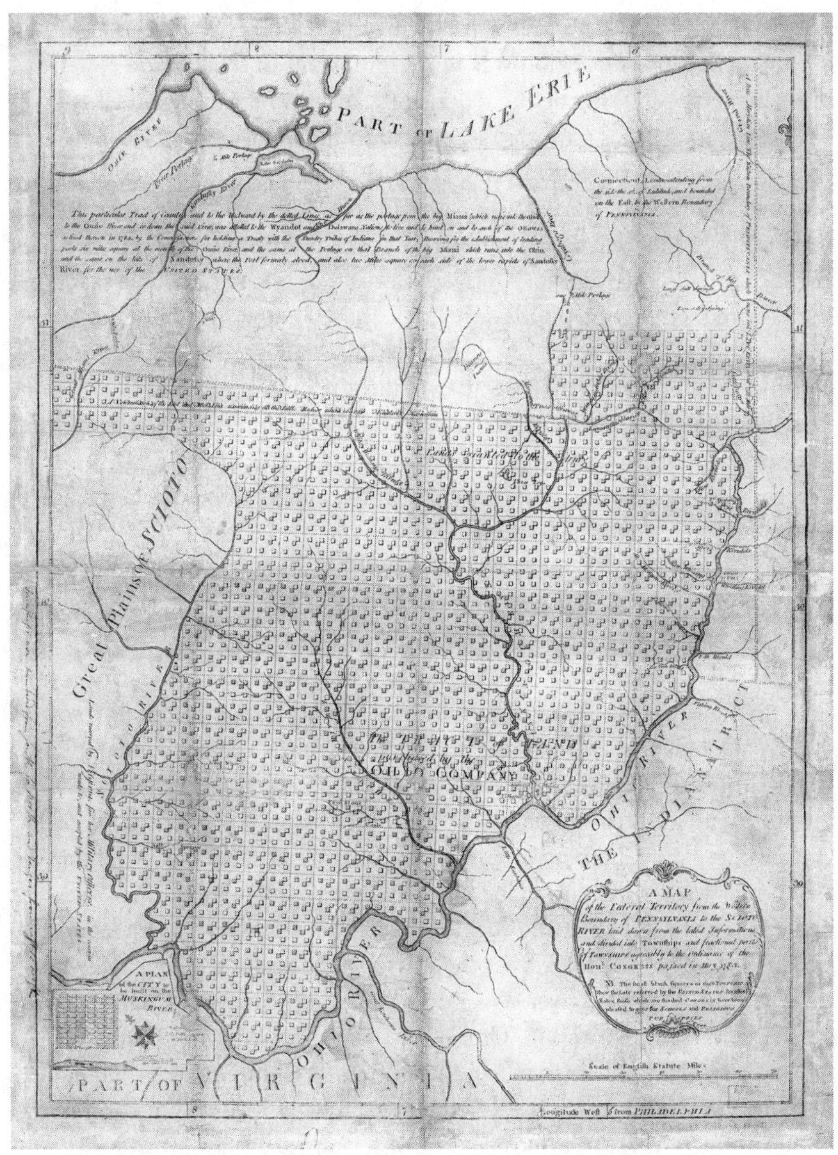

FIGURE 4. *Manasseh Cutler,* A Map of the Federal Territory from the Western Boundary of Pennsylvania to the Scioto River Laid Down from the Latest Information and Divided into Townships and Fractional Parts of Townships Agreeably to the Ordinance of the Honorable Congress Passed in May 1785. *[1788]. Geography and Map Division, G4081.F7 1785 .C8. Courtesy Library of Congress*

Speculators like Cutler and Imlay crowded into the Ohio country in the 1780s because no region was more important in that period to federal plans for removal. Long before federal officials set their sights on Cherokee, Creek, Choctaw, and Chickasaw country to the south, they cast their eyes on Miami, Delaware, Shawnee, Wyandot, Haudenosaunee, Ojibwe, Potawatomi, and Odawa lands to the north. In 1783, the Committee on Indian Affairs recommended that the federal government pursue land cessions north of the Ohio River first. Congress looked on the region "as a principal fund for redeeming the public securities of the United States." The cession of the Ohio country was a small concession, they argued—small enough to avoid the anger of Native people should they be "totally expelled" from their homelands. Between 1784 and 1786, U.S. commissioners forced the issue of the cession of Ohio country lands at a series of treaties. Although Congress had backed down from their initial claims to Native lands based on the right of conquest, commissioners in the field continued to treat with Natives as "conquered" peoples, and they demanded land cessions as the price of peace.[21]

Federal plans for removal were not a fait accompli. Native Americans and state leaders contested them on multiple fronts. Native leaders protested the Treaty of Paris and the cession of their lands to the United States. Creek diplomat Alexander McGillivray explained that Britain "has no right to give up a Country she never coud call her own." Together, the Creeks, Chickasaws, and Cherokees wrote to Spanish officials saying as much. Another delegation of Creeks, Cherokees, Chickasaws, Choctaws, Mohawks, Senecas, Delawares, Shawnees, and Tuscaroras met with British leaders at St. Augustine in 1782 to express their disgust at the agreement.[22]

North of the Ohio River, Wyandot, Delaware, Shawnee, Haudenosaunee, Wea, Miami, Kickapoo, Creek, and Cherokee representatives met in 1783 at Lower Sandusky to affirm their commitment to defend their rights. In the Shawnee towns on the Scioto River in what is now Ohio and in the

21. *JCC,* XXVII, 626 ("principal fund"), XXV, 682 ("totally"); Joseph Brant to Samuel Kirkland, Mar. 8, 1791, TPP, LXI, 208 ("conquered"); "The Virginia Cession of Territory Northwest of the Ohio," [Mar. 1, 1784], in Julian P. Boyd et al., eds., *The Papers of Thomas Jefferson,* 43 vols. (Princeton, N.J., 1950—), VI, 571–575. For state land cessions, see Thomas Perkins Abernethy, *Western Lands and the American Revolution* (New York, 1937); Merrill Jensen, "The Creation of the National Domain, 1781–1784," *Mississippi Valley Historical Review,* XXVI (1939), 323–342.

22. Alexander McGillivray to Stephen Merot [Miró], Mar. 28, 1784, in John Walton Caughey, *McGillivray of the Creeks* (Norman, Okla., 1938), 73 (quotation); DuVal, *Independence Lost,* 236–237.

Wea, Kickapoo, and Miami towns along the Wabash River in what is now Indiana, Native leaders led the opposition to U.S. negotiations. They wanted a return to the boundary agreed on at the 1768 Treaty of Fort Stanwix.[23]

Federal officials first tried to put removal into practice in a series of postwar treaties between 1784 and 1786. The arrival of federal treaty commissioners demanding land cessions divided Native communities. Some leaders responded by staying away altogether and refusing to participate, while others signed treaties under pressure or to keep the peace and then repudiated them afterward. All were shocked by federal demands. Rather than using councils to come to a mutual understanding, U.S. negotiators threatened Native leaders with war if they did not consent. Federal commissioners in the field called Native delegations with whom they treated conquered peoples, while Native leaders approached the councils as representatives of sovereign nations still at war with the United States.[24]

Federal commissioners told Native leaders that they represented the voice of all the states. It was clear, however, that their confederation was divided. Some states wanted to grasp Native land for themselves to sell to speculators and white migrants to pay their own war debts. The Articles of Confederation gave Congress the power to regulate trade and policy with "Indians, not members of any of the states," yet many states used their extensive charters that extended to the Mississippi River to claim the power to treat with Native peoples beyond state boundaries. Although federal commissioners worked to make their treaties, the states competed by negotiating their own agreements with Native nations. For example, when New York hoped to claim part of Iroquoia, state officials schemed to treat the Haudenosaunees as their subordinates, party to treaties with New York rather than the confederation government.[25]

23. Obadiah Robins to Josiah Harmar, May 17, 1785, JHP, II; "Transactions with Indians at Sandusky," Aug. 26–Sept. 8, 1783, *MPHC*, XX, 174–183; Dowd, *Spirited Resistance*, 93; Nichols, *Red Gentlemen and White Savages*, 26, 38, 91.

24. White, *Middle Ground*, 417; Nichols, *Red Gentlemen and White Savages*, 11, 26. For establishing common ground and for disillusionment at treaties, see James H. Merrell, *Into the American Woods: Negotiators on the Pennsylvania Frontier* (New York, 1999), 253–282; Nancy Shoemaker, *A Strange Likeness: Becoming Red and White in Eighteenth-Century North America* (New York, 2004), 65–76.

25. Articles of Confederation, 1777, art. IX (quotation); Nichols, *Red Gentlemen and White Savages*, 23, 29–30; DuVal, *Independence Lost*, 332–333; Ablavsky, "Savage Constitution," *Duke Law Journal*, LXIII (2014), 1013, 1016. For New York, see Alan Taylor, *The Divided Ground: Indians, Settlers, and the Northern Borderland of the American Revolution* (New York, 2006), 156; Sadosky, *Revolutionary Negotiations*, 131–132; Ablavsky, "Savage Constitution," *Duke Law Journal*, LXIII (2014), 1019–1024.

The divisions between New York and the federal government were on full display at Fort Stanwix in 1784, when a small Haudenosaunee delegation met with representatives of New York and Congress. Massachusetts, New York, and Pennsylvania all held colonial charters extending into Iroquoia. To preempt Massachusetts, New York's governor George Clinton began arranging a treaty with the Haudenosaunee to secure the state's interests. At the same time, Congress made preparations for a treaty with Haudenosaunee representatives to preempt New York. They asked New York and Pennsylvania to conduct their treaties concurrently. Though Pennsylvania agreed, New York refused. At the Treaty of Fort Stanwix, Haudenosaunee leaders met New York's commissioners, who arrived first. The Haudenosaunee delegation declined to make any agreements with the New Yorkers. Mohawk leader Brant gently chided them, "Here lies some Difficulty in our Minds, that there should be two separate Bodies to manage these Affairs, for this does not agree with our ancient Customs." Brant recognized the ambiguities and weaknesses of the postwar union of states. He insisted on meeting with the confederation's representatives rather than making agreements with several governments clearly in conflict with each other.[26]

Yet Haudenosaunees and their allies did not agree over policy, either. The states were not the only ones to present a divided front. In May 1783, Native delegates told the commanding officer at Fort Niagara that they "were free people, Allies not Subjects to the King of England, that He had no right to grant their lands, nor would they submit to it." Nonetheless, some Native leaders still favored negotiating with representatives of the crown, regardless of the damage done to the British-Native alliance by the Treaty of Paris. Brant no sooner expressed his anger at the British for their role in the agreement while speaking to New York commissioners at Fort Stanwix then he pronounced that he was "willing to Die for his Right and contry" and left shortly thereafter for Fort Niagara to speak with the governor of Canada. Oneida and Tuscarora allies of the United States, on the other hand, were more eager to stay to further negotiations. They enjoyed a privileged position at the council and wanted a guarantee that their lands would be protected. Mohawks, Onondagas, Cayugas, and Senecas who were still at war with the United States also hoped for peace, although not at the expense of their territory. Seneca leader Cornplanter, who had watched U.S. forces in-

26. "Extracts from the Proceedings of the Treaty of Fort Stanwix between New York and the Six Nations," [Sept. 4–10, 1784], in *EAID,* XVIII, 308 (quotation), "Proceedings of the United States and the Six Nations at Fort Stanwix," Oct. 3–21, 1784, 318; Taylor, *Divided Ground,* 154–157; Sadosky, *Revolutionary Negotiations,* 130–138; Nichols, *Red Gentlemen and White Savages,* 27–32.

vade Seneca homelands during the American Revolution, was one of those who stayed behind with Mohawk leader Aaron Hill to speak with the delegation.[27]

The Haudenosaunee emissaries who continued the talks were stunned when federal commissioners demanded all of Iroquoia west of Buffalo Creek as the price of peace. The proposal divided Haudenosaunee towns at Buffalo Creek in two. Given that Hill had made it clear at the beginning of the council that they were "free, and independent" and "not . . . under the influence of any," including Great Britain, Native diplomats found it extraordinary when federal commissioners insisted that the Haudenosaunees were not a "free and independent nation" capable of making "what terms you please." Instead, U.S. commissioners informed them, "It is not so. You are a subdued people; you have been overcome in a war which you entered into with us, not only without provocation, but in violation of most sacred obligations . . . . *You* now stand out *alone* against our *whole force.*" The United States claimed the right to grasp all of Iroquoia. Although Native speakers explained that they did not have the power to cede any lands — the Haudenosaunees had only sent a small delegation that did not have the authority held by the chiefs and clan matrons to make cessions — the remaining delegation nonetheless agreed to sign to placate U.S. commissioners, perhaps knowing that it would not stand because they were not authorized to make such a concession.[28]

When the Haudenosaunee delegates brought the treaty back to Buffalo Creek, it was swiftly rejected. The council determined that they would not give up their "Rights of the Soil" when it "actualy all belong[ed] to them." Haudenosaunee attendees of the Fort Stanwix meeting told a general at Fort Pitt that they had been "drove from their nation by their subjects — for selling this land to the United States which was their property." To the Haudenosaunees, the negotiations at Stanwix were theft.[29]

Federal commissioners sowed further distrust in Native councils as they

27. J. G. Simcoe to George Hammond, Aug. 24, 1793, in *CJGS,* II, 41 ("free people"); Thomas S. Abler, ed., *Chainbreaker: The Revolutionary War Memoirs of Governor Blacksnake as Told to Benjamin Williams* (Lincoln, Neb., 2005), 163–164 ("willing," 164); Taylor, *Divided Ground,* 157–158.

28. "Proceedings of the United States and the Six Nations at Fort Stanwix," Oct. 3–21, 1784, in *EAID,* XVIII, 319 ("free, and independent"), 323–324 ("free and independent," 323, "It is not so," 323–324); Taylor, *Divided Ground,* 159; Nichols, *Red Gentlemen and White Savages,* 30; Harper, *Unsettling the West,* 149–150.

29. Abler, ed., *Chainbreaker,* 170 ("Rights"); David Luckett to Josiah Harmar, July 10, 1785, JHP, II ("drove"), Michael Huffnagle to Harmar, July 1785; Nichols, *Red Gentlemen and White Savages,* 81.

moved west. At Fort McIntosh in Pennsylvania, they met with three hundred Shawnees, Delawares, Wyandots, Ojibwes, Ohio Senecas, and Odawas. They announced the right of conquest there, too. They brandished the Treaty of Paris and the 1784 Treaty of Fort Stanwix to argue that land cessions in the Ohio country—thirty million acres—were an unavoidable cost of war. Delaware and Wyandot speakers protested the demands before eventually agreeing to sign, but without engaging in the exchange of wampum that would have made the purchase valid. Moreover, while federal commissioners called the council a success, Shawnees, Weas, Miamis, and Kickapoos who had purposefully stayed away quickly declared it invalid.[30]

Federal commissioners again tried their hand at demanding the same land cessions from more than two hundred Shawnees, Miamis, and Kickapoos at Fort Finney in 1786. Congress sent three federal commissioners who all had a personal stake in land speculation. At Fort Finney, Shawnee war captain Kekewepellethe told them that "God gave us this country, we do not understand measuring out the lands, it is all ours." Most of the Shawnee representatives in attendance were Mekoche, the Shawnee division responsible for keeping the peace. After the Revolution, they had immediately returned their war belts to the British and had given up war against the United States. Mekoche attendees felt compelled by their responsibilities to smooth over the bellicosity of the federal commissioners who treated them as conquered people who had to atone for, in their words, "barbarously ravaging our frontier" during the American Revolution. Federal commissioners warned, "It rests now with you, the destruction of your women and children, or their future happiness, depends on your present choice." The attendees signed the treaty, but, as at Fort Stanwix and Fort McIntosh, the agreement only sowed division.[31]

Federal efforts to orchestrate removal met a different sort of challenge in the South, where the states made land grabs without consulting federal officials. North Carolina, Georgia, and Virginia all used their colonial charters

30. Josiah Harmar to Sarah Harmar, Jan. 10, 1785, JHP, II; Josiah Harmar to John Dickinson, [Jan. 15, 1785], in *EAID,* XVIII, 328–329; Merrell, *Into the American Woods,* 187–189; Nichols, *Red Gentlemen and White Savages,* 32–34; Harper, *Unsettling the West,* 150.

31. "Gen. Butler's Journal, Continued," Jan. 30, [1786], in Neville B. Craig, ed., *The Olden Time, a Monthly Publication . . . ,* II (Pittsburgh, Pa., 1848), 522 ("God"), also quoted in Colin G. Calloway, *The Shawnees and the War for America* (New York, 2007), 81; "Excerpts from the Journal of General Richard Butler at the Treaty of Fort Finney," Jan. 14–30, [1786], in *EAID,* XVIII, 346 ("barbarously"), 347 ("It rests"); White, *Middle Ground,* 435–438; Nichols, *Red Gentlemen and White Savages,* 38–42; Harper, *Unsettling the West,* 158–159; Ostler, *Surviving Genocide,* 88–90.

to claim Native lands running west to the Mississippi River. Between 1783 and 1785, the southern states' efforts to seize land were just as divisive as those in the North. North Carolina did not give up its western claims until 1789. The state aggressively pursued Native lands within the bounds of its charter, confiscating them outright by an act of the legislature. In the Tennessee Valley, a group of separatists from North Carolina declared themselves an independent state called Franklin. Franklinites concentrated on removal as one of their first priorities. In 1785, they made an arrangement with a small group of Cherokees who were not empowered to speak for the whole to buy their territory on the Holston and French Broad Rivers in what is now Tennessee. Over the next few months, hundreds of migrants moved to the region over the objections of Cherokee leaders.[32]

In Georgia, the state's leaders approached the Creeks as if they had conquered them, too. At the Treaty of Augusta in 1783, state commissioners presented Creeks with a demand for the lands that fell between the Ogeechee and Oconee Rivers. Hoboithle Miko of Great Tallassee and Neha Miko of Cussita headed the Creek delegation. Both men were responsible for securing the Creeks' relationship with Georgia and South Carolina—an assigned diplomatic role that made them eager to pursue peace. Georgia's demands stunned the Creek leaders, who protested that they did not have the power to cede any lands at all. Seeing few other options, Hoboithle Miko and Neha Miko signed nonetheless. Several dozen representatives of Creek towns jointly decried the cession foisted on them at Augusta.[33]

The southern states disputed the supremacy of federal officials as the architects of Indian removal, but Congress did not have the same goals for removal in the South as they outlined for the North. In 1784, a congressional committee decided that federal peace treaties with southern Native nations should confirm existing boundaries. They recommended that commissioners not "yield nor require too much" in order "to accommodate the Indians as far as the public good will admit" and to avoid a war. They worried that the rapaciousness of the states might spark a general conflict

32. "Treaty of Dumplin Creek," June 10, 1785, in *EAID,* XVIII, 386–387; Thomas Perkins Abernethy, *From Frontier to Plantation in Tennessee: A Study in Frontier Democracy* (Chapel Hill, N.C., 1932), 49–54; Kevin T. Barksdale, *The Lost State of Franklin: America's First Secession* (Lexington, Ky., 2008), 34, 65–66; Nichols, *Red Gentlemen and White Savages,* 63–64; Barksdale, "The State of Franklin: Separatism, Competition, and the Legacy of Tennessee's First State, 1783–1789," in Kristofer Ray, ed., *Before the Volunteer State: New Thoughts on Early Tennessee, 1540–1800* (Knoxville, Tenn., 2014), 167; DuVal, *Independence Lost,* 315–320.

33. Nichols, *Red Gentlemen and White Savages,* 23, 47; DuVal, *Independence Lost,* 251–253; Ostler, *Surviving Genocide,* 90.

in the West. Meanwhile, Georgia and North Carolina hoped to assert the power of their states to seize Native lands for themselves. Southern congressmen swiftly denounced federal plans for peace treaties. When Congress sent commissioners to meet with the Creeks at Galphinton, Georgia, and with the Cherokees at Hopewell, South Carolina, in 1785, the states asserted their power there. At Galphinton, only a small Creek delegation showed up. Federal commissioners and Georgia's representatives argued over whether or not they could use the occasion to demand more Creek lands. The disagreement amused Creek delegates, who marveled at the disunity of the United States. The federal commissioners and most Creeks left without any agreement. When only Hoboithle Miko and Neha Miko stayed to speak for the Creeks, Georgia commissioners again forced through more land cessions.[34]

Cherokees tried to take advantage of the division between the federal and state governments. They looked to the federal government as a competing power they could leverage to protect their core settlements from the encroachment of migrants, speculators, North Carolina, and the state of Franklin. Several thousand people had already crowded into Overhill Cherokee lands at the Holston and French Broad Rivers. Cherokee leaders used the Treaty of Hopewell in 1785 to demand that the United States address illegal migration into their territory and "remove the white people to their own side." U.S. commissioners were forced to admit that they were powerless to do much of anything to stop migrants or the states. As for those people who had settled illegally at the French Broad and Holston Rivers, the commissioners lamented that "they are too numerous for us to engage to remove," and they could only refer the case to Congress. Cherokee leaders signed the Treaty of Hopewell recognizing U.S. sovereignty, but it was clear that sovereignty was largely meaningless given the circumstances. In the contest over removal, the federal government never had control.[35]

34. *JCC,* XXVII, 456–457 (quotations, 456); Nichols, *Red Gentlemen and White Savages,* 45, 47; DuVal, *Independence Lost,* 299, also 298–300; Ablavsky, "Savage Constitution," *Duke Law Journal,* LXIII (2014), 1027–1029.

35. Henry Knox to George Washington, July 7, 1789, Enclosure A., No. 3., Hopewell on Keowee, Nov. 18–29, 1785, in *ASPIA,* I, 41 ("remove"), 43 ("too numerous"), Knox to Washington, July 7, 1789, 38, Knox to Washington, July 7, 1789, Enclosure A., No. 1, Benjamin Hawkins, Andrew Pickens, Joseph Martin, and Lach'n McIntosh to Richard Henry Lee, Dec. 2, 1785, 38–39; Nichols, *Red Gentlemen and White Savages,* 47–50; Barksdale, "State of Franklin," in Ray, ed., *Before the Volunteer State,* 167.

Throughout the 1780s, the federal government also competed with ordinary migrants as well as the states to control the work of removal. People were the building blocks of western state making. As one federal military officer observed, these "modes of population" went hand in hand with the march of an army or the construction of a blockhouse as a tool of removal. Federal planners and speculators depended on white migrants, in particular, to populate new territories. They needed migrants to purchase Native lands to fill federal coffers and speculator's pockets, and they needed them to link new settlements to the eastern states. These "modes of population" depended on women as much as men to be silent partners in settler colonial ventures. When federal officials imagined the ideal settlers, they pictured white agrarian families and households, rather than individuals. They needed their "progeny" to expand federal power over generations. At the same time, population could grow beyond the capacity of states to control it. When the Committee on Indian Affairs made their recommendations to Congress in 1783, they warned that U.S. sovereignty in the Ohio Valley would fall into disarray without a strong government to manage "the increase of feeble, disorderly and dispersed settlements" and to counteract "the depravity of manners which they have a tendency to produce."[36]

To channel population toward the proper ends, Congress passed a slate of ordinances in the 1780s governing the creation of new states. The ordinances outlined, in congressional delegate James Monroe's words, "a Colonial Govt. similar to that wh. prevail'd in these States previous to the revolution." The first ordinance outlined the creation of new states that would enter the union on equal terms with the original thirteen. The second encouraged compact settlements, a strategy that legislators imagined would tie migrants to the new nation through proximity and commerce. The final ordinance in 1787 created the Northwest Territory, which included all of the land claimed by the United States north of the Ohio River and west to the Mississippi River (present-day Ohio, Indiana, Illinois, Michigan, and Wis-

36. Henry Knox to Anthony Wayne, Jan. 5, 1792, in Richard C. Knopf, ed., *Anthony Wayne, a Name in Arms: Soldier, Diplomat, Defender of Expansion Westward of a Nation: The Wayne-Knox-Pickering-McHenry Correspondence* ([Pittsburgh, Pa.], 1960), 165–166 ("modes," 165), Knox to Wayne, July 27, 1792, 54–55; Arthur St. Clair to George Washington, "A Memorial Respecting the Territory of the United States North West of the River Ohio," August 1789, in *TPUS,* II, 212 ("progeny"); *JCC,* XXV, 690 ("increase"); Nichols, *Red Gentlemen and White Savages,* 15. For scholarship on gender, households, and settler colonialism, see Honor Sachs, *Home Rule: Households, Manhood, and National Expansion on the Eighteenth-Century Kentucky Frontier* (New Haven, Conn., 2015), esp. 7, 9; Shire, *Threshold of Manifest Destiny.*

consin). New states carved out of the territory needed to reach sixty thousand free inhabitants before applying for statehood. The Southwest Ordinance that organized lands south of the Ohio River in 1790 included the same population provisions. Population was the requirement for statehood, so migrants on the move literally made new states as they traveled west. Statehood depended on an imagined population replacement in which Natives would be removed and white settlers would take their place.[37]

Speculators also recognized that their wealth depended on population. Cutler of the Ohio Company of Associates imagined that "it is probable 20 years will not elapse, before there will be more people on the western than on the eastern waters of the United States." Kentucky speculator Imlay marveled at how quickly the region had grown "from an uninhabited wild, to the quantum of population necessary to govern and regulate its own administration." According to Cutler, eastern migrants would turn the Ohio Valley into "the centre of a great empire" by populating it. He could not see that the Ohio Valley already was "the centre of a great empire." On the eve of the Seven Years' War, European empires had competed for access to the region because of its fertility. The lush gardens and orchards that Miami and Shawnee women cultivated there demonstrated its abundance. Despite evidence that Native populations were growing in the Ohio Valley, both Imlay and Cutler insisted that they were "so extremely tardy" that they would eventually vanish and that U.S. modes of war and settlement would soon overtake their lands. Imlay accompanied his geography with neat population tables of Native nations to support his arguments.[38]

White migrants pursuing landed independence did set off a startling demographic shift. Briefly disrupted by the American Revolution, migra-

37. James Monroe to Thomas Jefferson, May 11, 1786, in Stanislaus Murray Hamilton, ed., *The Writings of James Monroe,* I, *1778–1794* (New York, 1898), 127 (quotation); *JCC,* XXVI, 148–150, 275–279, XXXII, 334–343; "An Act for the Government of the Territory South of the River Ohio," [May 26, 1790], in *TPUS,* IV, 18; Peter S. Onuf, *Statehood and Union: A History of the Northwest Ordinance* (Bloomington, Ind., 1987), 16–19; Saler, *Settlers' Empire,* 19–22, 25–26. These calculations about population were very different in Michigan and Wisconsin. See Michael Witgen, "Seeing Red: Race, Citizenship, and Indigeneity in the Old Northwest," *Journal of the Early Republic,* XXXVIII (2018), 581–611.

38. [Cutler], *An Explanation of the Map,* 22 ("probable"), 14 ("centre"); Imlay, *Topographical Description of the Western Territory of North America,* ii ("uninhabited"), 69 ("extremely"), 234–242. For abundance, see Sleeper-Smith, *Indigenous Prosperity and American Conquest.* For vanishing, see Jean M. O'Brien, *Firsting and Lasting: Writing Indians out of Existence in New England* (Minneapolis, Minn., 2010); Caroline Winterer, *American Enlightenments: Pursuing Happiness in the Age of Reason* (New Haven, Conn., 2016), 110–141.

tion from the East resumed at the war's conclusion. Although Congress forbade any settlements made in the western territories without the approval of the confederation government in 1783, white migrants largely ignored this proclamation, and their settlements along the Ohio River multiplied in the early 1780s. Migrants rushed to the Mohawk and Susquehanna River valleys in New York, the Monongahela and Allegheny valleys in Pennsylvania, the Tennessee Valley, and central Georgia. Between 1775 and 1790, the population of what would become Kentucky grew from three hundred to seventy-three thousand people, twelve thousand of whom were enslaved. Thousands of white migrants went to the headwaters of the Tennessee River and then on to the Cumberland River valley in the 1780s, bringing enslaved people with them. Despite that migration to Tennessee, unlike to Kentucky, was a steady stream rather than a flood, the population of the region nonetheless increased from ten thousand to thirty-six thousand people by the end of the decade. Free and forced migrants made their way toward the Appalachians from North to South.[39]

U.S. officials faced with such a demographic shift worried about managing the relentless mobility of Americans. They fretted that migrants might break away from the eastern states as the state of Franklin had in 1784, or from the United States altogether. In 1782, white migrants near Wheeling, Virginia, advertised a meeting "for all who wish to become members of a new State, on Muskingham," an eastern tributary of the Ohio River. As federal officials tried to keep new settlements near the old, they echoed British officials of the 1760s, who had labored to keep colonists on the coasts to ensure their attachment to the metropole.[40]

Some migrants did indeed contemplate allying with Spain. Spanish officials at St. Louis and New Orleans encouraged these attachments. They granted favorable inducements to white Americans willing to move across the Mississippi to Spanish territory. George Washington worried about the separatism that thrived in the West. If settlements formed a breakaway state, they might make for "a formidable and dangerous neighbor," he wrote in

39. *JCC,* XXIV, 503, XXV, 692–693; Cayton, *Frontier Republic,* 3, 7; Stephen Aron, *How the West Was Lost: The Transformation of Kentucky from Daniel Boone to Henry Clay* (Baltimore, 1996), 70–81; Nichols, *Red Gentlemen and White Savages,* 25, 58–59; Sachs, *Home Rule,* 30; DuVal, *Independence Lost,* 313–314.

40. William Irvine to George Washington, Apr. 20, 1782, with report, George Washington Papers, Ser. 4, General Correspondence, 1697–1799, Manuscript Division, LOC (quotation); Alan Taylor, "Land and Liberty on the Post-Revolutionary Frontier," in David Thomas Konig, ed., *Devising Liberty: Preserving and Creating Freedom in the New American Republic* (Stanford, Calif., 1995), 89. For Irvine to Washington, see also Cayton, *Frontier Republic,* 3, 9.

1784. U.S. citizenship itself was relatively new and unstable. Governor of the Northwest Territory Arthur St. Clair believed that westerners "have no country and indeed that attachment to the natale solum . . . is very little known in America." "Attachment" was a learned quality, however, that could be strengthened with the right conditions. St. Clair hoped to convince westerners that the federal government "was not a mere shadow" by granting lands liberally on credit and making a show of sending in federal troops to protect the blockhouses that now dotted the Ohio River. With a robust federal presence north of the Ohio River, these settlers' "progeny . . . would become the Nerves and Sinews of the Union."[41]

Federal officials saw population as a tool of state making, but they also feared that migration from the East was too rapid to secure the bloodless revolution in Native lands that they imagined. Separatist migrants complained that the federal government failed to protect them from raids by Native forces. Native peoples made the opposite demand. They asked the United States to remove migrants who settled on their lands illegally. Cherokee chief Old Tassel told U.S. officials that migrants were "rangeing through our Country, and marking our lands" and "when one goes off two comes in his place." Further north, white migrants began crossing the Ohio River and settling in Indian country without legal title. In 1783, Wyandot Half-King Dunquat complained that "Virginians are already encroaching upon our Lands." Free and forced migrants who went to Native lands put pressure on hunting grounds and hunters.[42]

U.S. officials fixated on migration into the Ohio Valley, the region which, in their eyes, bore so much import for the financial and moral foundations of the nation as a whole. Federal officials relied on partnerships with Kentucky militias to prosecute campaigns against Ohio country Natives, but they also deeply distrusted the independent will of those militias. As St. Clair wrote, if the federal government could not protect Ohio Valley migrants themselves, they would "march through that country, to redress

41. George Washington to Henry Knox, Dec. 5, 1784, in W. W. Abbot et al., eds., *PGW,* Confederation Series, 6 vols. (Charlottesville, Va., 1992–), II, 170–172 ("formidable," 171); Arthur St. Clair to John Jay, Dec. 13, 1788, ASCP, box 2, folder 6 ("have no country"); St. Clair to Washington, [August 1789], in Dorothy Twohig et al., eds., *PGW,* Presidential Series, 20 vols. (Charlottesville, Va., 1987–), III, 580–590 ("was not," 588); Cayton, *Frontier Republic,* 4; Sachs, *Home Rule,* 111–119.

42. "A Talk Delivered by the Old Tassel to Col. Joseph Martin . . . ," Oct. 10, 1784, in Walter Clark, ed., *State Records of North Carolina,* 26 vols. (Raleigh, N.C., 1886–1907), XVII, 175 ("rangeing"); "Transactions with Indians at Sandusky," Aug. 26–Sept. 8, 1783, *MPHC,* XX, 182 ("Virginians").

themselves, and the Government will be laid prostrate." St. Clair's fear was a self-fulfilling prophecy. Without having had some indication from the federal government that western lands might eventually be available for purchase, migrants might not have gone there. In the meantime, blaming federal actions on restless, violent, and unruly migrants justified the push of the federal government to dispossess Indigenous people.[43]

Ohio Valley federal officials filled their correspondence with population counts—of Natives in the lower Great Lakes, of eastern migrants at various stations along the Ohio River, of the number of dead after military campaigns. They feared the speed with which people moved west. Without the swift surveying of land, migrants would quickly "infest the frontiers of countries distant from the seat of government," explained the speculator Cutler. Squatters who disrupted U.S. plans for parceling out lands did not live up to the ideal households that federal planners had imagined. They labeled migrants "vagrants" or "a Banditty of Refugees not worthy of Congress's Notice." As Washington noted, there was little chance that the federal government would be able to stop the flood of new migrants onto Native land, but, if "you cannot stop the road, it is yet in your power to mark the way." "A little while, and you will not be able to do either," he intoned ominously. Washington drew on a deep cultural well of mistrust of mobile people as he fretted over migration.[44]

In the mid-1780s, federal officials simultaneously compelled Indian removal and signaled their intention to remove migrants north of the Ohio River. African slavery existed in parts of the Northwest Territory—in the slaveholding regions of the Illinois country, or Detroit, for example—before the United States claimed it in 1783, but eastern migrants who went to the Ohio country in the 1780s were largely free and white. Federal officials, however, made only half-hearted efforts to force white migrants from the region. After all, they still depended on migration to do the work of state making on the ground, and controlling migration was difficult given the paltry federal resources dedicated to policing the territories. Brigadier Gen-

43. Arthur St. Clair to George Washington, Sept. 14, 1789, in Twohig et al., eds., *PGW,* Pres. Ser., IV, 38–39 (quotation, 38); Hinderaker, *Elusive Empires,* 244; Griffin, "Reconsidering the Ideological Origins," in Cayton and Hobbs, eds., *Center of a Great Empire,* 13; Harper, *Unsettling the West,* 175.

44. [Cutler], *An Explanation of the Map,* 14 ("infest"); Extract of a Letter from Robert Patterson, July 12, 1786, JHP, V ("vagrants"); George Washington to Richard Henry Lee, Dec. 14, 1784, in Abbot et al., eds., *PGW,* Confed. Ser., II, 181–183 ("you cannot stop," 183); John Armstrong to Josiah Harmar, Apr. 13, 1785, JHP, II; Cayton, *Frontier Republic,* 5–8; Saler, *Settlers' Empire,* 22–24.

eral Josiah Harmar, the commander of Fort McIntosh on the Ohio River, counted thousands of migrants traveling downriver to settle without land titles. He was charged with tracking and evicting white migrants who made illegal settlements north of the Ohio River. From his post, he sent several expeditions to the other side of the river to dispossess white migrants on the orders of Congress. In April 1785, one expedition of twenty men commanded by John Armstrong went from door to door, warning out illegal migrants verbally and destroying their cabins and cornfields. During his travels, Armstrong noted upward of two thousand people settled in the eastern Ohio country. On his way between Fort McIntosh and Fort Harmar in November 1785, U.S. major John Doughty set fire to forty homes and structures situated on the west side of the Ohio River.[45]

Although federal officials called western migrants "lawless men," Armstrong mostly met white families north of the Ohio River. He dispossessed fourteen families over the course of four days in 1785. The destruction of homes and crops conferred significant hardship on white migrants. Migrants frequently asked Armstrong and his men for exceptions. They pressed on them sincere petitions describing their precariousness. Migrants John Nixon and William Hougland signed a petition on behalf of all the "Inhabitents on the Western Side of the Ohio," stating that "if we Cannot Get Liberty to Stay and gather our Crops, it will Totally Ruin us, for we have nothing to buy with." For his part, Doughty recognized the hardship that led many migrants to the West in the first place. "I am firmly of Opinion that many [cabins] will be rebuilt, for the poor Devils have no where to go," he wrote.[46]

The migrants Armstrong and Doughty encountered were undeterred

45. Daniel K. Richter, *Facing East from Indian Country: A Native History of Early America* (Cambridge, Mass., 2003), 226. The first census of the region shows only 337 African Americans and more than 46,000 white Americans in what would become Ohio in 1800. Although some free, enslaved, and indentured African Americans traveled to the Ohio country by force or by choice in the 1780s, free Black migration there did not increase until the 1810s. See Matthew Salafia, *Slavery's Borderland: Freedom and Bondage along the Ohio River* (Philadelphia, 2013), 31; "1800 Census Schedule of the Whole Number of Persons in the Territory North West of the Ohio, December 23, 1801," SEN 7A-EI, Records of the United States Senate, RG 46, NARA. For Armstrong and Doughty's expeditions, see Extracts of Instructions to Harmar by the Commissioners for Indian Affairs, Jan. 24, 1785, JHP, II; Cayton, *Frontier Republic,* 9–11.

46. Henry Knox to Josiah Harmar, May 12, 1786, JHP, II ("lawless"), Petition of John Nixon and William Hougland, Aug. 30, 1785 ("Inhabitents"), John Doughty to Josiah Harmar, Nov. 30, 1785 ("firmly"); Henry Knox, "Report of the Secretary at War Relative to Intruders on Public Lands," [Apr. 19, 1787], in *TPUS,* II, 27.

by federal removal. Doughty found that structures destroyed one summer were put up again the next. He and Armstrong posted orders from Congress prohibiting settlement north of the Ohio River at the public crossings on its east side, but migrants continued to move into the territory "by forties and fifties." On arriving at Mingo Bottom, north of the river, Armstrong read his instructions from Congress to migrant Joseph Ross, who, he reported, declared that, "if I destroyed his House he would build six more in the course of a week." Armstrong sent Ross back to Wheeling, Virginia, under an armed guard, while his men destroyed Ross's property. In Norristown, eleven miles down the Ohio, Armstrong was met by a group of about eighty men who had gathered to oppose his troops. In one Norristown cabin, Armstrong found that the inhabitants had "been making preparations for defense by cutting Loop holes in the front and barricading the door." When Armstrong explained his orders to another traveler, the man laughed and informed Armstrong that his company would continue down the Ohio the following day.[47]

The people Armstrong and Doughty met with made a novel set of moral and material claims against the new nation. Petitioners Hougland and Nixon reminded Armstrong that the confederation government "was our Choice with our fellow Citizens for which we fought and Sufferd in the Late Great Conflict for Liberty and which we are Jealously Determind to Defend to the Last." They demanded the "protection of Government." Contrary to the belief of federal officials, they hoped for more government, not less. They wanted federal resources to serve their interests in landownership and free movement. Western migrants brought with them their own revolutionary inheritances. Seventeenth- and eighteenth-century writers had encouraged British subjects to protect their rights by proclaiming them, which Britons did in the metropole and the colonies. Western migrants shared this penchant for naming rights. Among those they claimed was the right to free movement. In March 1785, migrant John Emerson called for an election among the migrants "for the forming of a constitution for the governing of the Inhabitants" on the west side of the Ohio River. Emerson proclaimed that "all mankind . . . have an undoubted right to pass into every vacant country." He asserted that "Congress is not empowered to forbid them." For Emerson, the Revolution had guaranteed him the right to free move-

47. Armstrong to Harmar, Apr. 13, 1785, JHP, II ("forties"), John Armstrong to Josiah Harmar, Apr. 12, 1785 ("if I destroyed"); Colonel Harmar to the President of Congress, May 1, 1785, in Smith, *St. Clair Papers,* II, 3–5.

ment across borders. In naming his right to move freely, he staked his place in a larger contest over whose vision of removal would prevail.[48]

Across the trans-Appalachian region in the 1780s, Native Americans countered federal plans for removal with removal efforts of their own. They demanded that Congress step in to drive intruders from their lands. At the Treaty of Fort Finney in 1786, Shawnee war captain Kekewepellethe warned treaty commissioners to remove squatters from their lands "or we will take up a Rod and whip them back to your side of the Ohio." Cherokee leader Old Tassel did the same at the Treaty of Hopewell in 1785, chiding commissioners for being unable to "do me justice" by ejecting squatters who had moved to the French Broad and Holston Rivers. "Are Congress, who conquered the king of Great Britain, unable to remove these people?" he asked. Meanwhile, Creek leader McGillivray promised that the Creeks would simply "send out parties to remove the people and effects from off the lands in question" on their own.[49]

Native leaders revived confederacy to push back migrants and to rebuff the surveyors who arrived in the wake of federal and state treaties. In the North, federationists cultivated British support. Officials in Canada sought to smooth over the betrayal of the Treaty of Paris with diplomacy, trade, and gifts, and they denounced U.S. interpretations of the treaty. In the South, McGillivray cultivated new ties with the Spanish to replace the Creeks' former British allies who had evacuated from St. Augustine. The Creeks formalized their connections with Spain during a visit to Spanish Pensacola in 1784. The Chickasaws and Choctaws did the same with a visit to Mobile. Federationists made diplomatic ties that spanned from the Great Lakes to the Gulf of Mexico. By 1784, Shawnees were sending war belts to the Creeks and Cherokees to ask them to join in their resistance against their

48. "To His Honor Commandent of the Party," Apr. 5, 1785, JHP, II ("our Choice"), John Emerson, "Advertisement," Mar. 12, 1785 ("forming"); Harper, *Unsettling the West,* 173–174. For rights in this context, see Nichols, *Red Gentlemen and White Savages,* 13; Hannah Weiss Muller, *Subjects and Sovereign: Bonds of Belonging in the Eighteenth-Century British Empire* (New York, 2017), 63. For free movement across borders, see Lawrence B. A. Hatter, *Citizens of Convenience: The Imperial Origins of American Nationhood on the U.S.-Canadian Border* (Charlottesville, Va., 2017).

49. Chiefs of the Shawanese, Mingoes, Delawares, and Cherokees, May 18, 1785, Great Britain Indian Department Collection, Box 1, CL ("or we will take up"); Knox to Washington, July 7, 1789, Enclosure A., No. 3., Hopewell on Keowee, Nov. 18–29, 1785, in *ASPIA,* I, 43 ("do me justice"); Alexander McGillivray to Andrew Pickens, Sept. 5, 1785, in *EAID,* XVIII, 388 ("send out"); Nichols, *Red Gentlemen and White Savages,* 47–50, 66; Ostler, *Surviving Genocide,* 90.

white neighbors. That summer, Shawnees attacked settlements across the Ohio Valley while the Creeks and more militant Cherokees called Chickamaugas carried out raids on eastern migrants in Kentucky and Tennessee. McGillivray hoped for "a Grand Indian Confederacy" of Native nations that would span the length of the continent. Federal officials worried about these efforts to make a "dangerous confederacy between . . . Indian nations."[50]

These alliances, like those that held together the United States, could be fractious. Federationists shared a common goal—to remove intruders from their lands—but they did not always agree on the means. They sometimes struggled to smooth over disagreements between Native nations. The Chickasaws refused to join a more general confederacy in 1784, for example, because they had long-standing grievances with the Kickapoos. Native leaders seeking to keep the peace with the United States agreed to cede some lands to U.S. commissioners to protect their most important towns. Chiefs and divisions responsible for the peacemaking functions of particular nations often defied federationists by seeking compromise. This was true for the Mekoche Shawnees who agreed to attend the Treaty of Fort Finney. This was also true for the Creeks. Federationists like McGillivray hoped to create a centralized Creek national council that would determine diplomacy for the nation, but he could not control civil chiefs like Hoboithle Miko and Neha Miko, whose power depended on their fulfillment of the diplomatic functions assigned to their towns.[51]

North of the Ohio River, federationists found common ground as they mobilized to protect their sovereignty in the face of the surveyors who arrived to mark out new boundaries after the federal treaties of 1784–1786. Geographer of the United States Thomas Hutchins traveled to western Pennsylvania in the fall of 1785 to launch the first survey in the region—seven ranges intended to be sold by the federal government. Over two years, Hutchins would survey 675,000 acres of Native land into townships in the company of a military escort. Delaware and Wyandot chiefs refused to accompany the surveyors as guides. By 1786, northern federationists met again at Brownstown, just south of Detroit, to oppose the invasion.

50. Alexander McGillivray to Esteban Miró, Oct. 4, 1787, in Caughey, *McGillivray of the Creeks,* 161 ("Grand"); "Report from H. Knox, Secretary of War, to the President of the United States," July 6, 1789, in *ASPIA,* I, 16 ("dangerous"), also quoted in Dowd, *Spirited Resistance,* 93–94; DuVal, *Independence Lost,* 247, 257, 294; Nichols, *Red Gentlemen and White Savages,* 27.

51. Nichols, *Red Gentlemen and White Savages,* 11, 54; Adam Jortner, *The Gods of Prophetstown: The Battle of Tippecanoe and the Holy War for the American Frontier* (New York, 2012), 52–53; DuVal, *Independence Lost,* 254–255, 296–297.

Chickamauga Cherokees joined them, as did Haudenosaunee leaders who stressed that only "Unanimity" would protect them from U.S. incursions in the West. "The Interest of any one Nation should be Interests of us all, the welfare of the one should be the welfare of all the others," they argued. At Brownstown, they took on the name the United Indian Nations. Creeks, Chickasaws, and Cherokees met simultaneously at Little Tallassee in Creek country to create a southern confederacy to protect their lands.[52]

By 1786, federationists in the North and the South called for a general war to address the crisis. North of the Ohio River, parties of Haudenosaunees, Wyandots, and Delawares crisscrossed the Ohio Valley to remove white Americans from their lands. South of the river, Ohio Iroquois, Cherokees, Shawnees, Weas, Miamis, Potawatomis, Piankeshaws, and Odawas attacked settlements in Kentucky and Tennessee. Meanwhile, Delawares traveled on a southern mission to cement an alliance with the Chickasaws. Federal officials tended to blame the violence north of the Ohio River on the Shawnees, Miamis, and Kickapoos, who were all at the forefront of resistance to the United States on the Wabash River in what is now Indiana. They called them "banditti," a term that referred to those who were lawless or unattached to a political community. But, by 1786, opposition to U.S. policy clearly ranged beyond a few scattered towns and militant young men. Rather, one anonymous deponent informed an American military officer that it was the opinion "of all the young men of the Indian Nations, who say, they will put their old men, women, and children behind their backs and will defend their country to the extremity."[53]

Native communities that tried to stay out of the conflict ended up joining with federationists when they had few other options for defending themselves. War in the Tennessee Valley continued to escalate after 250 militiamen burned the Cherokee town of Cowatee and forced Cherokee chiefs Old Tassel and Hanging Maw to cede more land. The state of Franklin retaliated against Chickamauga Cherokee campaigns by attacking the settlements

52. Speech of the Five Nations to the Western Indians, November 1786, Draper Mss., Frontier Wars, 23U 45–47 (quotations), quoted in White, *Middle Ground,* 441; "The Answer of the Waindots and Delawars to the Speech Sent to Them by General Richard Butler Esqr Superintendant of Indian Affairs and Delivered to Them by James Rankin 23d Sept 1786," enclosure in W. Ferguson to Josiah Harmar, Oct. 18, 1786, JHP, IV, Obidiah Robins to Richard Butler, Sept. 29, 1786; Ernst, *With Compass and Chain,* 37, 74–75; DuVal, *Independence Lost,* 296.

53. "Report of Congress," Oct. 20, 1786, JHP, IV ("banditti"), Thomas Hutchins to Josiah Harmar, Sept. 13, 1786 ("young men"), Report of W. Ferguson, Sept. 13, 1786, Robins to Butler, Sept. 29, 1786, "Answer of the Waindots and Delawars . . . 23d Sept 1786," enclosure in Ferguson to Harmar, Oct. 18, 1786.

of Cherokees who wanted to stay neutral alongside those of the Chickamaugas. In 1788, Old Tassel tried to intercept North Carolina militiamen as they invaded Cherokee country. Despite that Old Tassel was attempting to negotiate a truce, a militia officer killed him. Old Tassel's murder only added more people to the Chickamauga ranks. The Creeks went to war in 1786 as well, targeting migrants who had settled on their lands illegally. At Shoulderbone Creek in 1786, Georgia responded to Creek actions by taking civil chiefs Hoboithle Miko and Teha Miko and their party hostage to force the Creeks to give up more territory. Georgia only ended up pushing neutral people further toward federationists.[54]

The same was true north of the Ohio River. In October 1786, Benjamin Logan led nine hundred Kentucky militiamen on a retaliatory expedition for Shawnee raids against Shawnee towns on the Mad River, home of the Mekoche Shawnees who had worked hardest to keep the peace. When Logan and his men reached the towns, they found most of the men absent. They had gone to meet another Kentucky militia expedition headed toward the Wabash River, leaving "chiefly women and children" behind. Logan's Kentucky militia burned several Mekoche villages and took several dozen women and children captive. On Logan's militia's approach to the village of the Shawnee chief Moluntha, one of the Mekoche signers of the Treaty of Fort Finney who had worked to preserve peace, they found that Moluntha had "put up the Flagg (13 stripes) which he got at [the treaty]" to signify his alliance with the United States. Logan's men murdered Moluntha, despite the symbolic weight of the flag.[55]

Although federal planners spoke about Indian removal as a peaceful, natural process, people who lived at the western edges of U.S. settlements were more honest about the violence that U.S. removal entailed. Frontier people who had experienced the retaliatory violence of western warfare and Native raids during the Revolution carried Indian hating with them into the Ohio and Tennessee Valleys in the 1780s and 1790s. Near continuous raids after 1783 only produced more stories of so-called Native atrocities that lay the blame for the bloodletting on Indigenous people. In 1792, the missionary John Heckewelder observed the funeral of a Wea chief who was being held captive by U.S. officials in Cincinnati as a pawn to force western Natives

54. Dowd, *Spirited Resistance,* 96, 98; Nichols, *Red Gentlemen and White Savages,* 66; Barksdale, "State of Franklin," in Ray, ed., *Before the Volunteer State,* 168; DuVal, *Independence Lost,* 300–301.

55. A. Finney to Josiah Harmar, Oct. 31, 1786, JHP, IV (quotations); Dowd, *Spirited Resistance,* 95; Barksdale, "State of Franklin," in Ray, ed., *Before the Volunteer State,* 168; Harper, *Unsettling the West,* 162–163.

to treat for peace. Heckewelder was shocked when "malicious people dug up the body again at night, tore down the flag and post, threw them into a mud-hole and dragged the body down along the street and stood it up there." Military officials replaced the flag that had adorned the burial site and reburied the chief the next day only for the grave to be desecrated again the next evening. When one group of chiefs left Cincinnati for Philadelphia on a peace commission to President Washington, Heckewelder noted that they were met with curses all along their journey. At Limestone, soldiers on passing boats and men gathered on the Kentucky side of the river threatened them. Native leaders had predicted the ultimate goal of U.S. officials was their "extirpation"—and, indeed, federal officials themselves used that term often to refer to the "utter destruction" of particular towns they believed to be responsible for war. The violence of war seemed to bear that out.[56]

By 1787, war threatened to engulf the trans-Appalachian region from north to south. The federal government competed with the states to make policy, firm borders, and treaties with Native nations. Natives remained in control of their own territories, and the United Indian Nations posed an unshakeable obstacle to federal plans for removal as a means of financing and securing the nation's future. All of these issues weighed on the minds of the delegates to the Constitutional Convention when they gathered in Philadelphia in May 1787 to revise the Articles of Confederation. The Constitution they produced over the next several months was, as Gregory Ablavsky has written, "a wartime document," intended in part to respond to the failings of the Articles in shaping western policy. The Constitution made federal treaties the "supreme Law of the Land" and gave the federal government the ability to organize the territories. It also allowed Congress to fund a standing army through direct taxation. The fear of war in the West surely pushed some hesitant anti-Federalists toward ratification.[57]

56. M. C. Sprengel, ed., "Narrative of John Heckewelder's Journey to the Wabash in 1792," trans. Clara Frueauff, *Pennsylvania Magazine of History and Biography,* XII (1888), 34–54 ("malicious," 46), 165–184; Ostler, *Surviving Genocide,* 99 ("extirpation"); "Extract of a Letter, Dated Washington, in Kentucky, September 3, 1791," *Vermont Journal, and the Universal Advertiser,* Nov. 8, 1791, 2. For more on race making and on Indian hating, see Nancy Shoemaker, "How Indians Got to be Red," *American Historical Review,* CII (1997), 625–644; Joshua Piker, "Indians and Race in Early America: A Review Essay," *History Compass,* III (2005), 1–17; Peter Silver, *Our Savage Neighbors: How Indian War Transformed Early America* (New York, 2009); Harper, *Unsettling the West,* 165.

57. Ablavsky, "Savage Constitution," *Duke Law Journal,* LXIII (2014), 1038 ("wartime"), 1042 ("supreme"), 1045, 1049–1050, 1058, 1066.

Removal, however, continued to be just as contested after the ratification of the U.S. Constitution as before. The states persisted in treating Native peoples as if they were under their jurisdiction. Native leaders also grappled with internal debates about the best course for preserving their lands. This was particularly true north of the Ohio River, where federal policy—and thus the new power of the federal government—had the most impact. Leaders like Brant considered making peace with the United States while the Shawnees, Miamis, and Kickapoos held firm on their demand for an Ohio River border. The United Indian Nations renewed their alliance in 1789 after governor of the Northwest Territory St. Clair once again strong-armed them into confirming prior land cessions with threats of war and the right of conquest. U.S. plans to meet with Haudenosaunees and the other federationists separately to break the alliance only brought them closer together. As the 1780s came to a close, federationists' own defensive efforts north of the Ohio River demonstrated that federal plans were still on shaky ground. The United Indian Nations would test the policies, strength, and direction of the United States over the next several years. The Ohio Valley was not an empty Eden waiting for the projections of U.S. planners—it was Indian country.[58]

The inability of federal planners to counter Native power north of the Ohio River led to an anxious debate in Congress, among territorial officials, and among the public over removal policy. Native efforts to force interlopers from their lands called into question federal characterizations of removal as a peaceful process. In December 1788, St. Clair had only been in his position for five months when he wrote a note to the secretary of foreign affairs describing what he saw as the dire situation of his own territorial government. Native parties from the confederated nations in the Ohio country had attacked white settlements and the military contractors who brought provisions to poorly defended U.S. posts. Warfare had depressed land sales north of the Ohio River. Native resistance halted federal surveys north of the Ohio River after 1789. Between 1792–1796, public land sales accounted for a very

58. Arthur St. Clair to Henry Knox, July 16, 1788, ASCP, box 2, folder 4, St. Clair to George Washington, May 2, 1789, box 3, folder 1; Charles Thomas to St. Clair, Oct. 26, 1787, in *ASPIA,* I, 9. For the efforts of individual states to extend jurisdiction over Native people, see Deborah A. Rosen, *American Indians and State Law: Sovereignty, Race, and Citizenship, 1790–1880* (Lincoln, Neb., 2009); Nichols, *Red Gentlemen and White Savages,* 94, 96. For the 1789 Treaty, see ibid., 99–106; Alyssa Mt. Pleasant, "After the Whirlwind: Maintaining a Haudenosaunee Place at Buffalo Creek, 1780-1825" (Ph.D. diss., Cornell University, 2007), 78; Calloway, *Victory with No Name,* 55–57.

small percentage of federal revenues, while military campaigns cost the new federal government nearly five million dollars.[59]

St. Clair believed that Congress would need to approve a mission to "chastise" the western nations as soon as the winter snows receded. "It was always my Fear that our western Territory instead of a fund for paying the national Debt would be a source of Mischief and increasing Expenses," he warned. A federal campaign would need to begin quickly. Secretary of War Knox similarly believed that "a protracted indian war, would be destructive to the republic, under its present circumstances."[60]

The success of the United Indian Nations at contesting removal was apparent in 1790 and 1791, when the confederacy won two major military victories against U.S. forces. In October 1790, U.S. Brigadier General Harmar led a campaign up the Great Miami River to attack Miami villages. Miamis discovered the troops before they arrived, and they evacuated "as fast as they could procure horses to carry their women and children," as one Indigenous prisoner informed them. Harmar lost 183 men in the skirmishes that followed. The next fall, St. Clair organized a second military campaign against the confederacy's forces led by Miami Little Turtle, Shawnee Blue Jacket, and Delaware Buckongahelas. During the battle that came to be known as St. Clair's Defeat, St. Clair lost 623 men killed and 258 wounded out of 1,400 troops. As the survivors filtered into Fort Washington, they shared stories of a thoroughly botched campaign, hampered by supply issues and deserters. St. Clair asked for an investigation of the campaign, hoping to show that he was not at fault for the defeat. A special committee appointed by the House of Representatives cleared him of wrongdoing in 1792. Still, St. Clair spent the rest of his life trying to defend against his detractors.[61]

St. Clair's defeat prompted a sustained public debate in eastern newspapers about removal. Commentary on U.S. Indian policy dominated the

59. Onuf, *Statehood and Union,* 42; Taylor, "Land and Liberty," in Konig, ed., *Devising Liberty,* 98. Adam Jortner writes that these challenges made the United States a "failed state." See Jortner, *Gods of Prophetstown,* 51.

60. St. Clair to Jay, Dec. 13, 1788, ASCP, box 2, folder 6 ("chastise"), Henry Knox to Arthur St. Clair, Dec. 8, 1788 ("protracted").

61. "Copy of Lieut Denny's Report to the Secretary at War, Respecting the Expedition against the Maumee Towns," Jan. 1, 1791, ASCP, box 3, folder 7, 1 (quotation); Hendrik Booraem, V, *A Child of the Revolution: William Henry Harrison and His World, 1773–1798* (Kent, Ohio, 2012), 75. For the special committee and St. Clair's explanation of the defeat, see Arthur St. Clair to Henry Knox, Nov. 1, 1791, in Smith, *St. Clair Papers,* II, 249–251; ASCP, box 4, folder 5; Calloway, *Victory with No Name,* 132–137.

papers that winter, "excit[ing] much of the attention of the public." One writer complained that it was "nothing but the Indian war" in the papers. An observer from Princeton, New Jersey, wrote that no one in town talked of anything but St. Clair's defeat. As the news spread, eastern newspapers painted the confederacy's defense as without reason or cause, carried out by a few towns along the Miami and Wabash Rivers. One writer declared that "a thirst for blood and plunder" motivated the confederacy. Another commentator, who styled himself "Cassius" after the Roman senator, warned that "the Indians are determined upon war, and if you remove from the western country, they will follow you over the mountains, and butcher the wives and children of those on the frontier." Both comments invoked images of violence that Anglo-Americans had long used to dismiss Native sovereignty. The printer of the *Maryland Journal* ran an article recommending that western militias "surprise their towns in all quarters, and kill and burn without distinction." Advocates of war argued that further campaigns into Native homelands would bring Native people "to a sense of their duty."[62]

In New England, the Boston printer Ezekiel Russell used the victory of the confederacy to appeal to U.S. nationalism. Russell and his wife ran a print shop that specialized in small pamphlets and broadsides. In his patriotic broadside "The Columbian Tragedy: Containing a Particular and Official Account of the Brave and Unfortunate *Officers* and *Soldiers,* Who Were Slain and Wounded in the Ever-Memorable and Bloody Indian Battle," Russell announced the defeat with a row of coffins that he had previously used in a publication mourning the victims of the Battles of Lexington and Concord. Russell's broadside mixed triumphalism and lies. He exaggerated the number of Native fighters at five thousand—a Congressional report had put the number at five hundred to twelve hundred—in order to minimize the embarrassment of the U.S. military. Russell predicted that the memory of St. Clair's defeat would eventually be surpassed by "the future FREEDOM

62. "For the American Mercury," *American Mercury* (Hartford, Conn.), Feb. 27, 1792, [2] ("excit[ing]"); "Every Thing Has Its Season," *Gazette of the United States* (Philadelphia), Feb. 11, 1792, 331 ("nothing"); "Philadelphia, Jan. 2," *Dunlap's American Daily Advertiser* [Philadelphia], Jan. 2, 1792, [3] ("thirst"); "Philadelphia, Feb. 9," *The Mail; or, Claypoole's Daily Advertiser* (Philadelphia), Feb. 9, 1792, [1] ("Cassius," "Indians," "sense"); "Extract of a Letter from a Gentleman in the Western Country to His Friend in Philadelphia, Dated December 22," *Maryland Journal and Baltimore Advertiser,* Jan. 10, 1792, [2] ("surprise"); "New-York, January 14; Extract of a Letter from Princeton, New Jersey, January 9, 1792," *General Advertiser* (Philadelphia), Jan. 18, 1792, [2]; "For the National Gazette," *National Gazette* (Philadelphia), Feb. 6, 1792, 113–114; Calloway, *Victory with No Name,* 133–135.

MAJ. GEN. *RICHARD BUTLER*, Slain in the *Battle* at *Miami-Village*, Nov. 4.

THE

COLUMBIAN TRAGEDY:

CONTAINING A PARTICULAR AND OFFICIAL

ACCOUNT

Of the BRAVE and UNFORTUNATE *OFFICERS* and *SOLDIERS*, who were SLAIN and WOUNDED in the EVER-MEMORABLE and

BLOODY INDIAN BATTLE,

BLOODY INDIAN BATTLE, Fought at MIAMI VILLAGE, Nov. 4, 1791.

Perhaps the most shocking that has happened in AMERICA since its first Discovery; which continued *Six Hours*, with the most unremitted *Fury* and unparalleled *Bravery* on both Sides, having lasted from day-break, until near ten o'clock on *Friday Morning, Nov. 4, 1791*; between *Two Thousand* AMERICANS, belonging to the UNITED ARMY, and near *Five Thousand Wild Indian Savages*, at *Miami-Village*, near *Fort-Washington*, in the *Ohio-Country*, in which terrible and desperate *Battle* a most shocking Slaughter was made of *Thirty-nine gallant AMERICAN OFFICERS* and upwards of *Nine Hundred brave youthful SOLDIERS*, who fell *gloriously fighting* for their *COUNTRY*.—These *Particulars* and *Elegy* are now published in this SHEET by the earnest Request of the *Friends* to the DECEASED *WORTHIES*, who died in Defence of their *COUNTRY*, not only as a *Token* of *Gratitude* to the *DECEASED BRAVE*, but as a PERPETUAL MEMORIAL of this *important Event*, on which, perhaps may very essentially depend the future *FREEDOM* and *GRANDEUR* of *Fifteen* or *Twenty States*, that might, at some Period, be annexed to the *AMERICAN UNION*.

List of KILLED *and* Wounded *OFFICERS*.

KILLED; 1 *Maj. Gen.* RICHARD BUTLER.—2 *Col.* Oldham.—*Majors*; 3 Ferguson-4 Clark-5 Hart.—*Captains*; 6 Bradford--7 Phelon--8 Kirkwood--9 Price--10 Van Swearingin--11 Tipton--12 Smith--13 Purdy--14 Pratt--15 Guthrie--16 Cribbs-17 Newman—*Lieuts.* 18 Spear--19 Warren-20 Boyd 21 M'Math-22 Burgess-23 Kelso—24 Read—25 Little-26 Hopper--27 Lickins.--*Ensigns*; 28 Cobb—29 Balch—30 Chate—31 Turner-32 Willson-33 Brooks-34 Beatty-35 Purdy.-36 *Q. Mast.* Reynolds-37 Ward.-38 *Adj.* Anderson.-39 *Dr.* Grasson.

WOUNDED; 1 *Adj. Gen.* Sargent-2 *L. Col.* Gibson-3 Dark-4 *Major* Butler.—*Capts.* 5 Doyle--6 Trueman--7 Ford-8 Buchanan-9 Dark--10 Slough.--*Lts.* 11 Greaton 12 Davidson-13 DeButts-14 Price--15 Morgan-16 M'Crea-17 Lysle.-18 Thompson.--19 *Adj.* Whistler-20. Crawford. 21. *Ens.* Bines. 22. *Vis. Malartie*, Volunteer, *Aidecamp* to *Gen.* ST. CLAIR.

A

FUNERAL ELEGY on the Occasion.

2 SAMUEL, chap. i.

Ver. 19. *The Beauty of Israel is slain upon thy high places: How are the Mighty fallen!*—20. *Tell it not in* Gath, *publish it not in the streets of* Askelon: *Lest the Daughters of the* Philistines *rejoice, lest the* Daughters *of the* uncircumcised *triumph*.—21. *Ye Mountains of* Gilboa, *let there be no dew, neither let there be rain upon you, nor fields of offerings; for there the* Shield *of the* Mighty *is vilely* cast away.

YE Friends to men attend the Tale,
Ye brave ones all give ear,
With sympathetic grief bewail
And shed a sorrowing tear.

2. Behold the various scenes of
This hour is mirth and glee, [life!
The next we're free'd from care and strife,
And in eternity.

3. Joyful from *Boston's* happy Town,
These brave Men took their way,
Ah! soon were slain upon the ground,
To *BLOODY BRUTES* a prey!

4. Adieu to wanton songs and joys,
To idle tales that fill the ear,
A mournful theme my heart employs,
And hope the living will it hear.

5. A horrid *Fight* there hap'd of late,
The fourth day of *November*,
When a vast number met their fate,
We all shall well remember.

6. 'Twas on renown'd *Ohio's Land*,
And *fatal* prov'd of old,
Sad to relate! our FEDERAL *BAND*,
Were slain by *INDIANS* bold!

7. Ah cursed *Spot*! Ah rueful *Land*!
New-England will rejoin,
Where thousands of our *Countrymen*
Their wasted bones inshrine.

8. By much too dear the *Land* was bo't,
It's stain'd with *English* gore,
Where BRADDOCK fell! O sad to tell!
Full thirty years before.

9. Our *WASHINGTON* with chosen *Men*,
All ruddy, youthful too,
There rally'd some of *British* Train,
Coop'd by *infernal Crew*.

10. A horrid covert, where there lay
Whole legions of *black Men*.
But by the courage of that YOUTH,
They're hunted from their den.

11. A handful of *Columbians* led,
Their *Standard* sav'd from harm,
Full tatter'd when fam'd *Berwick* bled,
And *Tallard* felt its arm.

12. The flower of *British* pride was lost
In one great day they fell!
BRADDOCK's defeat, young SHIRLEY's loss
Our Annals all can tell!

13. Such scenes apart! my Muse still hear
The groans of dying *Friends*;
The horrid shrieks do fill the air,
Of wounded, dying Men.

14. Will not *Columba's Youth* now rouse,
And cheerful take the *Field*,
Columba's Cause they will espouse,
Nor to those BLOOD HOUNDS yield.

15. My Muse must quit that *mournful Tale*,
A *worse one* to record,
BOSTON shall weep and sore bewail
The stroke sent by the *LORD*.

16. Our COUNTRYMEN of *youthful bloom*,
Most in their vig'rous prime,
Are summon'd hence to meet their *GOD*,
And snatched out of time.

17. Brave GENERAL *BUTLER's* L[illegible] [illegible]eel,
And *OLDHAM's Death* bemoan,
Let's drop a tear when it we tell,
And view their hapless urn.

18. Young *NEWMAN* fell! and *TURNER*
With *PHELON* at their *Head*, (brave
No friendly arm there was to save,
They're number'd with the dead.

19. The names of *WARREN, BALCH* and
Let's mourn now o'er their grave, (*COBB*,
Who late with courage spilt their blood,
And fell with many brave.

20. Ah! *WARREN's* valor full was shewn,
A *Name* we'll now *renew*,
Who fell too soon! ah! much too soon!
Tho' *twelve fierce Brutes* he slew.

21. Let's sing of *BRADFORD* and whole
Of OFFICERS so brave, (scores
They're call'd to the *Elysian* shores,
And mingled in one grave.

22. We must relate the *Warrior's* fate
Of *GREATON*, young and brave!
A cruel shot his body pierc'd,
But yet his life was sav'd.

23. Of *Thirty* brave *Youth* in his core,
But *Three* surviv'd the *Brunt*,
Was ever such a scene before?
Ah! fatal *Indian Hunt*!

24. *Columba's Land* a scene presents,
Of blood and slaughter too,
The *Widow's* heart doth sore lament,
To bid their *Friends* adieu.

25. What shall we say when 'tis decreed,
By fate it must be so,
To see our dearest *Brethren* bleed,
And ev'ry vein to flow.

26. What heart that feels for others woe,
Can stop the gushing tear,
Or not the pangs of pity show,
When such events they hear.

27. But if such pity here imparts,
Think O! what griefs assail,
Their *Widow's* and their *Children's* hearts,
When they shall hear the tale!

28. The thought already fills each breast,
With kind condoling care,
And hope in Heav'n they'll meet at rest,
Their *Friends* and *Fathers* there.

29. We feel and sympathize for them
Who late in battle fell,
We mean those hardy, youthful men,
Their names to ages tell.

30. Though *Powers Immortal* are averse,
O LORD! the praise is thine!
The scene, O *GOD* of Grace reverse!
And make our arms to shine!

31. We'll scour all their *Thickets* then,
Make INDIANS sue for peace;
Hunt *lurking Savage* from his den,
When we shall win the chace.

32. If great *JEHOVAH* takes the shield,
And guards us round about,
No INDIAN will his *Tomax* wield,
Nor arrow dare to shoot.

33. My trembling hand can scarcely hold
My faint, devoted quill,
To write the actions of the *Bold*,
Their *valor* and their *skill*.

34. Let's not forget the SOLDIERS brave,
Who fell with *Indian* ax,
Who scorn'd to flinch their lives to save,
Nor on them turn'd their backs.

35. NINE HUNDRED hardiest of our Sons,
Some in their *early prime*,
Have fell a *victim* to their rage,
And are *cut off* from time.

36. Yes, numbers met an awful death,
In battle they were slain,
But we that live upon the earth,
Their mem'ry will sustain.

37. If that the *LORD* is on our side,
We need not fear our foe,
And if that gracious *Isr'el's GOD*
Now with our armies go;

38. Our heads he'll cover when in fight,
From harm he will us keep,
If that we seek his face aright,
Nor let our feet to slip.

39. With conq'ring might he will us shield,
And *INDIANS* all destroy,
He'll help us thus to win the field,
And slay those that annoy.

40. Our *Country* calls us far and near,
Columba's Sons awake,
For helmet, buckler and our spear,
The *LORD's* own arm we'll take.

41. His shield will keep us from all harm,
Tho' thousands 'gainst us rise,
His buckler we must sure put on,
If we would win the prize.

AMERICA: *BOSTON*; Printed by E. *RUSSELL*, for *THOMAS BASSETT*, of *Dunbarton*, (*New-Hamp.*)—[Pr. Six Pence.]

☞ Said BASSETT sells *Bickerstaff's* Almanack, for 1792, as CHEAP as at *this Office*.

FIGURE 5. *"The Columbian Tragedy: Containing a Particular and Official Account of the Brave and Unfortunate Officers and Soldiers, Who Were Slain and Wounded in the Ever-Memorable and Bloody Indian Battle." [1791]. Folio BrSides Cb4a. Courtesy Beinecke Rare Book and Manuscript Library, Yale University, New Haven, Conn.*

and *grandeur* of *Fifteen* or *Twenty States*" to be carved out of Native homelands in the west.[63]

The newspaper accounts were not all triumphal. Public debate just as often focused on anxieties about western expansion. Commentators argued that federal plans for the Ohio Valley were not just, nor were they winnable. Native power breathed new life into an old debate about the morality of removal that animated national newspapers in the early 1790s. Some writers protested that Natives had first possession of the soil and were its "legitimate proprietors." Another wondered how easterners could support U.S. military campaigns given that "scarcely an individual knows the principles of the war." The Philadelphia Quaker Meeting for Sufferings (representing Quakers in Pennsylvania, New Jersey, Delaware, and parts of Maryland and Virginia) sent a memorial urging the recognition of Native rights to the president and Congress that was reprinted by the Philadelphia newspapers.[64]

One commentator turned U.S. nationalism on its head by comparing the anticolonial resistance of Indigenous westerners to the recent revolution of the United States. The struggles of the United States to "emancipate the shackles of that power whose claims of dependency and vassalage were not more inequitable than ours with respect to the Indians of the western territory." Drawing a similar comparison, another asked, "Did the burning of Charlestown, Falmouth, Norfolk, etc. light the unquenchable flame of revenge in the bosoms of civilized christians—And will not the same cause, at Miami, St. Josephs', or the lake of woods, produce similar feelings" for federationists? The American Revolution was a flexible rhetorical tool because white Americans saw it as unmarred—an indisputable moral good in the political discourse of the early Republic. Those who did not foreground the Revolutionary comparison instead appealed to practicality, calling the war unwinnable. They suggested that the money would be better spent paying off the federal debt from the American Revolution directly.[65]

63. "The Columbian Tragedy: Containing a Particular and Official Account of the Brave and Unfortunate Officers and Soldiers, Who Were Slain and Wounded in the Ever-Memorable and Bloody Indian Battle" (Boston, [1791]), Collections of the Beinecke Rare Book and Manuscript Library, YUA.

64. "New-York, January 14; Extract of a Letter from Princeton, New Jersey," *General Advertiser,* Jan. 18, 1792, [2] ("legitimate"); "Miscellany; from the Independent Chronicle," *New-York Journal, and Patriotic Register,* Jan. 7, 1792, [2] ("scarcely"); "Philadelphia," *Connecticut Journal* (New Haven, Conn.), Jan. 4, 1792, [2].

65. "New-York, January 14; Extract of a Letter from Princeton, New Jersey," *General Advertiser,* Jan. 18, 1792, [2] ("emancipate"); "From the Argus; New Year–1792;

Washington and Knox cared that the public, both at home and abroad, would see wars of dispossession as necessary and just. They planned military campaigns to "extirpat[e]" Native nations that resisted U.S. claims. Washington warned Miamis of the "doom" and "destruction" they would meet with if they continued the contest over removal. They sent military campaigns into Indian country in the early fall before crops could be harvested so that they could burn Native American women's gardens and fields. In 1790, Harmar had destroyed five Miami towns along with vast fields of corn and vegetables abandoned by fleeing families. The destruction of Native towns was a hallmark of population warfare—war waged by U.S. armies against the subsistence of women and children as well as men. At the same time, Knox was uneasy lest these violent actions be recognized for what they were in the court of public opinion. Federal policy should not aim for the complete "extirpation" of Native people, he wrote, for "the favorable opinion and pity of the world is easily excited in favor of the oppressed . . . If our modes of population and War destroy the tribes the disinterested part of mankind and posterity" would judge U.S. policy harshly.[66]

In 1789, Knox proposed a new "liberal system of justice" that he believed would ensure the bloodless revolution in Native land that planners had always hoped for while preserving the moral high ground of the Revolutionary experiment through federal control of Indian affairs. Knox celebrated the ratification of a new Constitution that gave federal authorities firm control over Native American policy. He planned to appoint agents to live in Indian country to promote the "civilization" of Indigenous people. Knox hoped to minimize war by acknowledging that Native peoples had "the right of the Soil" that they could only lose after a "just War." "To dispossess them on any other principle would be a gross violation of the fundamental Laws of Nature and of that distributive justice which is the glory of a nation." Finally, Knox and Washington pushed Congress to enshrine these principles in federal statute. The resulting 1790 Trade and Intercourse

---

Retrospect," *New-York Journal, and Patriotic Register,* Jan. 18, 1792, [2] ("Did the burning"). For federal debt, see "New-York, January 14; Extract of a Letter from Princeton, New Jersey," *General Advertiser,* Jan. 18, 1792, [2].

66. George Washington to Richard Henry Lee, Mar. 15, 1785, in Abbot et al., eds., *PGW,* Confed. Ser., II, 437–438 ("extirpat[e]"); "The Message of the President of the United States to the Miami Indians," Mar. 11, 1791, TPP, LX, 41 ("doom," "destruction"); Knox to Wayne, Jan. 5, 1792, in Knopf, ed., *Anthony Wayne,* 165–166 ("extirpation," "favorable," 165); George Washington to the Marquis de Lafayette, Aug. 11, 1790, in Twohig et al., eds., *PGW,* Pres. Ser., VI, 233–235, "To the Miami Indians," VII, 550–552; Winthrop Sargent to Arthur St. Clair, Aug. 17, 1790, ASCP, box 3, folder 5.

Act regulated trade, justice, and land sales between Native nations and the United States.[67]

Dispossession after a "just War" was a large loophole in Knox's new "liberal system of justice," however. Although the Constitution never fully curbed state meddling in Indian affairs, it did give Congress the ability to reshape federal power in the west militarily. Congress could raise ever-larger armies to achieve removal. In January 1792, Knox asked Congress for $525,000 to fund a larger western campaign the following year. To support his request before a doubtful public, he wrote a full history of the war since 1783 that was published in newspapers and distributed to Congress. In the essay, Knox defended the treaties of 1784–1786 as councils that sought "a liberal peace." Only when Natives rejected peace did the federal government resort to "coercion"—meaning military campaigns. Knox argued that the United Indian Nations had no cause to wage war. A few Native towns that had "formed inveterate and incurable habits of enmity against the frontier inhabitants of the United States" were the source of the conflict in his telling. Taking up Knox's essay and his request, Congress debated war funding on moral and practical grounds. In the House, one representative opened discussion of Knox's request by calling the war "unjustly undertaken." The representative challenged his colleagues to consider a 1790 speech from Seneca leader Cornplanter complaining of the conduct of federal and state treaty commissioners. Cornplanter lamented that commissioners demanded "a great Country . . . as if our want of strength had destroyed our rights." "We hear nothing of the sufferings of the Indians," the representative remarked. A significant minority in the House rallied around the idea that the war itself was an unnecessary expense at a time when there was "scarcely a dollar in the Treasury."[68]

Congress ultimately funded Knox's campaign, dramatically enlarging a federal army commanded by Revolutionary War veteran General Anthony

67. "Enclosure," June 15, 1789, in Twohig et al., eds., *PGW,* Pres. Ser., II, 490–495 ("liberal system," 493, "right," 491); Bernard W. Sheehan, "The Indian Problem in the Northwest: From Conquest to Philanthropy," in Ronald Hoffman and Peter J. Albert, eds., *Launching the "Extended" Republic: The Federalist Era* (Charlottesville, Va., 1996), 190–222; Sadosky, *Revolutionary Negotiations,* 157–158.

68. *The Debates and Proceedings in the Congress of the United States . . . Second Congress: Comprising the Period from October 24, 1791, to March 2, 1793, Inclusive* (Washington, D.C., 1849), 1046 ("liberal"), 1050–1051 ("coercion," 1050, "formed," 1051), 337–338 ("unjustly undertaken," "We hear nothing," 337), 339, 341–342 ("scarcely," 341), 348; Seneca Chiefs to George Washington, [Dec. 1, 1790], in Twohig et al., eds., *PGW,* Pres. Ser., VII, 7–16 ("great Country," 8).

Wayne. The funding was a reminder of what the Constitution had wrought for eastern Native peoples. With the new ability under the Constitution to fund and marshal thousands of soldiers to do the work of removal, Congress could suddenly build a powerful state in the west to rival Native federationists. Just the same, Knox held violence and peace, war and so-called benevolence together. As Wayne marshaled his new army in the west, federal commissioners planned a peace treaty with the United Indian Nations for the summer of 1793. To supposedly satisfy "the dictates of humanity," federal officials would pursue peace and war simultaneously. But Washington's cabinet was sanguine about why they did so. In a private meeting, they noted that commissioners would make offers of peace "merely to gratify the public opinion" and "not from an expectation of success." Native leaders recognized the duplicity behind the simultaneous offers of peace and threats of war. At a meeting with federal commissioners at Niagara that summer, Brant offered a sharp rebuke, reminding them that they could not make peace while a U.S. Army marched toward their towns.[69]

Federal removal plans failed in the first decade after the American Revolution—a decade of uncertainty, expense, and Native power that has slipped out of the story of western expansion in the new nation. Migration, the meddling of the states, the proximity of the British and Spanish, and Native power made "disunion, anarchy, and underdevelopment" in the Appalachian region as likely as national prosperity. Native nations built diplomatic and military alliances across the North and South, and they aspired to create a broad confederacy to counter removal. Like U.S. federal officials, Native federationists grappled with disunion—they did not always agree on their strategies even if they shared a common goal. Nonetheless, they effectively exposed federal plans for bloodless removal as dishonest. By continuing the war long after the Revolution had ended in 1783, Native federationists forced federal and state officials to abandon their claims to

69. Henry Knox to Governor Blount, Apr. 22, 1792, in *TPUS,* IV, 139 ("dictates"); "Notes on Cabinet Opinions," Feb. 26, 1793, in Boyd et al., ed., *Papers of Thomas Jefferson,* XXV, 271–274 ("merely," 271); John Parrish, William Savery, John Elliott, and William Hartshorne to Benjamin Lincoln, Timothy Pickering, and Beverly Randolph, June 17 1793, TPP, LIX, 181, William Wilson to the Commissioners, June 17 1793, 182, Hendrick Aupaumut to Pickering, Aug. 6, 1793, 203A, "In Council at Navy Hall," July 7, 1793, LX, 154. For a powerful early national state in the West, see Max M. Edling, *Revolution in Favor of Government: Origins of the U.S. Constitution* (New York, 2003); William J. Novak, "The Myth of the 'Weak' American State," *American Historical Review,* CXIII (2008), 752–772; Ablavsky, "Savage Constitution," *Duke Law Journal,* LXIII (2014), 1078, 1082.

the right of conquest over Indigenous homelands. Military campaigns into Indian country exhausted the majority of the federal budget before 1795. In newspapers and in the halls of Congress, white Americans debated the "wreckages" of empire.[70]

Federal officials proposed removal as a gradual, peaceful process, but federationists did not give up their territory so willingly. Washington and Knox were protective of the standing of the United States among a community of European states and empires, and they felt themselves answerable not only to the people but also to posterity for their actions. As one commentator wrote, the United States was "a young empire" with "a federal government, scarcely established suspended on the slender thread of opinion." Removal threatened to break the thread. Knox's response was to hold violence and peace out simultaneously, an approach that would continue to be a hallmark of U.S. removal policy. It would take a more pernicious form in the future. That mixture of benevolence and plunder could only cause such devastation in the 1830s because it had been tested and tried from the beginning of the nation. In response to federal removal plans, Ohio Valley federationists argued for their right to remain as sovereign peoples. They strengthened their claims to Indian country, separate and apart from the British, Spanish, and U.S. territories on their borders.[71]

70. Onuf, *Statehood and Union,* 19 ("disunion); Paul A. Kramer, "Power and Connection: Imperial Histories of the United States in the World," *American Historical Review,* CXVI (2011), 1380 ("wreckages"), 1383.

71. "New-York, January 14; Extract of a Letter from Princeton, New Jersey," *General Advertiser,* Jan. 18, 1792, [2] (quotations).

CHAPTER 3
"A GREAT ROAD CUT"
Pursuing the Right to Remain in the Ohio Valley

In May 1793, Mohawk leader Joseph Brant, or Thayendanegea, traveled by boat southwest along the shoreline of Lake Erie from Brant's Town, the settlement he had founded set among lush gardens, meadows, and forests on the banks of the Grand River in Mississauga country and British Canada. He was accompanied by seventy Haudenosaunees and Delawares. The group moved through a land of contested borders. They rested at Detroit, then a small town of five dozen houses laid out along the Detroit River framing a Catholic chapel. The houses were British, but they were situated on what was supposedly U.S. soil. The British had traded away Detroit at the Treaty of Paris, but, in retaliation for the complacence of the United States in compensating British loyalists for their wartime losses, they had yet to relinquish it. According to the treaty, Detroit was part of the United States, while the plantations and houses across the Detroit River remained in British hands. The hand over of the town remained a sore point in British-U.S. relations. Leaving behind Detroit's disputes, Brant's group moved south along the Lake Erie shoreline before arriving at the foot of the rapids of the Maumee River in what is now northern Ohio, where Delaware and Shawnee communities gathered along the water's edge. The United Indian Nations of the Delawares, Haudenosaunees, Kickapoos, Miamis, Odawas, Ojibwes, Piankeshaws, Potawatomis, Shawnees, Weas, and Wyandots saw the land that Brant and his party passed through as a country held in common by Native people. U.S. commissioners and officials viewed it, like Detroit, as U.S. territory. Only from the perspective of the federal government, however, was this contested ground. For the United Indian Nations, there was no contest—it was theirs.[1]

1. E. B. Littlehales, "Journal from Niagara to Detroit," Feb. 7, 1793, in *CJGS,* I, 289, [Joseph] Brant, "Captain Brant's Journal of the Proceedings at the General Council Held at the Foot of the Rapids of the Miamis," May 17–Aug. 9, 1793, II, 5–17, "Message from the Western Indians to the Commissioners of the United States," Aug. 13, 1793, II, 17–20; Brant to Col. McKee, May 17, 1793, *MPHC,* XII, 49; John Parrish, "Journals to Indian Treaties," June 10, 1793, Ayer Collection, NL. Brant did not de-

For much of the eighteenth century, the Ohio Valley had been a place of refuge for Indigenous people. Miamis and Wyandots moved south in the late seventeenth century to pursue new opportunities for trade with the French. Delaware and Haudenosaunee migrants relocated there to escape land loss and violence at the hands of colonists in the East. Shawnees returned to their homelands along the Ohio River in the early eighteenth century. Long before white migrants moved into the Ohio Valley and lower Great Lakes, eastern Native peoples were the first migrants to the region. But, by century's end, U.S. policy threatened that refuge also. Federal plans for removal in the Ohio Valley and lower Great Lakes especially alarmed Ohio Valley Shawnees, Delawares, and Haudenosaunees because they had already experienced dispossession before. Brant's party was headed to a grand council of the United Indian Nations at the rapids of the Miami River southwest of Lake Erie to formulate a response to U.S. policy.[2]

Because the federal government promoted removal, Native Americans, amid intermittent warfare with the United States, spent the early 1790s developing rich arguments for their right to remain. In the Ohio Valley and lower Great Lakes, Native diplomats reached in all directions to make alliances to strengthen their case. They sought Anishinaabe and British support for the United Indian Nations to the north, and they went south to the Creeks and Chickamauga Cherokees to organize to defend their lands. By 1786, the United Indian Nations had developed a clear platform critiquing the pillars of postwar U.S. policy—the right of conquest, the right of preemption, and the idea that Native peoples would choose to alienate any lands at all. Their speeches outlined Native sovereignty, autonomy, and land rights, positions developed out of long experience with Euro-Americans.[3]

---

scribe his journey in detail, but it is likely he went by water, rather than the more tedious journey by land. For examples of both routes, see "A Narrative of an Embassy to the Western Indians, from the Original Manuscript of Hendrick Aupaumut, with Prefatory Remarks by Dr. B. H. Coates," *Memoirs of the Historical Society of Pennsylvania*, II, part 1 (1827), 78–86; Littlehales, "Journal from Niagara to Detroit," Feb. 4, 1793–Mar. 18, 1793, in *CJGS*, I, 288–292. For Detroit, see Catherine Cangany, *Frontier Seaport: Detroit's Transformation into an Atlantic Entrepôt* (Chicago, 2014); Tiya Miles, *The Dawn of Detroit: A Chronicle of Slavery and Freedom in the City of the Straits* (New York, 2017).

2. Helen Hornbeck Tanner, ed., *Atlas of Great Lakes Indian History* (Norman, Okla., 1987), 42–45; Eric Hinderaker, *Elusive Empires: Constructing Colonialism in the Ohio Valley, 1673–1800* (New York, 1999), 27–32; Sami Lakomäki, *Gathering Together: The Shawnee People through Diaspora and Nationhood, 1600–1870* (New Haven, Conn., 2014), 44–49.

3. For connections south, see Gregory Evans Dowd, *A Spirited Resistance: The North*

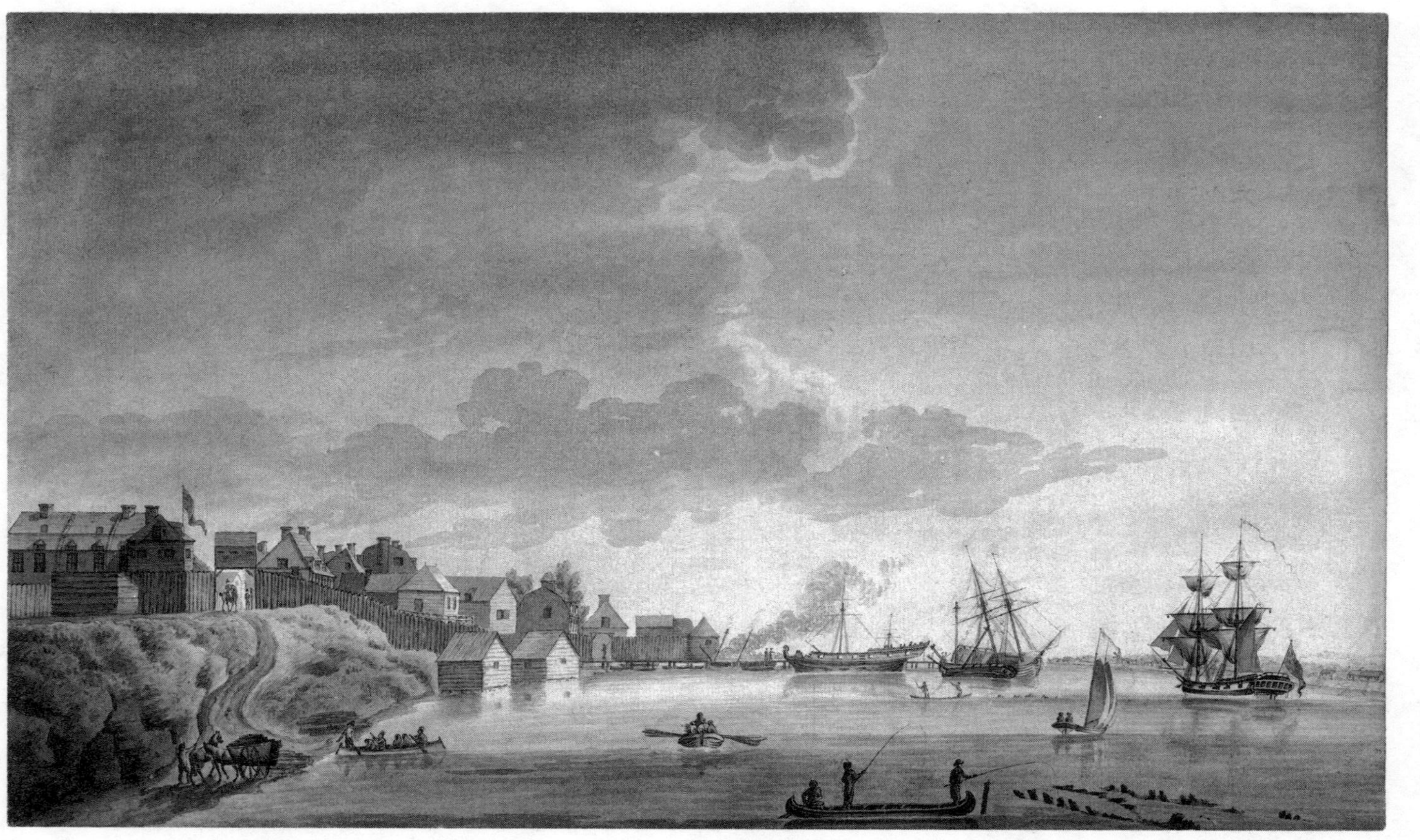

FIGURE 6. *[Edmund Henn]*, A View of Detroit. *July 25, 1794. Courtesy Burton Historical Collection, Detroit Public Library, Mich.*

Decades of war with white migrants had convinced Native leaders that they could only secure the right to remain if firm and clear borders set off Indian country as separate and distinct from the United States. The United Indian Nations pushed an antiremoval platform in which Natives held land in common. They considered the entire Great Lakes region to be, as Lisa Brooks has shown, a dish with one spoon, meaning it could not be divided or ceded without the consent of all who lived there. The United Indian Nations' emphasis on a border with the United States did not ignore the borders between Native nations, but it did try to give those Native borders new meaning. The confederacy made the borders between Indigenous lands and the United States paramount while deemphasizing those between Native people. The idea that borders should separate one group of homogenous peoples from another without enclaves was relatively new, both in Europe and the United States. The United Indian Nations was thus innovative on an Atlantic stage.[4]

American Indian Struggle for Unity, 1745–1815 (Baltimore, Md., 1993), 104–105, 109, 111. Colin G. Calloway and Michael A. McDonnell point out that connections to the north were more tenuous. Ojibwes, Odawas, and Potawatomis became more invested in militant resistance after the Treaty of Fort Harmar, but it is unclear if these were Ojibwe and Odawa peoples from the upper Great Lakes or around the Wabash River, Detroit, and Ohio Valley. Calloway says only "segments" of the Ojibwes, Odawas, and Potawatomis fought with the confederacy at any time. See Calloway, *The Victory with No Name: The Native American Defeat of the First American Army* (New York, 2015), 99; McDonnell, *Masters of Empire: Great Lakes Indians and the Making of America* (New York, 2015), 314–315.

4. See Brant, "Captain Brant's Journal of the Proceedings at the General Council," July 26, 1793, in *CJGS,* II, 12; Christina Snyder, "Native Nations in the Age of Revolution," in Andrew Shankman, ed., *The World of the Revolutionary American Republic: Land, Labor, and the Conflict for a Continent* (New York, 2014), 78. My account of Native space in the north and the Ohio Valley is especially indebted to Lisa Brooks, *The Common Pot: The Recovery of Native Space in the Northeast* (Minneapolis, Minn., 2008), 106–162. See also Jon Parmenter, *The Edge of the Woods: Iroquoia, 1534–1701* (East Lansing, Mich., 2010); Michael Witgen, *An Infinity of Nations: How the Native New World Shaped Early North America* (Philadelphia, 2012). For Native space more broadly, see Angela Pulley Hudson, *Creek Paths and Federal Roads: Indians, Settlers, and Slaves and the Making of the American South* (Chapel Hill, N.C., 2010); Robert Paulett, *An Empire of Small Places: Mapping the Southeastern Anglo-Indian Trade, 1732–1795* (Athens, Ga., 2012); Juliana Barr and Edward Countryman, eds., *Contested Spaces of Early America* (Philadelphia, 2014). For borders, see Alan Taylor, *The Divided Ground: Indians, Settlers, and the Northern Borderland of the American Revolution* (New York, 2006); Brooks, *Common Pot;* Juliana Barr, "Geographies of Power: Mapping Indian Borders in the 'Borderlands' of the Early Southwest," *William and Mary Quarterly,* 3d Ser., LXVIII (2011), 5–46; Sami Lakomäki, "'Our Line': The Shawnees, the United States, and Competing Borders on the Great Lakes 'Borderlands,' 1795–1832," *Journal of the*

The United States and the United Indian Nations used new ideas about boundaries to pursue two different models of statecraft. Responding to the demands of Indigenous councils, U.S. officials also urged clear boundaries that would end warfare in the Ohio Valley, yet they had ulterior motives for doing so. Although they promised to run a permanent border to protect Indian country, in actuality, they imagined a border that would mark the beginning of dispossession rather than the end of it. Even as they promised permanence, federal officials presumed that the boundary would eventually be superseded when the threat of war had passed. Establishing peace first would usher in the bloodless revolution in Native property that President George Washington and Secretary of War Henry Knox had hoped for in 1783. Although borders were traditionally intended to defend sovereign powers from outside encroachment, U.S. officials redefined them as tools of dispossession. The boundaries they imagined contained the seeds of removal.[5]

Native federationists disagreed about which borders would maintain the integrity of a country held in common. Just as the new United States had struggled to cement the union between the states, the United Nations also struggled to determine the best way to protect their right to remain. Which borders would situate people as too near neighbors, and which would keep the peace? Shawnees, Miamis, and Kickapoos, who stood at the front of the confederacy's resistance to the U.S., called for the removal of white migrants who had staked claims north of the Ohio River. Mohawk war chief and federationist Brant, Seneca war chief Cornplanter, and Mohican diplomat Hendrick Aupaumut along with some Wyandots and Delawares took up conciliation, searching for a compromise with U.S. officials. These Native leaders were not radicals or accommodationists; rather, they sought to balance the competing demands of other Native leaders and clan matrons with British and U.S. officials.[6]

Early Republic, XXXIV (2014), 597–624; Pekka Hämäläinen, "The Shapes of Power: Indians, Europeans, and North American Worlds from the Seventeenth to the Nineteenth Century," in Barr and Countryman, eds., *Contested Spaces of Early America,* 35.

5. For boundaries in European thinking, see Peter Sahlins, *Boundaries: The Making of France and Spain in the Pyrenees* (Berkeley, Calif., 1989), 93–102; Sahlins, "Natural Frontiers Revisited: France's Boundaries since the Seventeenth Century," *American Historical Review,* XCV (1990), 1434–1435, 1438–1443; Michael Biggs, "Putting the State on the Map: Cartography, Territory, and European State Formation," *Comparative Studies in Society and History,* XLI (1999), 374–405, esp. 386.

6. Antoinette Burton, "Introduction: Travelling Criticism? On the Dynamic Histories of Indigenous Modernity," *Cultural and Social History,* IX (2012), 491–492; James Joseph Buss, "Imagined Worlds and Archival Realities: The Patchwork World

The confederacy that Native westerners revived in 1783 was both a political and a spatial construct. Federationists promised to share land and to smooth over political divisions between Native peoples. At a council at lower Sandusky in 1783, the confederated nations determined that none would sell their land without the consent of all. At subsequent councils, "a Moon of Wampum and a Dish with one Spoon . . . Signified that the Country was in Common." The dish with one spoon was not a new invention. Brant told British trader Alexander McKee that "upwards of one hundred years ago" Native nations had first imagined the Ohio country as a space "with four roads leading to the center for the convenience of the Indians from different quarters to come and settle or hunt here." The land belonged to them all.[7]

In 1786, Haudenosaunee, Shawnee, Delaware, Wyandot, Ojibwe, Potawatomi, Odawa, Piankeshaw, Wea, Miami, and Cherokee delegates met at Brownstown where they put together a federationist platform critiquing U.S. policy, which disregarded Native lands as a country held in common. They argued against federal claims to the Ohio Valley based on the right of conquest—the idea that the United States had won Native lands per the Treaty of Paris. They protested U.S. preemption rights in Indian country as well. A Wyandot speaker would later express the thoughts of the council when he told U.S. officials: "Brothers, we never made any agreement with the King, not with any other nation, that we would give to either the exclusive right of purchasing our lands. And we declare to you that we consider ourselves free to make any bargain or cession of lands, whenever and to whomsoever we please." The United Indian Nations rejected U.S. pressure to sell land, making it clear that they did not plan to alienate any of their Ohio Valley territory. Among federationists, years of warfare created, in the words of one British official, "a firmness about them, to preserve their Rights."[8]

By 1790, federationists began to relocate to the Glaize—a long stretch of villages, gardens, and cornfields at the forks of the Auglaize and Maumee Rivers in what is now northwest Ohio. Eastern travelers would have ap-

---

of Early Nineteenth-Century Indiana," in Buss and C. Joseph Genetin-Pilawa, *Beyond Two Worlds: Critical Conversations on Language and Power in Native North America* (Albany, N.Y., 2015), 97–115.

7. Brant, "Captain Brant's Journal of the Proceedings at the General Council," July 26, 1793, in *CJGS,* II, 12 ("Moon"); Joseph Brant, Ms. 11F204–5, Draper Manuscript Collection, State Historical Society of Wisconsin (microfilm copy at Dartmouth College), quoted in Brooks, *Common Pot,* 124 ("upwards"); Brooks, *Common Pot,* 138–139.

8. Journey of the Western Commissioners, Aug. 16, 1793, TPP, LX, 173A ("Brothers"); Parrish, "Journals to Indian Treaties," June 12, 1793, Ayer Collection ("firmness").

MAP 3. *The Ohio Valley and Lower Great Lakes, 1792–1794. Drawn by Rebecca Wrenn*

proached the Glaize from the Shawnee and Delaware villages at the rapids of the Maumee River before moving further upriver. Within a few years, several thousand refugees had settled there to distance themselves from U.S. military campaigns. They clustered in towns named for prominent war chiefs like Shawnee Blue Jacket and Miami Little Turtle.[9]

Native people had long confederated as a strategy of political resistance. Ohio Valley and Great Lakes peoples had formed a strong confederacy dur-

9. Helen Hornbeck Tanner, "The Glaize in 1792: A Composite Indian Community," *Ethnohistory* (1978), 15–39; Calloway, *Victory with No Name,* 99–101; "Narrative of an Embassy," *Memoirs of the Historical Society of Pennsylvania,* II, part 1 (1827), 86, 97–98.

ing Pontiac's War in 1763, for example. More unusual was the idea of a country held in common, which was at odds with other conceptions of territorial sovereignty. Like Anglo-Americans, Native Americans had flexible and complicated ideas about how ownership and resource sharing worked. Native nations were organized around kinship, and they used kinship to organize property, too. Some people enjoyed the power to use the landscape in particular ways—for hunting, fishing, or agriculture—and particular clans or families acquired those use rights through negotiation and custom. The same was true for the edges of the territories of particular nations, where migrants might be permitted to share land at the invitation of Native hosts.[10]

Conceiving of land as a set of use rights rather than as property that could be fully alienated held political advantages. Land-sharing agreements benefitted all parties. In the Ohio Valley, Delawares and separatist Haudenosaunees settled on Miami and Wyandot lands to act as a buffer against outside military and political pressures. Villages in the Ohio Valley were a barrier for the peoples of the Great Lakes against white migrants from the United States. Land sharing blurred the borders between Indigenous people, but it did not undermine territoriality. Native diplomats still understood whose permission they had to secure to migrate beyond their homelands.[11]

The dish with one spoon was thus a creative adaptation. The common dish made the borders between Native lands and the United States paramount, while minimizing border drawing between Native nations. It was in keeping with the spirit of land sharing, but it also gave Native borders new meaning, privileging the idea of a national space aligned against the United States. In the post-Revolutionary period, the United Indian Nations adapted old modes of territorial expression to changing circumstances. Just as the United States crafted a "common cause" from a shared language of natural rights, representative government, and a fear of racialized others, so, too, did Indigenous people find a common cause in resistance to the United States that changed their sense of political space. That sense of political space extended beyond the Ohio Valley and lower Great Lakes to Anishinaabe, Cherokee, and Creek country.[12]

10. Taylor, *Divided Ground,* 36–38; Nancy Shoemaker, *A Strange Likeness: Becoming Red and White in Eighteenth-Century North America* (Oxford, 2004), 15–23; Alyssa Mt. Pleasant, "After the Whirlwind: Maintaining a Haudenosaunee Place at Buffalo Creek, 1780–1825" (Ph.D. diss., Cornell University, 2007), 69; Hämäläinen, "Shapes of Power," in Barr and Countryman, eds., *Contested Spaces of Early America,* 35.

11. John Graves Simcoe to unnamed recipient, Nov. 10, 1793, CO 42/318/10, TNA.

12. Robert G. Parkinson, *The Common Cause: Creating Race and Nation in the*

At the Glaize, the United Indian Nations marked their politics of resistance on the landscape. After the confederacy's 1790 victory over Brigadier General Josiah Harmar, federationists created a "large painted Encampment" of stripped trees nearly a half mile long at the Glaize, painted red with "Hieroglyphicks." One white captive, Matthew Bunn, remembered that his captors "spotted the trees around for some distance, and then made blacking of powder and marked the trees in all kinds of disfigured creatures." At Moraviantown, a Delaware village on the banks of the Thames River, a British official observed the same images in 1793. The trees were burned and marked with "various figures of Indians returning from battle with scalps, and animals drawn upon them descriptive of the Nations, Tribe and Numbers that had passed." When Quaker Gerard Hopkins traveled through the Ohio country a decade later, he "observed many curious and to us unintelegeble Indian Hieroglyphics cut upon the trees" and painted in bright colors. The markings were what Lisa Brooks has termed "a spatialized writing tradition," a form of writing on the landscape that was, significantly, incomprehensible to white observers. Like surveyors' marks, these forest paintings made a visual claim to land as Indian country. They also recorded Native resistance to the United States, an antiremoval conversation akin to that carried on in eastern newspapers.[13]

Holding together the idea of geographic unity was the idea of political unity among the confederacy's many parts. Native leaders promised not to alienate any land without unanimous consent. In the past, British and then U.S. negotiators had exploited divisions between leaders and nations to secure wide swaths of Indian country. Speculators and their allies in New York's state government, for example, took advantage of divisions in Haudenosaunee communities to seize large parts of Iroquoia after the Ameri-

---

American Revolution (Williamsburg, Va., and Chapel Hill, N.C., 2016); Snyder, "Native Nations," in Shankman, ed., *World of the Revolutionary American Republic,* 78, 81; Lakomäki, "'Our Line,'" *Journal of the Early Republic,* XXXIV (2014), 602. For the geographical reach of Native diplomats, see Dowd, *Spirted Resistance,* 104–105, 109, 111.

13. Winthrop Sargent to St. Clair, Jan. 8, 1792, Sargent Papers, typed transcript in the Shawnee File, 1792, Ethnohistory Archive, MHS, quoted in Dowd, *Spirited Resistance,* 106–107 ("large," 106, "Hieroglyphicks," 107); [Matthew Bunn], *A Narrative, of the Life and Sufferings of Matthew Bunn; Who Was Taken by the Indians, in 1791, and afterwards Made His Escape, to the British; Together with an Account of His Treatment, while with Them* (Peacham, Vt., 1806), 9 ("spotted"); Littlehales, "Journal from Niagara to Detroit," Feb. 14, 1793, in *CJGS,* I, 290 ("various"); Gerard Hopkins, Journal, Mar. 27, 1804, HSP ("observed"); Brooks, *Common Pot,* 12 ("spatialized"); Taylor, *Divided Ground,* 35; Philip H. Round, *Removable Type: Histories of the Book in Indian Country, 1663–1880* (Chapel Hill, N.C., 2010), 12–13.

can Revolution. Federal commissioners in the Ohio Valley had successfully used the same tactic at the Treaty of Fort Stanwix in 1784 and again at the Treaty of Fort Harmar in 1785. By the 1790s, U.S. officials hoped to divide the United Indian Nations, too. New York governor George Clinton warned that a convention of united Native nations would give Indigenous people "power and vigor, which we cannot with certainty direct, and over which we shall with much trouble and expense have an uncertain controul."[14]

Like the fledgling United States, however, the United Indian Nations already had its own internal divisions that served to challenge political unity. While white Americans in the Atlantic states debated whether removal was "just," federationists carried on their own antiremoval debate at the Glaize. Shawnees, Miamis, and Kickapoos led resistance to federal demands as white migrants threatened Miami lands in the Maumee and Wabash River valleys. Ojibwes, Odawas, and Potawatomis, whose towns sat at a greater distance from U.S. incursions, joined the confederacy, but they were less likely to be its leaders. Some Wyandots and Delawares, along with Haudenosaunees, were more interested in moderation, and some pursued compromise with the United States.[15]

Mohawk leader Brant's position as an advocate of compromise among federationists is representative of the internal divisions among the United Indian Nations. Brant saw unity as the only path toward peace, and he tried to pursue consolidation at his settlement on the Grand River in British Canada. In 1784, Sir Frederick Haldimand, governor of Quebec, had granted Brant and the Mohawks a tract of land purchased from the Mississaugas on the Grand River in recognition of their war service in the American Revolution. Haldimand imagined the Grand River lands as a buffer against white Americans. For British officials, this was a unique way of looking at a buffer state. For much of the eighteenth century, they had viewed white migrants as buffers protecting eastern settlements from Natives. Brant saw things still differently. He hoped that British forts would be a buffer against white migrants for *his* settlement, and he chose the Grand River location strategically. He wanted to consolidate all of the Haudenosaunees at what came to be known as Brant's Town.[16]

Brant's vision of unity and consolidation was nevertheless contested

14. George Clinton to Henry Knox, Apr. 27, 1791, TPP, LI, 212A (quotation); Taylor, *Divided Ground,* 21–22; Brooks, *Common Pot,* 127.

15. Calloway, *Victory with No Name,* 96–99.

16. Charles M. Johnston, "Joseph Brant, the Grand River Lands and the Northwest Crisis," *Ontario History,* LV (1963), 268 n4; Taylor, *Divided Ground,* 120–123.

even among Haudenosaunees. When he brought news of the reserve to the Haudenosaunee council at Buffalo Creek in New York, the clan matrons, who ultimately decided the location of Haudenosaunee villages, told the assembled chiefs that they would stay put. Most Mohawks left with Brant for the reserve, while the Senecas accompanied him, remained, or moved west to join Wyandot villages in the Ohio country. Some Tuscaroras followed Brant, but the Cayugas, Oneidas, and Onondagas largely remained in their homelands. "So every Nations have Saperated all Directions," recalled Seneca chief Chainbreaker decades later. The clan mothers, for their part, thought of the split differently. They saw the advantage of dividing the confederacy across the U.S.-Canadian border to hedge their bets. By staking a place among both colonial powers, Haudenosaunees could use borders to secure the right to remain on either side.[17]

Beyond Iroqouia, Native westerners also distrusted Brant as a leader of the United Indian Nations. Although he had been an important speaker at the 1786 Brownstown meeting when the confederacy put together their platform against the United States, the relationship between the Haudenosaunees and their western neighbors generally remained delicate. Shawnees, for example, were still angry over the Treaty of Fort Stanwix of 1768, when the Haudenosaunees had traded away Shawnee hunting grounds south of the Ohio River without consulting them. Haudenosaunee leaders had claimed Shawnee homelands as their own, giving them up as a bargaining chip in negotiations to draw stronger boundaries and protections around their own homelands in Iroquoia. The Fort Stanwix treaty set the boundary between British settlements and Indian country at the Appalachian Mountains, with a sharp dip into the Ohio country where the boundary cut along the Ohio River. In 1783, Dunquat, the Half-King of the Sandusky Wyandots, jabbed at Haudenosaunee leaders by reminding them of their cession at Fort Stanwix when he told them that "you know where the Boundary Line was fixed, since you were the people who fixed it."[18]

By the 1790s, Haudenosaunee councils were working hard to pursue

17. Thomas S. Abler, ed., *Chainbreaker: The Revolutionary War Memoirs of Governor Blacksnake as Told to Benjamin Williams* (Lincoln Neb., 2005), 168–169 (quotation). For the political role of clan matrons, see Taylor, *Divided Ground,* 123, 133–134; Mt. Pleasant, "After the Whirlwind," 65–66. On the Grand River lands, see Johnston, "Joseph Brant, the Grand River Lands, and the Northwest Crisis," *Ontario History,* LV (1963), 267–282; Charles M. Johnston, ed., *The Valley of the Six Nations: A Collection of Documents on the Indian Lands of the Grand River* (Toronto, 1964), 41–58, 70–119; Taylor, *Divided Ground,* 122–123.

18. "Transactions with Indians at Sandusky," Aug. 26–Sept. 8, 1783, *MPHC,* XX, 182.

peace through compromise with the United States, staying out of the conflict while placating their western neighbors. At a council at Newtown Point in 1791, when U.S. commissioner Timothy Pickering approached Haudenosaunee chiefs, asking them to stay neutral in the conflict between the United States and the western confederacy, they assured him they would. The Haudenosaunees were still recovering from the devastation of their homelands during the American Revolution, and they wanted to avoid another war. At the same time, the loss of the Ohio country would be disastrous for their hold on Iroquoia, sandwiching their lands between white settlements, so they continued to send emissaries to western federationists.[19]

Although U.S. officials saw Brant as a powerful leader who held the confederacy together and could sway western councils to pursue peace, far from making him a leader of the confederacy, as federal officials supposed, Brant's political machinations made him a figure of distrust. Brant spent the 1780s and 1790s triangulating between U.S., British, and federationist interests. By the early 1790s, Brant had earned the ire of federationists at the Glaize. In the spring of 1791, he tasked his nephew Tawalooth with bringing his input to the western councils when he could not travel himself. Tawalooth promised westerners that the Haudenosaunees would join them in a military engagement with the United States, but Brant was absent when the United Indian Nations defeated American forces under General Arthur St. Clair in 1791, which diminished his influence in western councils.[20]

The closer that Native leaders grew to federal officials, the more federationists mistrusted them. President Washington invited Seneca war captain Cornplanter and Mohican diplomat Hendrick Aupaumut, along with Brant and other Haudenosaunee leaders, to the U.S. capital in Philadelphia several times in the early 1790s to ask them to represent U.S. interests in western councils. Federal leaders paid emissaries for their work in hopes of encouraging their loyalty to the United States. Aupaumut and his traveling companions received individual payments. Aupaumut used his connections to press for resources for Mohicans, like a new sawmill and gristmill. For his part, Brant reported that he had declined federal payments. He might have been willing to pursue compromise, but he still advocated Native unity, and he was not willing to work for U.S. interests. At a western council in 1792, he asked Cornplanter, whom he particularly distrusted, why he had come

19. Mt. Pleasant, "After the Whirlwind," 58–64, 67, 86–87.

20. "Examination of Hendrick Aupaumut by Timothy Pickering," Feb. 15, 1793, TPP, LIX, 41; Presley Neville to Thomas Mifflin, Aug. 3, 1792, Ayer Collection; Taylor, *Divided Ground*, 253–260, 275–277. On Tawalooth's maneuverings, see "Narrative of an Embassy," *Memoirs of the Historical Society of Pennsylvania*, II, part 1 (1827), 85.

to the council with a "bundle of American speeches under your arm" from the U.S. capital in Philadelphia.[21]

Aupaumut, by contrast, went west partly to gain the favor of federal officials. But he also acted in order to claim a future place for his people in the dish with one spoon as a safeguard against dispossession. He had personal experience with land sharing. Aupaumut had been born in Stockbridge, Massachusetts. In the 1780s, the Oneidas invited Stockbridge Mohicans to settle near them after the American Revolution as buffers against white migrants. The Mohicans, faced with the prospect of being slowly forced out of their lands in New York and western Massachusetts, had taken them up on the invitation. The Mohicans formed a settlement called New Stockbridge on Oneida Creek that, alongside nearby Brothertown, quickly became a refuge for other Indigenous people. White migrants soon abutted this new settlement, too. When Aupaumut met with western federationists, they told him that they went to war with the United States to avoid the situation of Aupaumut's Mohicans, in which "we were shut up like so many hogs in a pen . . . surrounded by the Yankees in arms, who would not suffer us to go abroad." Across the U.S.-Canadian border, the chiefs at the Mohawk settlement at Grand River and at Delaware Moraviantown both invited the Mohicans to resettle near them.[22]

Federationist unease about any delegation that had met with the United States was on full display in the fall of 1792, when Haudenosaunee emissaries and Aupaumut went to meet with western councils carrying messages of peace from the United States. Shawnee and Delaware speakers were suspicious of eastern emissaries who had been to Philadelphia. Aupaumut believed that such was the ire of westerners toward the Haudenosaunees that they would do the opposite of what they recommended. One Shawnee warrior challenged them to live up to their previous calls for unity against the United States. He told them, "In our publick council you tell us, we whose are one colar, now have one heart and one head. If any Nation strikes us, we must all feel it. Now you must consider whether this is true what you

21. "Indian Council at the Glaize," Oct. 5, 1792, in *CJGS,* I, 224 (quotation); "Captain Hendrick's Narrative of His Journey to Niagara and Grand River, in February 1792," TPP, LIX, 19, Henry Knox to George Clinton, Apr. 12, 1791, LX, 51–52, Joseph Brant to Samuel Kirkland, Mar. 8, 1791, LXI, 208, Knox to Clinton, May 11, 1791, 217, Hendrick Aupaumut to Timothy Pickering, Oct. 7, 1794, LXII, 89; Taylor, *Divided Ground,* 257–258; Brooks, *Common Pot,* 127, 141–143.

22. "Capt Hendrick's Narrative of His Journey to Niagara and Grand River in July, August, Sept, and Oct, 1791," TPP, LIX, 11 (quotation), "Captain Hendrick's Narrative of His Journey to Niagara and Grand River, in February 1792," 19; Taylor, *Divided Ground,* 146.

told us." Chainbreaker, who traveled west with a group of Senecas, later remembered that the federationists they met in council called the Senecas "very coward Red men" who should be punished for acquiescing to the United States. Western federationists, on the other hand, would stand firm and "for our lands and Rights we will Die before we would give up to our enemy." Aupaumut, too, encountered the same challenges in bringing federal messages west, which he tried to do four times in the 1790s. Delawares accused him of being a spy for the United States, there merely "to number the Indians" and report back on their military strength.[23]

By carrying messages for the federal government, Aupaumut and Cornplanter sought to grasp some control over a moment when they had few good options. Mediators occupied positions of power, and they hoped to use that power for the benefit of themselves and their nations. Neither of these men thought of themselves as an accommodationist, although federationists sometimes saw them that way. The term does not fully account for their critique of U.S. policy. In December 1790, Senecas Cornplanter, Half Town, and Great Tree agreed to travel on a peace mission on behalf of the United States to the western councils, but they also used the occasion to chastise President Washington for taking Haudenosaunee lands since the end of the American Revolution. "We must know from you, whether you mean to leave us and our children any land to till," the chiefs asked. They were not torn between two worlds. Rather, they pursued the compromises and alliances they believed would best secure their futures.[24]

Although Aupaumut's work with the United States might seem naïve

23. "Narrative of an Embassy," *Memoirs of the Historical Society of Pennsylvania,* II, part 1 (1827), 115–117 ("In our," 117), 121, 128–130 ("number," 129); Abler, ed., *Chainbreaker,* 199 ("very coward," "lands and Rights"); "Newtown Point on the Tioga River, State of New York," 1791, TPP, LX, 72A; *The Debates and Proceedings in the Congress of the United States . . . Second Congress: Comprising the Period from October 24, 1791, to March 2, 1793, Inclusive* (Washington, D.C., 1849), Appendix, 1050–1051; Dowd, *Spirited Resistance,* 107–108. Aupaumut's position was also undermined by Joseph Brant. Both men spread rumors in the western councils that the other was not to be trusted. See "Capt Hendrick's Narrative of His Journey to Niagara and Grand River," TPP, LIX, 8, "Questions by Captain Hendrick, Feb., 11, 1793," 49, Samuel Kirkland to Timothy Pickering, May 31, 1792, LXII, 47–49; Brooks, *Common Pot,* 145–149.

24. "Speech of Cornplanter to the President of the United States," Dec. 5, 1790, TPP, LX, 9–15 (quotation, 15), "Third Speech of Cornplanter," Feb. 7, 1791, 29; Brooks, *Common Pot,* 130–131. For accommodationists, see Rob Harper, *Unsettling the West: Violence and State Building in the Ohio Valley* (Philadelphia, 2018), 174. For mediators and go-betweens, see Alan Taylor, "Captain Hendrick Aupaumut: The Dilemmas of an Intercultural Broker," *Ethnohistory,* XLIII (1996), 431–457; James H. Merrell, *Into the American Woods: Negotiators on the Pennsylvania Frontier* (New York, 1999).

in hindsight, he managed to make his own critiques of U.S. policy where he could. When he attended the 1791 council, he faithfully recorded the message of Delaware chief Big Cat, who wanted Aupaumut to carry his complaints about U.S. conduct back to Philadelphia. Big Cat told him that the United States would keep taking Native lands until there was nothing left, and he reminded Aupaumut of the massacre of Christian Delawares at Gnadenhutten in 1782 as well as the murder of Shawnee chief Moluntha, a U.S. ally, in 1786. He knew that federal officials could not, or would not, control the violence of white migrants, and he believed that "they would make slaves of us." Aupaumut took on the role of mediator, reassuring Big Cat that the U.S. Constitution, representative democracy, and strong laws could end these abuses. After recording this exchange, however, he took a moment for his own brief aside to his correspondents back in the federal capital: "In all my arguments with these Indians, I have as it were oblige to say nothing with regard of the conduct of Yorkers, how they cheat my fathers, how they taken our lands Unjustly, and how my fathers were groaning as it were to their graves, in loseing their lands for nothing, although they were faithful friends to the Whites; and how the white people artfully got their Deeds confirm in their Laws, etc." Aupaumut understood Delaware complaints because Mohicans had suffered in the same ways. He saw the limitations of federal promises, though he only aknowledged those limitations in brief glimpses.[25]

Federationists and their allies confronted fresh tensions over unity, consolidation, leadership, and compromise after St. Clair's defeat. Shawnee Blue Jacket came across a packet of papers after the battle revealing President Washington's intention to drive them out of the Ohio Valley. Native leaders told Captain Matthew Elliott, assistant to the British Indian superintendent at Detroit, that "from the American Speeches we find they are resolved to Persist in getting our Country—and banishing us out of it." Native leaders who joined together at the Glaize agreed that only a firm boundary could guarantee their right to remain. In 1792, federationists rejected outright all peace proposals from federal commissioners that did not guarantee an Ohio River boundary between the dish with one spoon and the United States. Weas, Piankeshaws, Potawatomis, Kickapoos, and Kaskaskias told a federal commissioner that they would only accept peace once the United States

25. "Narrative of an Embassy," *Memoirs of the Historical Society of Pennsylvania,* II, part 1 (1827), 122–131, 128 (quotations).

pledged to "accept this river as the frontier line." They wished for Natives and white migrants to "never live in too close proximity."[26]

By using the term *proximity,* Native speakers were taking up what was for the eighteenth-century Anglo-Atlantic a relatively new idea of border drawing. Borders were intended to separate unified peoples, eliminating strangers in their midst. To ensure that boundary, Native leaders wanted the removal of white migrants across the Ohio River. Two captives who escaped from Indian country told federal officials that Natives would not accept peace offers until white settlements on the north side of the Ohio River had been removed. British Indian agent McKee observed that there was a "general Union of Sentiment throughout all the Nations" that the United States should destroy their forts and settlements north of the Ohio River. For their part, British officials hoped that an Ohio River boundary would maintain Indian country as a "Barrier" or "a Line separating the British Territory and that of the United States." White migrants, wrote one official, were "too restless a neighbour." Upper Canada needed a Native buffer state to protect British boundaries from invasion.[27]

Federationists disagreed about where to draw the borders of the dish with one spoon. These disagreements became apparent in 1793, when U.S. commissioners went to Detroit to treat for peace with the confederacy. They planned to offer a large annuity in exchange for the recognition of previous

26. "The Western Indian Nations to Captain Mathew Elliott," May 16, 1792, in *CJGS,* I, 157 ("from"); M. C. Sprengel, ed., "Narrative of John Heckewelder's Journey to the Wabash in 1792," trans. Clara Frueauff, *Pennsylvania Magazine of History and Biography,* XII (1888), 171 ("accept"); "Proceedings of a General Council of the Several Indian Nations . . . at the Glaize on the 30th Day of September 1792 and Continued until, the 9th Day of October Inclusive," CO 42/317/32–33, TNA; Dowd, *Spirited Resistance,* 103–104; Helen Hornbeck Tanner, "The Glaize in 1792: A Composite Indian Community," *Ethnohistory* (1978), 15–39.

27. Alexander McKee to J. G. Simcoe, July 1, 1793, in *CJGS,* I, 374 ("general"), "Memorandum by J. G. Simcoe and Alexander McKee," n.d., 173 ("Line"), Charles Stevenson to Simcoe, Jan. 7, 1792, 101 ("too restless"), Stevenson to Evan Nepean, Jan. 11, 1792, 102; Simcoe to McKee, Aug. 30, 1792, CO 42/317/8, TNA ("Barrier"), Henry Dundas to Simcoe and Lt. Governor Clarke, May 5, 1792, CO 42/316/58–59, McTavish Frobisher, Forsyth Richardson, and Todd McGill to Simcoe, Dec. 9, 1791, CO 42/316/101–105, Simcoe and McKee to George Hammond, June 21, 1792, CO 42/316/137, Dundas to Simcoe, Oct. 2, 1793, CO 42/317/162; Don Heinrich Tolzmann, ed., *The First Description of Cincinnati and Other Ohio Settlements: The Travel Report of Johann Heckewelder* (1792) (Lanham, Md., 1988), 48; Taylor, *Divided Ground,* 279. On European and Anglo-American borders, see Sahlins, *Boundaries;* Sahlins, "Natural Frontiers Revisited," *American Historical Review,* XCV (1990), 1438–1443; Biggs, "Putting the State on the Map," *Comparative Studies in Society and History,* XLI (1999), 386.

treaties that had secured much of what is now southern Ohio for the United States. The commissioners were joined by six Quakers, carrying messages of peace from their Philadelphia meeting. The group ended their journey at Niagara, where they waited for Native emissaries to arrive. Meanwhile, the confederacy's delegates met separately with southern Creeks, Cherokees, and Shawnees at the rapids of the Maumee River in a grand council.[28]

At the grand council, Brant took a compromise position, proposing a boundary at the Muskingum River. That boundary ceded a small portion of what is now eastern Ohio to the U.S. government. Brant believed that letting American settlements across the Ohio River remain would prevent war while ensuring continued travel between southern Natives and the Glaize to foster their common cause. Although Brant had successfully pushed for this boundary several years before, most federationists now found Brant's stance unacceptable. The Shawnees, Miamis, and Kickapoos as well as some Delawares and Wyandots particularly objected. They argued that "the white People intended to take their whole Country from them, and deprive them from making a living for their Wives and Children." Moreover, Brant's opponents spoke from a position of strength. The confederacy had routed the United States twice in 1790 and 1791, white Americans wearied of war, and the federal government could ill afford to spend more on military engagements. At the Glaize, war chiefs—men like Blue Jacket, Little Turtle, and Tetapatchsit—had greater control over political affairs than civil chiefs and female councils. These men "were determined now to make a stand" for the Ohio River as the boundary.[29]

When Brant arrived at the rapids of the Maumee River to take part in the grand council, he was forced to send several messages before federationists would agree to meet with him. Meanwhile, he learned that Shawnees were spreading rumors that he was a traitor working in the interest of the United States. After Brant and fifty other delegates went to speak with federal commissioners at Niagara, Native speakers at the grand council berated him for his performance on his return. Delaware chief Buckongahelas grew angry

28. John Parrish, William Savery, John Elliott, and William Hartshorne to Benjamin Lincoln, Timothy Pickering, and Beverly Randolph, June 17, 1793, TPP, LIX, 181; Taylor, *Divided Ground,* 277–279.

29. Parrish, "Journals to Indian Treaties," June 12, 1793, Ayer Collection (quotations); J. G. Simcoe to Alured Clarke, Apr. 21, 1793, in *CJGS,* I, 317–318, Simcoe to Alexander McKee, Apr. 29, 1793, 323, Joseph Brant to Simcoe, July 28, 1793, 403; Timothy Pickering, "Journal of the Treaty," Aug. 10, 1793, TPP, LIX, Hendrick Aupaumut to Pickering, Aug. 6, 1793, 203–203A; Taylor, *Divided Ground,* 281; Brooks, *Common Pot,* 133–136; Adam Jortner, *The Gods of Prophetstown: The Battle of Tippecanoe and the Holy War for the American Frontier* (New York, 2012), 57.

when he realized that Brant had been the one to communicate the confederacy's position to U.S. commissioners at Niagara rather than a Shawnee emissary, who could better represent the federationist position. Buckongahelas interrupted Brant's speech to the council—a breach of protocol in the carefully scripted world of diplomacy. Shawnee, Wyandot, Miami, and Delaware federationists left to conduct their own private council. When they reemerged, they announced that they would brook none of Brant's compromises—the river would be the boundary.[30]

British boats with British flags carried the Native and U.S. delegations back and forth to Detroit twice to discuss peace. That July, twenty-five Shawnee and Delaware chiefs met federal commissioners at Matthew Elliott's estate at the mouth of the Detroit River. Wyandot chief Carry-One-About stood at the center of the group to communicate the confederacy's decision through an interpreter. "The line has been fixed long ago," he told the U.S. delegation. The commissioners objected that removing white settlements in the Ohio country would be prohibitively expensive, particularly given the cost of paying settlers for the improvements to their land. Carry-One-About summarized the impasse bluntly: "You know you have houses and people on our lands. You say you cannot move them off; and we cannot give up our lands."[31]

Back at the Miami Rapids, Shawnee war captain Kekewepellethe placed a moon of wampum and the dish with one spoon in the grand council once again. He passed a pipe and tobacco to the Creek warrior beside him, solidifying the alliance with southern federationists, who told of threats to the south. Producing four strings of wampum, Kekewepellethe told the council that "altho these our Strings are small they are full of meaning, our Confederacy is a like a house with four Doors and all the Indian Country is

30. Parrish, "Journals to Indian Treaties," June 12, 1793, Ayer Collection; Aupaumut to Pickering, Aug. 6, 1793, TPP, LIX, 203–203A; "Minutes of a Council with the Indians," July 9, 1793, in *CJGS,* I, 381, Brant, "Captain Brant's Journal of the Proceedings at the General Council," May 17, 22, 24, June 3, July 23, 24, and 25, 1793, II, 5, 8–10; Brooks, *Common Pot,* 151–153.

31. Benjamin Lincoln, "Journal of a Treaty Held in 1793, with the Indian Tribes North-West of the Ohio, by Commissioners of the United States," MHS, *Collections,* 3d ser., V (Boston, 1836), Aug. 1, 1793, 150 (quotations); Parrish, "Journals to Indian Treaties," July 29–Aug. 1, 1793, Ayer Collection; Western Indians to the Commissioners of the United States, July 27, 1793, in *CJGS,* I, 401–402, B. Lincoln, Beverley Randolph, and Timothy Pickering, "The Speech of the Commissioners of the United States to the Deputies of the Confederate Indian Nations Assembled at Rapids of the Miamis River," July 31, 1793, 405–409; U.S. Commissioners of Indian Affairs to Confederate Indian Tribes, July 31, 1793, Lewis Cass Papers, box 5, folder 24, CL.

FIGURE 7. *Lewis Foy,* The Great Indian Council. *Circa 1793. Pen and ink, watercolour and gouache over traces of graphite. Gift of Messrs. G. Ronald Jackson and Michael Jackson, 1967.1575. Photo: The Montreal Museum of Fine Arts, Christine Guest. Courtesy The Montreal Museum of Fine Arts.*

Lewis Foy's painting depicts the 1793 meeting at Matthew Elliott's estate on the Detroit River. A Native orator, perhaps Carry-One-About, addresses the group; the British officer beside him is likely either Alexander McKee or Matthew Elliott; the commissioners for the United States are seated to the right; Quaker observers, including John Parrish, stand in hats behind them.

in common." The eastern door, Kekewepellethe said, was the most in danger from war with the United States if the confederacy continued to resist further cessions, "but we are determined that no part of it shall suffer if in our power to support it." Over Brant's objections, Kekewepellethe asked the council to reject peace. They did so, ending the grand council with a feast and a war song celebrating the British alliance and encouraging an active defense of the dish with one spoon.[32]

Two Wyandots were appointed to carry the grand council's speech to the U.S. commissioners back at Detroit. The speech denounced the commissioners' request for a "concession" of land from the confederacy. "It appears strange that you should expect any from us, who have only been defending our just Rights against your invasion," they said. The speech also rejected the idea that the United States had the right of preemption over Indian country. The council told the commissioners that if George III had indeed given them such a right, "It is an affair which concerns you and him and not us. We have never parted with such a power." They concluded by informing the commissioners that they had no use for the funds offered by the United States to purchase their land. Instead, the commissioners should apply them to removing and "satisfying their own people, who have settled and made improvements on the Indian Lands." Quaker observer John Parrish called the speech "mortifying to the Commissioners." Their party left the following day.[33]

The grand council's speech was an articulation of antiremoval arguments decades in the making. Long before the antiremoval debates of the 1820s and 1830s, the grand council formulated their own three-point rejection of removal. They highlighted the inconsistency and injustice of the core tenets of U.S. Indian policy—the right of conquest, the right of preemption, and the purchase of Indian lands. They recalled the long history of invasion that had pushed some Indigenous people into the Ohio country in the first place. They asked only for "the peaceable possession of a small part of our once great Country. Look back and view the lands from whence we

32. Brant, "Captain Brant's Journal of the Proceedings at the General Council," Aug. 7, 1793, in *CJGS,* II, 12 (quotations), 15, "From Heckewelder's Journal," Aug. 16, [1793], II, 24.

33. "Message from the Western Indians to the Commissioners of the United States," Aug. 13, 1793, in *CJGS,* II, 19–20 ("concession," 19, "affair," 20); Parrish, "Journals to Indian Treaties," Aug. 16, 1793, Ayer Collection ("satisfying"); Journey of the Western Commissioners, Aug. 16, 1793, TPP, LX, 173–173A; U.S. Commissioners of Indian Affairs to Confederate Indian Tribes, July 31, 1793, Lewis Cass Papers, box 5, folder 24, CL.

have been driven to this spot," the council told the commissioners. They informed them that "we can retreat no further, because the country behind hardly affords food for its present inhabitants. And we have therefore resolved, to leave our bones in this small space, to which we are now confined." Ultimately, the confederacy demanded the removal of white migrants in 1793.[34]

After the confederacy rejected federal terms and insisted on their right to remain in Indian country, President Washington and Secretary of War Knox waged a war to compel removal. U.S. general Anthony Wayne led an enlarged federal army—three thousand troops—into the Ohio country that summer. His troops kept busy. In December, they built Fort Recovery on the site of St. Clair's 1791 battle. The following summer, they marched to the Glaize. A deserter warned residents there of the advance of the army, and they evacuated to nearby British Fort Miamis. Seven miles from the fort, federal forces defeated the United Indian Nations at the Battle of Fallen Timbers. When the confederacy's men retreated to the safety of Fort Miamis, the fort's commanding officer refused them entry. As it became clear that their British allies had no intention of coming to their aid, federationists abandoned the field.[35]

After Fallen Timbers, Wayne's army destroyed the villages at the Glaize along with acres of cornfields and gardens that had fed thousands. Their crops and homes ruined, refugees of the Glaize moved into the vicinity of British Fort Miamis at the mouth of the Maumee River. In the immediate aftermath of the destruction, they depended on Fort Miamis for three thousand rations a day. By September, the banks of the Maumee "were thickly occupied with Indian huts and wigwams."[36]

According to American and British reports circulating that winter, the

34. "Message from the Western Indians to the Commissioners of the United States," Aug. 13, 1793, in *CJGS,* II, 20 (quotations); "To the Chiefs and Warriors of the Indian Nations Assembled at the Foot of the Miami Rapids," Aug. 16, 1793, TPP, LIX, 208. Quakers later interpreted this moment pithily as a negotiation interrupted by "bad spirits." See "Address from the Quakers in Pennsylvania, New Jersey, and Other Neighbouring Governments, by Their Representatives, Assembled at Philadelphia . . . ," May 22, 1795, AWP, XLI, 13.

35. Anthony Wayne to Thomas Posey, Jan. 21, 1794, Thomas Posey Collection, IHS; Dowd, *Spirited Resistance,* 113; Jortner, *Gods of Prophetstown,* 68.

36. William Mayne, "Memoranda by Lieut. Wm. Mayne on the Expedition to Detroit, Turtle Island, Fort Miamis, etc.," Sept. 26, 1794, in *CJGS,* III, 74 (quotation), R. G. England to J. G. Simcoe, Sept. 17, 1794, 96, "J. G. Simcoe's Diary of Journey to the Miamis River," September [1794], 98.

confederacy was deeply rent by British and Spanish politics. Brant observed that federationists were "in much Confusion" and "in bad Temper" over the British betrayal at Fallen Timbers. The negotiation of the Jay Treaty, completed in November 1794, resolved some of the long-standing diplomatic issues that had strained the relationship between the United States and Britain—most notably the arbitration of loyalist claims. Of significance for geopolitics in the western country, the Jay Treaty also confirmed the withdrawal of the British military from forts within the territory ceded to the United States in 1783. The negotiations had devastating effects for Native people north of the Ohio River. British withdrawal from the northwest posts left them without a powerful ally and strengthened a U.S. presence along the lower Great Lakes. Creek and Chickamauga Cherokee federationists faced new challenges in the South, too. They lost Spanish aid after Spain went to war with France in 1793. White Americans mounted a military campaign against Chickamauga Cherokees in 1794, and the resulting Treaty of Tellico Blockhouse temporarily ended their resistance.[37]

Meanwhile, through the winter, federationists sat in council at Detroit, debating whether to end the war by attending a council with the United States. One by one, the confederacy's leaders promised to participate in negotiations at the new U.S. fort at Greenville in what is now western Ohio. Some of the confederacy's war chiefs who had led resistance—Miami Little Turtle, Potawatomi Five Medals, and Shawnee Blue Jacket—eventually agreed to go, seeing few other options. As Oneida trader Sally Ainse reported to Brant, who had tried without success to maintain the unity of the Confederacy through the winter, "I am much afraid that your wampum and Speeches will be to little effect with the Indians, as they are sneaking off to General Wayne every day." At Greenville in the summer of 1795, 1,130 Delawares, Shawnees, Miamis, Wyandots, Ojibwes, Odawas, Potawatomis, Kickapoos, Weas, Piankeshaws, and Kaskaskias gathered for the council. Spectators and U.S. Army officers gathered, too, although they would be kept out of the council house "in ignorance" of the proceedings inside.[38]

37. "Extract of a Letter from Captain Joseph Brant to Joseph Chew Secretary of Indian Affairs . . . ," Oct. 22, 1794, in *CJGS,* III, 140–141 (quotations, 140). For the consequences of the Jay Treaty, see Timothy Pickering to Anthony Wayne, Apr. 15, 1795, AWP, XL, 50, Wayne to Thomas Pasteur, June 11, 1795, XLI, 59, Pickering to Wayne, June 17, 1795, XLI, 76; Dowd, *Spirited Resistance,* 112–113.

38. Sarah Ainse to Joseph Brant, Feb. 5, 1795, in *CJGS,* III, 287 ("I am much afraid"), R. G. England to J. G. Simcoe, Jan. 27, 1795, 274; John F. Carmichael, Diary, July 18, 1795, 47 ("ignorance"), 48, John F. Carmichael Collection, typed transcript, OHC; Anthony Wayne to Thomas Hart, Jan. 24, 1795, AWP, XXXIX, 32, "Summary of Speeches Delivered by Blue Jacket and Nyanymsecah, Two Shawanoe Chiefs and Tebe-

Both parties used geographic metaphors to open negotiations. In an adaptation of the Haudenosaunee Condolence ceremony, U.S. and Native representatives began their conferences by using spatial metaphors to clear the ground of the physical remains of warfare. In their speeches, they buried the bones of the dead. Wyandot headman Tarhe went through the steps of burying the bodies of the American soldiers "that they may never again be seen by our posterity." Wayne echoed Tarhe so that "no bloody traces will ever lead to the graves of your departed heroes." Symbolically burying the dead was crucial to the Condolence ceremony, which was meant to welcome outsiders into Haudenosaunee villages by ameliorating their burdens and grievances. The ritual's conventions had become such a vital part of diplomacy in eastern North America over the course of the seventeenth and eighteenth centuries that federal officials also readily adopted it. Emissaries on both sides took turns removing obstructions from the paths that had led them to the council, thus clearing the landscape of violence so that all communications could be clearly heard.[39]

Federal officials made dramatic concessions at the 1795 Greenville Treaty. Secretary of War Pickering had earlier instructed Wayne to negotiate for all of the Ohio Valley west to what is now Illinois. After six years of war, however, Pickering decided to settle for a different land cession, one that would open only two-thirds of what is now Ohio to white settlement. The line would run south to the Ohio River from the meeting point of the Miami and St. Mary's Rivers. All of the land north and west of the Greenville line (what is now Indiana, Illinois, Michigan, and Wisconsin) would remain Indian country. Pickering explained that this change in federal policy was necessary, "for *peace* and not *increase* of *territory* has been the object

---

bockiska a Delaware Chief at Greenville to Major General Wayne," 56, Wayne to Henry Knox, Feb. 12, 1795, 60; Wayne, "To the Cherokees, Now Settled on the Head Waters of Scioto," Aug. 3, 1795, in *ASPIA,* I, 582; Cayton, "'Noble Actors' upon 'the Theatre of Honour': Power and Civility in the Treaty of Greenville," in Cayton and Fredrika J. Teute, eds., *Contact Points: American Frontiers from the Mohawk Valley to the Mississippi, 1750–1830* (Williamsburg, Va., and Chapel Hill, N.C., 1998), 256–257. For the spectacle of eighteenth-century treaties, see Merrell, *Into the American Woods,* 256–270.

39. "Minutes of a Treaty with the Tribes of Indians Called the Wyandots, Delawares, Shawanese, Ottawas, Chippewas, Pattawatamies, Miamies, Eel River, Kickapoos, Piankeshaws, and Kaskaskias, Begun at Greenville, on the 16th Day of June, and Ended on the 10th Day of August, 1795," in *ASPIA,* I, 571 ("that they may never"), 573 ("no bloody"); Merrell, *Into the American Woods,* 20–22; David Andrew Nichols, *Red Gentlemen and White Savages: Indians, Federalists, and the Search for Order on the American Frontier* (Charlottesville, Va., 2008), 172–173; Colin G. Calloway, *Pen and Ink Witchcraft: Treaties and Treaty Making in American Indian History* (Oxford, 2013), 16.

of this expensive War." Pickering's comments were, of course, disingenuous. Increase of territory had certainly been the object of the war. But, after years of expensive and debilitating conflict in the West, federal officials had taken up some arguments of the confederacy about Native rights to the soil. Pickering proposed a different boundary "for the sake of peace."[40]

Throughout the Greenville Treaty proceedings, speakers argued about the proper geographic form the boundary should take. At issue were multiple, conflicting ways of imagining the land north of the Ohio River. The attendees clarified those differences when debating how to organize the territory to avoid conflict and how to mark each party's claims on the landscape. On the eve of negotiations, for example, Wayne, mulling the consequences of the proposed border for a lasting peace, suggested that the boundaries chosen by Pickering and the War Department "will make the White and Red people too near neighbours, and be productive of constant and mutual distrust, animosity and murders." Wayne instead wished "that a kind of consecrated ground" should separate them. That buffer would be held by Congress, and the government would "neither sell or suffer it to be settled upon any occasion or pretext whatever."[41]

Like others who promoted removal in the 1790s, Wayne was creating his own theory of separation. What distance would position white and Native neighborhoods too close together? Wayne imagined that an uninhabited buffer zone between settlements might solve the problem of proximity. By moving Native peoples away at a distance, he presumed that the "consecrated ground" between the two neighborhoods would foreclose any interaction—violent or peaceful. Yet he also issued a caveat to his idea of a neutral buffer zone. The space between U.S. and Native territory would not be settled by anyone "until some distant and future day, when circumstances might render it expedient and proper." Wayne foresaw a "future day" when a buffer zone would no longer be necessary, although he gave little indication of how that might come about.[42]

40. Timothy Pickering to Anthony Wayne, Apr. 8, 1795, AWP, XL, 35 (quotations), Pickering to Wayne, Apr. 15, 1795, 49, Pickering to Wayne, June 29, 1795, XLI, 115.

41. Wayne to Pickering, May 13, 1795, AWP, XL, 114 (quotations), Wayne to Pickering, Feb. 2, 1795, XLII, 87; Wayne to Pickering, May 15, 1795, in Richard C. Knopf, ed., *Anthony Wayne, a Name in Arms: Soldier, Diplomat, Defender of Expansion Westward of a Nation: The Wayne-Knox-Pickering-McHenry Correspondence* ([Pittsburgh, Pa.], 1960), 417. For neighborhood, see James E. Lewis, Jr., *The American Union and the Problem of Neighborhood: The United States and the Collapse of the Spanish Empire, 1783–1829* (Chapel Hill, N.C., 1998); Paulett, *Empire of Small Places,* 184–185.

42. Anthony Wayne to Timothy Pickering, May 13, 1795, AWP, XL, 114 (quotations),

For Native leaders, the proposed boundary tested the unity of a country held in common. The goal of the United Indian Nations had been to consider the entire Ohio Valley as belonging to the whole so as to secure the right to remain for all, but many chiefs began to press their own claims by specifying their borders. Ojibwe leader Masass used the treaty to insist that Ojibwes, Odawas, and Potawatomis also claimed ownership over the Ohio country and thus should be paid for ceding it. For his part, Miami Little Turtle insisted that the Ohio country from the Scioto River to the Wabash belonged to the Miamis. Meanwhile, Wyandot chief Tarhe tried to keep the confederacy's understandings of the dish with one spoon at the forefront of negotiations even as he acquiesced to Wayne's boundary line. He reminded the council "that no one in particular can justly claim this ground; it belongs, in common, to us all."[43]

Little Turtle made an alternative argument to explain Miami claims. Since the beginning of English colonization, Anglo-Americans had accused Natives of underusing the land, and they attacked Native land rights by arguing that white migrants would put it to better employment. Little Turtle also posited that a history of use determined rights to land, and he pointed to physical evidence to make his case. "The print of my ancestors' houses are everywhere to be seen in this portion," he explained. Little Turtle made territorial claims by referencing physical structures on the landscape and a long history of occupation by one's ancestors. Wayne countered that the marks of French possessions or "houses"—forts—were also everywhere in the Ohio Valley, and those structures were now in the possession of the British who would, for their part, turn them over to the United States. Miami rights to the soil could not be proven through the remains of houses, Wayne argued, because structures, like territory, changed hands. Physical evidence of use and occupation could not override, in his eyes, treaty marks on a piece of paper.[44]

When Little Turtle suggested an alternative boundary line further east, Wayne dismissed it as too "crooked." In treaty negotiations, a boundary line had its own inherent properties. When Wayne used the word *crooked,*

Wayne to Pickering, Feb. 2, 1795, XLII, 87; Wayne to Pickering, May 15, 1795, in Knopf, ed., *Anthony Wayne,* 417; Pickering to Wayne, June 29, 1795, AWP, XLI, 115.

43. "Minutes of a Treaty with the Tribes of Indians . . . Begun at Greenville," in *ASPIA,* I, 570–572 (quotation, 571); Carmichael, Diary, July 21, 1795, 58–59, July 22, 1795, 62–65, Carmichael Collection; Lakomäki, "'Our Line,'" *Journal of the Early Republic,* XXXIV (2014), 603.

44. "Minutes of a Treaty with the Tribes of Indians . . . Begun at Greenville," in *ASPIA,* I, 570 (quotation), 573.

he meant that the line was deceptive. In this case, Wayne professed that the line might be unrecognizable or misunderstood because multiple roads ran parallel to it. He was also calling on Anglo-American expectations about the proper way to delineate landed property. Europeans had been demarcating property through survey, in which land was parceled out by a grid, since the sixteenth century. The grid made ownership "legible" and thus "governable" by the state. Federal plans for the Ohio country depended on grid surveys. The 1787 Northwest Ordinance and promotional literature used the grid to rationalize and claim land. Manasseh Cutler's 1787 map of the Ohio Company Purchase, for example, overlaid a series of perfect squares onto the natural features of the Ohio Valley in a neat calculation of the promise of property ownership in the Ohio Company settlement.[45]

It was the boundary line proposed by the U.S., however, that departed from convention. Most treaty lines followed topographical features, rather than the straight lines of the cadastral survey. The Proclamation Line of 1763 followed the Appalachian Mountains. The 1768 Treaty of Fort Stanwix followed the Ohio River for much of its course. And Joseph Brant's proposed Muskingum boundary followed the Muskingum River. Native peoples used rivers to mark boundaries between themselves and other Indigenous polities. So did Europeans, who appreciated the geographical determinism of natural boundaries by the mid-eighteenth century. Rivers seemed relatively permanent and stable in a world marked by boundaries that could be otherwise easily shifted. The Greenville line, by contrast, connected significant historical or military markers but followed no particular topographical markers. It is the Greenville line that appears "crooked" when drawn on a map, stretched in a series of imposing straight lines across a vast swath of land that later became Ohio.[46]

Wayne did not root his boundary in the supposed rationality of the cadastral survey but in emotion and sentiment. The line turned at historically significant junctures—Loramie's store, Fort Recovery, and the mouth of the Kentucky River created, in Wayne's opinion, incontrovertible markers that would dispel confusion. Pierre Loramie's trading post, for example, had been built in 1769 on one of the principle routes taken by Natives moving

45. Ibid., 578 ("crooked"); Martin Brückner, *The Geographic Revolution in Early America: Maps, Literacy, and National Identity* (Williamsburg, Va., and Chapel Hill, N.C., 2006), 20–21 ("legible," 21); Manasseh Cutler, *The First Map and Description of Ohio: 1787*, ed. P. Lee Phillips (Washington, D.C., 1918).

46. Sahlins, *Boundaries*, 97–98; Sahlins, "Natural Frontiers Revisited," *American Historical Review*, XCV (1990), 1435–1436; Hudson, *Creek Paths and Federal Roads*, 19–20; Paulett, *Empire of Small Places*, 52–53.

between the Great Lakes and the Ohio River. Loramie's store had been a common launching point for Shawnee raids in Kentucky during the Revolution, so infamous that General George Rogers Clark had burned it to the ground during a 1782 campaign against the Shawnee.[47]

Where the line turned south at Fort Recovery, Wayne insisted that the spot would also be recognizable to Native peoples and white Americans alike, as it was "made famous by two Memorable actions." Wayne built Fort Recovery on the site of the United Indian Nations' victory over St. Clair's army in 1791. The construction of Fort Recovery purposefully reclaimed that ground as U.S. territory. Wayne argued that Fort Recovery was an appropriate location to mark the line because the United States had been "*severely* defeated, so as to leave an indelible impression upon the minds of the present Generation, but also upon the minds, of their Children and Childrens Children to the end of time." The powerful memory of defeat, he believed, would make Fort Recovery consecrated ground, and that history would be apparent to future generations. Both locations thus turned on a history of conflict to create a shared geography. Wayne's choice of Loramie's store and Fort Recovery justified the cession and federal conquest by calling on the regenerative violence of war. His invocation of war gave white Americans a claim to the land through their bloodshed. Federal officials had often portrayed Native boundary marking as rooted in sentiment rather than enlightenment rationality, but Wayne flipped the script. His boundary line was profoundly emotional.[48]

The Treaty of Greenville brought peace to the Ohio River valley through the coerced consent of the Delawares, Shawnees, Miamis, Wyandots, Ojibwes, Odawas, Potawatomis, Kickapoos, Weas, Piankeshaws, and Kaskaskias, who were forced to give up their claims to land north of the Ohio River. After nearly two months in council, all of the confederacy's delegates except Little Turtle signed the Treaty of Greenville on August 2. The treaty agreement ceded two-thirds of what would become Ohio and a portion of southern Indiana to white settlement and guaranteed free passage to white Americans through Indian country to and from sixteen U.S. forts and trading posts on smaller reserves across the Great Lakes region. Ten days later,

47. "Treaty with the Wyandot, etc., 1795," in Charles J. Kappler, ed., *Indian Affairs: Laws and Treaties,* II, *Treaties* (Washington, D.C., 1904), 39–40.

48. Anthony Wayne to Timothy Pickering, Sept. 2, 1795, in Knopf, ed., *Anthony Wayne,* 448 (quotations); R. Douglas Hurt, *The Ohio Frontier: Crucible of the Old Northwest, 1720–1830* (Bloomington, Ind., 1996), 208–209; Richard Slotkin, *Regeneration through Violence: The Mythology of the American Frontier: 1600–1860* (Norman, Okla., 2000).

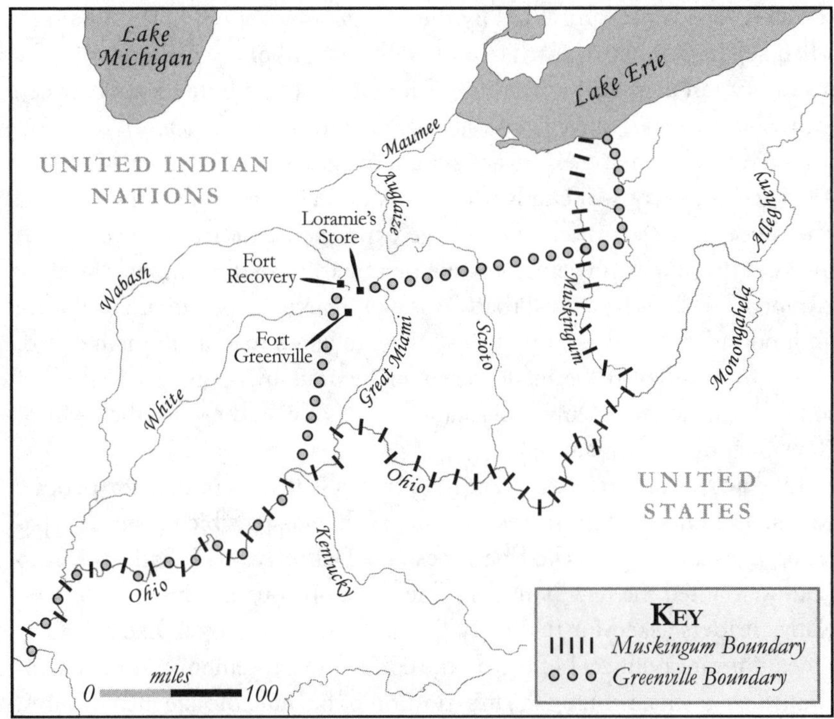

MAP 4. *Treaty of Greenville, 1795. Drawn by Rebecca Wrenn*

in a private meeting with Wayne, Little Turtle, left with few options, also accepted the terms of the treaty.[49]

U.S. commissioners promised to run a permanent border to protect Indian country and to secure the right of Native peoples to remain. For the sake of peace, Federal officials made a permanent boundary the focus of the negotiations at Greenville and their aftermath. The work of carving out the line prompted a string of correspondence and negotiations over the proper form the boundary should take so as to assure its permanence. Wayne wanted the line between Fort Recovery and the mouth of the Kentucky River to be "a wide avenue." The idea of an open road as a boundary was reminiscent of Wayne's theory that peace could be ensured by a "con-

49. The fullest account of the Greenville proceedings is Cayton, "'Noble Actors' upon 'the Theatre of Honour,'" in Cayton and Teute, eds., *Contact Points,* 235–269. See also Dowd, *Spirited Resistance,* 113; Richard White, *The Middle Ground: Indians, Empires, and Republics in the Great Lakes Region, 1650–1815* (1991; rpt. New York, 2011), 471–472; Taylor, *Divided Ground,* 294; James Joseph Buss, *Winning the West with Words: Language and Conquest in the Lower Great Lakes* (Norman, Okla., 2011), 15–41.

secrated" space held unsettled by the federal government until some time when separation between white and Native neighbors would no longer be necessary. An unsettled, open border might serve as a buffer zone between the two territories. Native people also wanted the line to be a road. Requesting ten to twelve "axe-men" to assist him, the line's surveyor, Israel Ludlow, informed Surveyor General Rufus Putnam that "some of the Chiefs of the Shawanoe and Delaware nations have expressed a desire to have a great road cut that it may prevent the white people from settling on their hunting grounds." Although "a great road" was a more expensive and unusual form for a boundary to take, all parties seemed to agree that, as Putnam noted, "these lines ought to be made very conspicuous by opening a Vestige of some feet in width." Only a permanent vestige would secure the right of Native peoples to remain.[50]

Like a river or stream, a great road was not just a conduit for people, goods, and information. It was also one of the most visible means of separating two landscapes. The Shawnees and Delawares who had spoken to Ludlow wanted the new boundary line to be obvious to white interlopers. Native leaders asked for the treaty line to be clear and open like a road—a metaphor for political honesty in the condolence ceremony. Putnam complained that when running the first portion of the line, the axe men he hired had "effected nothing." "That line," he continued, "is no more conspicuous than any other line of survey in the woods." Putnam understood that "what the Indians want is a line so opened that a person will not be likely to pass without seeing it." Both Native and Federal officials were determined that the line should be an open space, so wide that it could mark the end of one territory and the beginning of another.[51]

No matter how open and clear a border appeared to be, many of the Greenville Treaty's Native attendees remained opposed to the cession itself. Federationists continued to resist the line, even as Ludlow went about his work. In 1799, when Ludlow returned to the Ohio country to finish marking the Greenville line, his Native escorts did not show up to meet him. Surveys were an extension of the treaty-making process, and federal officials

50. Wayne to Pickering, Sept. 2, 1795, in Knopf, ed., *Anthony Wayne,* 448 ("wide"); Wayne to Pickering, Feb. 2, 1795, AWP, XLII, 87 ("consecrated"); Rufus Putnam to Oliver Wolcott, Mar. 15, 1799, ASCP, box 5, folder 3 ("axe-men"); Putnam to [Wolcott], Jan. 25, 1797, in *TPUS,* II, 589 ("these lines ought"), Putnam to [Wolcott], May 18, 1797, 606.

51. Putnam to Wolcott, Mar. 15, 1799, ASCP, box 5, folder 3 (quotations). For roads as spaces of encounter, see Hudson, *Creek Paths and Federal Roads,* 6; Paulett, *Empire of Small Places,* 115–141.

who wanted land cessions to be accepted in Indian country always asked Native emissaries to be present for the running of the lines. Ludlow vaguely noted that the Shawnees and Odawas he spoke with appeared alarmed by reports of Chickasaw raids, but he insisted that the failure of his escorts to appear was "some kind of policy" to prevent the running of the line. Secretary of War James McHenry blamed the dissension on "the insinuations and practices of interested Indians."[52]

McHenry dismissed the opposition, but there was real and widespread organization against the Greenville cessions. That summer, some Shawnees circulated speeches against the running of the line that were stoked by rumors in the backcountry about the sale of Louisiana to the French in 1798—a prospect that signaled the potential return of their French alliance of the early eighteenth century. The Shawnees met in council to discuss a revision of the Greenville Treaty. Federal officials observed with trepidation that fewer Native visitors trickled into Detroit, which had switched from British to U.S. hands in 1796 as a result of the Jay Treaty. On their way to assist Ludlow with the running of the line, two soldiers were detained near Greenville by a group of Natives who "told them that they must go no farther" and "that they would all be killed if they continued on." Their objections made apparent the depth of ongoing Native resistance to dispossession years after the Treaty of Greenville made the Ohio cessions seem like a certainty in the East.[53]

While Ludlow ran the lines in the Ohio country, federal officials and legislators in Philadelphia wrote the new boundary into federal law. In the 1790s, Congress passed several Trade and Intercourse Acts that codified the relationship between the federal government and Native nations in trade, diplomacy, justice, and land sales. The 1796 iteration of the Trade and Intercourse Acts defined Indian country in federal statue law for the first time, naming the new northern boundaries alongside the southern boundaries that protected Creek and Cherokee lands from Georgia and Tennessee migrants.[54]

52. Israel Ludlow to Rufus Putnam, July 20, 1799, in *TPUS,* III, 59 ("some"), Putnam to [Oliver Wolcott], Aug. 15, 1799, 61; James McHenry to Arthur St. Clair, Aug. 15, 1799, War Department Papers, NL ("insinuations").

53. Rufus Putnam to [Oliver Wolcott], Sept. 18, 1799, in *TPUS,* III, 68 (quotations); James McHenry to Arthur St. Clair, Aug. 30, 1799, War Department Papers; McHenry to the Chiefs and Warriors Representatives of the Wyandots, Delawares, Shawanoes, Ottawas, Chipewas, Potawatimes, Miamis, Eel River, Weeas, Kickapoos, Piankashaws, and Kaskaskias, n.d., Lewis Cass Papers, box 1, folder 3, CL.

54. Francis Paul Prucha, *American Indian Policy in the Formative Years: The Indian Trade and Intercourse Acts, 1790–1834* (Cambridge, Mass., 1962), 48–49.

Promises of permanence, however, were at odds with the language that federal legislators and officials used to describe the new boundary line. The Greenville Treaty itself laid the groundwork for dispossession by giving the right of preemption to the United States and determining that future agreements would be made with individual nations rather than the confederacy, a significant imposition on Native sovereignty that was intended to break apart unity. The 1796 Trade and Intercourse Act provided for the boundaries of Indian country to be clearly marked. Yet it also included the provision that if the lines were "varied" by subsequent treaties, the act's provisions would apply to the newly delineated territory. Federal officials expected future land sales. Pickering, for example, informed Wayne that he should not ask for too large of a cession at Greenville. Rather, he should look forward to a time after the British evacuation of Great Lakes posts when land dispossession would be supposedly simpler and "we can obtain every thing we shall want with a tenth part of the trouble and difficulty which you would now have to encounter."[55]

It was no accident that the line sowed the seeds of future removal. The most valuable and most desired lands fell along survey lines, pushing settlement forward to the edges. Although mapmakers effortlessly recorded the treaty line on maps as a straight line running across the upper third of the state of Ohio, this is not how Ludlow himself experienced his laborious work between 1797 and 1799. As Angela Pulley Hudson has noted, through the eighteenth century, surveying and land speculation went hand in hand. Surveyors "performed a sort of resource reconnaissance as they passed through Indian lands." Ludlow himself was both a speculator and surveyor, and his account of the running of the line makes this evident. As he marked trees on the landscape and distances in his journal, he also took detailed notes about land quality: "Through a brushy plain of a good quality for the production of small grain" or "Salt may probably be made here," he noted. The journal was a precise record of his path and the agricultural promise of the ceded lands. The information that surveyors like Ludlow recorded could be used for future profit and speculation.[56]

55. An Act to Regulate Trade and Intercourse with the Indian Tribes, and to Preserve Peace on the Frontiers, Pub. L. No. 4-30, 1 Stat. 469 (1796) ("varied"); Timothy Pickering to Anthony Wayne, Apr. 15, 1795, in Knopf, ed., *Anthony Wayne,* 405 ("we can obtain"); Taylor, *Divided Ground,* 293.

56. Hudson, *Creek Paths and Federal Roads,* 42 ("performed"); Israel Ludlow, "Field Notes of the Indian Boundary Line from Lorramie's Creek to the Muskingum River as Determined by the Treaty of Greeneville," Aug. 3, 1795, Israel Ludlow Papers, 1 ("brushy"), 31 ("Salt"), OHC.

Ludlow, Pickering, and other federal officials anticipated future land sales because the demand for Ohio country land was so high in the Atlantic states. As metaphors, roads could signify open communication and clear boundaries, but they could also set the terms for future land sales. Roads encouraged travel and linked white Americans in the East to what they thought of as the backcountry. Soon after the Battle of Fallen Timbers in 1794, eager migrants capitalized on the changing political tides in the Northwest Territory and set out for the Ohio country by the thousands. In 1795, Richard England, the British commandant at Detroit, reported to Governor John Graves Simcoe that "purchases are daily making in all quarters from the Indians, with hopes of their being ratified by Congress or General Wayne" at the Greenville council. Between 1790 and 1800, the white and Black population of the Ohio country rose from three thousand to more than forty-five thousand. Another observer likened the great tide of migrants swelling west to madness, a greedy "passion which amounts to a species of mania for migrating to the Westward."[57]

Access shaped the geography of new settlements in the Ohio Valley. Migrants clustered along the Ohio River and in the Scioto and Miami River valleys on the tracts of land that were most affordable and accessible from the East and South. For decades, white migrants had made their way into the territory by embarking on the Ohio River at Pittsburgh, or crossing by ferry at Wheeling, Virginia. In 1796, Virginia colonel Ebenezer Zane successfully petitioned Congress to lay out an overland route through what is now southern Ohio. Completed the following year, Zane's Trace remained little more than a path for the next decade, but it was the shortest route into the territory and the only overland road bringing migrants into the Ohio country before the War of 1812. Such schemes promoted affordable land acquisition and enriched speculators' pockets. Their effect was striking. In 1800, new towns clustered along the Ohio River, which had long been the major conduit into the Ohio Valley. By 1810, nearly half of U.S. migrants lived a considerable distance north of the Ohio River, in the Virginia Military Tract, above Cincinnati, or along Zane's Trace.[58]

The realities of dispossession on the ground together with the conflicting language of federal officials created strange cultural dissonances in the work

57. R. G. England to J. G. Simcoe, June 18, 1795, in *CJGS,* IV, 29 ("purchases"); John T. Griffith, *Rev. Morgan John Rhys, "The Welsh Baptist Hero of Civil and Religious Liberty of the Eighteenth Century"* (Lansford, Pa., 1899), 115 ("passion"); Patrick Griffin, *American Leviathan: Empire, Nation, and Revolutionary Frontier* (New York, 2008), 252.

58. Hurt, *Ohio Frontier,* 197, 262.

of U.S. geographers. They quickly celebrated the Greenville line as permanent. The line appeared on many period maps published by Connecticut minister Jedidiah Morse and the Philadelphia printer Mathew Carey. Morse and Carey marked the treaty line in their primers to celebrate the victory of the United States over the confederacy. In 1796, Morse explained a map of the Ohio Territory by declaring that "the settlement of this country was checked for several years by an unhappy Indian war. Peace is now restored, and an advantageous treaty concluded with the Indians, by General Wayne, at Greenville, in June, 1795." Maps in the early Republic celebrated national expansion. Like Wayne, early national geographers justified the Greenville line by rewriting the 1790s as a story of land purchase through suffering and bloodshed.[59]

Mapmakers, geographers, and printers embedded the Greenville line in national memory and consciousness through the War of 1812. Charlestown, Massachusetts, printer Samuel Etheridge reproduced the line in an 1804 map. In 1805, Carey was still using the pages of his own pocket atlas to celebrate the "vast tract of country" that "was peaceably ceded to the United States" at Greenville. Carey continued to mark the line through the 1814 edition of his *General Atlas.* Massachusetts minister Thaddeus Harris portrayed the Greenville boundary when he reprinted Rufus Putnam's *Map of the State of Ohio* in his 1805 text about his journey to the Ohio country. By 1812, Scottish mapmaker John Melish's neat survey of the Ohio country portrayed the state as a series of orderly surveys with a blank empty space above the Greenville line to represent Indian country.[60]

In practice, however, federal officials never enforced the border. Local

59. Jedidiah Morse, *Geography Made Easy: Being an Abridgement of the American University Geography; Containing Astronomical Geography; Discovery and General Description of America; General View of the United States; Particular Accounts of the United States of America, and of All the Kingdoms, States, and Republics in the Known World, etc.*, 5th ed. (Boston, 1796), 207.

60. [Mathew Carey], *Carey's American Pocket Atlas; Containing Twenty Maps . . . with a Brief Description of Each State, and of Louisiana: Also, the Census of the Inhabitants of the United States, for 1801; the Exports from the United States for Ten Years*, 3d ed. (Philadelphia, 1805), 79 (quotations); "The State of Ohio," in Carey, *Carey's General Atlas, Improved and Enlarged: Being a Collection of Maps of the World and Quarters, Their Principal Empires, Kingdoms, etc.* . . . (Philadelphia, 1814); Samuel Etheridge, *Map of the Northern Parts of the United States of America by Abraham Bradley Jr. Corrected by the Author* ([Charlestown, Mass., 1804]); "Map of the State of Ohio," in Thaddeus Mason Harris, *The Journal of a Tour into the Territory Northwest of the Alleghany Mountains; Made in the Spring of the Year 1803; with a Geographical and Historical Account of the State of Ohio; Illustrated with Original Maps and Views* (Boston, 1805); John Melish, *Ohio* ([Columbus, Ohio, 1812]).

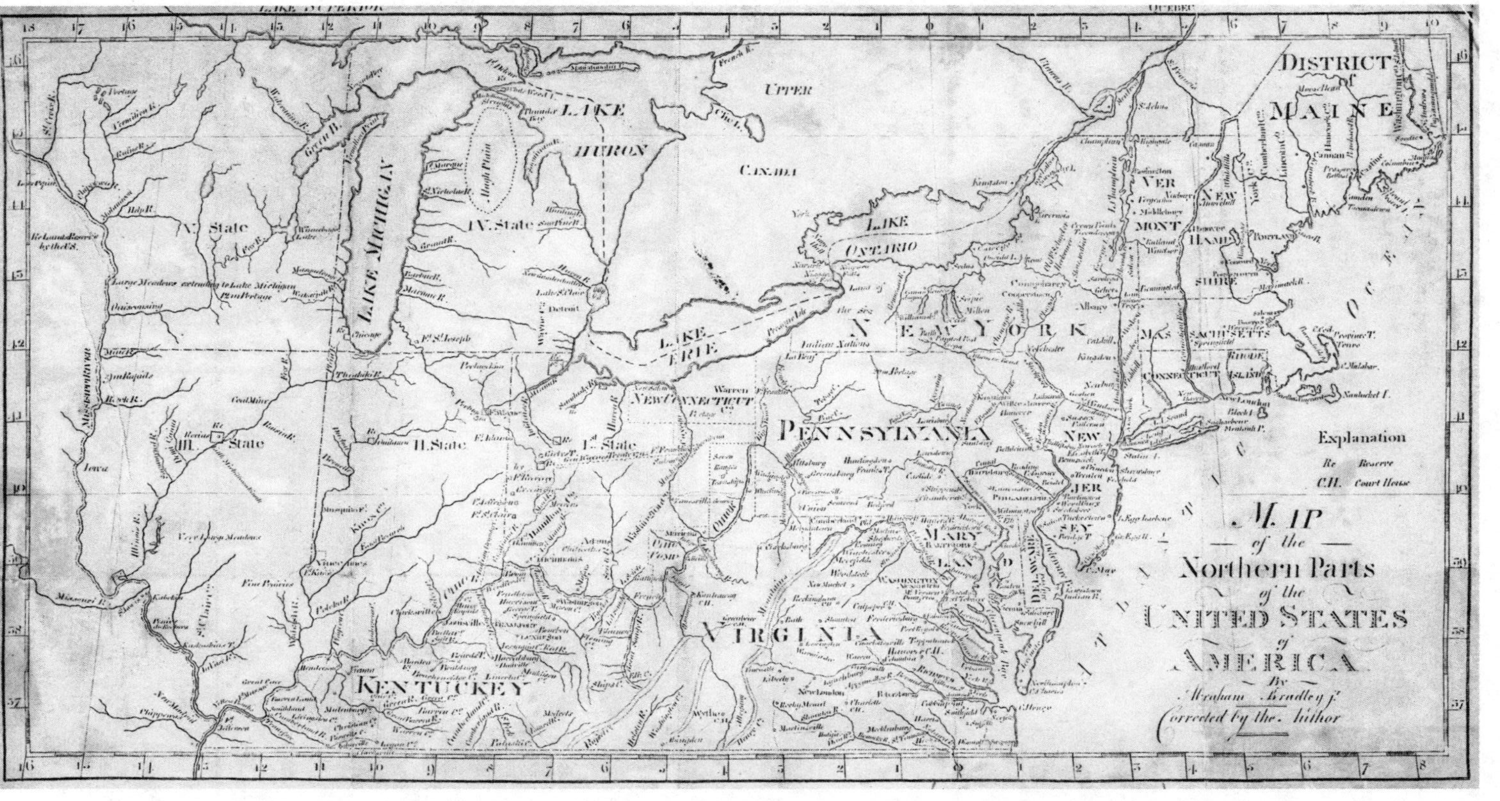

FIGURE 8. *Abraham Bradley,* Map of the Northern Parts of the United States of America. *1804. Lionel Pincus and Princess Firyal Map Division. Maps of North America. Courtesy New York Public Library*

FIGURE 9. *Rufus Putnam,* Map of the State of Ohio. *[1805]. From Thaddeus Mason Harris,* The Journal of a Tour into the Territory Northwest of the Alleghany Mountains: Made in the Spring of the Year 1803 . . . Illustrated with Original Maps and Views. *[Boston, 1805]. Geography and Map Division, G4080 1804 .P8. Courtesy Library of Congress*

FIGURE 10. *John Melish,* Ohio. *[1812]. Geography and Map Division, G4080 1812 .M4. Courtesy Library of Congress*

officials had wide discretion in curtailing migration. The federal government had only weak coercive power in the territories. As a result, individuals in the Ohio country determined what the border would mean. Moreover, federal officials never intended the boundary to be permanent, despite demands by Miami and Wyandot speakers and federal promises that it should be clearly marked for posterity. Indeed, only eight years later, the Jefferson administration would once again open negotiations to amend the boundary line created by Greenville.

It became harder for Indigenous people to preserve the right to remain in the Ohio country after 1795. Those who remained sometimes did so by moving further north of the treaty line to the Maumee and Lake Erie watersheds. Despite the wide "vestige" that federal officials promised, the treaty failed to stem the racial conflict that had characterized Ohio Valley land dispossession for decades. In 1803, the eastern end of the dish with one spoon was renamed Ohio and admitted to the union as the seventeenth state on the heels of Kentucky (1792) and Tennessee (1796). The remaking of Indian country north of the Ohio River made it more difficult for Shawnees, Delawares, Wyandots, Miamis, Odawas, Ojibwes, Senecas, and Shawnees in the southern Great Lakes to remain north of the Ohio River—although they did remain.

After 1803, when the United States purchased a swath of land west of the Mississippi that the French called Louisiana, it changed the pace of removal, but not its calculus. In 1800, Spain restored Louisiana to French control with the Treaty of San Ildefonso. In 1803, reeling from the impact of the Haitian Revolution in Saint Domingue, Napoleon decided to sell New Orleans to U.S. commissioners. The Louisiana Purchase doubled the size of the United States, setting off many decades of discussion and argument over the purpose to which those lands should be put. The Mississippi River boundary might have slowed white migration west before 1803, but after the Louisiana Purchase, there was little barrier to stop it. Federal Indian policy quickly adapted to the new sense of national space. After 1803, the Republican presidents of the early nineteenth century—Thomas Jefferson, James Madison, and James Monroe—imagined the Mississippi River as the natural boundary that would separate Native and white settlements.

Although U.S. officials expressed the importance of firm boundaries, they also presumed that later cessions would follow. They envisioned the kind of bloodless revolution that Washington had outlined but had not realized after the end of the American Revolution in 1783. The ease with which federal officials broke old boundaries and replaced them with new ones accelerated removal in the era before Andrew Jackson. Despite the attempts of Native negotiators to use the Greenville treaty line to protect their right to remain, borders were no longer defenses against invasion from outsiders—they were the means of dispossession.[61]

61. Lakomäki, "'Our Line,'" *Journal of the Early Republic*, XXXIV (2014), 598.

CHAPTER 4
THE TOOLS OF "CIVILIZATION"
Restricting Migration in the West

In 1807, the Odawa messenger Le Maigouis left his village L'Arbre Croche on the eastern shore of Lake Michigan and journeyed north to Lake Superior to spread news of a prophet who had arisen among the Shawnee. Le Maigouis traveled across what would become Michigan and Wisconsin, working his way from village to village—from Michilimackinac to Grand River, Saginaw Bay to Sault Ste. Marie, and on to Whitefish Bay. At every stop, he told assembled men, women, and children that Tenskwatawa, a Shawnee prophet sent by the Great Spirit, promised that those who renounced their corrupting relationships with whites would reap spiritual and material rewards. From Le Maigouis, Tenskwatawa's message passed to other emissaries, who brought it as far north and west as the Red River and Lake Winnipeg, where it circulated among the Saulteaux. Tenskwatawa had assembled his followers at Greenville, the site of the Treaty of Greenville, and told them to give up alcohol, domestic animals, Euro-American styles of dress, and their business with white traders. He preached racial separation—"My White and Red Children were thus marked with different colours, that they might be a separate people," he said. His religious message came amid the economic dislocations wrought by European colonialism. Le Maigouis told each assembly that white Americans "grew from the Scum of the great water, when it was troubled by the Evil Spirit—And the froth was driven into the Woods by a strong east wind .... They are unjust—They have taken away your Lands which were not made for them." When the U.S. agent at Michilimackinac learned of Le Maigouis's travels, he saw danger not just in the Prophet's words but also in Le Maigouis's ability to carry them vast distances.[1]

1. J. Dunham to William Hull, May 20, 1807, *MPHC,* XL, 123–127, "Speech of Indian Chief to Various Tribes [Enclosure in Dunham to Hall, May 20]," 127–133 ("my White," 131, "grew from the Scum," 129); Laura Peers, *The Ojibwa of Western Canada, 1780 to 1870* (St. Paul, Minn., 1994), 85–87; Adam Jortner, *The Gods of Prophetstown: The Battle of Tippecanoe and the Holy War for the American Frontier* (New York, 2012), 135–136; John Tanner, *The Falcon: A Narrative of the Captivity and Adventures of John Tanner* (New York, 1994), 144–147; Harry W. Duckworth, ed., *Friends, Foes, and Furs: George*

The agent sprang to action, promising his superiors that he would send people to arrest the Odawa messenger and his party on their return and jail them for their insidious mobility. In the meantime, Le Maigouis's speech had already begun circulating far beyond the places he had visited. It appeared in newspapers up and down the Atlantic coast from Savannah, Georgia, to Portland, Maine, causing panic among state officials and stirring up fear among residents of Ohio. The circulation of his words raised the specter of war and of the pan-Indian alliance that had halted U.S. expansion in the 1780s and 1790s.[2]

Le Maigouis's words were exceptional, but his travels were not. For centuries, the peoples of the Ohio country and the Great Lakes had been in motion. In the upper Great Lakes, Anishinaabe peoples like Le Maigouis's Odawas excercised power through kinship and migration. Exogamous marriage bound together patrilineal lineages into a world of mobile villages—an "expansive weave of relations" that allowed the Anishinaabeg to control most of the Great Lakes region and the activities of the European empires that attempted to trade there. In the seventeenth century, Wendats, Odawas, Eries, Potawatomis, and Miamis in the region all relocated to avoid Haudenosaunee warfare or in response to the spread of European diseases. By the early eighteenth century, the Ohio Valley and lower Great Lakes—depopulated by disease, slaving, and raiding in the seventeenth century—were home to thousands of refugees of dispossession and to Native people who had moved to capitalize on the fur trade. Natives who filled the Ohio country used travel to make new political alliances for their own protection. Movement was important to securing subsistence, to gathering together in composite towns, and to practicing diplomacy. When Le Maigouis became an emissary of pan-Indianism in 1807, he journeyed on routes that others had traveled many times before.[3]

Nelson's Lake Winnipeg Journals, 1804–1822 (Montreal, 2019), 102–104. Thank you to Doug Winiarski for sharing these sources from his forthcoming work with me.

2. Dunham to Hull, May 20, 1807, *MPHC,* XL, 125. For fear of a pan-Indian alliance, see Robert M. Owens, *Red Dreams, White Nightmares: Pan-Indian Alliances in the Anglo-American Mind, 1763–1815* (Norman, Okla., 2015); Patrick Bottiger, *The Borderland of Fear: Vincennes, Prophetstown, and the Invasion of the Miami Homeland* (Lincoln, Neb., 2016).

3. Michael A. McDonnell, *Masters of Empire: Great Lakes Indians and the Making of America* (New York, 2015), 8 (quotation); Dunham to Hull, May 20, 1807, *MPHC,* XL, 125. For Anishinaabe mobility and kinship ties, see Michael Witgen, *An Infinity of Nations: How the Native New World Shaped Early North America* (Philadelphia, 2012), esp. 42, 55, 69–115; McDonnell, *Masters of Empire,* esp. 7–13. For dispersal and re-

Precisely because travel was so important to creating political connections across the Ohio Valley and Great Lakes, U.S. territorial officials indicted Indigenous people as peculiarly mobile. U.S. agents, legislators, and reformers believed that movement proved Natives were unsteady in their political attachments, or were hunters rather than farmers, and thus had no rights to land. In the early nineteenth century, U.S. agents held in their hands only paper claims to power in Indian country. They believed that the control of movement would make those paper claims real. Early national policy—"civilization" plans, trading houses, the imposition of federal law—turned on the conceit of "attaching" Native people to the United States and to particular locations. All of these programs were designed to further removal by thwarting movement as a strategy of resistance. The early nineteenth century was a period of profound social change for Natives in the Ohio country. That period of change was rooted as much in a contest over movement as it was in a contest over religion, political economy, and culture.[4]

The Shawnee, Potawatomi, Miami, Wyandot, and Kaskaskia leaders who participated in these federal schemes had their own ideas about the contest over movement. They used federal programs to extract money and resources and to establish relationships of mutual obligation between themselves and the United States that would shore up their own political power in a period of turbulence and uncertainty. They turned the instruments of removal to their advantage when they could. They created bounded national

---

location in the Ohio Valley and Great Lakes, see, for example, Michael N. McConnell, *A Country Between: The Upper Ohio Valley and Its Peoples, 1724–1774* (Lincoln, Neb., 1992), 5–60; Eric Hinderaker, *Elusive Empires: Constructing Colonialism in the Ohio Valley, 1673–1800* (New York, 1999), 10–17; Kathryn Magee Labelle, *Dispersed but Not Destroyed: A History of the Seventeenth-Century Wendat People* (Vancouver, B.C., 2013). For literature on Native travel, see, in particular, John P. Bowes, *Exiles and Pioneers: Eastern Indians in the Trans-Mississippi West* (New York, 2007); Angela Pulley Hudson, *Creek Paths and Federal Roads: Indians, Settlers, and Slaves and the Making of the American South* (Chapel Hill, N.C., 2010); Laura Keenan Spero, "'Stout, Bold, Cunning and the Greatest Travellers in America': The Colonial Shawnee Diaspora" (Ph.D. diss., University of Pennsylvania, 2010). A new vein of scholarship has examined the transatlantic movement of Indigenous people. See Coll Thrush, *Indigenous London: Native Travellers at the Heart of Empire* (New Haven, Conn., 2016); Jace Weaver, *The Red Atlantic: American Indigenes and the Making of the Modern World, 1000–1927* (Chapel Hill, N.C., 2017); Nancy Shoemaker, *Native American Whalemen and the World: Indigenous Encounters and the Contingency of Race* (Chapel Hill, N.C., 2017).

4. Richard White, *The Middle Ground: Indians, Empires, and Republics in the Great Lakes Region, 1650–1815* (1991; rpt. New York, 2011), 474.

spaces, clarified their borders, and gathered together to secure the right to remain.[5]

Beginning in 1805, a new Native confederacy took a different tack, using a flurry of diplomatic travel to urge a return to an Ohio River boundary between the United States and Indian country. What had begun as a series of visions experienced by Tenskwatawa turned into a movement spread by diplomats like Le Maigouis that demanded the expulsion of white Americans across the Ohio River. Native messengers traveled across the Great Lakes region sharing news of Tenskwatawa's visions and calling a confederation into being. The Prophet and his followers revived the idea of a multiethnic country held in common, linked by travel.[6]

Native leaders who took different approaches in the contest over movement did not necessarily see themselves as accommodationists or militants. Rather, they believed they were doing what they could to secure their futures amid U.S. colonialism. Those who tried to mark out sovereign national boundaries believed that consolidation and fixity would secure the right to remain. They competed against the Prophet and his vision of a vast empire of Native peoples bound together by long-distance travel. Over the early nineteenth century, U.S. policies steadily undermined both approaches. As territorial officials pressured Natives in what is now Indiana and Illinois to sign treaties, migration created controversies about who had the power to sell land. Ultimately, it was white migration that most clearly advanced removal in the Ohio Valley. U.S. officials saw population as a crucial tool of state making, and they would increasingly use it to justify and achieve the removal of eastern Indigenous prople across the Mississippi.[7]

Throughout the 1780s and 1790s, federal officials overseeing U.S. policy in the trans-Appalachian West lamented travel as a problem to be managed. Their goal in the immediate aftermath of the Revolution was to secure the

5. Sami Lakomäki, *Gathering Together: The Shawnee People through Diaspora and Nationhood, 1600–1870* (New Haven, Conn., 2014); Lori J. Daggar, "The Mission Complex: Economic Development, 'Civilization,' and Empire in the Early Republic," *Journal of the Early Republic,* XXXVI (2016), 467–491; Bottiger, *Borderland of Fear,* 59.

6. For scholarship on Tenskwatawa, see, for example, R. David Edmunds, *The Shawnee Prophet* (Lincoln, Neb., 1983); Gregory Evans Dowd, *A Spirited Resistance: The North American Indian Struggle for Unity, 1745–1815* (Baltimore, Md., 1993), 123–147; Stephen Warren, *The Shawnees and Their Neighbors, 1795–1870* (Urbanna, Ill., 2008), 13–42; Jortner, *Gods of Prophetstown;* Lakomäki, *Gathering Together,* 143–152; Bottiger, *Borderland of Fear,* 59.

7. Antoinette Burton, "Introduction: Travelling Criticism? On the Dynamic Histories of Indigenous Modernity," *Cultural and Social History,* IX (2012), 492.

new nation by removing Indigenous people from their lands north of the Ohio River. At first, white travel was as much of a challenge to their plans as Native travel. In the 1770s and 1780s, thousands of white migrants began to crowd at the edges of the Ohio River in western Pennsylvania, western Virginia, and New York. Speculators and boosters tended to celebrate the insatiable movement of white migrants as a sign of U.S. energy and prosperity. Federal and territorial officials in the Washington administration were more pessimistic, condemning unchecked movement as an obstacle to orderly state making. They dismissed free migrants as "a Banditty of Refugees not worthy of Congress's Notice," in the words of one speculator and territorial official.[8]

They applied the same terms to Natives to argue that they were dangerous enemies or had no legal claim to their lands. In making these statements, they participated in a tradition in Euro-American thought stretching back to the seventeenth century. Colonizers had long argued that Indigenous people were mobile and placeless, while Euro-Americans were settlers. During the colonial period, British officials had dubbed Natives "wandering Indians" or "roving Indians" or "vagrant Indians." As Jean O'Brien has shown for New England, the English never understood Indigenous "social relations that held 'mobility' and 'fixity' in tension" through seasonal migration and usufruct rights that shifted over time and space.[9]

These semantic choices had consequences for land dispossession from the beginnings of English colonization. In his *Second Treatise on Government,* John Locke argued that property rights arose from mixing one's labor with the land—a claim that was repeated by countless colonial writers. When colonial writers described Native people as "wandering" or "roving," they refused to see how they mixed their labor with the land. The labor theory of property specifically targeted those who wandered as landless, which was consistent with a general mistrust of mobile people in contemporaneous English writing. Such arguments were self-serving. The placeless

8. Extract of a Letter from Robert Patterson, July 12, 1786, JHP, V (quotation).

9. Robert Montgomery, *A Discourse concerning the Design'd Establishment of a New Colony to the South of Carolina* . . . (London, 1717) ("wandering"); [Anthony Benezet], *A Short Account of That Part of Africa, Inhabited by the Negroes* . . . , 2d ed. (Philadelphia, 1762), 72 ("roving"); Lawrence Henry Gipson, ed., *The Moravian Indian Mission on White River: Diaries and Letters, May 5, 1799, to November 12, 1806,* trans. Harry E. Stocker, Herman T. Frueauff, and Samuel C. Zeller (Indianapolis, Ind., 1938), 374 ("vagrant"); Jean O'Brien, "'They Are So Frequently Shifting Their Place of Residence': Land and the Construction of Social Place of Indians in Colonial Massachusetts," in Martin Daunton and Rick Halpern, eds., *Empire and Others: British Encounters with Indigenous Peoples, 1600–1850* (Philadelphia, 1999), 204–216 ("social").

had no homes of their own to defend and no fields of their own to protect. By the late eighteenth century, U.S. troops who burned Native villages during the campaigns of Brigadier General Josiah Harmar or territorial governor Arthur St. Clair could have seen how inaccurate those beliefs were if they wanted to. The Glaize, for example, was a place of extraordinary agricultural abundance, and Native peoples there enjoyed a more comfortable lifestyle than did many white Americans. Yet white Americans persisted in arguments about placelessness.[10]

When Native federationists challenged the presumption that their lands were "conquered," federal officials eventually abandoned the conceit. They never gave up the idea, however, that Natives were particularly mobile and without land rights. In the immediate postwar years, federal restrictions on who could purchase Native land (private citizens versus the states versus the federal government) transformed U.S. legal understandings of Indigenous control over territory. So, too, did arguments about Native mobility. Between the 1790s and the 1820s, early national legislators, officials, and jurists revived the colonial-era belief that Natives were hunters without property rights. That conviction also fueled a new market in preemption rights in which speculators purchased lands in Indian country on the presumption that they would eventually be ceded to the federal government. Preemption's proponents believed it was a more democratic means of distributing federal lands to purchasers, rewarding those who settled on the land, rather than large speculators. Preemption's opponents argued that it impinged on Native land rights. Preemption did allow migrants to imagine Indian territory as land that was salable at some point in the future. In essence, it transformed "settler[s] into speculators."[11]

Preemption rights only made sense as legally protected purchases if Natives had the right of tenancy rather than fee simple property rights—meaning the ability to own land absolutely without limitations. In 1795,

10. Stuart Banner, *How the Indians Lost Their Land: Law and Power on the Frontier* (Cambridge, Mass., 2007), 151–160. For prosperity, see Susan Sleeper-Smith, *Indigenous Prosperity and American Conquest: Indian Women of the Ohio River Valley, 1690–1792* (Williamsburg, Va., and Chapel Hill, N.C., 2018); Colin G. Calloway, *The Victory with No Name: The Native American Defeat of the First American Army* (New York, 2015), 31–32.

11. Joseph Brant to Samuel Kirkland, Mar. 8, 1791, TPP, LXI, 208 ("conquered"); Jessica Intrator, "From Squatter to Settler: Applying the Lessons of Nineteenth Century U. S. Public Land Policy to Twenty-First Century Land Struggles in Brazil," *Ecology Law Quarterly*, XXXVIII (2011), 207 ("settler[s]"); Paul W. Gates, *History of Public Land Law Development* (Washington, D.C., 1968), 219–247; Banner, *How the Indians Lost Their Land*, 135–139, 160–168.

Congress debated the issue when discussing whether or not those who had purchased preemption rights to land in Cherokee country that was ultimately confirmed to the Cherokees should receive restitution. The debate in Congress largely split along party lines, with Federalists defending Indigenous land rights and Republicans denying them. Republicans argued that Indigenous people were "tenants at will" of land owned by first the British and then the U.S. government. Most vociferously opposed to Native land rights was Thomas Blount of North Carolina, who told representatives that they were wanderers and thus could make no claim to having improved the land. "To walk across a country, and to shoot in it, was different from an occupation," he declared.[12]

Federal officials also used the trope of Native people as "wandering" to argue that they were untrustworthy in their attachment to the United States. They routinely labeled Natives who traveled "banditti"—those who were lawless. Secretary of War Henry Knox asserted in 1786 that war was prosecuted solely by "the predatory incursions of a banditti collected from a number of tribes," particularly Shawnee and Cherokee confederationists. Vagrancy was a charge leveled at Natives in the Ohio country as well. Quakers called Indigenous people on the Wabash River "wandering." Moravians living on the White River in 1805 described visiting Native families as "vagrant Indians" who "do not hesitate to ask for the last mouthful." They betrayed a distaste for people on the move and the dependency that movement implied—an echo of conceits about vagrancy stretching back to the early modern period.[13]

Long-distance travel was a strategy for Native peoples in the Ohio Valley and lower Great Lakes. They traveled to pursue trading opportunities.

12. *The Debates and Proceedings in the Congress of the United States . . . Fourth Congress—First Session; Comprising the Period from December 7, 1795, to June 1, 1796, Inclusive* (Washington, D.C., 1855), 895 ("tenants"), 898–901; *The Debates and Proceedings in the Congress of the United States . . . Third Congress: Comprising the Period from December 2, 1793, to March 3, 1795, Inclusive* (Washington, D.C., 1855), 1153 ("walk"); David Andrew Nichols, *Red Gentlemen and White Savages: Indians, Federalists, and the Search for Order on the American Frontier* (Charlottesville, Va., 2008), 180.

13. Henry Knox to Josiah Harmar, June 27, 1786, JHP, II ("banditti"), Knox to Harmar, May 12, 1786 ("predatory"); Philadelphia Yearly Meeting, Minutes of the Indian Committee, Mar. 11, 1795, 1, 5, HQC ("wandering"); Gipson, ed., *Moravian Indian Mission on White River*, trans. Stocker, Frueauff, and Zeller (Indianapolis, Ind., 1938), 374 ("vagrant"); *The Debates and Proceedings in the Congress of the United States . . . Second Congress: Comprising the Period from October 24, 1791, to March 2, 1793, Inclusive* (Washington, D.C., 1849), 1048, 1051; Baltimore Yearly Meeting, Standing Committee on Indian Concerns, Mar. 4, 1807, 151, FHL.

Others moved to find safety from dangerous neighbors or to escape overhunting and resource extraction that undermined their livelihoods as the Delawares had in the early eighteenth century. Travel was instrumental to diplomacy, too. Shawnees were exceptional diplomats because they were diasporic peoples whose identities became bound up with long-distance travel. Forced from the Ohio Valley by war and disease between the 1640s and the 1670s, Shawnees nonetheless maintained their language, kin groups, and rituals by reconstituting distinct towns in what is now Alabama, Tennessee, Georgia, Illinois, and Pennsylvania. In 1752, one Cherokee called the Shawnees "a People of no Settlement but rambling from Place to Place," while a colonial observer labeled them "the greatest Travellers in America." The importance of mobility to trade and to political alliances made Native movement an object of ire for U.S. officials. As they moved, Indigenous people formed polyglot, multiethnic villages and ties that would become the basis for confederation building in the 1780s and 1790s and the first decade of the nineteenth century. From the perspective of federal officials, travel looked dangerous.[14]

As the United States began to account for its citizens more fully at the turn of the century, the secretary of war, territorial governors, and Indian agents tried to control Native movement to the ends of state making. The control of movement took on renewed importance in the 1790s as white Americans debated who belonged in the new nation. Just as censuses ordered U.S. citizens in the Atlantic states, federal officials put in place new systems of surveillance west of the Appalachians. Indian agents were tasked with reporting on Native movements in a "regular journal of facts," tracking down "foreign agents" who moved through Indian country, and reporting on "hostile movements" against the U.S. government. Others surveyed Indigenous people within their agencies to record the populations of their towns.[15]

14. Tasattee of Hywassee to Governor Glen, Nov. 28, 1752, in William L. McDowell, Jr., ed., *Documents relating to Indian Affairs, May 21, 1750–August 7, 1754* (Columbia, S.C., 1958), 363, quoted in Stephen Warren and Randolph Noe, "'The Greatest Travelers in America': Shawnee Survival in the Shatter Zone," in Robbie Ethridge and Sheri M. Shuck-Hall, *Mapping the Mississippian Shatter Zone: The Colonial Indian Slave Trade and Regional Instability in the American South* (Lincoln, Neb., 2009), 163–187 ("People," 164); Edmund Atkin, *The Appalachian Indian Frontier: The Edmund Atkin Report and Plan of 1755,* ed. Wilbur R. Jacobs (1954; rpt. Lincoln, Neb., 1967), 165 ("greatest Travellers"), quoted ibid., 164; Warren, *Shawnees and Their Neighbors,* 13–42.

15. Henry Dearborn to William Lyman, July 14, 1801, Letters Sent by the Secretary

Trading houses were instrumental to these goals. Successive federal laws called the Trade and Intercourse Acts, along with a new coterie of federal Indian agents and a series of federally funded trading houses, were all meant to bring Indigenous people in the Ohio Valley into the orbit and interests of the U.S. government. Beginning in 1796, the federal government opened a series of trading houses supported by a $150,000 capital fund that purchased furs from Native peoples with the aim of undercutting the prices private traders offered for goods. U.S. officials were particularly suspicious of British traders, who often had long-standing ties with Native communities and were, according to Indiana territorial governor William Henry Harrison, "one reason of the contempt with which the American Traders are treated by the Indians." Undercutting British competition was not just economic—it was largely a political goal. For Indigenous people, trade and trading posts secured strong alliances that extended outward over vast distances. For federal officials, trade was a means of control, designed to restrict movement and to encourage dispossession. Secretary of War Henry Dearborn hoped that the trading factories would in their words attach Natives to the United States and detach them from "the influence of neighboring Governments," meaning Britain and Spain. The concern of federal officials with attachment shows how they thought about political alliances in spatial terms as a matter of travel and proximity.[16]

U.S. agents and factors at trading posts were crucial intermediaries in the project of attachment. Thomas Jefferson authorized the construction of twelve new factories while he was president. Four were established north of the Ohio River during his administration—at Detroit and Fort Wayne in 1802, Chicago in 1805, and Sandusky in 1806. Each location was chosen

---

of War relating to Indian Affairs, 1800–1824, M15, reel 1, 98 ("regular," "hostile"), 93, NARA, Henry Dearborn to Indian Agents, July 9, 1803, 360–361; Dearborn to William Henry Harrison, Apr. 15, 1803, WHH, reel 1, 547 ("foreign"); Dearborn to Silas Dinsmoor, May 8, 1802, in *TPUS,* V, 146–150. For legibility, see John Torpey, "Coming and Going: On the State Monopolization of the Legitimate 'Means of Movement,'" *Sociological Theory,* XVI (1998), 241; James C. Scott, *Seeing Like a State: How Certain Schemes to Improve the Human Condition Have Failed* (New Haven, Conn., 1998).

16. William Henry Harrison to Thomas Jefferson, Dec. 30, 1801, in *TPUS,* VII, 42 ("one reason"); Statement by H[enry] Dearborn, Dec. 8, 1801, in *ASPIA,* I, 655 ("influence"), "Northwestern Frontiers; Communicated to the House of Representatives," June 13, 1812, I, 797; "An Act to Regulate Trade and Intercourse with the Indian Tribes, and to Preserve Peace on the Frontiers," May 19, 1796, in *The Public Statutes at Large of the United States of America, from the Organization of the Government in 1789, to March 3, 1845 . . . ,* I (Boston, 1845), 469–474. See also Jefferson to [Dearborn], Aug. 12, 1802, in *TPUS,* VII, 68.

strategically: Detroit to undercut British traders posted across the Detroit River at Malden; Fort Wayne to monitor a key portage controlling access to the Wabash River valley; Chicago to watch the portage between the upper Mississippi River valley and the Great Lakes as well as nearby Odawa and Potawatomi towns; and Sandusky to cement ties to the Wyandot community there. The federal officials posted at each location passed along information to territorial governors. Governors revoked the licenses of traders who they suspected of undermining U.S. policy. When Secretary of War Dearborn ordered Harrison to remove British and Spanish agents working as traders in the territory, he used trading posts as his source of information. U.S. officials even hoped to control warfare between Native peoples, such as raids by Potawatomis, Kickapoos, Sacs, and Mesquakies on the Osages across the Mississippi River, through such channels. In reality, of course, they could not prevent war parties from crossing the Mississippi or trading with British or Spanish agents. In some cases, they could not even protect the factories themselves. In 1803, Fort Wayne agent John Johnston reported that someone had burned the factor's house at Fort Wayne in Indiana Territory, ruining several thousand dollars of trading goods and symbolically striking at the heart of U.S. policy in the Ohio Valley.[17]

Native leaders transformed methods of surveillance like trading houses to serve their own interests. They treated the factories as "de facto embassies" of foreign guests (the factors themselves) in Indian country, and they used them as way stations, expecting to receive hospitality and goods on credit as they traveled. Fort Wayne, for example, was located at an ideal spot for factors to keep watch over movement in the region, and it became a central location for U.S. treaty making in the early nineteenth century. It occupied the former site of Kekionga, a complex of Miami towns and a regional trading center located at the eight-mile portage connecting the Wabash and Maumee Rivers. It was what one eighteenth-century observer had called "a glorious gate" linking the Great Lakes to the Ohio River to the Missis-

17. H[enry] D[earborn] to W[illia]m H[enry] Harrison, Sept. 3, 1802, in *TPUS,* VII, 74, [Dearborn] to Harrison, Feb. 21, 1803, 87, [Dearborn] to Harrison, Apr. 15, 1803, 108, [Dearborn] to Harrison, June 20, 1805, 296; R. David Edmunds, "Main Poc: Potawatomi Wabeno," *American Indian Quarterly,* IX (1985), 261; Nichols, *Red Gentlemen and White Savages,* 193; David Andrew Nichols, *Engines of Diplomacy: Indian Trading Factories and the Negotiation of American Empire* (Chapel Hill, N.C., 2016), 47–48, 104–106; Royal B. Way, "The United States Factory System for Trading with the Indians, 1796–1822," *Mississippi Valley Historical Review,* VI (1919), 224. For the burning of the factor's house, see Goods Arriving at Fort Wayne, 1803, Records of the Office of Indian Trade, Daybooks, 1804–1806, folder 1, NARA.

sippi. The site was chosen with the help of Miami chief Little Turtle, and his collaboration in the venture was telling. He did not see it as an instrument of control but as a source of goods that he could manage toward his own ends. In other cases, the location of trading houses supported some leaders in their contests for the control of annuities. Shawnees led by Black Hoof, who founded a town at Wapakoneta in 1796, asked for their annuities to be delivered to Fort Wayne rather than Detroit in 1809. Fort Wayne factor Johnston interpreted the request as stemming from the Wapakonetans' weariness over the distance they had to travel to Detroit. It is just as likely that Black Hoof's Wapakonetans were attempting to wrest control over the Shawnee annuity from other leaders closer to Detroit, cementing the status of their town as the political center of a consolidated Shawnee nation—an innovation given the diasporic identity that had been embraced by the Shawnee for centuries.[18]

Federal plans to control movement also depended on the consolidation of Native nations in particular locations through fenced-in fields and European-style dwellings. What were known as federal civilization plans encouraged Natives to take up Euro-American forms of private property and gendered labor, with men tilling fields and women performing domestic labor. First proposed by Henry Knox in 1789, these plans were pushed forward by successive presidential administrations. Beginning with the 1793 Trade and Intercourse Act, Congress authorized the president to spend twenty thousand dollars each year on "useful domestic animals, and implements of husbandry" that would be sent west. Meanwhile, federal treaty commissioners used treaties as instruments of so-called civilization, too. They urged Native people to take their annuities in the form of plows, hoes, and spinning wheels rather than money. Treaties included clauses promising blacksmiths, missionaries, and mills to those who signed away their lands.[19]

18. Nichols, *Engines of Diplomacy,* 4 ("de facto"), 7–8, 47–48; Wallace A. Brice, *History of Fort Wayne, from the Earliest Known Accounts of This Point, to the Present Period* (Fort Wayne, Ind., 1868), 38 ("glorious"), quoted in Bottiger, *Borderland of Fear,* 15 (quotation), 20; John Johnston to William Eustis, Apr. 15, 1809, in *TPUS,* VII, 648; Baltimore Yearly Meeting Standing Committee on Indian Concerns, Oct. 13, 1802, 60, FHL; Gerard T. Hopkins, Journal, Mar. 31, 1804, HSP.

19. "An Act to Regulate Trade and Intercourse with the Indian Tribes," Mar. 1, 1793, in *Public Statutes at Large of the United States of America,* I, 329–332 ("useful domestic," 331); "A Treaty of Peace and Friendship, Made and Concluded between the President of the United States of America, on the Part and Behalf of the Said States, and the Undersigned Kings, Chiefs, and Warriors, of the Creek Nation of Indians . . . ," Aug. 7, 1790, in *ASPIA,* I, 81–82 ("useful domestic," 82), Henry Knox to George Washington, July 7, 1789, I, 54; Banner, *How the Indians Lost Their Land,* 155; Daniel K.

Knox encouraged missionaries to partner with the federal government to create model farms in Indian country and to act as the "friends and fathers" of Native nations. North of the Ohio River, Presbyterians and Baltimore Quakers took the lead in establishing missions at Miami chief Little Turtle's town in 1804, the Wyandot town of Lower Sandusky in 1805, and the Shawnee town Wapakoneta in 1807. Quakers were particularly active in collaborating with the federal government to attach Natives to the United States. They believed that without employing plow agriculture, gendered forms of labor, and adopting private property, Native people were doomed to "extreme want and distress" and "annihilation."[20]

Federal officials and missionaries were determined not to see Eastern Woodlands peoples—most of whom relied far more on the agricultural skills of Native women than on hunting—as farmers. When they wrote that Indigenous people should learn to farm, they meant that Native men should farm as Euro-American men did. Baltimore Friends insisted that women were too weak to perform agricultural labor. Others made assumptions about the efficiency of Euro-American modes of cultivating the soil in contrast to those of Native methods, which were, in their words, "precarious" or full of "fatigue and toil." In 1796, President Washington told a delegation of Wyandots, Delawares, Shawnees, Odawas, Ojibwes, Potawatomis, Miamis, Weas, Kickapoos, Piankeshaws, and Kaskaskias at Philadelphia that raising domestic animals would allow them to "procure the conveniencies and necessaries of life in greater abundance and with less trouble than you do at present."[21]

Richter, "'Believing That Many of the Red People Suffer Much for the Want of Food': Hunting, Agriculture, and a Quaker Construction of Indianness in the Early Republic," *Journal of the Early Republic,* XIX (1999), 611–612. See also R. Pierce Beaver, "Church, State, and the Indians: Indian Missions in the New Nation," *Journal of Church and State,* IV (1962), 18.

20. Knox to Washington, July 7, 1789, in *ASPIA,* I, 54 ("friends and fathers"); Baltimore Yearly Meeting Standing Committee on Indian Concerns, Oct. 7, 1797, 19 ("extreme"), FHL, Oct. 13, 1802, 60, Oct. 15, 1804, 81, Mar. 4, 1807, 151 ("annihilation"); *A Brief Account of the Proceedings of the Committee Appointed in the Year 1795 by the Yearly Meeting of Friends of Pennsylvania, New-Jersey, etc., for Promoting the Improvement and Gradual Civilization of the Indian Natives* ([1805]; rpt. London, 1806), 49; Philadelphia Yearly Meeting, Minutes of the Indian Committee, Jan. 20, 1798, 1, 67.

21. Benjamin Hawkins, "General View; Communicated to Congress," Dec. 8, 1801, in *ASPIA,* I, 646–648 ("precarious," 646); Baltimore Yearly Meeting Standing Committee on Indian Concerns, Oct. 7, 1797, 19 ("precarious"), Oct. 15, 1804, 77 ("fatigue"), 80; "George Washington to Chiefs and Warriors, Representatives of the Wiandots, Delawares, Shawnoes, Ottawas, Chippewas, Potawatamies, Miamis, Eel River, Weas, Kicka-

Native leaders who asked for "implements of husbandry" or worked with Quaker missionaries did so to secure their political positions and to strengthen their relationship with the United States. Eastern Native peoples had been selectively taking up European goods and tools for centuries, and they were already fully ensconced in a market economy. Odawas, Wyandots, and Delawares who traded at the Sandusky Factory, for example, went looking for silver spoons, wine glasses, stoves, and hardware and tools with which to adorn their houses. Miami chief Little Turtle, Shawnee chief Black Hoof, and Tarhe, headman of the Sandusky Wyandots, whose towns were closest to the new border that set off Indian country, saw partnerships with missionaries and the pursuit of what they called civilization goods as a means of protecting their homelands during a period of aggressive efforts by the United States to acquire their lands. Little Turtle visited Philadelphia, Washington, and Baltimore several times in 1798 and 1802 to secure Quaker and federal funds. Wyandot leader Tarhe and his wife joined one of these meetings at the Fourth Street Meeting House in Philadelphia in 1798, as did Potawatomi Five Medals. Quakers, meanwhile, sent messages to the Miamis urging them to give up the ways of "the strolling hunter." Little Turtle, dressed in European garb and an experienced statesman who had met with both Washington and John Adams, was far from the strolling hunter they imagined.[22]

In 1804, Baltimore Quakers heeded Little Turtle's and Five Medals's requests, and they sent Philip Dennis to establish a mission near Fort Wayne that became one of the longest in operation. Little Turtle's connections served him well. Quakers brought hoes, axes, ploughs, horses, and cows with them. They labored on Native farms, built mills at their own expense, and constructed a two-story house for Little Turtle. Jefferson's administration appointed Little Turtle's son-in-law, William Wells, a salaried Indian agent at Fort Wayne, cementing Little Turtle's own connections to the federal government. Little Turtle chose a spot for Dennis's mission at the forks

---

poos, Piankeshaws, and Kaskaskias, Given at Philadelphia, Nov. 29, 1796," Lewis Cass Papers, box 5, folder 26, CL ("procure"); Matthew Dennis, *Seneca Possessed: Indians, Witchcraft, and Power in the Early American Republic* (Philadelphia, 2010), 148–178.

22. Philadelphia Yearly Meeting, Minutes of the Indian Committee, Feb. 17, 1798, 1, 17 (quotation); Max L. Carter, "John Johnston and the Friends: A Midwestern Indian Agent's Relationship with Quakers in the Early 1800s," *Quaker History,* LXXVIII (1989), 37–47; Dowd, *Spirited Resistance,* 131–136; Dennis, *Seneca Possessed,* 151, 162–167; Nichols, *Red Gentlemen and White Savages,* 179; Daggar, "Mission Complex," *Journal of the Early Republic,* XXXVI (2016), 467–491, esp. 479–483; Nichols, *Engines of Diplomacy,* 106.

of the Wabash, the meeting point of the Little River and the Wabash River close to his village. It was, Little Turtle professed, a "most public" spot that "would afford passengers an opportunity of seing what was done more than any other we could point out." Anyone who passed by would see the resources Little Turtle mobilized. In his meetings with Quakers, he and Five Medals inflated their own power, suggesting that they spoke for all of the Potawatomis, Miamis, Delawares, Shawnees, Weas, Piankeshaws, Kickapoos, and Kaskaskias in the region and that they would bring Quaker speeches from the Wabash River to the Mississippi and up to Michilimackinac. For Little Turtle, especially, such a claim was an assertion of Miami power over the many Native migrants who had settled in Miami territory on the Maumee and Wabash rivershebs—one he felt empowered to make because of his connections to the federal government.[23]

Black Hoof also partnered with Quakers to build a mission with a mill and a demonstration farm at Wapakoneta in what is now Ohio. He attempted to use the program to increase the power of the Mekoche and Chalagawtha divisions of the Shawnee, who remained in Ohio after 1795. In 1807, the federal government sent Quaker William Kirk to establish a model farm at Wapakoneta. Nearby Shawnee villages at Hog Creek and Lewiston took up Kirk's plans as well. Fort Wayne factor Johnston observed two years later that Wapakoneta boasted a saw mill and had nearly completed a grist mill, too. "The settlement bears the marks of industry," Johnston noted approvingly. After the War of 1812, Black Hoof convinced the federal government to pay for Shawnee property and the Wapakoneta mill that had been destroyed during campaigns in Ohio. For Black Hoof, accepting civilization goods was a means of staking out a place for the Shawnee where they could come together in Ohio. Accepting Kirk's help also did not rearrange Shawnee social relations in the way that Johnston thought it had. Men had traditionally helped to clear and fence land, for example, though white observers saw these activities as new innovations. Quakers bragged that a Wabash village had "planted a large field of Corn Potatoes and many

23. "To the Yearly Meeting Now Sitting," in Baltimore Yearly Meeting Standing Committee on Indian Concerns, [Oct. 16, 1806], 142, FHL (quotations); Baltimore Yearly Meeting Standing Committee on Indian Concerns, Oct. 10, 1803, 62, Oct. 15, 1805, 112, Oct. 13, 1807, 164, Aug. 8, 1808, 184–185, Dec. 31, 1808, 215; "Proceedings of the First Conference," in Baltimore Yearly Meeting Standing Committee on Indian Concerns, [May 24, 1802], 48–49; Philadelphia Yearly Meeting, Minutes of the Indian Committee, Feb. 17, 1798, 1, 17; Daggar, "Mission Complex," *Journal of the Early Republic*, XXXVI (2016), 478, 484–488; Bottiger, *Borderland of Fear*, 7–8, 32, 48–49.

garden Vegetables," although they did so by following their own methods rather than Quaker prescriptions for the use of plows.[24]

Federal officials and their Quaker partners believed that so-called civilization plans would suspend Native movement across the Ohio Valley by encouraging consolidation. Missionaries and federal officials put particular emphasis on the trappings of private property—land held in fee simple, permanent dwellings, fences, pigs, cattle—as a means of discouraging mobility. Quaker writers asserted that agriculture and "ideas of distinct property" went hand in hand. New Yorker Silas Wood hoped that "civilization" plans would "introduce the notion of private property, of a fixed residence and agriculture." Wood willfully misunderstood that Native communities already had comparable and defined conceptions of property that determined how land was used and who could use it. Wells and Baltimore Quakers similarly argued that Native peoples should embrace fixity and consolidate their towns. Federal officials hoped those locations would serve U.S. interests. The mission towns occupied strategic places in the Ohio Valley where they reinforced the goals of U.S. factories. Joseph Badger of the Connecticut Missionary Society located his Presbyterian mission to the Wyandots at Lower Sandusky the year before the founding of the Sandusky trading post. Quakers began their mission at Little Turtle's town on the heels of the establishment of the Fort Wayne trading post. Indeed, Fort Wayne supplied the Quaker mission project, stocking the hoes, axes, and plows that would transform Miami and Potawatomi lives of supposed mobility into those of fixity.[25]

Wells and Wood wanted consolidation and fixity, but so, too, did leaders like Black Hoof and Little Turtle. Black Hoof hoped to use federal annu-

24. Johnston to Eustis, Apr. 15, 1809, in *TPUS,* VII, 648 ("settlement"); Baltimore Yearly Meeting Standing Committee on Indian Concerns, Oct. 13, 1807, 161 ("planted"); Dennis, *Seneca Possessed,* 158, 167–178; Lakomäki, *Gathering Together,* 135–137; R. David Edmunds, "A Patriot Defamed: Captain Lewis, Shawnee Chief," in Stephen Warren, ed., *The Eastern Shawnee Tribe of Oklahoma: Resilience through Adversity* (Norman, Okla., 2017) 17–18.

25. *Brief Account of the Proceedings of the Committee Appointed in the Year 1795 by the Yearly Meeting of Friends,* 47 ("ideas"); [Silas Wood], *Thoughts on the State of the American Indians by a Citizen of the United States* (New York, 1794), 35 ("civilization"); Baltimore Yearly Meeting Standing Committee on Indian Concerns, Oct. 15, 1804, 77, Committee on Indian Concerns to Little Turtle, Five Medals, Le Gris, Mar. 12, 1806, 132; William Wells to Henry Dearborn, Dec. 31, 1807, in *TPUS,* VII, 510; Carter, "John Johnston and the Friends," *Quaker History,* LXXVIII (1989), 40; Lakomäki, *Gathering Together,* 135. For fixity, see O'Brien, "'They Are So Frequently Shifting Their Place of Residence,'" in Daunton and Halpern, eds., *Empire and Others,* 208–210, 212.

ities and the tools and assistance provided by civilization programs to draw Shawnees back to Wapakoneta. He envisioned Wapakoneta as the center of a place-bound Shawnee nation. Given how central movement was to Shawnee identity, Black Hoof's idea to consolidate Shawnee divisions in one place was a novel one. He was successful at collecting some Shawnees together. By 1809, the population of Wapakoneta had reached five hundred Chalagawtha and Mekoche Shawnees, and other Shawnees and Senecas formed two more settlements close by. Leaders from the clustered towns met as a national council at Wapakoneta by the early nineteenth century. The Mekoche who accepted federal programs pursued what they believed to be the best options available to them given the circumstances. Across the Ohio Valley and lower Great Lakes, people used federal programs for their own purposes, subverting attempts to manage mobility. For Little Turtle, defined boundaries and fixity were already a part of Miami politics. Missions and the civilization project did little to change that. Miamis had long invited outsiders to join them as a means of reinforcing their claim to place in the Wabash and Maumee River valleys.[26]

Factories surveiled Native movement, civilization plans supposedly imposed fixity, and other measures were intended to control travel back and forth across the borders between the United States and Indian country. The Greenville Treaty of 1795 allowed for the free movement of Natives across the new border, and it promised hunting rights to Natives south of it. In theory, travelers from the United States did not have the same legal power to move back and forth across the line. The Treaty of Greenville determined that boundary crossers from the United States were out of the "protection"

26. Lakomäki, *Gathering Together,* 138–141. Sami Lakomäki argues that while many historians have portrayed Black Hoof's choices as "Americanizing," they were actually efforts to renew Shawnee spiritual power. See Lakomäki, "'Our Line': The Shawnees, the United States, and Competing Borders on the Great Lakes 'Borderlands,' 1795–1832," *Journal of the Early Republic,* XXXIV (2014), 614 (quotation); James Joseph Buss, "Imagined Worlds and Archival Realities: The Patchwork World of Early Nineteenth-Century Indiana," in Buss and C. Joseph Genetin-Pilawa, eds., *Beyond Two Worlds: Critical Conversations on Language and Power in Native North America* (Albany, N.Y., 2015), 98–99. For Shawnee "fluidity" and a defense of Shawnee leaders who worked with the United States, see R. David Edmunds, "Patriot Defamed," in Warren, ed., *Eastern Shawnee Tribe of Oklahoma,* 36 ("fluidity"); Edmunds, "'A Watchful Safeguard to Our Habitations': Black Hoof and the Loyal Shawnees," in Frederick E. Hoxie, Ronald Hoffman, and Peter J. Albert, eds., *Native Americans and the Early Republic* (Charlottesville, Va., 1999), 162–199. See also Edmunds, "Redefining Red Patriotism: Five Medals of the Potawatomis," *Red River Valley Historical Review,* V, no. 2 (Spring 1980), 13–24. For Miami claims to place, see Bottiger, *Borderland of Fear,* 7–8, 59.

of the federal government. The Trade and Intercourse Acts also prohibited their travel through Indian country without a passport. The army could enforce the law, and federal Indian agents could prosecute trespassers in federal courts. In practice, however, federal officials did not make a great effort to control white movement. After 1795, the federal government moved U.S. troops further north into posts on the Great Lakes, leaving Natives to police the boundaries of Indian country themselves.[27]

In the case of the Greenville Treaty, the slow and belabored marking of the treaty's boundary line created a contested legal culture of travel in the Ohio country. In the early nineteenth century, the most common complaint of Native leaders was that white interlopers passed over the boundary with impunity. In 1802, Little Turtle visited Secretary of War Dearborn and demanded that he guard the border more closely. Although white American border crossers admittedly forfeited the protection of the United States, Little Turtle worried that punishing them would bring violence on the Miamis, and he asked the United States to call its citizens to account. A few months later, Black Hoof led a delegation of Shawnee and Delaware visitors to the capital, where he, too, asked Jefferson to control white migrants. He demanded that U.S. officials "stop your people from killing our game" on lands that were not their own. "At present they kill more than we do." The Shawnee chiefs compared the animals in their territory to those of white farmers, explaining that they "would be angry if we were to kill a cow or hog of theirs, the little game that remains is very dear to us." Though Dearborn promised that he would uphold the law, he did little to stop white interlopers from hunting in Indian country.[28]

By contrast, the federal government had easy recourse against Natives accused of crossing the border to commit property theft. The 1796 Trade and Intercourse Act determined that federal officials could deduct remuneration for property crimes from treaty annuities. If Indigenous people refused to pay for a horse they were accused of stealing or a cabin they were accused of destroying, the federal government could directly assess fines by dock-

27. Charles J. Kappler, ed., *Indian Affairs: Laws and Treaties,* II, *Treaties* (Washington, D.C., 1904), II, 42 (quotation); "An Act to Regulate Trade and Intercourse with the Indian Tribes, and to Preserve Peace on the Frontiers," May 19, 1796, in *Public Statutes at Large of the United States of America,* I, 470; White, *Middle Ground,* 473; Anthony F. C. Wallace, *Jefferson and the Indians: The Tragic Fate of the First Americans* (Cambridge, Mass., 1999), 216–218.

28. "Conference with Delaware and Shawnee Deputations," [1802], Letters Sent by the Secretary of War relating to Indian Affairs, 1800–1824, M15, reel 1, 151 (quotations), 158, NARA; Henry Dearborn to William Henry Harrison, Feb. 23, 1802, WHH, reel 1, 265–266.

ing annuities. This is exactly what federal officials did in 1805 when they paid seventy-eight dollars to Abraham Brinker for a stolen horse directly from the 1806 Delaware annuity. Federal officials also used land cessions to settle their balance sheets for supposed property crimes. In an 1804 treaty with the Delawares, the United States agreed to pay all claims outstanding against them for stolen horses in return for land cessions.[29]

Federal attempts to control Native mobility were linked to removal. Jefferson believed that fixity would make Natives eager to sell their lands to the United States. In a private message to Indiana governor William Henry Harrison, Jefferson explained that trading houses selling goods on credit would send Indigenous people into debt. In combination with private property and the fixity imposed by civilization plans, federal policy would convince Natives to sell their homelands through the coercion of the marketplace rather than violence of warfare, he wrote. Jefferson reasoned that, "when they withdraw themselves to the culture of a small piece of land, they will perceive how useless to them are their extensive forests, and will be willing to pare them off from time to time in exchange for necessaries for their farms and families." When those "necessaries" got Native peoples into debt, they would "become willing to lop them off by a cession of lands." Jefferson's statement symbolizes the predatory nature of federal civilization policy.[30]

Missions that encouraged consolidation and private property were key to federal plans. Agriculture made territory more "legible" and "manipulable" and opened a door to private property and land sales. Indian agent Wells remarked that collecting nations together might make them more willing to give up "surpl[u]s" land. Private property also had the potential to dismantle Native sovereignty. In 1808, Jefferson advised a delegation of Miami, Potawatomi, Delaware, and Ojibwe visitors that civilization programs would prepare them "to possess property, to wish to live under regular laws, to join us in our governments, to mix with us in society and

29. "An Act to Regulate Trade and Intercourse with the Indian Tribes," May 19, 1796, in *Public Statutes at Large of the United States of America,* I, 470, 473; White, *Middle Ground,* 473; William Henry Harrison to Henry Dearborn, Nov. 29, 1805, WHH, reel 2, 422; Harrison to William Eustis, Oct. 3, 1809, Fort Wayne Indian Agency Letter book, 1809–1815, 29–30, CL; James McHenry to Arthur St. Clair, Aug. 15, 1799, War Department Papers, NL.

30. Thomas Jefferson to William Henry Harrison, Feb. 27, 1803, WHH, reel 1, 519–520 (quotations); Thomas Jefferson, "Trade; Communicated to Congress," Jan. 18, 1803, in *ASPIA,* I, 684; Jortner, *Gods of Prophetstown,* 86–88; Lakomäki, *Gathering Together,* 135.

your blood and ours united will spread again over this great Island." The replacement of customary laws with the "regular laws" of the United States was fundamental to Jefferson's own narrative of population replacement in which Native people would become "culturally indistinguishable" from white Americans.[31]

The relationship between the control of movement and removal had always been clear to Native leaders, even when federal officials hid their thinking in secret correspondence. By the early nineteenth century, removal as an end goal of civilization policy was no longer hidden in secret correspondence but was openly discussed. In 1816, Fort Wayne Indian agent Johnston could write that the civilization project "would pave the way for extinguishing the Indian title to most of the lands within this state."[32]

U.S. policy did begin to put pressure on Native movement, but not because of civilization plans or trading houses. Rather, backhanded deals and treaties began to undermine traditions of land sharing in the early-nineteenth-century Ohio Valley. Miamis, Shawnees, Potawatomis, Wyandots, and Kaskaskias who capitalized on U.S. schemes for new trading houses and civilization plans had their own ideas about property and fixity. Their conception of property rights included land held communally, the mutual recognition of use rights, and invitations to other Native nations to share lands based on political alliances. Natives across the Ohio Valley and lower Great Lakes were clear about the borders of their lands even when they allowed others to settle on them. Land sharing accommodated long-distance travel and the relocation of people pushed west by settler colonialism while preserving the territorial integrity of various Native nations.

Yet land sharing had already begun to show cracks by 1795. The United Indian Nations spent much of the 1780s and early 1790s creating a confederation that claimed the entire Ohio Valley and lower Great Lakes as common territory—a dish with one spoon. The most ardent proponents of the dish with one spoon insisted that the boundary between U.S. and

31. Scott, *Seeing Like a State,* 2 ("legible"); Wells to Dearborn, Dec. 31, 1807, in *TPUS,* VII, 510 ("surpl[u] s"); Thomas Jefferson to Miamis, Potawatomis, Delawares, and Chippewas, Dec. 21, 1808, Lewis Cass Papers, box 5, folder 29, CL ("possess"); White, *Middle Ground,* 473 ("culturally"); Jefferson to Delawares, December 1808, in Logan Esarey, ed., *Messages and Letters of William Henry Harrison,* I, *1800–1811* (Indianapolis, Ind., 1922), 333–335.

32. John Johnston to William Crawford, June 4, 1816, Johnston Account Book, Beinecke Rare Book and Manuscript Library, YUA ("would pave"); Lewis Cass to William Crawford, June 6, 1816, Lewis Cass Papers, box 2, BHC.

Native territories was more important than those between Native nations. This hierarchy of borders deemphasized tribal spaces and accentuated a Native-settler divide. Nevertheless, at the Treaty of Greenville in 1795, a country held in common came under strain. Masass, an Ojibwe leader, used the council to explain that Ojibwes, Odawas, and Potawatomis were the true owners of Ohio country lands. Masass's statement was odd in that the Anishinaabeg had no strong claim to the Ohio Valley. From his perspective, however, the Anishinaabeg were important power brokers in the larger Great Lakes region, and making such a statement in a public council might have been a way to grasp political and diplomatic power. Little Turtle disputed Masass's claims. "Listen and I will tell you who has the right of soil," he told the assembly. He used his own speech to lay out the bounds of Myaamionki, or Miami territory, which he said extended from Detroit along the Scioto River and the Ohio River to the Wabash River and then up to Chicago—both the center of Miami territory and its larger hinterlands. Little Turtle asserted that the line the United States proposed "cuts off from the Indians a large portion of country, which has been enjoyed by my forefathers time immemorial, without molestation or dispute."[33]

Anthony Wayne, who negotiated on behalf of the United States at Greenville, was tasked with creating a permanent treaty line. It was not nearly so permanent as he claimed. Over the course of the Jefferson administration, U.S. agents and territorial governors negotiated thirty treaties that sold two hundred thousand square miles of Native homelands to the United States. Fifteen of those treaties were negotiated by William Henry Harrison. They included hasty deals for Indigenous territory in Ohio and nearly half of all the lands in what would become Indiana and most of the future Illinois. Harrison focused negotiations on the lands along the Ohio and Mississippi Rivers because Jefferson hoped to monopolize travel and trade along both rivers in order to "present as strong a front on our western as on our eastern border, and plant on the Mississippi itself the means of its own defence."[34]

33. John F. Carmichael, Diary, July 21, 1795, 58–59, July 22, 1795, 62–65, 64 ("Listen"), John F. Carmichael Collection, typed transcript, OHC; "Minutes of a Treaty with the Tribes of Indians Called the Wyandots, Delawares, Shawanese, Ottawas, Chippewas, Pattawatamies, Miamies, Eel River, Kickapoos, Piankeshaws, and Kaskaskias, Begun at Greenville, on the 16th Day of June, and Ended on the 10th Day of August, 1795," in *ASPIA,* I, 570–572 ("cuts off," 570); Bottiger, *Borderland of Fear,* 16. For the Anishinaabeg as power brokers in the Great Lakes, see McDonnell, *Masters of Empire;* Witgen, *Infinity of Nations.*

34. Jefferson to Harrison, Feb. 27, 1803, WHH, reel 1, 521 (quotation); Robert M. Owens, "Jeffersonian Benevolence on the Ground: The Indian Land Cession Treaties

Ohio Valley Native peoples responded to the steady loss of their homelands by gathering together on lands borrowed from other nations. They made composite towns, strategically relocating away from white migrants by finding safety further west and north. For those who shared their land, like the Miamis, relocating easterners created buffer settlements and protection from white migrants. At the same time, U.S. policy increasingly took advantage of these strategies of relocation, diaspora, and land sharing. As territorial officials pressured Natives to sign treaty agreements, migration caused controversies about who had the power to sell land. Harrison deliberately targeted those who had the weakest claims to divide Native nations against each other. His aggressive negotiating strategy made the treaty system, in Bethel Saler's words, "self-regenerative." When some leaders agreed to make land cessions, others were forced to follow or risk walking away from a council with no remuneration for stolen lands. In 1812, Wyandot Maera and seven other Wyandot leaders from Brownstown on the Detroit River petitioned the U.S. government against the treaty system. "When the United States want a particular piece of land, all our nations are assembled; a large sum of money is offered; the land is occupied probably by one nation only . . . if the particular nation interested refuses to sell, they are generally threatened by the others. . . . Fathers, this is the way in which this small spot, which we so much value, has been so often torn from us," they wrote.[35]

From the beginning of his tenure as governor, Harrison exploited Native histories of movement. He was particularly eager to clarify the boundaries of U.S. settlements around Vincennes because it was the seat of Indiana's territorial government. Little Turtle was likewise eager to clearly delineate boundaries, as he was worried about encroachment on Miami lands in the region. In 1803, Harrison called for a council at Fort Wayne to address the issue. He threatened to withhold the Greenville Treaty annuities if Delaware, Shawnee, Potawatomi, Miami, and Kickapoo leaders did not appear at Fort Wayne to sell more than one million acres of land around Vincennes. When Little Turtle agreed to sign away Miami lands in exchange for a clear boundary setting off Miami territory, other leaders representing competing claims had little choice but to follow him. Black Hoof and two other Shaw-

---

of William Henry Harrison," *Journal of the Early Republic,* XXII (2002), 409; Kappler, ed., *Indian Affairs,* II, 64–105.

35. Bethel Saler, *The Settlers' Empire: Colonialism and State Formation in America's Old Northwest* (Philadelphia, 2015), 73–76 ("self-regenerative," 73); "The Wyandots; Communicated to the House of Representatives," Feb. 28, 1812, in *ASPIA,* I, 796 ("When"); Thomas Jefferson to the U.S. Senate, Dec. 31, 1804, WHH, reel 2, 11.

nee leaders signed for the Shawnees, though they also angrily renounced the treaty. So, too, did Potawatomi Five Medals and Delawares Buckongahelas, Hockingpomska, and Kechkawhanund.[36]

Harrison repeated this strategy the following year when he opened up negotiations with the Delawares for lands on the Wabash and Ohio Rivers. In the 1770s, the Piankeshaws had invited Delawares to settle on the White River in what is now Indiana, and most Delaware towns relocated to the west fork of the White River after 1795. As white migrants flooded the Ohio country in the early nineteenth century, many Delawares considered relocating again to join kin across the Mississippi River. Harrison rushed to negotiate with the Delawares before they left. Extracting land sales from the Delawares was underhanded. The Piankeshaws were part of the Miami Confederacy that claimed the White River as the "common property in several nations." Delawares were merely guests with no authority to sell, as Harrison well knew. He approached the Delawares first because they had lesser ties to the tract in question. In 1804, they sold lands between the Wabash and Ohio Rivers in return for three thousand dollars of civilization goods. The Piankeshaws, whose "ancestors . . . resided on [the land] for Many generations," Harrison acknowledged, were forced to agree to the cession, too.[37]

Native people had created composite towns across the Ohio Valley that, by the early nineteenth century, became a liability. The Delaware treaty prompted an outcry from the Miami Confederacy. The Miamis had allowed Delawares to live on the ceded lands, but they "strenuously contended that the declaration which they made on that occasion meant nothing more than an assurance to the Delawares that they should occupy the country as long as they pleased but that they had no intention to convey an exclusive right." Little Turtle protested that the Miamis had invited outsiders to their lands but they had not given them up. In Delaware towns, too, young men denounced the treaty's signatories, who also complained bitterly about Harrison's tactics soon after they left his company. They agreed that they could

36. H[enry] D[earborn] to W[illia]m H[enry] Harrison, Jan. 23, 1802, in *TPUS,* VII, 46–47, D[earborn] to Harrison, July 29, 1802, 62–63; Owens, "Jeffersonian Benevolence on the Ground," *Journal of the Early Republic,* XXII (2002), 417–419; Jortner, *Gods of Prophetstown,* 90–91; Bottiger, *Borderland of Fear,* 42–43, 48–49.

37. Henry Dearborn to William Henry Harrison, Jan. 17, 1805, WHH, reel 2, 79 ("common"), Harrison to Thomas Jefferson, May 12, 1804, reel 1, 797–799 ("ancestors"); Owens, "Jeffersonian Benevolence on the Ground," *Journal of the Early Republic,* XXII (2002), 420; Jortner, *Gods of Prophetstown,* 92.

not sign away Miami territories. Moreover, the Treaty of Greenville had supposedly guaranteed the territory in perpetuity. Forced to backtrack, Harrison invited Delaware, Miami, and Potawatomi leaders to his estate, Grouseland, in 1805 and grasped title from them there. Already, he looked to future divisions and sales. Of the Miami's Wabash lands, he wrote that "I conceive that it will be no difficult matter to get them in the course of a few years to make a division of the land that they now hold in Common."[38]

Harrison's unscrupulous treaties jeopardized layered rights to land. This was particularly clear in negotiations he undertook with the Kaskaskias in 1803. An 1803 treaty with the Kaskaskias exemplified how swift U.S. negotiations challenged overlapping claims. The Kaskaskias were one of fourteen subgroups of Illinois speakers who colonized the southern Illinois valley by the early seventeenth century. They formed close ties to French missionaries and traders at the Grand Village of the Kaskaskias, a populous group of settlements in what is now Illinois. In the early eighteenth century, the Kaskaskias moved to the mouth of the Kaskaskia River, where they were closely linked to the Miamis. When George Rogers Clark arrived in Illinois with U.S. forces during the American Revolution, many French inhabitants abandoned Illinois. Most of the Illinois eventually did so as well, permanently relocating west of the Mississippi River. Some Kaskaskias remained, however, and, under the leadership of Jean Baptiste Ducoigne, they ultimately tied their fortunes to the United States. The Kaskaskias were frequently at war with their Native neighbors. In the 1770s, for example, they went to war with the Mesquakies. The Mascoutens and Mesquakies attacked them again in 1787. The wars took a toll on the Kaskaskias who chose

38. William Henry Harrison to Henry Dearborn, Aug. 26, 1805, WHH, reel 2, 324 ("strenuously"), 326 ("I conceive"), Dearborn to Harrison, Mar. 3, 1805, 104–108, John Gibson and Francis Vigo to Harrison, July 6, 1805, 236–237, Harrison to Dearborn, July 10, 1805, 246, Harrison to Dearborn, Dec. 24, 1805, 442, Harrison to Dearborn, Jan. 27, 1808, reel 3, 103, Dearborn to Harrison, Mar. 11, 1808, 123; Dearborn to William Wells, Oct. 26, 1804, Letters sent by the Secretary of War relating to Indian Affairs, 1800–1824, M15, reel 2, 21–23, NARA, Dearborn to Wells, Dec. 24, 1804, 35, Dearborn to Harrison, Oct. 11, 1805, 119; [Dearborn] to Harrison, May 24, 1805, in *TPUS,* VII, 287–288; Gipson, ed., *Moravian Indian Mission on White River,* trans. Stocker, Frueauff, and Zeller, 328–329; Delaware Indians to Wells, Mar. 30, 1805, in Esarey, ed., *Messages and Letters of William Henry Harrison,* I, 117–118, William Patterson, a Delaware, to Wells, Apr. 5, 1805, 121–123, Harrison to Henry Dearborn, Apr. 26, 1805, 125–126; Owens, "Jeffersonian Benevolence on the Ground," *Journal of the Early Republic,* XXII (2002), 420–423; Robert M. Owens, *Mr. Jefferson's Hammer: William Henry Harrison and the Origins of American Indian Policy* (Norman, Okla., 2007), 99–105; Bottiger, *Borderland of Fear,* 48–49.

to remain. By 1796, federal officials counted only twenty families living on four thousand acres of land.[39]

When Harrison set his sights on the Illinois country, he approached the Kaskaskias first, rather than the Sauks and Mesquakies, who also claimed it as their own. Led by Ducoigne, six Kaskaskias sold more than eight million acres of Illinois land to the United States in exchange for the promise of U.S. protection, a small reservation, and an annuity of one thousand dollars to be divided by the government between individual families. Written into the treaty was the administration's own investment in their narrative of Native declension—the federal government would discontinue annuities individually after the death of each recipient. For the Sauks and Mesquakies who were not included in the treaty, the message was clear—those who did not attend Harrison's councils would find their homelands sold out from under their feet.[40]

Ducoigne's motivations were obvious to see. The sale strengthened his alliance with the United States at a time when the Kaskaskias badly needed it. They had recently been engaged in intermittent raids with the Missouri Shawnees, and federal officials also believed that they were on the verge of war with the Potawatomis. Ducoigne himself received a house built with federal funds and completed three years later. He continued to invest in the federal relationship, lobbying for more civilization funds for the Kaskaskias and for an additional annuity to buy more furniture, chocolate, coffee, sugar, and wine to show other chiefs, in Dearborn's estimation, "how much like a gentlemen he lives." Beyond personal emoluments, the Kaskaskias would receive U.S. protection.[41]

Yet promises of protection were quickly put to the test. In June 1807, a party of Kickapoos killed Ducoigne's brother-in-law and stole his property. By accepting U.S. protection, the Kaskaskias were technically prohib-

39. Robert Michael Morrissey, *Empire by Collaboration: Indians, Colonists, and Governments in Colonial Illinois Country* (Philadelphia, 2015), 19, 28, 232–234; Morrissey, "The Power of the Ecotone: Bison, Slavery, and the Rise and Fall of the Grand Village of the Kaskaskia," *Journal of American History,* CII (2015), 667–692.

40. "Treaty with the Kaskaskia Made in Vincennes," Aug. 13, 1803, WHH, reel 1, 632–636; "The Kaskaskia and Other Tribes; Communicated to the Senate," Oct. 31, 1803, in *ASPIA,* I, 687; Jortner, *Gods of Prophetstown,* 91.

41. Henry Dearborn to William Henry Harrison, May 24, 1804, WHH, reel 1, 802 (quotation), Jefferson to Harrison, Feb. 27, 1803, 521, Jefferson to the U.S. Congress, Oct. 17, 1803, 637, Dearborn to Harrison, Feb. 25, 1806, reel 2, 152, Michael Jones to Harrison, Jan. 5, 1806, 476; Robert M. Owens, "Jean Baptiste Ducoigne, the Kaskaskias, and the Limits of Thomas Jefferson's Friendship," *Journal of Illinois History,* V (2002), 109–136.

ited from pursuing retributive justice of their own. Ducoigne demanded that Harrison deliver the murderer to the Kaskaskias and guarantee them "a protection as effectual as that which is enjoyed by our own Citizens as guaranteed to him by their Treaty." Although Harrison agreed, he had a fuzzier sense of what protection meant. In reality, he had little power to demand the handover of a murderer from the Kickapoos, who declined to fulfill his request. Ducoigne angrily criticized the double bind of U.S. protection: "Yes when I meet an Indian I must stand until he shoots me down, and then make a defence, and thus lose my life and the lives of my people." Ducoigne's appeal to U.S. protection demonstrates, on the one hand, how smaller nations like the Kaskaskias sought to use treaties to their advantage. On the other hand, it shows the resistance of Ducoigne's neighbors to the imposition of U.S. law in their affairs.[42]

Just as Harrison made a decision to exploit land sharing to his advantage, leaders like Shawnee chief Black Hoof made similar choices to use the treaty system to consolidate their own alliances and territory. Shawnees hoped that the U.S. government would recognize them as a centralized, territorial nation to protect them from dueling land claims. In 1795, Black Hoof's Shawnees settled at Wapakoneta on the headwaters of the Auglaize River at the invitation of the Miamis and Wyandots. The Shawnees at Wapakoneta tried to secure their power to remain there by working with the Jefferson administration. In 1802 and 1807, Black Hoof traveled to Washington, once in company with other Shawnees and Delawares, to ask for a deed to a Shawnee reserve where they might bring together Shawnee bands that had been dispersed by conflict over several centuries. They declared their desire to "live in one place and never move." Not all Shawnees agreed with Black Hoof's centralizing goals, however. Black Hoof also sought power for the Wapakonetans as spokesman for a Shawnee nation at the expense of Shawnee peoples elsewhere.[43]

In the decade before the War of 1812, federal officials relied on the treaty system to dispossess Native peoples of most of their Ohio and Indiana lands

42. William Henry Harrison to Henry Dearborn, July 11, 1807, WHH, reel 2, 840 ("protection"), Michael Jones to Harrison, May 4, 1807, 779–780 ("Yes"), Dearborn to Harrison, June 20, 1807, 815, Harrison to Dearborn, May 23, 1807, 802, "Orders to Pierre Menard," May 18, 1807, 794, 796; Saler, *Settlers' Empire,* 74–76.

43. Speech of Blackbeard, 1806 [1807], Shawnee File, Ohio Valley-Great Lakes Ethnohistory Archive, Glenn A. Black Archaeology Laboratory, Indiana University, Bloomington ("live"), quoted in Lakomäki, "'Our Line,'" *Journal of the Early Republic,* XXXIV (2014), 614; Lakomäki, *Gathering Together,* 140–142; Edmunds, "Patriot Defamed," in Warren, ed., *Eastern Shawnee Tribe of Oklahoma,* 16–17.

as well as those in Illinois. Enterprising leaders like Black Hoof and Ducoigne tried to manipulate the treaties to their advantage by securing independent, national reserves out of overlapping claims. Others left altogether and moved west of the Mississippi River or north in the late eighteenth century. They left in search of autonomy and political independence outside the boundary claims of the United States. Some wagered that moving away from what had been a country held in common was a safer route than fighting for the power to remain.[44]

Harrison's machinations were part of a renewed contest over removal by confederated Native nations and the United States. In 1803, the Louisiana Purchase added 827,000 square miles to the United States and prompted Jefferson to reconsider the geography of removal. He put forward a plan to "transplant our Indians into [the Louisiana Territory], constituting them a Marechaussée to prevent emigrants crossing the river, until we shall have filled up all the vacant country on this side." Jefferson drafted two constitutional amendments to incorporate the Louisiana territory into the United States. Both included a proposal to exchange the lands of eastern Native peoples for those west of the Mississippi River. Congress followed suit. In 1804, it directed Jefferson to purchase Native lands east of the Mississippi in exchange for lands west of the river secured by the Louisiana Purchase, an instruction that they would repeat in 1817. By 1804, Secretary of War Dearborn and Harrison were already discussing a land exchange with the White River Delawares.[45]

While Jefferson's administration embraced removal across the Mississippi River, a new nativist movement spread across the Great Lakes region that demanded the removal of white Americans across the Ohio River. In the early nineteenth century, several Native prophets began to reject the

44. Lawrence Kinnaird, ed., *Annual Report of the American Historical Association for the Year 1945: Spain in the Mississippi Valley, 1765–1794,* IV (Washington, D.C.,1946), xxx–xxxi; Kathleen DuVal, *The Native Ground: Indians and Colonists in the Heart of the Continent* (Philadelphia, 2007), 162–163.

45. Thomas Jefferson to Pierre Samuel Du Pont de Nemours, Nov. 1, 1803, in Julian P. Boyd et al., eds., *The Papers of Thomas Jefferson,* 43 vols. (Princeton, N.J., 1950—), XLI, 647–648 (quotation, 648); "Exchange of Lands with the Indians; Communicated to the Senate," Jan. 9, 1817, in *ASPIA,* II, 123–124; "Drafts of an Amendment to the Constitution," [July 1803], in Paul Leicester Ford, ed., *The Writings of Thomas Jefferson,* VIII, *1801–1806* (New York, 1897), 243; [Henry Dearborn] to W[illia]m H[enry] Harrison, June 21, 1804, in *TPUS,* VII, 203; Wallace, *Jefferson and the Indians,* 224; John P. Bowes, *Land Too Good for Indians: Northern Indian Removal* (Norman, Okla., 2016), 57; Banner, *How the Indians Lost Their Land,* 193–194.

responses of chiefs like Black Hoof, Little Turtle, and Tarhe to U.S. colonialism. Foremost among them was Shawnee prophet Tenskwatawa, who had a series of visions in 1805–1806 that he shared with a growing group of followers. Tenskwatawa railed against U.S. civilization plans. He invented a traditional Shawnee past free from the influence of colonizers, and he ignored the female councils that had held power in Shawnee communities. Tenskwatawa taught his followers to abandon U.S. trade goods, Christianity, and gendered agricultural labor. In the 1790s, Wayne reclaimed the sites of U.S. military defeats by building a string of forts across the Ohio country. Tenskwatawa did the same at the site of the infamous Treaty of Greenville. He gathered his followers together there, building a longhouse and dozens of dwellings for a permanent settlement.[46]

Tenskwatawa revived the idea of a country held in common for his followers. Black Hoof's Wapakonetans preached consolidation, defined national borders, and Shawnee nationhood. Tenskwatawa took the opposite tack. He argued that all Native peoples were part of a single nation linked by long-distance travel and mobility. As with the United Indian Nations a decade prior, Tenskwatawa claimed that the only line that mattered was the one that separated the United States from Indian country. At Greenville, Tenkswatawa and his brother Tecumseh built a multiethnic community to counter U.S. policy. In 1808, Tenskwatawa moved his followers to a new site he called Prophetstown on the Wabash and Tippecanoe Rivers. He relocated at the suggestion of Main Poc, a Potawatomi war and religious leader, who had led raids against the Osages and white migrants in what is now southern Illinois from his village at Red Rock Creek and the Kankakee River to increase his own economic power in the region. From the vantage point of Prophetstown, Tenskwatawa could better protect his followers from U.S. attacks. It was far from U.S. factories at Fort Wayne and Chicago. From that location, Tenskwatawa believed "they would then be able to watch the Boundry Line between the Indians and white people—and if a white man put his foot over it that the warriors could Easly put him back." Tenskwatawa renewed a central objective of the confederation of the 1780s and 1790s to remove white Americans across the Ohio River.[47]

46. Jortner, *Gods of Prophetstown,* 103, 134; White, *Middle Ground,* 503–509.

47. William Wells to Henry Dearborn, Apr. 20–23, 1808, in *TPUS,* VII, 558 ("they would"), also cited in Edmunds, *Shawnee Prophet,* 69–70; John Gibson to William Hargrove, Oct. 4, 1807, WHH, reel 3, 1, William Henry Harrison to Dearborn, May 19, 1808, 156; White, *Middle Ground,* 514; Edmunds, "Main Poc," *American Indian Quarterly,* IX (1985), 260, 262; Dowd, *Spirited Resistance,* 144–145; William Franz, "'To Live by Depredations': Main Poc's Strategic Use of Violence," *Journal of the Illinois State*

Tenskwatawa's message was met with fear and repression at U.S. posts and with criticism by Indigenous leaders who had embraced fixity or bounded national spaces. Harrison himself demanded the "removal of the Impostor from our [United States] Territory." He sent an agent to Greenville telling Tenskwatawa to disband his followers. Little Turtle also opposed the Shawnee prophet. Prophetstown was sited on Miami lands. When Little Turtle heard that Tenskwatawa intended to move there, he tried to stop the group from relocating. Little Turtle confronted them in the midst of their travels, but Tenskwatawa refused to change his plans. Their goals ran counter to each other. Little Turtle wanted defined boundaries for the Miamis to protect their power in a rapidly changing world. Tenskwatawa, by contrast, was more expansive. He hoped to do away with tribal territories altogether to create one vast multiethnic empire of Indigenous peoples. Neither was an accommodationist or a militant—they pursued very different strategies to mitigate the effects of U.S. colonialism, and their interests were at odds with each other.[48]

Tenskwatawa insisted that he had never sent for his followers, but, in fact, Native diplomats ranged far and wide to spread his message. By 1805, Le Maigouis and eventually Main Poc, as well, began traveling across the Great Lakes, calling a new confederation into being. Main Poc spent several months at Greenville in 1807, where he was courted by Tenskwatawa and took up many, although not all, of his teachings. Indian agent Wells called Main Poc, "the pivot on which the minds of all the Western Indians turned"—surely an overstatement but nonetheless a symbol of his perceived power as an emissary, religious figure, and war leader among the Potawatomis. A U.S. agent similarly dubbed Le Maigouis a "Herald of this new Religion." Le Maigouis brought Tenskwatawa's teachings to a broad

---

Historical Society, CII (2009), 238–247; Gregory Evans Dowd, "Thinking outside the Circle: Tecumseh's 1811 Mission," in Kathryn E. Holland Braund, ed., *Tohopeka: Rethinking the Creek War and the War of 1812* (Tuscaloosa, Ala., 2012), 35; Jortner, *Gods of Prophetstown,* 138–139.

48. William Henry Harrison to Henry Dearborn, Sept. 5, 1807, in Logan Esarey, ed., *Messages and Letters of William Henry Harrison,* I (Indianapolis, Ind., 1922), 247 ("removal"), also quoted in Jortner, *Gods of Prophetstown,* 138, 139, 143–148. Adam Jortner has argued that Prophetstown was a Native city-state, with its own legal code, military, and national religion. I use the term *empire* here to stress the differences between the Prophet's vision and that of Little Turtle. See Wells to Dearborn, Apr. 20–23, 1808, in *TPUS,* VII, 558–559; Edmunds, *Shawnee Prophet,* 69–70; Dowd, "Thinking outside the Circle," in Braund, ed., *Tohopeka,* 36; Buss, "Imagined Worlds and Archival Realities," in Buss and Genetin-Pilawa, eds., *Beyond Two Worlds,* 97–116; Lakomäki, *Gathering Together,* 150; Bottiger, *Borderland of Fear,* 59.

audience beyond Prophetstown. Le Maigouis's emphasis on the injustice of U.S. policy appealed to Native people of the Great Lakes, motivating them to visit Greenville and then Prophetstown. To eastern Americans, these movements and messages were terrifying. Native solidarity and the specter of a pan-Indian alliance stoked racial fears in the Atlantic states and increased the clamor for removal in Ohio.[49]

After 1808, Tecumseh also traveled to gain the support of the British at Amherstburg; he moved to the upper Mississippi and to Ohio, and he went south to bind the Creeks and Cherokees to the Prophet's cause in 1811. Harrison marveled that Tecumseh was "in constant motion. You see him today on the Wabash and in a short time you hear of him on the shores of Lake Erie or Michigan, or on the banks of the Mississippi." Tecumseh, however, was not as exceptional as Harrison thought. Shawnee nativists had a long history of traveling south to cement alliances. It made sense that the Shawnee brothers were at the center of a political and religious movement that depended on long distance travel. They were of the Kishpokotha division that relocated between the Creeks and the Ohio River Valley in the eighteenth century. In the 1780s, some Kishpokotha Shawnees had gone to live with the Chickamauga Cherokees in Tennessee, while a decade later, others ended up on the White River. They remained staunchly opposed to the Treaty of Greenville and to any accommodation with the United States of the sort undertaken by Black Hoof.[50]

The Shawnee brothers sent messages and emissaries far and wide to the Haudenosaunees, to the Detroit River region, and west to the Sac, Mesquakies, Potawatomis, Kickapoos, and Ho-Chunks. The Prophet found followers among the Shawnees, Wyandots, and Delawares in Indiana and Ohio. The Wyandots, for example, sent a delegation to visit Greenville in 1807. His most eager audiences were among Natives in what would become Illinois, Michigan, and Wisconsin. Kickapoos, who were some of the Prophet's first converts, Potawatomis, Odawas, and Ojibwes all traveled to hear his teach-

49. Wells to Dearborn, Apr. 20–23, 1808, in *TPUS,* VII, 556 ("pivot"); Dunham to Hull, May 20, 1807, *MPHC,* XL, 123–127 ("Herald," 125), "Speech of Indian Chief to Various Tribes [Enclosure in Dunham to Hall, May 20]," 127–133; Dowd, *Spirited Resistance,* 144; Franz, "'To Live by Depredations,'" *Journal of the Illinois State Historical Society,* CII (2009), 241–242; Owens, *Red Dreams, White Nightmares,* 185; Jortner, *Gods of Prophetstown,* 135–138, 169; Bottiger, *Borderland of Fear,* 57–58, 113–115.

50. William Henry Harrison to William Eustis, Aug. 7, 1811, in Esarey, ed., *Messages and Letters,* I, 549 (quotation); White, *Middle Ground,* 514; Edmunds, *Shawnee Prophet,* 71, 118; Dowd, *Spirited Resistance,* 144–145; John Sugden, "Tecumseh's Travels Revisited," *Indiana Magazine of History,* XCVI (2000), 150–168, esp. 167; Dowd, "Thinking outside the Circle," in Braund, ed., *Tohopeka,* 32; Lakomäki, *Gathering Together,* 143.

ings at Greenville in 1807 and carried his words back to towns on Saginaw Bay, to Sault Ste. Marie, and to the Wabash River. By the following year, the Prophet's message had circulated even further north and west, eventually appearing one thousand miles away from Prophetstown along the Red River and Lake Winnipeg. Native travelers on their way to see the Prophet passed through Fort Wayne and Chicago. At Chicago in 1807, Indian agent Charles Joett counted one thousand Native travelers "crouding down upon us from the Green Bay on their way . . . to see the Shawonee at Greenville." Trading houses intended by the United States to prevent and control movement instead became way stations in the relentless motion inspired by the Prophet.[51]

U.S. officials were largely powerless to stop the continual arrival of Native diplomats and visitors to Prophetstown. They disparagingly labeled the Prophet's followers as an "assemblage of vagabond Indians"—a reference to their movements. Indian agents followed the travels of various parties on their way to Greenville. They tried to intercept British speeches. They reported that British agents were spreading rumors that George III was going to send ships and soldiers "to releave his red children from oppression and restore their country to them again." Secretary of War Dearborn directed agents to discover the "real feelings and Intentions" and to "penatrate the veiws of the Indians." At Fort Wayne, Indian agent Wells, gave eight hundred dollars worth of gifts to Main Poc, hosting him and his party for five months from December 1807 to April 1808 in an attempt to sever his ties and travels to the Prophet. On receipt of these gifts, Main Poc appeased Wells, telling him, "My friend you have caught me: like a wild Horse is caught with a Lick of Salt you have Hobled me—that I can no longer range the woods as I please." Main Poc agreed to travel to Washington where he met with Jefferson, who asked him to end Potawatomi raids on the Osages. U.S. attempts to attach Main Poc to the federal agenda, however, were not successful. He refused to give up raids on the Osages, and he returned to Prophetstown the following year. He was far from "caught."[52]

51. Charles Jouett to Henry Dearborn, Dec. 1, 1807, in *TPUS,* VII, 496 (quotation), William Wells to Dearborn, Mar. 6, 1808, 531; Wells to Harrison, June 1807, WHH, reel 2, 827, Harrison to Dearborn, July 11, 1807, 841, Harrison to Dearborn, May 19, 1808, reel 3, 156; White, *Middle Ground,* 511–513; Sugden, "Tecumseh's Travels Revisited," *Indiana Magazine of History,* XCVI (2000), 167; Tanner, *Falcon,* 144–147; Duckworth, ed., *Friends, Foes, and Furs,* 102–104; Jortner, *Gods of Prophetstown,* 134–135.

52. John Johnston to Henry Dearborn, Dec. 31, 1807, RG 107, M221, roll 9, NARA, quoted in Lakomäki, *Gathering Together,* 148 ("assemblage"); William Wells to Henry Dearborn, Dec. 5, 1807, in *TPUS,* VII, 498 ("releave"), Dearborn to Charles Jouett, Jan. 26, 1808, 519 ("real"), Wells to Dearborn, Dec. 31, 1807, 510 ("penatrate"), 556

In their correspondence, U.S. officials portrayed these movements as a cacaphony of which they simply could not make sense. In 1811, U.S. troops under Harrison marched to Prophetstown to destroy Tenskwatawa's empire. At the Battle of Tippecanoe on November 7, a small group of Shawnee, Piankeshaw, Ho-Chunk, and Potawatomi warriors were unable to protect the settlement against Harrison's troops. When Britain and the United States went to war later that year, most Natives in the region who participated fought on the side of the British. They hoped that the British government would help deliver a secure homeland in the Ohio Valley—what the British called a "barrier state" and what some Native leaders had long conceived of as a country held in common. Some Shawnees fought for the British at the Battle of the Thames in 1813, where Tecumseh was killed by U.S. troops. Tenskwatawa's movement faltered soon after, although resistance to U.S. colonialism never disappeared.[53]

Despite the aspirations of Britain's Native allies, the Treaty of Ghent that ended the War of 1812 returned the relationship between Britain and the United States to the status quo antebellum. The treaty did not establish a barrier state. Article IX promised to return Native rights and possessions to their prewar status. The status quo antebellum was nevertheless difficult to pinpoint in the Ohio Valley, where federal treaties had rapidly remade Native homelands on the ground. At one postwar peace treaty between the United States and Wyandot, Delaware, Seneca, Shawnee, Miami, Ojibwe, Odawa, and Potawatomi chiefs in 1815, the signatories confirmed land cessions made long before the war at Greenville in 1795. Reviewing the 1795 cessions, one Potawatomi chief "gave his consent, though with reluctance." The chief determined that he would no longer fight against the Greenville Treaty. "If, however, it were to do again, he would pause; he would reflect. He would look at his children in the cradle, and ask what right he had to injure those innocents? what authority he had to deprive them of their rights?"[54]

Ultimately, federal officials who discouraged Native movement had little control over Indigenous politics and long-distance travel. They were much

("My friend"); Edmunds, "Main Poc," *American Indian Quarterly*, IX (1985), 262–265; Franz, "'To Live by Depredations,'" *Journal of the Illinois State Historical Society*, CII (2009), 242.

53. Colin G. Calloway, "Suspicion and Self-Interest: The British-Indian Alliance and the Peace of Paris," *Historian*, XLVIII (1985), 57 (quotation); Owens, *Red Dreams, White Nightmares*, 187–192; Nichols, *Red Gentlemen and White Savages*, 201.

54. "Journal of the Proceedings of the Commissioners Appointed to Treat with the Northwest Indians at Detroit," Sept. 6, 1815, in *ASPIA*, II, 25 (quotations).

more successful at changing the region by encouraging migration from the Atlantic states. As Tenskwatawa and Tecumseh settled on removal as a tactic of resistance, white migrants were already transforming Native space. The federal government encouraged their movements by opening land offices and building roads in Ohio and Indiana Territory. In 1800, Congress had passed a new land law that opened up the acquisition of government land to smaller purchasers and created new land offices west of the Appalachians. Buyers could pay for lands slowly, and they only had to secure 320 acres at a time. In combination with Harrison's treaties, the land law sent white migrants and a small number of Black migrants scrambling across the Appalachians. A new land office opened at Vincennes in 1804 did a brisk business. New migrants purchased fifty thousand acres of Indiana Territory land each year. They transformed the landscape in other ways, marking out bounded private property in fee simple with fenced-in fields.[55]

Territorial officials and new migrants were overwhelmingly concerned with population as a building block of state making. Their concerns were not unlike those of the British officials who had wielded population growth as a political tool in the mid-eighteenth century. Those who went to Indiana were young people with high fertility rates. As a result, the population of the territory increased dramatically over the first two decades of the nineteenth century.[56]

Indian agents managed the population boom by working with it instead of against it, as had the first generation of federal officials. They pressed for changes that would encourage migration from the East. They petitioned for new roads to increase the value of the lands they purchased. They created wagon roads that pushed new settlements away from the major arteries of the Ohio and Wabash Rivers and toward the interior. The experience of the War of 1812 convinced federal officials that new roads crossing Native lands were necessary for military transportation. In 1815, President James Madi-

55. Report to the U.S. House of Representatives, Feb. 18, 1800, WHH, reel 1, "Circular," May 14, 1800; "An Act to Amend the Act Intituled 'An Act Providing for the Sale of the Lands of the United States, in the Territory Northwest of the Ohio, and above the Mouth of the Kentucky River," May 10, 1800, in *The Public Statutes at Large of the United States of America, from the Organization of the Government in 1789, to March 3, 1845 . . .*, II (Boston, 1845), 73–78; Malcolm J. Rohrbough, *The Land Office Business: The Settlement and Administration of American Public Lands, 1789–1837* (New York, 1968), 19–41; Andrew R. L. Cayton, *Frontier Indiana* (Bloomington, Ind., 1996), 179–180, 184–185, 264–267; Nichols, *Red Gentlemen and White Savages,* 194, 198–199.

56. "Petition to Congress by Inhabitants of Knox, St. Clair, and Randolph Counties," [Oct. 22, 1803], in *TPUS,* VII, 126; Lewis Cass to Elkanah Watson, Nov. 3, 1815, Lewis Cass Papers, box 2, BHC.

son's first postwar message to Congress argued that the United States, more than any other nation, needed extensive national roads that were essential to "binding" the country together. By 1818, seventy miles of a western military road stretched from the rapids of the Miami to Detroit. New roads incentivized migration and drove up the price of public lands. By 1810, more than one million migrants from the East had migrated to land west of the Appalachians.[57]

After the War of 1812, federal officials quickly countered previous demands for a Native buffer state in the Ohio Valley with their own plans for the removal of Native peoples from those same lands. By 1816, federal officials turned to focus more intently on making the settlement of the various new western states "more compact" by pushing Indians to cede all of their lands in individual states. To Indigenous people who held fast to their homelands in the Ohio Valley and lower Great Lakes, they likely saw such changes, not as a sudden transformation of federal demands into a removal period, but as part of a longer transformation in the contest over movement in the Ohio country.[58]

57. James Madison, "Seventh Annual Message," Dec. 5, 1815, in James D. Richardson, [ed.], *A Compilation of the Messages and Papers of the Presidents, 1789–1897,* I (Washington, D.C., 1896), 567 (quotation); Cass to Watson, Nov. 3, 1815, box 2, Lewis Cass Papers, BHC, Alexander Macomb to John C. Calhoun, Nov. 2, 1818, box 4; Drew R. McCoy, *The Last of the Fathers: James Madison and the Republican Legacy* (New York, 1989), 94–95; Cayton, *Frontier Indiana,* 184–185, 281–282.

58. William H. Crawford to [William] Clark, [Ninian] Edwards, and [Auguste] Chouteau, May 7, 1816, in *ASPIA,* II, 97 (quotation).

Part 2

The American Revolution spurred a revolution in race and rights. The efforts of enslaved people to free themselves during and after the war, the natural rights tradition that emerged alongside revolution, Quaker-led lobbying campaigns, and individual freedom suits all pushed forward a wave of abolitionist action. Political organizing by Black and white abolitionists led to an injunction against the participation of U.S. traders in the Atlantic slave trade in 1794 and to the abolition of the trade in 1808. State legislatures in New England and the mid-Atlantic, beginning with Pennsylvania in 1780, passed gradual emancipation laws freeing enslaved people born after the passage of the acts when they reached adulthood. By 1804, seven states had either mandated immediate abolition or laid out a plan for gradual emancipation. Growing numbers of white Americans were beginning to understand slavery as wrong or were no longer willing to defend it.

At the same time, slaveholding expanded rather than diminished across the South after the American Revolution. Virginia, Maryland, and Delaware liberalized laws allowing enslavers to manumit people but took no other action. The arguments of Black and white abolitionists barely registered in the lower South, where both Georgia and South Carolina reopened the Atlantic slave trade while they could in the two decades after the war. From the vantage point of enslaved people, emancipation looked like a long process that spanned the nineteenth century.

Even where African Americans won their freedom, they had to fight for belonging. White legislators debated who constituted *the people.* They generally agreed that some Native Americans who lived in the United States were still not a part of the new nation—though they might be in the future. In the case of free African Americans, the question was more complicated. In some states, free African Americans had all the rights of white citizens. In others, they lacked the right to vote, settle, change residence, or practice certain trades. Free African Americans who built on the legal gains they secured after the Revolution by fighting for particular rights prompted a backlash. In response to their successes, white legislators, jurists, and reformers who hoped to temper the radical equality inherent in *the people* proposed colonization.

Just as Native Americans watched their borders to protect their right to remain, so, too, did African Americans. They read colonizationist writings to anticipate the borders between exclusionary language and the actual practice of exclusion. They looked to the borders between states, developing a nuanced understanding of where their rights shifted under their feet as they moved. Finally, they came to know the borders of their own communities. It was at the local level that free people secured the right to remain.

CHAPTER 5
"A GOOD CITIZEN OF THE WHOLE WORLD"
Colonization in the Era of Gradual Emancipation

When Moses Fisk, a white teacher at Dartmouth College in Hanover, New Hampshire, gave his Thanksgiving Day oration in 1795, he used the occasion to appeal for abolition. The crowd before him had gathered to celebrate many blessings. Fisk listed them: suffrage rights, "plenty in our habitations," the "destruction of the Indians" at the Battle of Fallen Timbers, and peace with the British after the Jay Treaty. It brought "shame to the whole union" that enslaved people could celebrate none of those things, he told them. "They are not of the nation; and, therefore, have no national blessings to acknowledge. They have no share in the commonwealth. They are politically nothing. And by celebrating this day, we subscribe to their nonexistence." Fisk wanted an immediate end to slavery. He did not, however, think that freed people could be immediately included in the blessings he had just named. He told the crowd that colonization—the removal of free African Americans from the nation—should follow emancipation. Free African Americans would have to leave the nation that had subscribed them to "nonexistence" and escape white prejudice, he believed, in order to seize political rights.[1]

Like many Americans, white and Black, Fisk hoped that colonization would follow emancipation. Hardly an outlier, colonization ideology accompanied the first wave of gradual emancipation that began in the 1780s. White enslavers, ministers, and opponents of slavery invoked it in debates about slavery and freedom and the rights of free African Americans. They discussed it in private letters, parlor conversations, public orations, antislavery pamphlets, and newspaper editorials. Free African Americans in northern cities broached the idea of creating an independent settlement

1. [Moses Fisk], *Tyrannical Libertymen; A Discourse upon Negro-Slavery in the United States: Composed at——, in Newhampshire; on the Late Federal Thanksgiving-Day* (Hanover, N.H., 1795), 12.

as a response to white racism in petitions, correspondence, and at public meetings. But if colonization talk was common, its proponents disagreed about the ends it should serve. It vaguely referred to the planting of a new colony—and thus to a range of strategies that were alternately voluntary or coercive, separatist or prejudiced.[2]

Colonization was a broad concept that appealed to white writers whose opposition to slavery grew from very different concerns. Fisk believed that the creation of a Black state would accelerate emancipation. He and other colonizationists thought that free African Americans could never find equality in the United States because of white racism. They argued that free African Americans lived within the nation but did not belong to it. Like Fisk, they understood removal to resolve that contradiction by creating a republic based on whiteness. Enslavers in the upper South and colonizationists scattered across the mid-Atlantic thought that freed people might create a faction and tear the Republic apart from within. Meanwhile, white ministers in New England saw colonization in West Africa as a missionary venture that would suppress the slave trade. A wave of scholarship has shown that early national abolitionism, spearheaded by Black and white activists associated with antislavery societies like the Pennsylvania Abolition Society (PAS), was a far more radical and interracial movement than scholars have previously imagined. At the same time, the gradualism and environmentalist ideas about race that underpinned early abolitionism shared an uncomfortable kinship with colonization, a tension that became more obvious the further one traveled from Pennsylvania.[3]

2. For the centrality of colonization to late-eighteenth-century antislavery, see Christa Dierksheide, *Amelioration and Empire: Progress and Slavery in the Plantation Americas* (Charlottesville, Va., 2014), 25–66; Nicholas Guyatt, *Bind Us Apart: How Enlightened Americans Invented Racial Segregation* (New York, 2016). For early colonization and emigration in the United States before 1816, see Peter S. Onuf, *Jefferson's Empire: The Language of American Nationhood* (Charlottesville, Va., 2000), 174–188; David Kazanjian, *The Colonizing Trick: National Culture and Imperial Citizenship in Early America* (Minneapolis, Minn., 2003), 89–126; Cassandra Pybus, *Epic Journeys of Freedom: Runaway Slaves of the American Revolution and Their Global Quest for Liberty* (Boston, 2006); James Sidbury, *Becoming African in America: Race and Nation in the Early Black Atlantic* (New York, 2007), 17–155; Alexander X. Byrd, *Captives and Voyagers: Black Migrants across the Eighteenth-Century British Atlantic World* (Baton Rouge, La., 2008), 125–244; Christopher Cameron, *To Plead Our Own Cause: African Americans in Massachusetts and the Making of the Antislavery Movement* (Kent, Ohio, 2014), 100–113.

3. For the broader context in the upper South, see Eva Sheppard Wolf, *Race and Liberty in the New Nation: Emancipation in Virginia from the Revolution to Nat Turner's Rebellion* (Baton Rouge, La., 2006), 85–129. For the radicalism of early national aboli-

Some free African Americans in northern cities also worked with white colonizationists. Their involvement might seem unexpected given colonization's later history in the United States. Separatism took many forms in free African American communities after the American Revolution. Black ministers, tradesmen, and lay leaders pursued self-determination by building independent churches, mutual aid societies, and schools. They also sought to remove their families from the grasp of white supremacy by exploring emigration to West Africa. Black northern proponents of the idea believed that a West African venture they controlled themselves could deliver political rights and land grants that offered economic independence. As these men sought to make a new world after the American Revolution, their interests converged for a time with white ministers and antislavery reformers who promoted colonization. Their plans had meaningful differences: self-determination motived most African American emigrationists while exclusion motivated most white colonizationists. Despite these differences, both colonizationists and emigrationists drew on the the language of Christian missions and a diasporic return to describe their projects.[4]

---

tion, see Manisha Sinha, *The Slave's Cause: A History of Abolition* (New Haven, Conn., 2016), 5; Nicholas P. Wood, "A 'Class of Citizens': The Earliest Black Petitioners to Congress and Their Quaker Allies," *William and Mary Quarterly*, 3d Ser., LXXIV (2017), 113; Paul J. Polgar, *Standard-Bearers of Equality: America's First Abolition Movement* (Williamsburg, Va., and Chapel Hill, N.C., 2019), 4, 15. For a more pessimistic view of the period, see Shane White, *Somewhat More Independent: The End of Slavery in New York City, 1700–1810* (Athens, Ga., 1991); Joanne Pope Melish, *Disowning Slavery: Gradual Emancipation and "Race" in New England, 1700–1860* (Ithaca, N.Y., 1998); Leslie M. Harris, *In the Shadow of Slavery: African Americans in New York City, 1626–1863* (Chicago, 2004); James J. Gigantino, II, *The Ragged Road to Abolition: Slavery and Freedom in New Jersey, 1775–1865* (Philadelphia, 2015).

4. Scholars of the antebellum period have pointed out this distinction by calling Black-led plans "emigrationist" and white-led migration plans "colonizationist." For important discussions of the terms *colonization* and *emigration* in scholarship about the United States, see, for example, Kazanjian, *Colonizing Trick,* 94–95; Ousmane K. Power-Greene, *Against Wind and Tide: The African American Struggle against the Colonization Movement* (New York, 2014), xix; Martha S. Jones, *Birthright Citizens: A History of Race and Rights in Antebellum America* (New York, 2018), 37–38. These early plans were intertwined with British colonization at the mouth of the Sierra Leone River. See Christopher Fyfe, *A History of Sierra Leone* (Oxford, 1962); James W. St. G. Walker, *The Black Loyalists: The Search for a Promised Land in Nova Scotia and Sierra Leone, 1783–1870* (New York, 1976); Ellen Gibson Wilson, *The Loyal Blacks* (New York, 1976); Sylvia R. Frey, *Water from the Rock: Black Resistance in a Revolutionary Age* (Princeton, N.J., 1991), 192–202; Deirdre Coleman, *Romantic Colonization and British Anti-Slavery* (Cambridge, 2005), 106–133; Sidbury, *Becoming African in America,* 80–86, 91–129; Padraic X. Scanlan, *Freedom's Debtors: British Antislavery in Sierra Leone in the Age of Revolution* (New Haven, Conn., 2017).

Yet that convergence was fleeting. The split over colonization that would define later abolitionism had its origins in the 1790s. By the mid-1790s, free African Americans had largely abandoned the public campaign for West African emigration after observing the failures of Britain's experiment with colonization in Sierra Leone. At courthouses and in legislatures, they partnered with white abolitionists in places like Philadelphia and New York to pursue the right to remain in the United States. Emigration did not emerge as a mass movement again until the 1820s. By contrast, some white writers in the upper South and mid-Atlantic never abandoned colonization. They continued a separate conversation about it for decades.

White colonizationists looked west more often than they looked east. Indian removal in the trans-Appalachian West enabled and influenced colonization plans. White colonizationists borrowed from the realm of Indian affairs when they formulated their ideas. From slaveholding statesman Thomas Jefferson to New Divinity minister Samuel Hopkins, white colonizationists learned to think about emancipation by taking ideas from civilization plans directed at Native Americans. They harkened back to abolitionists Granville Sharp and Anthony Benezet, whose proposals for doling out *"compact little Farms"* to African Americans in Indian country looked similar to those proposed by Quaker agents who were also involved in Indian affairs. Some of the most supposedly benevolent white writers took details formulated for Indian country—the idea that Native Americans and white migrants could not be neighbors, that Native people could only pursue self-determination beyond the United States, or that they should be sent with teachers and "implements of household and of the handicraft arts" to pursue the right to remain elsewhere—and reworked them for emancipation. When white writers imagined the place for an African American colony, they turned to Indian country more often than West Africa. Black writers never did the same. That difference is revealing. For most white writers, colonization did not mean Christian missions to Africa or a diasporic return; it meant removal.[5]

Removal linked the experiences of Native Americans and African Americans. Fisk, who urged his listeners to embrace abolition in 1795, likely understood these connections. He went to Dartmouth, founded in 1769 to teach Native students. By the time he matriculated, no Native scholars were in

5. Granville Sharp to Benjamin Rush, July 18, 1775, in John A. Woods, "The Correspondence of Benjamin Rush and Granville Sharp, 1773–1809," *Journal of American Studies,* I (1967), 15 *("compact");* Thomas Jefferson, *Notes on the State of Virginia,* ed. William Peden (Williamsburg, Va., and Chapel Hill, N.C., 1982), 138 ("implements").

residence, nor would they be for the next fifteen years. The year after he gave his oration in Hanover, Fisk migrated to the Cumberland Plateau, where he speculated in Cherokee lands. Fisk saw opportunity there in 1796 because the Treaty of Greenville and an agreement with the Lower Cherokees in 1794 made dispossession and land speculation possible. Before the Revolution, white migrants had tried to move into the region, "but the Indians have always been troublesome," Fisk wrote to a friend. Although white migrants had been barred from the region by Cherokees in the past, he wrote, "Peace now opens the way for their spreading." Fisk described colonization and Indian removal as benign processes. In his telling, removal was peaceful and passive. In a period in which the relationship between race and belonging was up for debate, men like Fisk thought that colonization and Indian removal would quietly resolve the contradictions of Native American sovereignty and African American rights in a republic based on whiteness.[6]

The American Revolution transformed the scattered plans for West African colonization put forward by missionaries, antislavery activists, and free African American petitioners in the 1770s. Sixty thousand loyalists left the United States during and after the war. Several thousand of those émigrés were formerly enslaved people who traveled on British transport ships to start new lives in London or Nova Scotia. As British officials considered the refugee crisis created by the war, they gravitated toward West African settlements. One such proposal was put forward by white British naturalist and entrepreneur Henry Smeathman. In 1771, Smeathman secured funding for a scientific journey to West Africa and the West Indies from a group of wealthy philanthropists. By 1783, he was meeting with London Quakers to drum up funds for a new journey. This time, he proposed a broader venture to form a free Black colony in West Africa. In a 1786 pamphlet that he wrote to publicize the scheme, Smeathman promised prospective émigrés three months provisions, transportation, and as much land as they could cultivate.[7]

Smeathman's ambition paid off. He gained the support of London abolitionist Sharp, who was troubled by the refugee crisis. The city was flooded

6. Moses Fisk to Timothy Green, Mar. 12, 1796, Moses Fisk Papers, folder 6, Tennessee State Library and Archives, Nashville (quotations); Colin G. Calloway, *The Indian History of an American Institution: Native Americans and Dartmouth* (Hanover, N.H., 2010), 166.

7. Christopher Leslie Brown, *Moral Capital: Foundations of British Abolitionism* (Williamsburg, Va., and Chapel Hill, N.C., 2006), 314–316.

with thousands of soldiers who had fought in the American war. Sharp was concerned that Black refugees who had served in the British army were having difficulty finding housing and work in London. He created a Committee for the Relief of the Black Poor to give short-term aid to claimants who could not access help under the city's settlement laws. After meeting with Smeathman, Sharp also folded colonization into the committee's work. He met with free Black Londoners to discuss the plan, gathered funds from London abolitionists, and offered a government bounty to anyone who wished to go to West Africa. Writer Ottobah Cugoano lent his patronage, and abolitionist Olaudah Equiano served as the commissary for the initial voyage, although they both soon became disillusioned with the project. The colony's backers imagined that the settlement would be a base for religious missions to Christianize Africans. This was not unlike how religious leaders in North America envisioned the role of missions to Indian country. They also hoped that a West African colony would produce free labor goods to compete with those of the Atlantic slave trade. A new "commercial nation" would bring about the abolition of slavery by proving that free labor was also profitable. In February 1787, 441 Black and white Londoners left Plymouth, England, for the mouth of the Sierra Leone River. They called the settlement the Province of Freedom.[8]

Black and white Americans who heard about the Province of Freedom considered supporting it themselves. African American men in New England and the mid-Atlantic circulated news about the Province of Freedom through mutual aid societies they had organized beginning in the 1770s. Black male elites and tradesmen formed these institutions to encourage the moral values—thrift, hard work, and education—that they believed could secure their rights. Black mutual aid societies thrived in New England's towns. In 1775, leather dresser Prince Hall formed the African Lodge of the Honorable Society of Free and Accepted Masons of Boston, the first Black freemason lodge in the world. African Americans in Newport, Rhode Island,

8. William Thornton to John Coakley Lettsom, May 20, 1787, in C. M. Harris, ed., *Papers of William Thornton*, I (Charlottesville, Va., 1995), 56 (quotation); Walker, *Black Loyalists*, 96–100; Brown, *Moral Capital*, 316–317; Pybus, *Epic Journeys of Freedom*, 108–117; Byrd, *Captives and Voyagers*, 121–122, 125–153. For Cugoano and Equiano on colonization, see Vincent Carretta, *Equiano, the African: Biography of a Self-Made Man* (New York, 2006), 202–235; David Kazanjian, *The Brink of Freedom: Improvising Life in the Nineteenth-Century Atlantic World* (Durham, N.C., 2016), 59–65. For Christian missions and free labor goods, see Henry Thornton to John Clarkson, Dec. 30, 1791, John Clarkson Papers, I, 38, 40, BL, William Wilberforce to John Clarkson, Apr. 27, 1792, I, 83; Walker, *Black Loyalists*, 102–103; Brown, *Moral Capital*, 259–330.

constituted the Free African Union Society in 1780. In 1787, Philadelphia ministers Richard Allen and Absalom Jones organized the Free African Society, a mutual aid society that supported burials, apprenticeships, and education and provided for the poor, sick, widowed, and orphaned. Other mutual aid societies followed in Providence and New York City. Women could not be members of the Free African Society, but they established their own benevolent societies. In Philadelphia, a Female Benevolent Society that emerged out of St. Thomas's African Episcopal Church provided aid and burial assistance. The societies corresponded with each other and became vehicles for publicizing emigration ideas.[9]

The identification of men's mutual aid societies with Africa made them the backbone of support for emigration in New England in the 1780s and 1790s. The leaders of these institutions expressed their goals through early forms of African nationalism, what James Sidbury has described as a diasporic identity based on a shared past shaped by slavery. In the early 1790s, members of Newport's Free African Union Society self-identified as "Africans, the Natives of Africa, residing in Newport." When Bristol Yamma was elected the vice president of Newport's Free African Union Society in 1789, he delivered "a very handsome speech respecting Africans in General . . . ." Yamma himself was born in Africa, as were some other society members, but many people of African descent identified as African in a diasporic sense in the late eighteenth century, regardless of where they were born.[10]

After the Revolution, mutual aid societies carried on a lengthy correspondence to consider the Sierra Leone venture. The New England societies likely heard of the Province of Freedom just as the first migrants prepared to journey there in late 1786. They learned more about the plans from Tortola Quaker William Thornton, who toured Philadelphia, New York,

9. Patrick Rael, *Black Identity and Black Protest in the Antebellum North* (Chapel Hill, N.C., 2002), 118–156; Harris, *In the Shadow of Slavery,* 82–86; Cameron, *To Plead Our Own Cause,* 95–98; Sinha, *Slave's Cause,* 131–135. For the Free African Society, see Julie Winch, *Philadelphia's Black Elite: Activism, Accommodation, and the Struggle for Autonomy, 1787–1848* (Philadelphia, 1988), 4–8; Bruce Dorsey, *Reforming Men and Women: Gender in the Antebellum City* (Ithaca, N.Y., 2002), 25–26. For the Female Benevolent Society, see Erica Armstrong Dunbar, *A Fragile Freedom: African American Women and Emancipation in the Antebellum City* (New Haven, Conn., 2008), 52, 60–62.

10. "Proceedings of the Free African Union Society . . . ," in William H. Robinson, ed., *The Proceedings of the Free African Union Society and the African Benevolent Society, Newport, Rhode Island, 1780–1824* (Providence, R.I., 1976), Sept. 8, 1792, 86 ("Africans"), Nov. 16, 1789, 60 ("very handsome"); Rael, *Black Identity and Black Protest,* 84–91; Sidbury, *Becoming African in America,* 6–7.

Newport, Providence, and Boston in 1786 and 1787 to gather support for the colony. Thornton had inherited part of his father's Tortola estate—a parcel of land and upward of seventy people who labored there in chains whom he planned to emancipate. Thornton happened to meet Smeathman in Paris where he became apprised of the idea for a West African colony. He quickly pledged his support. Newport's Free African Union Society held a copy of Smeathman's book proposing a Sierra Leone colony—perhaps a gift from Thornton. At the same time, whaling merchant and white antislavery Quaker William Rotch traveled home from Europe with news of the venture from Friends in London back to the Rhode Island Yearly Meeting in Newport in 1787. He might have shared what he had learned with the Free African Union Society, too. Both Rhode Island societies organized a circular letter to free Black organizations in other states soliciting support for an African settlement. For the next several years, the committees in Boston, Newport, Providence, and Philadelphia replied to the circular, debating the merits of a move to Africa.[11]

Thornton blustered that he could muster at least two thousand people to board ships to Sierra Leone if the first émigrés were successful in planting a settlement. The correspondence of the men's societies reveals that if they took Thornton's proposals seriously, they did not take his words at face value. Samuel Stevens declared on behalf of the Boston African Society that "we do not approve of Mr. Thornton's going to settle a place for us; we think it would be better if we could charter a Vessel, and send some of our own Blacks." Anthony Taylor, president of the Free African Union Society, was charged with opening a correspondence with Thornton on behalf of the membership. They welcomed the project, but they also made clear the terms of their involvement: they wished to control the venture themselves. Taylor wrote to Thornton to give him "a more particular and full idea of our proposal" for an independent emigration plan. He proposed that "a number of Men from among Ourselves shall be sent to Affrica to see if they can obtain, by gifts or purchase of some Kings, or chief people, Lands proper

11. Harris, ed., *Papers of William Thornton,* I, xxxix–xliii, William Thornton to John Coakley Lettsom, Nov. 18, 1786, 31, "General Outlines of a Settlement on the Tooth or Ivory Coast of Africa," [1786], 40, Thornton to Jacques Pierre Brissot de Warville, Nov. 29, 1788, 82, Lettsom to Thornton, Jan. 29, 1789, 87; Gaillard Hunt, "William Thornton and Negro Colonization," American Antiquarian Society, *Proceedings,* New Ser., XXX (1920), 32–61; Lamont D. Thomas, *Rise to Be a People: A Biography of Paul Cuffe* (Urbana, Ill., 1986), 19–21; Guyatt, *Bind Us Apart,* 211–215. For the activism of the Newport group in particular, see Sidbury, *Becoming African in America,* 77–80; Sinha, *Slave's Cause,* 131–133.

and sufficient to settle upon." Stevens and Taylor expected that the colony should not just be independent of Thornton and other white abolitionists. It should also be independent of empire. Taylor and Stevens's insistence on "a perfect independence" seemed to have had a great effect on Thornton. After his meetings in Rhode Island, Thornton was adamant in letters to his British correspondents that a Black colony could never be truly free or successful unless it was self-governing.[12]

Hall and the members of the African Lodge also petitioned the Massachusetts legislature for funds to send their own representatives to West Africa in January 1787. Hall and forty-five others excoriated the prejudice they met with in Boston. They were excluded from certain trades, exposed to violence from white people in the streets, and denied spots in Massachusetts free schools. The petitioners expressed interest in emigration as an escape from the "disagreeable and disadvantageous circumstances" in which they found themselves, "most of which must attend us, so long as we and our children live in America." Emigration was a response to prejudice, appealing as an opportunity for self-determination. Rather than let Thornton take the lead, Hall, Taylor, and the Newport society insisted that they manage the project themselves.[13]

Their concerns were well-placed. For a prediction of what white-led ventures might hold, they need not have looked further than Nova Scotia. New Englanders had likely received word of the disappointments of Black refugees who fled on British transport ships to Nova Scotia at the end of the war. By 1783, twenty-seven thousand troops and refugees had arrived in the province from St. Augustine, Charleston, Savannah, and New York. The British government had promised all refugees free land grants without quitrents for ten years. In Nova Scotia, three thousand Black refugees spent years waiting for the promised land grants. In the meantime, they labored as tenant farmers, eking out a difficult subsistence on poor, rocky soil and giving up half of their produce each season to pay for rented land. Black

12. Samuel Stevens to Anthony Tiler [Taylor], June 1, 1787, in Robinson, ed., *Proceedings of the Free African Union Society and the African Benevolent Society,* 18 ("we do not"), Anthony Taylor to [William Thornton], Jan. 24, 1787, 16 ("more particular"); Thornton to John Coakley Lettsom, May 20, 1787, in Harris, ed., *Papers of William Thornton,* I, 56 ("perfect"), Thornton to Lettsom, Feb. 15, 1787, 44, 47, Thornton to Lettsom, July 26, 1788, 71, Thornton to Samuel Hopkins, Sept. 29, 1790, 117–118.

13. Petition of Samuel Stevens et al., 1787, Massachusetts Anti-Slavery and Anti-Segregation Petitions, House Unpassed Legislation, Docket 2358, SC1/Ser. 230, Massachusetts Archives, Boston (quotations); Gary B. Nash, *Race and Revolution* (Lanham, Md., 2001), 65–66; Sidbury, *Becoming African in America,* 75–77.

Nova Scotians could not vote or serve on juries, and they had difficulty collecting wages from white employers.[14]

Eighteenth-century political economy linked virtue, citizenship, and personal liberty with landownership. In their correspondence, Black mutual aid societies in Newport and Providence stressed that they wanted to control any emigration venture in order to guarantee that they would find "sufficient" land wherever they went. The Providence group could only obtain the political rights they desired if they could secure land and "proper and good title to it." Moreover, their ability to form patriarchal families and to ensure the independence and comfort of their children also depended on land title. Taylor was adamant that "we want to know by what right or tenor we shall possess said Lands, when we settle upon them, for we should think it not safe, and unwise for us to go and settle on Lands in Affrica unless the right and fee of the Land is first firmly, and in proper form, made over to us, and to our Heirs or Children." Once title had been obtained, he proposed that a company of men would proceed alone to prepare the land for their families. Rather than leave the specifics to Sharp or Thornton, Taylor wished to know exactly how land might be apportioned and land title guaranteed. The Newport group wanted to ensure legal title and their right to remain.[15]

African American emigrationists kept these economic goals at the forefront of their plan for making a settlement. One Philadelphia petition signed by fifty-five men, perhaps intended for Congress but never presented, suggested founding "an Assalem . . . similar to the one prepared by the British in Sereallione so that such of us that are favoured with Liberty may have it in our power to become more Usefull to the Community at Large who are now at a loss for a livelihood for ourselves and familys." Although white colonizationists often pinned their arguments on the so-called problem of Black citizenship in the new nation, the Philadelphia petitioners bypassed citizenship rights as the end goal of emigration. Rather, they focused on economic independence and the ability of "the Community at Large" to care for itself. Their interest in Sierra Leone shows that the idea of creating a separate colony had many different meanings after the Revolution. It could

14. "Remarks Halifax," [1791], John Clarkson Papers, II, 8–9, 16, 22–23; Walker, *Black Loyalists*, 21–30; Pybus, *Epic Journeys of Freedom*, 148–149; Byrd, *Captives and Voyagers*, 167–171.

15. Taylor to [Thornton], Jan. 24, 1787, in Robinson, ed., *Proceedings of the Free African Union Society and the African Benevolent Society*, 16.

be an escape from racism, when led by Black proponents, or an expression of it, when led by white proponents.[16]

The location of that asylum mattered. All of the mutual aid societies that corresponded about emigration trained their eyes on Africa as a God-appointed homeland and a site for Christian missions. It mattered to emigrationists in Newport or Providence that they kept their schemes separate from those of white colonizationists. At the same time, they shared similar ideas about a colony as a vehicle for civilizing Africa through trade and religion. The Newport group saw their colony as a Christian mission that would address "the unhappy state and circumstances of our brethren, the nations in Africa," whom they found to be "in heathenish darkness and barbarity." They expressed an African identification that arose from their interpretation of God's own intentions, which linked all people of African descent to the African continent. In 1789, the Newport group sent a circular to Philadelphia's Black elites offering emigration as a solution to "the calamitous state into which we are brought by the righteous hand of GOD, being strangers and outcasts in a strange land, attended with many disadvantages and evils, with respect to living, which are like to continue on us and on our children, while we and they live in this country." West Africa, they felt, was the opposite of a "strange land"—a place where they could achieve autonomy for themselves and their children. They harkened back to earlier missionary ventures that had galvanized some of their membership before the American Revolution. Bristol Yamma, who had trained to be a missionary in the 1770s with New Divinity minister Hopkins, was a member of the Newport group, for example.[17]

The idea that Africa might be a homeland was appealing to Prince Hall and his 1787 copetitioners in Boston. They preferred to pursue emigration to "our native country . . . for which the God of nature has formed us." They envisioned a separate colony both as a political venture—supported by an independent political constitution—and a religious venture—guided by their own Black ministers and bishops. Hall was likely influenced by his correspondence with the Black clergyman John Marrant, who had been

16. "Petition," [circa 1792], Cox-Parrish-Wharton Papers, box 9, folder 7, HSP (quotation); Richard S. Newman, Roy E. Finkenbine, and Douglass Mooney, "Philadelphia Emigrationist Petition, Circa 1792: An Introduction," *William and Mary Quarterly*, 3d Ser., LXIV (2007), 161–166.

17. Members of the Free African Society to Henry Steward, Sept. 1, 1789, in Robinson, ed., *Proceedings of the Free African Union Society and the African Benevolent Society*, 25 (quotations), "To All the Affricans in Providence," July 27, 1789, ibid., 19.

born free in New York and was converted as a teenager in South Carolina by George Whitefield. Marrant was impressed into the British navy during the American Revolution. After he was released, Marrant met Selina Hastings, the Countess of Huntingdon, in London, and he joined the Huntingdon Connexion of Calvinistic Methodists. In the late 1780s, Marrant had traveled to preach in Nova Scotia to Black refugees who had run to British lines during the American Revolution and then left for Canada on British ships at the end of the war. He became a freemason and corresponded with Hall, preaching a sermon in Boston in 1789. Marrant's travels linked Black communities in London, Nova Scotia, and Boston at a moment when emigration was a pressing debate. His support for the Sierra Leone project likely influenced Hall.[18]

Meanwhile, in Philadelphia, a committee appointed to consider the Newport invitation on behalf of the Free African Society pushed back against the idea that Africa had a greater claim on their belonging than any other place. They were more circumspect. Rather, they argued that "every pious man is a good citizen of the whole world." The Philadelphia correspondents espoused a broader Christian universalism. They claimed a wider moral vision and a right to belonging that went beyond narrow conceptions of race and geography. They had the same ability to be "citizens of the world" as their white correspondents.[19]

The Sierra Leone venture that Taylor, Hall, and Stevens watched so carefully was troubled from the beginning. The group arrived in the midst of the rainy season, which prevented them from growing crops. Faced with inadequate food and shelter, many members of the group, including all three surgeons and a chaplain from the Society for the Propagation of the Gospel, left the settlement to work for European slave-trading forts along the coast. By March 1788, only 130 people remained. Sharp accused those who left of being "bought over by the Lure of Large Salaries," but he significantly

18. Petition of Samuel Stevens et al., 1787, Massachusetts Anti-Slavery and Anti-Segregation Petitions, House Unpassed Legislation, Docket 2358, SC1/Ser. 230 (quotation); John Saillant, "'Wipe Away All Tears from Their Eyes': John Marrant's Theology in the Black Atlantic, 1785–1808," *Journal of Millennial Studies,* I, no. 2 (Winter 1999), [7]; Sidbury, *Becoming African in America,* 86–89.

19. Cyrus Bustill et al. [Committee of the Free African Society] to the [Free African Union Society], n.d., in Robinson, ed., *Proceedings of the Free African Union Society and the African Benevolent Society,* 30 (quotation); Sarah M. S. Pearsall, "'Citizens of the World': Men, Women, and Country in the Age of Revolution," in Leonard J. Sadosky et al., eds., *Old World, New World: America and Europe in the Age of Jefferson* (Charlottesville, Va., 2010), 66.

underestimated the difficulties they faced on arrival. In 1789, the Temne ruler King Jimmy destroyed Granville Town in a dispute over the original land purchase. Back in London, Sharp lobbied Parliament to incorporate a trading company that could send factors and agents to aid the fledgling colony. When he failed to get government assistance, Sharp gathered donations from British abolitionists and formed the Sierra Leone Company. The company aimed to provide a base for free labor goods to rival the slave trade and support for a Christian mission.[20]

Even as Granville Town withered away on the coast, Black refugees in Nova Scotia still considered emigration as a reaction to the material disappointments of Nova Scotia. In 1790, they sent lay leader Thomas Peters to London to petition for land grants that had been promised to them by the crown. Peters was taken captive as a child in the Atlantic slave trade and enslaved in North Carolina. During the Revolution, he seized his freedom by serving in the Black Company of Pioneers for the British Army. Peters's 1790 mission worked. British officials ordered Nova Scotia's governor to fulfill the promised grants. British officials also offered an alternative to Black Nova Scotians: anyone who wished to go to Sierra Leone would be granted free passage there. Peters brought this new promise home alongside white abolitionist John Clarkson, who was appointed as a government agent to recruit émigrés. Clarkson promised Black refugees free land in the new colony and the ability to govern the settlement themselves. Some people told Clarkson they wanted to emigrate to protect their children from exploitative apprenticeship agreements. Others said they had not yet received the promised land or provisions from the British government. Overall, one-third of Black Nova Scotians, or 1,196 people, left for Sierra Leone to found Freetown on the former site of Granville Town in March 1792. They departed as members of congregations and communities, led by elites like Peters and Baptist minister David George. They wanted self-determination, political rights, access to economic opportunity, and the right to remain in a place where they could claim independence from white racism.[21]

New England's Black mutual aid societies shared these political goals, and they watched the Sierra Leone project closely. In late 1794, the Provi-

20. Granville Sharp to John Coakley Lettsom, Oct. 13, 1788, Thomas Clarkson Papers, box 1, HL (quotation); Walker, *Black Loyalists,* 104–105; Pybus, *Epic Journeys of Freedom,* 139–142; Sidbury, *Becoming African in America,* 80–83; Byrd, *Captives and Voyagers,* 200–243.

21. "Remarks Halifax," [1791], John Clarkson Papers, II, 8–9, 16, 22–23; Byrd, *Captives and Voyagers,* 177–199; Walker, *Black Loyalists,* 105–107, 115–138; Pybus, *Epic Journeys of Freedom,* 153; Sidbury, *Becoming African in America,* 93–94, 98.

dence African Union Society sent one of their members, James Mackenzie, to visit the colony. He likely arranged passage with help from Congregational minister Hopkins, who had never lost interest in colonization himself. When Mackenzie arrived in January 1795, he was introduced to the Sierra Leone Company's council. Mackenzie told the council that potential émigrés from the Providence society wished to pay for their own passage in return for "a portion of Land and the right of Citizenship, which they say is denied them in America." The council invited twelve Providence families to join the colony. They would receive land grants and all of the rights of British subjects. To receive the grants, each family had to arrive with a certificate from Hopkins and a second clergymen or the president of Rhode Island's abolition society attesting to their good character. The colony's governor, Zachary Macaulay, wanted assurances that potential émigrés planned to participate in the colony's Christian mission. He complained that Freetown's residents had been too influenced "by the age of reason." The colony's leadership held Anglican services, but colonists gathered for worship with their own dissenting Baptist, Methodist, and Huntingdon Connexion preachers who had led the exodus of entire congregations from Nova Scotia.[22]

It is likely that Mackenzie was not impressed by what he found in Sierra Leone because the Providence group decided to stay put. By the time Mackenzie made his tour of the colony, many of Freetown's residents felt disillusioned with it. Clarkson had recruited Nova Scotian émigrés with promises of free land and self-government. But while he was off recruiting, the newly incorporated Sierra Leone Company met in London and altered the arrangement of the colony. The company changed the settlement's constitution to impose closer regulation, quitrents, and a new company-appointed

22. For Mackenzie's journey, see Zachary Macaulay and James Watt to the Chairman and Court of Directors of the Sierra Leone Company, Jan. 31, 1795, CO 268/5/16, TNA ("portion"), Macaulay to Samuel Hopkins, Mar. 19, 1795, 21–23 ("age of reason," 22), Macaulay to the Chairman and Court of Directors of the Sierra Leone Company, Mar. 8, 1795, 18–19, In Council, Jan. 26, 1795, CO 270/3/23, In Council, Feb. 21, 1795, 27–28, In Council, Mar. 19, 1795, 39; Sidbury, *Becoming African in America,* 121–123. George E. Brooks, Jr., and Floyd J. Miller write that Mackenzie's voyage was likely facilitated by Hopkins's friend Moses Brown, a Rhode Island abolitionist who was an investor in the ship that Mackenzie sailed in. See Brooks, "The Providence African Society's Sierra Leone Emigration Scheme, 1794–1795: Prologue to the African Colonization Movement," *International Journal of African Historical Studies,* VII (1974), 192–193; Miller, *The Search for a Black Nationality: Black Emigration and Colonization, 1787–1863* (Urbana, Ill., 1975), 17–18. For religion, see Pybus, *Epic Journeys of Freedom,* 169–170.

council and governor. Residents had little say in politics, defense, prices for company goods, or company wages. It was several years before colonists held their first elections. Meanwhile, according to one observer, disease struck six hundred people at the same time in the summer of 1793, reducing the settlement to a "starving condition."[23]

Freetown's residents also suffered from a lack of protection that would have seemed especially dangerous to Mackenzie. The colony had a mandate to prevent slave trading, but traders operating along the coasts threatened the settlers and occasionally kidnapped them. In September 1794, a French fleet briefly occupied Freetown, destroyed the company's buildings, and plundered their contents. Freetown's inhabitants had no arms with which to defend themselves, and they complained of the "most Scandolas Manner" in which the company's agents had given up the settlement to an invader. Colonists appropriated the lumber, rice, molasses, and rum that they recovered from the French for their own use. The company's agents viewed the settlers' actions as theft, and they denied them access to doctors and schools until the missing stores had been returned.[24]

Mackenzie might have been most discouraged by the news that the Freetown settlers had not yet received their land grants on the terms they had been promised. The Providence African Union Society saw emigration as an opportunity for self-determination and property ownership. The Sierra Leone Company had thus far failed to deliver both of those things. The

23. Isaac Dubois to John Clarkson, May 1, 1793, John Clarkson Papers, III, 41 (quotation). Samuel Hopkins apparently wrote to Governor Zachary Macauley about "the intended emigration of 12 Families from thence," but the letter does not appear in the archives. See Macaulay to the Chairman and Court of Directors of the Sierra Leone Company, May 16, 1796, CO 268/5/81, TNA. Scholars have suggested varied reasons why the Providence group never left. Floyd J. Miller and George E. Brooks, Jr., suppose that Hopkins refused to sign the certificates of good character. See Brooks, "Providence African Society's Sierra Leone Emigration Scheme," *International Journal of African Historical Studies,* VII (1974), 183; Miller, *Search for a Black Nationality,* 19. For land grants and quitrents, see Macaulay and Thomas Gray to the Chairman and Court of Directors of the Sierra Leone Company, Oct. 7, 1796, 123, CO 268/5/19, TNA. On Sharp's plan for the colony's political system, see Sharp to Lettsom, Oct. 13, 1788, Thomas Clarkson Papers.

24. James Liaster to John Clarkson, Mar. 30, 1796, John Clarkson Papers, III, 120–121 (quotation), Thomas Clarkson to John Clarkson, July 17, 1792, I, 148, Luke Jordan and Isaac Anderson to John Clarkson, June 28, 1794, III, 112, Jordan et al. to John Clarkson, Nov. 19, 1794, III, 114–115; Zachary Macaulay to Henry Thornton, Dec. 23, 1794, CO 268/5/10, TNA, Macaulay to unidentified recipient, Sept. 30, 1796, 132, In Council, Sept. 25, 1794, CO 270/3/9, In Council, Oct. 14, 1794, 9–11, In Council, Oct. 20, 1794, 12–13, In Council, Jan. 17, 1795, 21–22, In Council, Apr. 28, 1795, 77–78; Pybus, *Epic Journeys of Freedom,* 180–182; Sidbury, *Becoming African in America,* 109–110.

company was slow to lay out the farmlands promised to each émigré, so Freetown's residents built homes along the waterfront in the first years of the settlement. The company, however, soon reclaimed the coast for colonial defense. When the company's employees began fencing off the waterfront for a new fort, one of them watched as "the whole neighbourhood assembled—and unanimously said if we offered to fence in another inch of ground then what we had—they would pull the fence down."[25]

Two groups of emissaries, including David George and prominent church leaders Fortune Rivers, Cato Perkins, and Isaac Anderson took their concerns to London. Perkins and Anderson wanted to know what "they had to depend upon" given the difference between the promises they had received in Nova Scotia and the company's conduct in Sierra Leone. In a petition delivered by Perkins and Anderson, the inhabitants of Freetown made a series of complaints. Their wages on the company's works could not match the prices the company charged for goods, so "we have nothing to lay out for a rainy Day or for our Children after us." The majority of their lands had not been surveyed. Anderson and Perkins reported that the company refused to answer the petition, and they "send us back like Fools." Company officials were affronted when the émigrés pressed for a greater say in the governing of the colony. Governor Macaulay privately vented that the colonists had "fallacious notions of civil rights (a thing not to be wondered at in emancipated slaves)." Precisely because they had experienced slavery and risked everything by leaving Nova Scotia, Freetown's residents thought they should have a say in the company's operations. Governor Macaulay argued that these were matters of "favor" rather than matters of "right." Because company officials had funded the venture, they thought they should also control it. The attitude of the company's men made many of Freetown's inhabitants fearful that they might never achieve the independence and self-determination they believed emigration should deliver. On the eve of Mackenzie's visit, the émigrés wrote that the company's agents treated them "just as bad as if we were all slaves which we cannot bear." When Freetown's émigrés compared their lack of political power to slavery, their words had power because they had experienced bondage themselves.[26]

25. "Journal of Mr. Dubois," Dec. 31, 1792–Feb. 16, 1793, John Clarkson Papers, III, 20 (quotation), 25–27; Pybus *Epic Journeys of Freedom,* 171–174.

26. Cato Perkins and Isaac Anderson to John Clarkson, Oct. 26, 1793, John Clarkson Papers, III, 97 ("they had to depend"), "Petition of the Nova Scotians to the Chairman and Court of Directors of the Sierra Leone Company," 99 ("we have nothing," "just as bad"), Anderson and Perkins to Clarkson, Nov. 9, 1793, 105 ("send us back"), Clarkson to Richard Crankepone, n.d., 62, Clarkson to Mr. Guagon, July 30, 1793, 73,

In Nova Scotia, reports circulated about the difficulties faced by Sierra Leone's émigrés, and Black Nova Scotians stopped making applications to leave. New England mutual aid societies likely turned away from Sierra Leone for the same reason. For nearly a decade, African American mutual aid societies had debated whether they should remove from the nation or fight for full inclusion as citizens within the United States. The conflict between emigration and the struggle to remain paralleled debates in Indian country about whether or not to look to white interlopers as neighbors or to move west to avoid them. Neither was more radical than the other—they were choices made by individuals in difficult circumstances. For Black leaders in New England, the example of Sierra Leone encouraged a turn, instead, toward the fight for equal citizenship.[27]

Changing political conditions in the various states might have dampened the enthusiasm of Black mutual aid societies for emigration, too. By the mid-1790s, a wave of institution building supported the struggle to remain. In the upper South, mid-Atlantic, and in New England, some Black ministers built independent churches where they could worship away from the segregation of white-led congregations. Black communities also formed separate schools supported by their churches and Quaker philanthropists to serve their children, who had been denied an education by the public free schools.[28]

These new institutions stopped considering emigration and began working to secure rights at the state and federal levels. Black ministers, tradesmen, and entrepreneurs drafted antislavery petitions and sought legal help for community members who had been wrongly enslaved. Black leaders partnered with white antislavery organizations formed in the 1780s to push for state-level gradual emancipation laws. Quakers were the backbone of these organizations. Quakers buttressed the work of the PAS with anti-

---

Perkins and Anderson to Clarkson, Oct. 30, 1793, 101, Jordan et al. to Clarkson, Nov. 19, 1794, 114; Zachary Macaulay to Samuel Hopkins, Mar. 19, 1795, CO 268/5/22, TNA ("fallacious"), Macaulay, "Remarks to Tythingmen and Hundreders," Mar. 7, 1795, CO 270/3/33 ("favor," "right"); Sidbury, *Becoming African in America,* 100–101. For slavery as a metaphor, see François Furstenberg, "Beyond Freedom and Slavery: Autonomy, Virtue, and Resistance in Early American Political Discourse," *Journal of American History,* LXXXIX (2003), 1300–1301.

27. John Clarkson to Moses Wilkinson, [n.d.], John Clarkson Papers, III, 83–84.

28. For separate churches and burial societies, see Harris, *In the Shadow of Slavery,* 82–84; Dorsey, *Reforming Men and Women,* 27; Sidbury, *Becoming African in America,* 131–145; Sinha, *Slave's Cause,* 130–144. For the persistence of interracial congregations, see Richard J. Boles, "Dividing the Faith: The Rise of Racially Segregated Northern Churches, 1730–1850" (Ph.D. diss., George Washington University, 2013).

slavery advocacy and lobbying. They organized through the Philadelphia Meeting for Sufferings (PMS), a group that met under the auspices of the Pennsylvania Yearly Meeting to support their antislavery testimony. The PAS recruited lawyers, philanthropists, and tradesmen to promote emancipation as well. The state societies coordinated with each other. They began meeting annually to address slavery as a national problem beginning in 1794. These groups often worked on behalf of individuals. Black leaders and the white men who joined the societies pursued individual freedom suits, protected people from kidnappers, and negotiated apprenticeship agreements for children.[29]

Black and white abolitionists worked to bring about legal changes at the state level that would have a wider impact. They traveled to state capitals to convince legislators to introduce gradual emancipation bills. Their efforts resulted in acts that made manumission legal in Virginia, Maryland, and Delaware as well as gradual emancipation acts in Pennsylvania, Connecticut, Rhode Island, and eventually New York and New Jersey. African American leaders petitioned Congress to legislate against the slave trade. In 1794, Congress did finally prohibit ships fitted out in American ports from participating in the transatlantic slave trade. Given the halting, but significant, political accomplishments of the period, pursuing the right to remain within the United States might have seemed more important to northern mutual aid societies by the mid-1790s than it had a decade before. In 1787, one group of Black leaders in Philadelphia rejected the idea of African emigration, explaining that the members of their mutual aid society wished to remain in Philadelphia because of their partnership with white abolitionists who were "sacrificing their own ease, time and property for us."[30]

The collaboration between white colonizationists and Black emigrationists in New England shows how flexible the idea of a separate West African settlement was in the post-Revolutionary decades. It resonated with both Black and white elites. Black emigrationists' interest in Sierra Leone largely faded by the mid-1790s. Yet that was not true for white colonizationists.

29. For more on interracial activism and the PAS and PMS, see Sinha, *Slave's Cause,* 113–122; Wood, "'Class of Citizens,'" *William and Mary Quarterly,* 3d Ser., LXXIV (2017), 109–144; Polgar, *Standard-Bearers of Equality.* Gary B. Nash has called the PAS "the first freedmen's bureau in the new nation." See Nash, *Forging Freedom: The Formation of Philadelphia's Black Community, 1720–1840* (Cambridge, Mass., 1988), 100 (quotation), 108.

30. Bustill et al. [Committee of the Free African Society] to ?, n.d., in Robinson, ed., *Proceedings of the Free African Union Society and the African Benevolent Society,* 30.

White antislavery moderates like Moses Fisk or white Quakers like Philadelphian John Parrish toyed with colonization ideas into the early nineteenth century. Enslavers in the upper South were the strongest and most consistent proponents of colonization. For them, colonization was not about Black economic autonomy or political independence. Rather, its purpose was to preserve white supremacy in the South.

Freedom appeared to be a problem to elites in Virginia, Maryland, and Delaware because these states had the largest enslaved populations of any state that seriously debated emancipation in the early Republic. In the 1780s, all three passed manumission laws that gave enslavers the ability to manumit individuals. Black freedom blossomed in the upper South thereafter. Colonization became important to white writers in the upper South as they observed the growth of Black freedom in the 1780s and 1790s. The Chesapeake produced liberal leaders—men like Luther Martin and Gustavus Scott of Maryland, Caesar Rodney of Delaware, and Patrick Henry and Thomas Jefferson of Virginia—who believed that slavery was a great evil and that the natural love of liberty held dear by all people might also one day lead enslaved people to grasp their freedom.[31]

These men also believed that their commitment to enslaving others would one day lead to violence, though they were ultimately unwilling to give up the profits of slaveholding. Jefferson hoped that emancipation might proceed "with the consent of the masters, rather than by their extirpation." His sentiments aligned with the liberal philosophy that fueled the American Revolution. In his *Second Treatise on Civil Government,* John Locke had written that "he who attempts to get another man into his Absolute Power, does thereby *put himself into a State of War* with him." In any number of pamphlets, white Revolutionaries explained that their support for abolition stemmed from the idea that enslaved people lived in the constant state of war that Locke had described. Benjamin Franklin argued in 1776 that "slaves rather weaken than strengthen the State" in their capacity for insurrection. In his 1788 antifederalist pamphlet, Luther Martin, attorney general of Maryland and delegate to the Constitutional Convention, made a similar argument for slavery's impact on the health of the state. At the same time, when enslaved people did not choose rebellion over bondage, some white writers concluded that they did not have the virtue to be free.[32]

31. Nash, *Race and Revolution,* 12–13, 15.

32. Jefferson, *Notes on the State of Virginia,* ed. Peden, 163 ("with the consent"); John Locke, *Two Treatises of Government,* ed. Peter Laslett, student ed. (Cambridge, 1988), 279 ("he who attempts"); John Adams, "[Notes of Debates on the Articles of Confederation, Continued]," July 30, 1776, in L. H. Butterfield et al., eds., *Diary and*

If slaveholding Virginians saw enslaved people as "internal enemies," they saw free African Americans as an equally destabilizing force. Although some upper South enslavers called bondage a great evil, they nonetheless regarded manumission and emancipation with a sense of impending disaster. Virginia's Revolutionary leaders argued that they could free enslaved people only if there was no danger in it, and they invoked the specter of rebellion whenever they considered gradual emancipation plans. They believed that freed people would side with the enslaved in the event of a rebellion. In their minds, in a republic based on whiteness, both free and enslaved African Americans were "a captive nation" in a constant state of war. It was slavery itself that held that state of war in check. Virginia governor Edmund Randolph could thus declare in 1788 that he supported abolition, but "the situation of the country" could not allow him to work for it, even though "as a private man . . . I am free to declare, that whensoever an opportunity shall present itself, which shall warrant me, as a *citizen* to emancipate the slaves, possessed by me, I shall certainly indulge my feelings." Black freedom could be destabilizing in a region committed to slavery.[33]

Colonization particularly appealed to moderate Virginia enslavers and liberal Revolutionaries because it resolved the state of war that Locke had explained. Virginia colonizationists laid out their thinking in several publicly circulated statements. The most influential of these was the colonization plan devised by Jefferson that he included in his *Notes on the State of Virginia.* Jefferson had first drawn up the plan in the midst of the American Revolution when the Virginia General Assembly revised its laws. Under Jefferson's plan, all enslaved children born after a particular date would be free but bound out in an apprenticeship system to teach them a trade at the expense of the state. On reaching adulthood, they would be sent with supplies "to declare them a free and independant people" protected by the state "till they shall have acquired strength." Jefferson's plan imagined that Black colonists traveled and moved under the protection of the United States.[34]

Autobiography of John Adams, II, *Diary 1771–1781* (Cambridge, Mass., 1961), 245–246 ("slaves rather weaken," 246); "From the Maryland Gazette; Mr. Martin's Information to the House of Assembly," *Independent Gazetteer; or, The Chronicle of Freedom* (Philadelphia), Feb. 11, 1788, [2]; Onuf, *Jefferson's Empire,* 147–188; Furstenberg, "Beyond Freedom and Slavery," *Journal of American History,* LXXXIX (2003), 1303.

33. Alan Taylor, *The Internal Enemy: Slavery and War in Virginia, 1772–1832* (New York, 2014); Onuf, *Jefferson's Empire,* 149–150 ("captive," 149); Edmund Randolph to Benjamin Franklin, Aug. 2, 1788, Pennsylvania Abolition Society Incoming Loose Correspondence, Pennsylvania Abolition Society Papers, folder 4, 1–167, HSP ("situation").

34. Jefferson, *Notes on the State of Virginia,* ed. Peden, 138 (quotations). Jefferson and George Wythe devised the plan as an amendment to a bill on enslaved Virginians,

Jefferson did not make his colonization plan public until he included it in his *Notes on the State of Virginia.* Yet it was still slow to circulate. Jefferson began the manuscript in 1780 as a primer on Virginia intended for his immediate circle while he was in France. Even after he privately published the text in 1785, he only distributed a few dozen copies among his acquaintances. It did not begin to enjoy a broader readership in the United States until 1787, after the book leaked out in French translation, then in an English edition with Jefferson's permission, and finally in pieces in American newspapers. Part of Jefferson's reluctance to share his *Notes on the State of Virginia* more widely in the United States centered on his worry that the passages on race and colonization might anger his Virginia neighbors because they embraced emancipation. Most white antislavery men who read *Notes on the State of Virginia* at the time understood it as an antislavery text, despite that it contained passages proclaiming the permanent inferiority of African Americans. Colonization in the upper South was always more closely aligned with moderate antislavery views and gradual emancipation than with proslavery arguments. It is notable that colonization never gained a foothold in the proslavery strongholds of South Carolina and Georgia, for example.[35]

Colonization garnered many adherents in Jefferson's Virginia by the 1790s, perhaps because of the circulation of *Notes on the State of Virginia* there among influential white men by 1787. St. George Tucker, a legal scholar at William and Mary, wrote his own colonization plan that responded directly to Jefferson's, and he brought Jefferson's ideas to his pupils, some of whom also became colonizationists. In 1795, the Baptist minister Morgan John Rhees visited with one Virginia planter who professed that he was "willing to emancipate his negroes provided they could be colonised." William Thornton reported that James Madison did not believe emancipation could ever proceed in Virginia without colonization. Other Virginians took up Jefferson's ideas in print. Virginia enslaver Ferdinando Fairfax published his own plan in 1790 that called for a free Black colony in Africa, referencing the Sierra Leone scheme. Fairfax published his plan in the *American Museum,* a popular magazine.[36]

---

but they never presented it to the Virginia General Assembly. See Onuf, *Jefferson's Empire,* 151, 174; Cara J. Rogers, "Jefferson's Sons: *Notes on the State of Virginia* and Virginian Antislavery, 1760–1832" (Ph.D. diss., Rice University, 2018), 66–67.

35. For the publication history of *Notes on the State of Virginia* and its reception, see Rogers, "Jefferson's Sons," 3–4, 15, 147–174, 180–181.

36. John T. Griffith, *Rev. Morgan John Rhys, "The Welsh Baptist Hero of Civil and Religious Liberty of the 18th Century"* (Lansford, Pa., 1899), 118 (quotation); William

Colonization gained attention again in 1796, when Virginia jurist St. George Tucker revived Jefferson's plan for gradual emancipation in his own *Dissertation on Slavery*. Tucker proposed an emancipation scheme in which freed people could choose to voluntarily emigrate to the Louisiana or Florida territories. Tucker presented his *Dissertation* to the Virginia House of Delegates in 1796, but as one legislator reported, resistance to emancipation was so strong that the delegates refused to table the pamphlet, so it could not be taken up at a later date. Legislators objected to any kind of action to end slavery in the state. Like Jefferson, Tucker attempted to resolve what he saw as the problem of emancipation by embracing removal as its necessary counterpart. Born in Bermuda, Tucker moved to Virginia before the Revolution. In 1778, he married Virginian Frances Bland Randolph, a wealthy widow and enslaver. In his *Dissertation,* Tucker insisted that the spirit of the Revolution demanded abolition and that to "tolerate a practice incompatible therewith, is such an evidence of the weakness and inconsistency of human nature, as every man who hath a spark of patriotic fire in his bosom must wish to see removed from his own country." Yet, in the course of the Revolution, when enslaved people at Mataox freed themselves by running for British lines in 1781, Tucker pursued them. Tucker supported emancipation, but on his own terms, and those terms included colonization.[37]

Upper South colonizationists simply could not imagine that the Republic could accommodate African American citizenship. In *Notes on the State of Virginia,* Jefferson predicted that the prejudices of white people and the

---

Thornton to Etienne Clavière, [Nov. 7, 1789], in Harris, ed., *Papers of William Thornton,* I, 106; Ferdinando Fairfax, "Plan for Liberating the Negroes within the United States," *American Museum, or, Universal Magazine* (Philadelphia), December 1790, 285–287; Nash, *Race and Revolution,* 43; Guyatt, *Bind Us Apart,* 217; Rogers, "Jefferson's Sons," 18, 260–271, 278–280.

37. St. George Tucker, *A Dissertation on Slavery: With a Proposal for the Gradual Abolition of It, in the State of Virginia* (Philadelphia, 1796), 30 (quotation); Robert McColley, *Slavery and Jeffersonian Virginia,* 2d ed. (Urbana, Ill., 1973), 135; Douglas R. Egerton, *Gabriel's Rebellion: The Virginia Slave Conspiracies of 1800 and 1802* (Chapel Hill, N.C., 1993), 15; Christopher Leonard Doyle, "Lord, Master, and Patriot, St. George Tucker and Patriarchy in Republican Virginia, 1772–1851" (Ph.D. diss., University of Connecticut, 1996), 136; Phillip Hamilton, "Revolutionary Principles and Family Loyalties: Slavery's Transformation in the St. George Tucker Household of Early National Virginia," *William and Mary Quarterly,* 3d Ser., LV (1998), 531–556. In 1790, Tucker had proposed that enslaved people should be manumitted to "a portion of the western territory." See St. George Tucker to John Page, Mar. 29, 1790, Pennsylvania Abolition Society Incoming Loose Correspondence, Pennsylvania Abolition Society Papers, folder 6, 2–135.

injustices suffered by the formerly enslaved would "divide us into parties and produce convulsions, which will probably never end but in the extermination of one or the other race." In the 1790s, partisan battles waged in the halls of the legislature, at the ballot box, and on the streets fanned fears that political factions would destroy individual liberties. White colonizationists harnessed the language of partisanship to argue that general emancipation without removal would give rise to a Black faction or, in the words of Fairfax, "a separate interest from the rest of the community" that would tear apart the Republic from within. Their fear of political factions stemmed from concern over proportionate populations and the ability of a slave "interest" to overpower a white monopoly on violence. Fairfax believed, for example, that, if given "*all* the privileges of citizens," free African Americans would naturally form a political faction of significance to challenge white supremacy, or what he called "the peace of society." Read against the grain, these were also strong claims about the power of African American political resistance in the early Republic as well as the potential racial solidarity that could animate those politics.[38]

Intellectuals who wrote about factionalism reflected on the real example of a successful slave rebellion in the French colony of Saint Domingue. By the end of the eighteenth century, enslaved people who toiled in Saint Domingue produced more sugar and coffee beans than in any other place in the world. In 1791, capitalizing on the upheavals of the French Revolution, an enslaved head driver named Boukman started a revolt in the northern parishes of the island. Boukman's successor, Touissaint Louverture, led enslaved forces to control the island after 1793. As Britain invaded Saint Domingue in 1794, French forces abolished slavery and recruited from among the plantations. Reports on the storming of the port city of Le Cap in 1793 by enslaved forces were particularly well publicized in U.S. newspapers. After June 1793 as Le Cap burned, fifteen thousand Saint Dominguans left the island as refugees bound for Philadelphia, Charleston, Boston, and Norfolk. Enslaved and free people made up at least one-third of the refugees.[39]

In the wake of the Haitian Revolution, white Virginians expressed their

38. Thomas Jefferson, *Notes on the State of Virginia,* quoted in Tucker, *Dissertation on Slavery,* 86 ("divide"); Fairfax, "Plan for Liberating the Negroes," *American Museum, or, Universal Magazine,* December 1790, 285 *("all"),* 286 ("separate," "interest," "peace").

39. Laurent Dubois, *Avengers of the New World: The Story of the Haitian Revolution* (Cambridge, Mass., 2004), 19–26; Ashli White, *Encountering Revolution: Haiti and the Making of the Early Republic* (Baltimore, Md., 2010).

fear of slave rebellion, but they also denied that the enslaved could lead resistance themselves. White writers presumed that enslaved people and free African Americans were dependents, without the self-ownership or property to guarantee their political independence. They wrote that free African Americans could be easily swayed in a delicate republic. "May they not even become the auxiliaries of domestic faction; or the fit engine of any artful and enterprising leader?" queried Virginia lawyer and colonizationist George Tucker, cousin to St. George Tucker.[40]

Colonization plans did not go unanswered. Virginia Quaker and abolitionist Robert Pleasants scoffed at the idea that extending equal rights to free African Americans would produce factionalism. In 1790, he excoriated Fairfax's colonization plan and argued that "a union of interests" secured through equal rights for freed people would bring stability to the new nation. Corresponding with St. George Tucker about his notes in 1797, Pleasants made the same critique, to which Tucker responded that accommodating the racism of slavery's defenders was necessary to advance emancipation. Kentucky land speculator Gilbert Imlay similarly argued against colonization plans intent on "banishing a numerous class of men who might be made useful citizens." Other writers criticized colonization on the matter of practicality. Imlay and Pleasant both wondered, in Imlay's words, "From what country is the vacancy" caused by the departure of so many thousands of people "to be filled?" George Tucker believed that white laborers from the North or Europe would replace enslaved laborers. Lexicographer and cofounder of the Connecticut Society for the Abolition of Slavery Noah Webster, on the other hand, worried that expulsion would cause a steep decline in the southern states, and he looked to historical parallels. After Phillip III's expulsion of several hundred thousand descendants of Spain's Muslims between 1609 and 1614, Webster warned, the economy had suffered.[41]

Virginia colonizationists wanted to use colonization to create a white re-

40. [George Tucker], *Letter to a Member of the General Assembly of Virginia, on the Subject of the Late Conspiracy of the Slaves; with a Proposal for Their Colonization* (Baltimore, Md., 1801), 16.

41. "Humanity" [Robert Pleasants], *Virginia Independent Chronicle, and General Advertiser* (Richmond, Va.), July 7, 1790, [1] ("union"); G[ilbert] Imlay, *A Topographical Description of the Western Territory of North America . . . to Which Is Annexed, a Delineation of the Laws and Government of the State of Kentucky* . . . (London, 1792), 187 ("banishing"); [Tucker], *Letter to a Member of the General Assembly of Virginia,* 20; Noah Webster, *Effects of Slavery on Morals and Industry* . . . (Hartford, Conn., 1793), 36; Robert Pleasants to St. George Tucker, May 30, 1797, Robert Pleasants Papers, LVA; Rogers, "Jefferson's Sons," 269.

public. They hoped the removal of free African Americans would give rise to a strict sense of racial belonging in the new United States to counter post-Revolutionary emancipation. The French general Francois Jean de Beauvoir, marquis de Chastellux, imagined something similar when he authored his own colonization plan for the United States. In his *Travels in North America,* Chastellux wrote that Black men should be removed from the nation and that new laws should encourage marriages between white men and Black women. Chastellux, who had served alongside George Washington in the American Revolution and corresponded with Jefferson about *Notes on the State of Virginia* and his own manuscript, might have picked up his interest in colonization from the two Virginia leaders. He differed from them in that he believed that free African Americans should possess equal rights and citizenship. Nonetheless, he still chose removal as the means to achieve both.[42]

Chastellux also might have developed his ideas in conversation with those discussed in Virginia and directed at Indigenous peoples. The Virginia legislature nearly passed a similar scheme in 1784 promising bounties to white men and women who married Native men and women and had children. The committee in charge of the bill supposed that these marriages "may have great effect in conciliating the friendship and Confidence" of Native men and women, "whereby not only their Civilization may in some Degree, be finally brought about, but in the mean time their hostile inroads be prevented." Chastellux's colonization plan subtly linked policies proposed for Indian country with those fitted out for emancipation. Of his own plan, Chastellux wrote that, over several generations, through removal and marriage, "the colour should be totally effaced." Whether these ideas were directed at Native Americans or at African Americans, removal underpinned them all.[43]

Although free Black leaders of northern mutual aid societies had looked to West Africa as a site of opportunity and liberation, white writers in and beyond the upper South frequently shared a different geographical referent: what they thought of as the western territory. Alongside plans for West Afri-

42. Guyatt, *Bind Us Apart,* 129–131; Rogers, "Jefferson's Sons," 142–144.

43. "A Bill for the Encouragements of Marriages with the Indians, December 2nd," Original and Engrossed Bills, Resolutions and Joint Resolutions, and Related Attachments of the House of Delegates, box 9, LVA ("may have great effect");"The State of Slavery in Virginia and Other Parts of the Continent, from the Marquis de Chastellux's Travels in America," *Columbian Magazine* (Philadelphia), June 1787, 479, 480 ("colour"); Guyatt, *Bind Us Apart,* 115–194.

can settlements, white colonizationists projected free Black colonies west of the Appalachian Mountains. By contrast, African American correspondence and petitions never mentioned North America as the site for a colony. Rather, they wrote about West Africa as a divinely ordained homeland and a site of patriarchal independence. White writers after the 1790s had no similar intentions. What colonizationists called the "immense unsettled territory on this continent" figured in their writings as empty space ready for American migrants without any of the religious and cultural connotations that West Africa had held for northern mutual aid societies. West Africa did not appear as often in the writings of white colonizationists because colonization was not, for them, a missionary project or a diasporic return. It was removal.[44]

Colonization plans that looked west depended on Indian removal. Continental visions of colonization called on assumptions that the territories at the edges of empire were both empty and simultaneously the home of other internal enemies: Native people. By "unsettled territory," of course, colonizationists most likely meant Native homelands west of the Appalachians. They did not acknowledge that Indigenous people controlled the land to which they referred. Nevertheless, they registered a Native presence in their writings in other ways. Reflecting back on his 1786–1787 American tour thirty years later, William Thornton described how several members of the Massachusetts Assembly had, at that time, expressed interest in supporting a Black colony. He recalled that when he explained "the intention of taking the Blacks to Sierra Leone," the legislature "expressed an unwillingness to send them out of the limits of the U.S., and wished a Settlement to be made in the most southern part of the back Country between the whites and Indians." The Massachusetts Assembly members imagined a kind of buffer state in which Black migrants would form a defensive-edge settlement against Native peoples. Colonization plans depicted the territories as empty space available for the taking, without Native inhabitants. Yet these writings also invoked a Native presence to suggest the territory as an appropriate location for those who seemed to threaten the political coherence and racial homogeneity of the early Republic.[45]

Even writers who were familiar with the U.S. war against Native Ameri-

44. Tucker, *Dissertation on Slavery,* 95 (quotation). Fairfax, an exception, does mention missionizing in his 1790 plan as an argument for why West Africa would be the best place for a colony. See Fairfax, "Plan for Liberating the Negroes," *American Museum, or Universal Magazine,* December 1790, 286.

45. Hunt, "William Thornton and Negro Colonization," American Antiquarian Society, *Proceedings,* New Ser., XXX (1920), 58–59 ("intention," 58, "expressed," 59).

cans in the trans-Appalachian West projected new colonies onto Native homelands. Quaker John Parrish, for example, wrote about western colonization in an 1806 pamphlet despite, or perhaps because of, the fact that he had spent the previous three decades engaged in Indian affairs. In draft form, Parrish's pamphlet adopted an antislavery position that his contemporaries would have deemed radical; he expressed support for slave rebellion as a means of forcing abolition. In his notes in the text, Parrish signaled support for full citizenship rights for Black Americans. In published form, however, Parrish walked back some of those claims, instead warning his readers that slavery posed a danger to white people because it made rebellion inevitable. In both versions, Parrish expressed support for a western Black colony. He defended emancipation against its white detractors by explaining that colonization would prevent marriages across the color line. Emancipation would be accompanied by separation. Parrish proposed a model of Black family landownership in the West that he believed would convince newly freed people to remove there voluntarily. The legislature should, he wrote "assign a tract within some part of the western wilderness (where there are millions of acres likely to continue many ages unoccupied) for the colonization of those who are already free" and would choose to remove. "And if from one to two hundred acres were set off to each family, according to their number and strength," he continued, "it would be an inducement to others, as they became free, to repair to the colony." Even Parrish saw Native land as empty space with the transformative potential to alter the character of the nation.[46]

Quaker concerns with Indian affairs and with emancipation frequently overlapped. PAS president James Pemberton compared missionary work in Sierra Leone with Quaker-led federal "civilization" plans in Iroquois country. Philadelphia Friend Ann Mifflin participated in missions to the Senecas while also communicating with London Quaker William Dillwyn about colonization in 1805. Mifflin's correspondents, who were part of the London African Institution founded to foster so-called civilization in West Africa, lauded Quaker missions in Iroquouia as a model for Sierra Leone.[47]

46. John Parrish, *Remarks on the Slavery of the Black People; Addressed to the Citizens of the United States, Particularly to Those Who Are in Legislative or Executive Stations in the General or State Governments; and Also to Such Individuals as Hold Them in Bondage* (Philadelphia, 1806), 42, 43 (quotations).

47. James Pemberton to Paul Cuffe, Aug. 6, 1808, in Rosalind Cobb Wiggins, *Captain Paul Cuffe's Logs and Letters, 1808–1817: A Black Quaker's "Voice from within the Veil"* (Washington, D.C., 1996), 77; Gary B. Nash, *Warner Mifflin: Unflinching Quaker Abolitionist* (Philadelphia, 2017), 317n44. For the African Institution, see Wayne Acker-

Colonizationists began to look west in the 1790s precisely because U.S. military campaigns for Indian removal had just come to a temporary halt across much of the trans-Appalachian region in 1795. Thornton, Fairfax, and Madison had all expressed skepticism about a western colony in the 1780s, in the midst of war between the U.S. and Native people. If African American colonists settled too close to white Americans and Native people, a western settlement would foster conflict. By 1795, however, the United States had signed treaties with the Cherokees, the United Indian Confederacy, Britain, and Spain that led to frenzied land speculation and westward migration. The putatively empty space to the west appealed to colonizationists because it promised the right amount of distance from the Atlantic states and it seemed large enough to accommodate all without making anyone "too near neighbours," as Anthony Wayne had remarked in deliberations over the Greenville treaty line.[48]

When white colonizationists considered appropriate distance, they made plain their estimations of population growth over time in relation to the availability of Native lands. They made these calculations more easily after 1790, when Congress passed the first census act, which required marshals to count U.S. inhabitants by household. In his own anonymous pamphlet published in 1801, Virginian George Tucker shared none of the concerns about proximity that Fairfax, Thornton, and Madison put forward a decade earlier. Tucker had likely observed the many thousands of migrants who had left for western lands in the past few years. He expressed faith in the explosive growth of white settlements in Native homelands west of the Appalachians. He declared that "the impolicy of planting an enemy on our frontier" should not be troublesome; white population growth would always outstrip, and therefore overpower, the growth of a Black colony. Western space seemed useful to these writers as a means of neutralizing Native Americans and free African Americans as political forces.[49]

Tucker's cousin St. George Tucker similarly considered proximity and distance in his *Dissertation on Slavery*. He proposed an emancipation

---

son, *The African Institution (1807–1827) and the Antislavery Movement in Great Britain* (Lewiston, N.Y., 2005), 16–48, 52–53; Thomas, *Rise to Be a People*, 34–35; Julie Winch, *A Gentleman of Color: The Life of James Forten* (New York, 2003), 178.

48. Anthony Wayne to Timothy Pickering, May 13, 1795, AWP, XL, 114 (quotation); William Thornton to Clavière, [Nov. 7, 1789], in Harris, ed., *Papers of William Thornton*, I, 106.

49. [Tucker], *Letter to a Member of the General Assembly of Virginia*, 20 (quotation); "An Act Providing for the Enumeration of the United States," Mar. 1, 1790, *The Public Statutes at Large of the United States of America, from the Organization of the Government in 1789, to March 3, 1845 . . .*, I (Boston, 1845), 101–103.

scheme in which freed people could voluntarily emigrate to Gulf South territories "more congenial to their natural constitutions." He identified Virginia's land as being "ours" (referring to white Virginians) and declared Black Virginians to be more biologically suited to the "immense unsettled territory" beyond the state's borders. When Tucker was specific about location, he tellingly honed in on North American land outside of national borders. "The Florida's, Louisiana, and the Country south of the Mouth of the Mississippi would I should hope afford a continual drain for them," he wrote. The territories that Tucker identified notably fell outside of U.S. territorial claims, west of the Mississippi and south of the thirty-first parallel territorial line that divided Anglo-American and Spanish territory after 1795. Tucker judged that if the colony were located in Spanish territory, then "at that distance they could never be formidable to us." He might have assumed that a colony situated outside of the nation could never be at odds with Anglo-American settlements. East and West Florida already had a reputation as havens for enslaved people escaping bondage in the lower South. From the late seventeenth century until 1790, Spanish officials had guaranteed sanctuary to enslaved fugitives who ran from plantations in Carolina, and later Georgia.[50]

When colonizationists discussed distance, they also subtly explained the relationship of a future colony to the United States. Their ideas mirrored conversations among federal policymakers about whether Native Americans constituted sovereign nations or colonized peoples. At issue was whether a colony would eventually become part *of* the United States or stay separate from it. Western colonizationists addressed the status of a Black colony by invoking the relationship between Native people and the federal government. William Craighead, a planter and presiding magistrate of Lunenberg County, Virginia, presented his own plan for a western colony to his state assembly. Craighead imagined that the relationship of the colony to the federal government would "be something analogous to that in which the Indians now stand. The position "in which the Indians now stand" had been clarified with the first Trade and Intercourse Act of 1790, which accepted Native tribes as sovereign nations that should be negotiated with through

50. Tucker, *Dissertation on Slavery,* 95 ("more congenial"); St. George Tucker to Jeremy Belknap, Nov. 27, 1795, 4, Jeremy Belknap Papers, MHS ("Florida's"). Tucker's reference to "the Country south of the Mouth of the Mississippi" could refer to the swamplands formed by the silt that the Mississippi River deposits in the Gulf of Mexico, which had a reputation for being a dangerous disease environment adverse to white settlement. See Jane Landers, *Black Society in Spanish Florida* (Urbana, Ill., 1999), 25, 79.

treaties. On the ground, however, the rights of eastern Native peoples to control trade and justice, as well as to refuse treaties with the United States, were increasingly challenged by the federal government in the early Republic. Craighead essentially thought the settlement might have a colonial relationship to the federal government.[51]

Other white colonizationists suggested that a free Black settlement might eventually become part of the United States. In Jefferson's *Notes on the State of Virginia,* the colony he outlined would be "a free and independant people." *Free people* could mean either *free individuals* or an *independent nation,* distinct from the United States. But Kentucky abolitionist David Rice suggested that some portion of the western territories be cordoned off for a new free Black "state," a term that suggested it would become part of the union. Moses Fisk similarly proposed that a colony should be "formed into a state, and, in due time, have a voice in Congress." Fisk imagined a settlement that would be brought into the federal system in stages just as new states were. His plan mirrored the federal territorial model outlined only a few years prior in 1787 in the Northwest Ordinance. White colonizationists had no difficulty imagining varying modes of political incorporation when Congress was in the midst of conversations about the incorporation of western territories into the federal system. A profitable and industrious state, Fisk suggested, would add revenue and manpower to the nation. Meanwhile Virginian Ferdinando Fairfax, in outlining an African colony, determined that it would only be an American colony "until the colonists should themselves become competent" to govern themselves and become "an independent nation."[52]

Ultimately, white writers focused on the West for the same reason thousands of eastern migrants, promoters, land speculators, and utopians also imagined their future there: defined as untrammeled or empty space, Native land offered the chance for people to remake themselves away from the corruption of the overpopulated East. White writers believed that "new situations make new minds," as Dierdre Coleman has written. The Americas had

51. Archibald Alexander, *A History of Colonization on the Western Coast of Africa* (Philadelphia, 1846), 62 (quotation); H. N. Sherwood, "Early Negro Deportation Projects," *Mississippi Valley Historical Review,* II (1916), 489–490; Guyatt, *Bind Us Apart,* 218.

52. David Rice to William Rogers, Nov. 4, 1794, Pennsylvania Abolition Society, Committee of Correspondence, Letter book, II, 1794–1809, Pennsylvania Abolition Society Papers, 19–20 ("state"); [Fisk], *Tyrannical Libertymen,* 10 ("formed"); Fairfax, "Plan for Liberating the Negroes," *American Museum, or, Universal Magazine,* December 1790, 286 ("until the colonists").

long called to Europeans as a space where they could begin anew. Colonizationists centered their attention on the trans-Appalachian West for similar reasons. They saw it as a landscape that promised the regeneration of individuals and families. Native land might alter the character of individuals along with that of the nation.[53]

Romantic ideas about the capacity of new places to transform individuals appeared across colonization thinking in the United States. Colonizationists justified removal by arguing that free African Americans could find citizenship only away from the prejudices of white people, a kind of paternal benevolence that echoed the language of U.S. Indian policy. Federal policymakers warned that Native Americans in the East risked being corrupted by the influence of whites who sold them alcohol or stole their lands. Some advocates of removal suggested that only distance could counteract that corruption and eventually turn Native Americans into citizens. Colonizationists similarly insisted that free Black men and women could never become political actors until they acquired some distance from Anglo-American society. Fisk wrote that "they will never be men, till they are treated like men; they will never be citizens, till they feel themselves so." Like many proponents of colonization, Fisk appealed directly to Black masculinity in his pamphlet, even while he invoked African American women as silent participants in the settlement project.[54]

Colonizationists mirrored U.S. Indian policy, too, when they argued that free African Americans should be sent outside the borders of the nation as part of a "preparation state" that would usher them into freedom. In the case of both Native Americans and African Americans, proponents of removal saw the stadial theory of Scottish Enlightenment thinkers as an important influence. By the mid-eighteenth century, Scottish philosophers began to articulate a uniform theory of social development that all individuals and communities passed through over time. They posited that communities moved from a state of hunting and gathering, to pasturage, to subsistence farming, to trade and commerce. The architects of federal Indian policy put Native Americans in the first stage of social growth. In the Revolutionary period, white abolitionists also began to argue that slave traders had preyed on a people still in the first stage of social growth.[55]

Colonizationists believed that slavery and the slave trade were corrupting

53. Coleman, *Romantic Colonization and British Anti-Slavery*, 4.

54. [Fisk], *Tyrannical Libertymen*, 10.

55. Ibid., 10 (quotation); Drew R. McCoy, *The Elusive Republic: Political Economy in Jeffersonian America* (Williamsburg, Va., and Chapel Hill, N.C. 1980), 17–21.

forces that could only be ameliorated by removal. Writers like Fisk focused on the transformative impact of distance on the capacity of individuals to act as free people or as citizens. Removal to "a portion of our new territory," Fisk suggested, would allow formerly enslaved people to "go through their non-age or preparation state in the wilderness." By nonage, Fisk meant people in their legal minority, who needed to be prepared for citizenship. John Locke had described nonage as a state of ignorance during "the imperfect state of Childhood" in which parents had a duty to direct the actions of a child who "has not *Understanding* of his own to direct his *Will*." Those in a state of nonage needed to be directed in their actions by fictive parents who could exercise reason on their behalf. Fisk had a decidedly Lockian idea of nonage; he imagined that freed people had no conception of reason to direct their own affairs. For Fisk, the state of minority that freed people inhabited was temporary, unlike the constant state of minority of enslaved people—it was "a state of dependence and discipline," not servitude. "If they are not fit for freedom, they must be fitted," Fisk determined.[56]

Fisk's plan and others that mentioned a preparatory state were in this sense consistent with the gradualism embraced by white abolitionists. That both colonizationists and abolitionists looked favorably on the idea complicates an easy division between opposing sides. Most gradual emancipation laws freed enslaved people when they reached the age of majority, or adulthood, between the ages of eighteen and twenty-five, partly out of adherence to the idea that enslaved people needed to be fitted for freedom. Manumission societies in northern and mid-Atlantic cities argued that freed African Americans needed schooling, apprenticeships, training, and oversight to prepare them for emancipation. When members of the PAS reconstituted the organization in 1789, it encompassed a broad set of moral reform projects aimed at free people—from education to religion. In a broadside they issued that year, the PAS declared that slavery "is such an atrocious debasement of human nature, that its very extirpation, if not performed with solicitous care, may sometimes open a source of serious evils." They wanted to change the so-called conduct of free Black men and women, much like Quakers who worked in Indian country. Prominent Philadelphia Quaker women simultaneously established the Committee to Inquire into the Con-

56. [Fisk], *Tyrannical Libertymen*, 9–10 ("portion," "go through," 10, "state," "If they are not," 9); Locke, *Two Treatises of Government*, ed. Laslett, 306 ("imperfect," "has not"); Holly Brewer, *By Birth or Consent: Children, Law, and the Anglo-American Revolution in Authority* (Williamsburg, Va., and Chapel Hill, N.C., 2005), 91–93.

dition of Freed Slaves. The committee undertook regular visitations to free Black homes to encourage Quaker modes of conduct, church attendance, indentures, and education for free Black children. The PAS and the Free African Society, both of which took on home visits in the 1780s and 1790s to evaluate the conduct of free African Americans, also absorbed that message. David Brion Davis has argued that early critics of slavery focused on replacing the "labor discipline" of slavery, even as they concerned themselves with liberty as a natural right. Discussions about poverty, prisons, and the management of wage labor accompanied the rise of antislavery in the British Atlantic world.[57]

Colonization located that labor discipline at a distance from the United States. By removing to the "wilderness," enslaved people could become industrious yeoman farmers. Fisk argued that a trio of "guardians, governours, and instructors" would teach freed people "some honest method of acquiring a livelihood" and acquaint them with the "rights and duties" of citizenship. Fairfax determined that the first emigrants should be "properly educated and instructed" in order "to forward their progress in the useful arts, and to qualify them for the business of legislation." Just so, Noah Webster similarly suggested colonization on a "portion of land in the United States" where free people would be sent "with means of cultivation." All of these thoughts repeated Jefferson's language in *Notes on the State of Virginia,* when he insisted that free Black colonists would be given wagons, livestock, clothing, and other supplies. Colonizationists determination that freed people should be sent out with teachers and instruments to farm, spin, and sew also invoked the civilization plans directed at Native people that were a significant component of Federalist and then Jeffersonian Indian policy after the Revolution.[58]

57. *An Address to the Public, from the Pennsylvania Society for Promoting the Abolition of Slavery, and the Relief of Free Negroes, Unlawfully Held in Bondage* (Philadelphia, 1789) ("such an atrocious"); David Brion Davis, *The Problem of Slavery in the Age of Revolution, 1770–1823* (Ithaca, N.Y., 1975), 306 ("labor discipline"), 358, 455; Harris, *In the Shadow of Slavery,* 61–66; Nash, *Forging Freedom,* 89; Dorsey, *Reforming Men and Women,* 48. Paul Polgar argues that the manumission societies embraced immediatist goals of equal rights for African Americans and that their emphasis on a "preparation state" before those rights could be conferred was a response to slavery's defenders. See Polgar, *Standard-Bearers of Equality,* 23, 123–124, 133, 140–141, 162.

58. [Fisk], *Tyrannical Libertymen,* 9 ("guardians"); Fairfax, "Plan for Liberating the Negroes," *American Museum, or, Universal Magazine,* December 1790, 286 ("properly"); Webster, *Effects of Slavery on Morals and Industry,* 36 ("portion"); Jefferson, *Notes on the State of Virginia,* ed. Peden, 138. Thornton also mentioned "such utensils

Even after Black mutual aid groups abandoned their interest in West African emigration in the 1790s, white colonizationists kept writing about the possibility of a separate Black settlement. They altered some of their calculations about western colonization after 1803, when the completion of the Louisiana Purchase added 827,000 square miles of Native lands to the federal domain. Colonization plans often meditated on distance, meaning the physical space between two settlements that were elastic and would grow over time with their populations. White colonizationists did not worry about "filling up" western land, despite that many other writers did turn their pens to that question. Thomas Malthus's claim that population growth was bound to inevitably outstrip food supply had wide purchase in Europe. To Americans, Malthus's ideas seemed to have little relevance. Intellectuals in the United States used his work to demonstrate the boon of a population boom across a vast continent, rather than to chart the eventual decline of the nation. By the time Jefferson considered Malthus's writings in a letter to the French economist Jean-Baptiste Say in early 1804, he could conclude that the completion of the Louisiana Purchase would prevent American population growth from "filling up" western land for many hundreds of years.[59]

White colonizationists also argued that the West contained plenty of space for their projects. John Parrish concluded in his pamphlet that the Louisiana lands would be "many ages" unoccupied and thus a good place for African Americans to begin an independent colony. Radical intellectual Thomas Paine suggested that enslaved people should be given passage by Congress to New Orleans. On their arrival, they could be indentured to Louisiana planters for several years to "learn plantation business." Paine imagined that when the indentures ended, enslaved people would be given their freedom and a tract of land to cultivate. Former slave trader turned antislavery pamphleteer Thomas Branagan conjectured that the national government would lose little by giving free Black settlers "some distant part of the national domains." Louisiana, he noted, "is farther from us than some

---

as will be required to cultivate the lands." See "General Outlines of a Settlement on the Tooth or Ivory Coast of Africa," [1786], in Harris, ed., *Papers of William Thornton,* I, 39. For civilization plans, see David Andrew Nichols, *Red Gentlemen and White Savages: Indians, Federalists, and the Search for Order on the American Frontier* (Charlottesville, Va., 2008), 122; Daniel K. Richter, "'Believing That Many of the Red People Suffer Much for the Want of Food': Hunting, Agriculture, and a Quaker Construction of Indianness in the Early Republic," *Journal of the Early Republic,* XIX (1999), 601–628.

59. Thomas Jefferson to [John] Breck[i]nridge, Aug. 12, 1803, in *State Papers and Correspondence Bearing upon the Purchase of the Territory of Louisiana* (Washington, D.C., 1903), 235 (quotation); McCoy, *Elusive Republic,* 189–195, 200; Nicole Eustace, *1812: War and the Passions of Patriotism* (Philadelphia, 2012), 4–18.

parts of Europe." That land was so vast that it far outweighed demand and "will not be worth a cent to government" for hundreds of years.[60]

When white colonizationists argued that freed people could only become citizens outside the space of the nation, they joined a broader conversation about Black rights that animated the halls of state legislatures in the decades after the American Revolution. Few white colonizationists insisted that colonization should be mandatory, at least tacitly recognizing that African Americans had rights in the states. St. George Tucker, for example, did not approve of compulsory removal, but he did argue that Black citizenship was unlikely and undesirable in the new union. Tucker drew on an emerging biological racism. He justified colonization by highlighting what Jefferson argued were "the *real distinctions* which *nature* has made" between white and Black people. Tucker emphasized that colonization should be voluntary but that African Americans would be compelled to remove to a new colony because of the denial of citizenship rights in the United States. Rather than force people to leave, Tucker wanted to prompt movement by excluding free African Americans from the body politic.[61]

Even as Tucker penned his plan, the state legislatures had already begun to deny basic rights to free African Americans. The 1790s represented a turning point in the struggle to preserve and extend Black rights. In 1790, federal legislators passed a federal naturalization act that excluded anyone who was not white from immigrating to the United States. Even as abolitionists worked to protect Black citizenship, the state legislatures reacted to the growth of Black freedom with the "denization" of free African Americans—the gradual exclusion of free Black people from certain rights in individual states. In the 1790s, state legislatures passed new laws prohibiting marriage across the color line, the participation of Black children in public education, and the ability of freed people to work in certain trades or to

60. Parrish, *Remarks on the Slavery of the Black People,* 43 ("many"); Thomas Paine to [Thomas Jefferson], Jan. 25, 1805, Thomas Jefferson Papers at the Library of Congress, Ser. 1, General Correspondence, 1651–1827, Thomas Jefferson Papers, 1606–1827, Manuscript Division, LOC ("learn"); Thomas Branagan, *Serious Remonstrances, Addressed to the Citizens of the Northern States, and Their Representatives: Relative to the Impolicy of Keeping Three Hundred Thousand Well Informed and Aspiring Negroes in the Bowels of Their States: Especially on an Event, of the Citizens Being Necessitated to March to the Frontiers to Repel an Invading Foe* (Philadelphia, 1805), 22–23 ("distant," 22–23, "farther," 22, "will not be worth," 23).

61. Jefferson, *Notes on the State of Virginia,* quoted in Tucker, *Dissertation on Slavery,* 86 (quotation). For compelling movement through coercion, see K-Sue Park, "Self-Deportation Nation," *Harvard Law Review,* CXXXII (2019), 1878–1941.

carry arms. In North Carolina, New York, New Jersey, Pennsylvania, Massachusetts, Rhode Island, New Hampshire, Delaware, Maryland, and Vermont, free Black men could vote in state and local elections if they met the requisite property qualifications. These states gradually restricted Black suffrage. In the first decades after the American Revolution, colonization was a proxy for ideas about belonging and citizenship for free African Americans. By the early nineteenth century, the state legislatures began to bring removal into effect by passing laws restricting migration and residency, too.[62]

Colonization came to have a single meaning after 1816, when a group of influential enslavers, politicians, and ministers founded the American Colonization Society (ACS). They distilled a variety of ideas into a specific organization that administered a colony in Liberia supported by state fundraising societies and a national mouthpiece in the *African Journal and Colonial Repository*. The founding of the ACS, which was predicated on the presumption that Black Americans did not belong in the nation, made colonization anathema to most free Black northerners after 1816. Historians have long suggested that anticolonization activism emerged in 1817, when a group of Black Philadelphians held a public meeting to protest the newly founded ACS.

Black Philadelphians denounced colonization so readily in 1817 because these ideas were not new, though they began to take a more virulent form. They had reckoned with them for decades. The split between Black and white abolitionists over colonization had begun in the 1790s, when African Americans abandoned emigration after the failure of the Sierra Leone project. In the face of such exclusions, Black men and women formed institutions to insist on their right to remain in the United States. Their work in the first three decades after the American Revolution laid the groundwork for the anticolonization movement after 1816.

62. Douglas Bradburn, *The Citizenship Revolution: Politics and the Creation of the American Union, 1774–1804* (Charlottesville, Va., 2009), 235–271, esp. 262–265 (quotation, 238); "An Act to Establish an Uniform Rule of Naturalization," Mar. 26, 1790, in *Public Statutes at Large of the United States of America,* I, 103–104; Ira Berlin, *Slaves without Masters: The Free Negro in the Antebellum South* (New York, 1974), 90–99; James H. Kettner, *The Development of American Citizenship, 1608–1870* (Williamsburg, Va., and Chapel Hill, N.C., 1984), 313.

CHAPTER 6

"SHUT EVERY STATE AGAINST HIM"

Restricting Migration between the States

John Hope came to his trade during Revolutionary times. Kidnapped into the transatlantic slave trade as a child, he arrived in Virginia in 1743 as the property of Yorktown tavern owner Benjamin Catton who registered his name as "Caesar." Hope was made to learn the art of barbering in Catton's wigmaking shop. It was a trade that would serve him well. Yorktown was a short distance from Williamsburg, the seat of royal government in colonial Virginia. Barbering facilitated connections to Virginia's Revolutionary leaders. Men like Thomas Jefferson passed through Catton's shop. In 1775, at the start of the war, when Virginia's royal governor, John Murray, fourth earl of Dunmore, fled from the capital to the safety of the British ship *HMS Fowey,* Hope might have heard that hundreds of enslaved people just to the southeast of Yorktown were joining the British fleet in a bid for freedom. Many of these men, women, and children left on British ships for New York and then, later, for Nova Scotia and Sierra Leone. Hope himself did not escape with them. His son was enslaved by another Yorktown family, and he wagered that he could use his connections and his trade to make a place for his family in a newly independent Virginia. He bet correctly. He was manumitted in the midst of war in 1779, and he cast aside the name "Caesar" for a new one of his own choosing: John Hope.[1]

John Hope experienced the promise of antislavery in post-Revolutionary Virginia, the largest slaveholding state in the new nation, as well as the backlash against it only two decades later. He might have imagined that the language of natural rights would eventually inspire legislation ending slavery in Virginia. This was the case in the northern and mid-Atlantic states, which implemented immediate or gradual emancipation between 1780 and 1804. State legislatures in Delaware, Maryland, and Virginia only loosened re-

1. Michael L. Nicholls, "Aspects of the African American Experience in Eighteenth-Century Williamsburg and Norfolk," 1990, Colonial Williamsburg Foundation Library Research Report Series-330 (Williamsburg, Va., 1991), 144–145; Douglas Walter Bristol, Jr., *Knights of the Razor: Black Barbers in Slavery and Freedom* (Baltimore, Md., 2009), 8–12, 24–25.

strictions that had previously prohibited manumission but went no further. Nonetheless, thousands of enslaved people in the upper South were manumitted by their enslavers or purchased themselves in the post-Revolutionary decades. In Maryland and Delaware, the number of manumissions was so great that slavery declined dramatically by the early nineteenth century. African Americans and white enslavers used manumission so often that it became much more than a limited measure.

Virginia legislators reacted to the expansion of Black freedom by bringing colonization out of parlor conversations and into the law. They were responding in part to slave rebellion. In 1800, an enslaved blacksmith named Gabriel Prosser planned to march on Richmond to capture the capital and overturn slavery. After Governor James Monroe uncovered the plan, support in and beyond the Virginia General Assembly for colonization led to the passage of an 1806 Virginia statute that included a provision exiling all newly freed people from the state within a year of their manumission. The Virginia statute had national ramifications. Neighboring Maryland and Delaware passed their own migration restrictions in response. They closed their borders to Black migrants, whether they were free or enslaved. One by one, states expanded their control over legitimate movement within their borders. The domino effect spread across the middle states—Virginia, Delaware, Maryland, Ohio, Kentucky, and later Indiana and Illinois all restricted Black migration and threatened unauthorized migrants with removal or reenslavement. Just as removal and the control of migration were conjoined in Indian country, colonization and migration restrictions were also mutually reinforcing. These laws promised to resolve the contradiction of Black freedom in a nation committed to slavery.

Black migration seemed threatening to white Virginians because movement was fundamental to becoming free in the upper South. Thousands of freed people left for neighboring states where they hoped that their rights and opportunities would be more secure. Others moved locally to growing towns like Baltimore, Petersburg, Philadelphia, or Wilmington, Delaware, to take up trades and earn money to purchase the freedom of enslaved family members. Hope eventually followed the political connections that had served him so well. He relocated to Richmond after the Revolutionary state government moved there in 1780. He purchased a hillside lot on the slope of Shockoe Hill, a short walk from the new neoclassical capitol building. In those same years, Hope worked to build a future for his family. Over the next several decades, he labored as a barber to purchase his son, Aberdeen, his wife, Tenah, and their daughter, Judith. By moving to Richmond, Hope made a telling political choice about where freedom felt the richest. His journey was akin to the paths that enslaved people took "out of the house of bondage" during and after the Civil War.[2]

Precisely because movement was an important means of self-determination for newly freed people, localities and states sought to control mobility with local policing and state statutes. Slave patrols surveilled enslaved people as they traveled country roads or the docks and streets of urban centers. Passes and fugitive ads monitored their movements. The logic of slavery continued into the experience of freedom. Free African Americans carried papers, too, and they were liable to be jailed and re-enslaved if they could not prove their freedom. State statutes restricted who had the right to move freely through public space. Registration laws limited whether freed people could settle in towns and counties. In the early national period, federal, state, and local officials defined the movements of African Americans and Native Americans as threatening to the peace of the Republic. They struggled to contain the movement of free African Americans in the upper South, just as they tried to make white migrants in the trans-Appalachian West or Native Americans in the Great Lakes legible, too. Free movement was politicized and contested rather than natural or unimpeded.[3]

2. Thavolia Glymph, *Out of the House of Bondage: The Transformation of the Plantation Household* (New York, 2008); Petition of Judith Hope, Dec. 21, 1819, VLP, box 278, folder 18, Petition of Judith Hope, Dec. 11, 1820, box 278, folder 20, Petition of Judith Hope, Dec. 14, 1821, box 285, folder 70; Bristol, *Knights of the Razor,* 31–32. For migration out of slavery during and after the Civil War, see also Tera W. Hunter, *To 'Joy My Freedom: Southern Black Women's Lives and Labors after the Civil War* (Cambridge, Mass., 1997), 20–30; Stephanie M. H. Camp, *Closer to Freedom: Enslaved Women and Everyday Resistance in the Plantation South* (Chapel Hill, N.C., 2004), 117–138; Susan Eva O'Donovan, *Becoming Free in the Cotton South* (Cambridge, Mass., 2007); Steven Hahn, *The Political Worlds of Slavery and Freedom* (Cambridge, Mass., 2009), 55–114; Yael A. Sternhell, *Routes of War: The World of Movement in the Confederate South* (Cambridge, Mass., 2012), 93–154.

3. John Torpey, "Coming and Going: On the State Monopolization of the Legitimate 'Means of Movement,'" *Sociological Theory,* XVI (1998), 239. For the policing of movement under slavery, see Sally E. Hadden, *Slave Patrols: Law and Violence in Virginia and the Carolinas* (Cambridge, Mass., 2001); Camp, *Closer to Freedom;* Rashauna Johnson, *Slavery's Metropolis: Unfree Labor in New Orleans during the Age of Revolutions* (New York, 2016); Marisa J. Fuentes, *Dispossessed Lives: Enslaved Women, Violence, and the Archive* (Philadelphia, 2016), 13–45; Shauna J. Sweeney, "Market Marronage: Fugitive Women and the Internal Marketing System in Jamaica, 1781–1834," *William and Mary Quarterly,* 3d Ser., LXXVI (2019), 206, 213–216; Simone Browne, *Dark Matters: On the Surveillance of Blackness* (Durham, N.C., 2015), 31–88. For the policing of movement for free African Americans, see Edlie L. Wong, *Neither Fugitive nor Free: Atlantic Slavery, Freedom Suits, and the Legal Culture of Travel* (New York, 2009); Eliza-

The restrictive migration laws that stemmed from colonization ideas were reactions to the efforts of African American men, women, and families to determine their own futures by moving toward them in the postwar decades. Free African Americans asserted their right to pass freely and to settle where they pleased in the late eighteenth century. They remade the geography of slavery and freedom in their choices to stay or go, and state legislatures reacted strongly as a result. The states had always had the power to control immigration and migration. They decided who was "foreign" within their borders. At the same time, the free passage of people between the states gave meaning to the nation itself. When state legislatures rescinded the right of free African Americans to pass freely and to settle, they issued a stark challenge to the concept of union—one the framers had not anticipated because free African Americans had so changed the political terrain of the early Republic. The middle states attempted to form a bloc that would not accept African American migrants. Black migrants in search of a refuge in the early Republic thus faced a problem within the federal system: in a period in which the states determined the meaning of citizenship, migration restrictions could render one—in theory—stateless, without a home.[4]

In Virginia, Maryland, and Delaware, the post-Revolutionary period was a brief window when the language of natural rights was translated into legislation against slavery. In colonial Virginia and Maryland, slaveowners could not manumit people without special permission from the royal governor and assembly. Since 1740, Delaware had required that enslavers give security to ensure that freed people would not become a public charge. For most of

---

beth Stordeur Pryor, *Colored Travelers: Mobility and the Fight for Citizenship before the Civil War* (Chapel Hill, N.C., 2016); Kristin O'Brassill-Kulfan, *Vagrants and Vagabonds: Poverty and Mobility in the Early American Republic* (New York, 2019), 84–111.

4. For state control of immigration in this period, see Kunal M. Parker, *Making Foreigners: Immigration and Citizenship Law in America, 1600–2000* (New York, 2015), 4 (quotation), 50–80; Hidetaka Hirota, *Expelling the Poor: Atlantic Seaboard States and the Nineteenth-Century Origins of American Immigration Policy* (New York, 2017). For debates about African American citizenship before Dred Scott, see, for example, James H. Kettner, *The Development of American Citizenship, 1608–1870* (Williamsburg, Va., and Chapel Hill, N.C., 1984), 287–333; Douglas Bradburn, *The Citizenship Revolution: Politics and the Creation of the American Union, 1774–1804* (Charlottesville, Va., 2009), 235–271; Martha S. Jones, *Birthright Citizens: A History of Race and Rights in Antebellum America* (New York, 2018); Christopher James Bonner, *Remaking the Republic: Black Politics and the Creation of American Citizenship* (Philadelphia, 2020). For statelessness, see Linda K. Kerber, "The Stateless as the Citizen's Other: A View from the United States," *American Historical Review*, CXII (2007), 15–18.

the eighteenth century, such restrictions went largely unchallenged. A small but vocal minority of upper South elites began to push back against these prohibitions in the late eighteenth century. They were motivated in part by natural rights ideas coming out of the American Revolution. The strength of Baptist and Methodist revivals in the coastal Tidewater region also gave a religious foundation to white antislavery action. Before the 1780s, southern white evangelicals had aimed their moral weight at Christianizing slavery, rather than dismantling it; as evangelicalism became more widely accepted in the postwar period, ministers increasingly sought to end the institution within their own congregations or in the halls of the state legislature. At the same time, the economic concerns of many older Tidewater elites—fluctuating tobacco prices and the declining fertility of their fields—dovetailed with antislavery ideas. Many enslavers became convinced that their futures did not lie in slave-grown tobacco.[5]

Yet antislavery action in the post-Revolutionary period did not just arrive naturally out of latent, liberatory promises within the language of natural rights or evangelicalism. If these ideas did lead to abolition, that inevitability was produced over and over again by enslaved people who used mobility to grasp freedom for themselves during and after the war. Thousands of enslaved people had run to British lines over the course of the Revolution. When planters, evangelicals, and legislators did not embrace antislavery, enslaved people seized on small openings to emancipate themselves. In a 1773 letter to white Virginia Quaker Robert Pleasants, who had been pressing Virginia's Revolutionary leaders to take antislavery action, Patrick Henry called slavery a "lamentable Evil" and attested that he abhorred the institution. Still, he regretted that he was "drawn along by the general Inconvenience of living without them." Ralph Henry, enslaved by

5. On manumission restrictions, see James M. Wright, *The Free Negro in Maryland, 1634–1860* (New York, 1971), 58; Patience Essah, *A House Divided: Slavery and Emancipation in Delaware, 1638–1865* (Charlottesville, Va., 1996), 39–41; Eva Sheppard Wolf, *Race and Liberty in the New Nation: Emancipation in Virginia from the Revolution to Nat Turner's Rebellion* (Baton Rouge, La., 2006), 3, 28–29. On evangelicalism, see James D. Essig, *The Bonds of Wickedness: American Evangelicals against Slavery, 1770–1808* (Philadelphia, 1982), 20–21, 61–65; Peter Joseph Albert, "The Protean Institution: The Geography, Economy, and Ideology of Slavery in Post-Revolutionary Virginia" (Ph.D. diss., University of Maryland, 1976), 178–181. On economic motivations, see T. H. Breen, *Tobacco Culture: The Mentality of the Great Tidewater Planters on the Eve of Revolution* (Princeton, N.J., 1985), 30–31; Lorena S. Walsh, *Motives of Honor, Pleasure, and Profit: Plantation Management in the Colonial Chesapeake, 1607–1763* (Williamsburg, Va., and Chapel Hill, N.C., 2010), 526–530, 624, 633.

Patrick Henry, did what he would not. In 1776, Ralph Henry emancipated himself by running to join the British Army.[6]

As enslaved people found freedom, they challenged white assumptions about the future of slavery. By the 1780s, elites like Henry reconciled their philosophical objections to slavery with their economic self-interest by suggesting that bondage would end naturally at some point in the future. One Virginia observer reported that there were many "strong advocats for the liberty of the Black's" in the Virginia General Assembly at the time and that most legislators expected emancipation to become "universal." Although most white Virginians took no action, African Americans did, and their struggles to move out of bondage by emancipating themselves became antislavery's driving force in the upper South.[7]

Important, too, were the actions of Quakers and other reformers, who, meanwhile, translated antislavery ideas into law by lobbying against manumission restrictions in the colonial and state assemblies. Slaveholding Friends took issue with manumission restriction because it barred them from taking action on a vital new application of Quaker peace testimony. Northern Friends began banishing enslavers from their society in the late eighteenth century. Quakers in the upper South could not do the same because of legal restrictions against manumission. They skirted the law by arranging private manumission agreements outside of the courts, and such arrangements were not uncommon for non-Quakers as well. In 1792, for example, Scottish merchant David Ross manumitted Christopher McPherson, an enslaved man who managed his store in Fluvanna County. McPherson had served alongside Ross when he was the commercial agent for Virginia during the American Revolution. When Ross registered McPherson's manumission, he noted that McPherson had already been living as a free man for some time.[8]

6. Copy of Patrick Henry to Robert Pleasants, Jan. 18, 1773, manuscript collection 968, Haverford College, Haverford, Pa. (quotations); Cassandra Pybus, *Epic Journeys of Freedom: Runaway Slaves of the American Revolution and Their Global Quest for Liberty* (Boston, 2006), 212.

7. John Parrish, "Notes on a Journey to Virginia," [1782], Parrish Family Papers, folder 6, [14], FHL (quotations); Robert Pleasants to John Townshend, Jan. 25, 1788, Robert Pleasants Letter book, 142–143, LVA; Alan Taylor, *The Internal Enemy: Slavery and War in Virginia, 1772–1832* (New York, 2014), 23–28. Thank you to Nicholas Wood for sharing Parrish's "Notes on a Journey to Virginia" with me.

8. Albert, "Protean Institution," 168–169; Christopher McPherson, *A Short History of the Life of Christopher McPherson, Alias, Pherson, Son of Christ, King of Kings and Lord of Lords: Containing a Collection of Letters etc. Written by Himself,* 2d ed. (Lynchburg, Va., 1855), 12. Some Quakers deeded their slaves to their meetings, and they lived

For the enslaved, freedom under such conditions could be precarious. The courts did not recognize private agreements, and the white heirs of those who made them did not always honor them. In his will, Virginia Quaker John Pleasants freed those he kept in bondage when they turned thirty and the manumission laws would "admit of it without transportation." But Pleasants died before manumission was legalized, and only one of his children, abolitionist Robert Pleasants, followed his wishes. During the American Revolution, Robert Pleasants made a private agreement to allow the enslaved people he had inherited from his father to "go at large" as free people. Pleasants was brought up on grand jury presentments after his neighbors complained about the arrangement.[9]

Quakers in the upper South spent the 1780s seeking protection for these private agreements by lobbying state assemblies to ask for the ability to manumit enslaved people. In Virginia, Quaker petitioning and the persistent lobbying of Pennsylvania Quaker John Parrish and Delaware Quaker Warner Mifflin led to a 1782 law that permitted manumission by individuals. After the passage of the law, Pleasants petitioned the Virginia General Assembly for help in forcing his family members to fulfill his father's wishes to manumit the enslaved people they had inherited. It was only after the younger Pleasants brought a suit against his extended family in 1799 that those who were owned by John Pleasants were emancipated.[10]

---

as emancipated people. See, for example, Robert Pleasants to Samuel Pleasants, July 8, 1776, Robert Pleasants Letter book, 39.

9. John Pleasants, Will, Pleasants Family Papers, Brock Collection, box 12, folder 18, HL ("admit"), "Robert Pleasants to the Governor and Council of Virginia, The Memorial of Robert Pleasants," n.d., box 13, folder 12 ("go at large"); Robert Pleasants to Joseph Lewis, July 29, 1778, Robert Pleasants Letter book.

10. John Parrish and Warner Mifflin traveled to Richmond in 1782 for nineteen days to visit with members of the Virginia General Assembly, and they attended each day of debate on the bill. For Quaker lobbying in Virginia, see Parrish, "Notes on a Journey to Virginia," [1782], Parrish Family Papers, folder 6. For Quaker petitions, see Petition of Quakers, Nov. 29, 1780, VLP, box 289, folder 107, Petition of Committee of Quakers, May 29, 1782, box 290, folder 23; Robert Pleasants to John Thomas, July 1782, Robert Pleasants Letter book, 126. For the law, see "An Act Directing the Trial of Slaves, Committing Capital Crimes; and for the More Effectual Punishing Conspiracies and Insurrections of Them; and for the Better Government of Negros, Mulattos, and Indians, Bond or Free," May 1723, in William Waller Hening, *Statutes at Large; Being a Collection of All the Laws of Virginia, from the First Session of the Legislature, in the Year 1619*, IV (Richmond, Va., 1820), 132. For the Pleasants case, see *Virginia: In the High Court of Chancery, March 16, 1798; Between Robert Pleasants, Son and Heir of John Pleasants, Dec'd; Pltf; and Mary Logan; Widow and Administratrix of Charles Logan, and Devisee of John Pleasants and Jonathan Pleasants* . . . (n.p., n.d.); Christopher Leonard Doyle,

In the first decade of the early Republic, all three upper South states made it possible for African Americans to find freedom amid slavery. In Delaware, petition campaigns by Quaker and Methodist meetings and abolition societies from the 1780s to the 1810s put emancipation on the legislative agenda. Although the campaigns failed to shepherd a gradual emancipation bill through the legislature, they did spur Delaware to drop surety bonds as a requirement for manumission in 1787. In 1790, the Maryland legislature repealed the state's prohibition on manumission by will for all but the elderly. It was important that the new laws permitted manumission rather than mandated emancipation. They represented respect for property rights, including property rights in people, as much as antislavery ideas.[11]

Manumission reform might appear limited, given that other states passed gradual emancipation acts in the same period. Nevertheless, it was still controversial. Emancipation was pushed forward by a small cadre of Black and white abolitionists, quietly endorsed by some white moderates, and protested by a significant proslavery interest. Manumissions recorded in county deed books often began with formulaic language about the reason for manumission. Virginian Samuel Hargrave emancipated Jane and Nancy in 1791 because he was "persuaded that freedom is the natural right of all mankind and being desirous of doing to others as I would be done by." The language of careful reflection around the question of slavery and natural rights was common in deeds of manumission. But it did not reflect the will of the majority of enslavers in the upper South, most of whom did not choose to manumit enslaved people after 1782. In fact, the proportion of white men and women in Virginia who owned slaves increased significantly after the war. By the turn of the century, half of white households in the state kept people in bondage. Even manumitters like Hargrave did not free all those he enslaved outright. Thirteen-year-old Sary and eight-year-old Aggy had to wait until they turned eighteen to receive their free papers, and thirteen-year-old William was bound to Hargrave until he turned twenty-one. For Sary, Aggy, and William, it must have been an agonizing wait.[12]

"Lord, Master, and Patriot, St. George Tucker and Patriarchy in Republican Virginia, 1772–1851" (Ph.D. diss., University of Connecticut, 1996), 147–148.

11. Petition of Wilmington Monthly Meeting of Friends, Dec. 27, 1785/Dec. 28, 1786, Loose Petitions, DHS; "Petition of the Society of Quakers in Favor of the Negro Slaves," Jan. 9, 1786, Delaware Legislative Papers, DPA; "An Act to Prevent the Exportation of Slaves, and for Other Purposes," Feb. 3, 1787, *Laws of the State of Delaware . . .*, II (New Castle, Del., 1797), 884–888.

12. Charles City County Deed Book 4, 1789–1802, Jan. 20, 1791, 33, LVA (quotation); Taylor, *Internal Enemy*, 46–47.

In Virginia, enslavers reacted to antislavery action with vitriol, waging a petition war across the state. In 1785, antislavery Methodists in the western Piedmont passed around petitions after worship proposing gradual emancipation. Proslavery activists responded by collecting signatures in shops and taverns for their own petitions against manumission. The majority of the proslavery petitioners came from the Southside, a tobacco-growing region just north of the North Carolina border that would become the center of slavery in the new nation. One petition suggested that the manumission law was an opening toward a "general Emancipation" that would lead the country toward ruin and "the disturbance of Governmente." Another insisted that "the harbours [and] the houses of . . . manumitted negroes would probably afford them and other outlying slaves" protection in the event of a rebellion. Like colonizationists, the petitioners thought that Black freedom would tear apart the Republic from within. Their protests had real effects. In some counties and towns across the state, there was a stretch of manumissions immediately after the passage of the 1782 act, followed by a dip during the proslavery campaign. The legislature also took the proslavery petitions seriously, drawing up an unsuccessful bill to end voluntary manumission.[13]

Freed people made the new laws their own by more strongly asserting their liberty in the 1780s and 1790s than they had been able to before. In Maryland and Virginia, the post-Revolutionary decades yielded unprecedented opportunities for enslaved people to grasp freedom by legal means. Black and white abolitionists in both states had success in encouraging voluntary manumission in the first few decades after the Revolution. Twenty-five thousand people in Maryland became free in the two decades after manumission reform. There were only three thousand freed people living

13. Petition of Inhabitants of Lunenberg, Nov. 29, 1785, VLP, box 150, folder 15 ("general"), Petition of Citizens of Accomack, June 3, 1782, box 1, folder 10 ("harbours"). For more examples, see Petition of Freeholders and Inhabitants of Henrico, Nov. 16, 1784, VLP, box 116, folder 24, Petition of Freeholders and Inhabitants of Hanover, Nov. 16, 1784, box 105, folder 28, Petition of Inhabitants of Mecklenburg, Nov. 8, 1785, box 160, folder 13, Petition of Inhabitants of Brunswick, Nov. 10, 1785, box 39, folder 20, Petition of Inhabitants of Halifax, Nov. 10, 1785, box 97, folder 21, Petition of Citizens of Amelia, Nov. 10, 1785, box 9, folder 21; Frederika Teute Schmidt and Barbara Ripel Wilhelm, "Early Proslavery Petitions in Virginia," *William and Mary Quarterly*, 3d Ser., XXX (1973), 133–146; Albert, "Protean Institution," 185–187; Allan Kulikoff, *Tobacco and Slaves: The Development of Southern Cultures in the Chesapeake, 1680–1800* (Williamsburg, Va., and Chapel Hill, N.C., 1986), 432; Philip D. Morgan, *Slave Counterpoint: Black Culture in the Eighteenth-Century Chesapeake and Lowcountry* (Williamsburg, Va., and Chapel Hill, N.C., 1998), 659.

in Virginia in 1782. By 1800, twenty thousand Black Virginians had purchased their freedom or had been given free papers.

In Delaware, when Quaker and Methodist activists failed to shepherd a gradual emancipation bill through the legislature, white and Black activists crafted Delaware into a "free" state through other means. The state legislature subjected slaveholders to heavy fines if they sold enslaved people to the Carolinas, Georgia, the West Indies (and later Virginia and Maryland) without the permission of the courts. Enslaved people brought into the state to be sold would be freed. Without the ability to legally sell enslaved people out of the state, enslavers manumitted them instead. These laws made it possible for Black Delawareans and their Quaker and Methodist allies to protect and encourage Black freedom, making Delaware into something resembling a free state in a matter of decades.[14]

Black and white abolitionists in Delaware transformed manumission reform from a limited measure into something akin to gradual emancipation. Abolitionist societies organized largely by white Quakers and Methodists in Dover, Wilmington, and Sussex put the protection of those who were "detained by fraud or violence" at the center of their mission. Black Delawareans worked with the societies to pursue freedom suits, halt kidnappers, and uncover illegal sales of slaves for a term—those who would become free at adulthood under gradual emanicipation—across state lines where their indentures might be converted to permanent slavery. It was so common for enslaved people to use the law to their advantage that slaveholders petitioned the legislature in 1810, complaining that the societies had involved them in an excess of freedom suits. The Wilmington Society reported that they had used the courts to free eighty people from slavery in less than a decade. Delaware was an early leader in the antislavery movement in both the mid-Atlantic and the upper South, despite that the state never passed an emancipation bill. The rapid decline of slavery in Delaware outpaced that of its mid-Atlantic neighbors for several decades—including New York until 1820 and New Jersey until 1830. In 1790, 70 percent of Black Delawareans were enslaved. Twenty years later, that number had dropped to 24 percent. Manumission laws were part of the general move toward gradual emancipation in the northern states, not separate from it.[15]

14. "An Act to Prevent the Exportation of Slaves, and for Other Purposes," Feb. 3, 1787, *Laws of the State of Delaware,* II, 884–888, "An Additional Supplementary Act to an Act, Intitled, an Act to Prevent the Exportation of Slaves, and for Other Purposes," Feb. 3, 1789, 942–944.

15. "Constitution of the Delaware Abolition Society," Abolition Society of Delaware Minute Book, 2–3 (quotation), 64, Pennsylvania Abolition Society Papers, HSP;

African Americans in the upper South extended the impact of manumission reform by moving. They pursued economic opportunity within states that were committed to slavery. They reimagined their communities and towns as free spaces. Some envisioned the upper South as a watery regional corridor along the Chesapeake Bay leading to northern free communities. Their choices about whether to go or to stay were political decisions about which spaces could protect them from the long reach of slavery. Enslaved people developed "rival geographies"—understandings of places where they might find a modicum of freedom within the plantation. Freed people created rival geographies of their own. Because the surveillance of Black mobility was so integral to southern slavery, free African Americans keenly understood the power of moving toward interstitial spaces—the northern borderlands, for example, or thriving Black communities in Petersburg, Baltimore, or Philadelphia—in a region devoted to bondage. In doing so, they produced new understandings of the geopolitical space of the upper South for everyone.[16]

Urbanization shifted the gravity of free Black life and created places where people could find a semblance of security. The ease with which both free and enslaved people moved in and out of towns, and through taverns and homes and streets, was a means of asserting self-possession. Late-eighteenth-century fugitive ads printed in Virginia newspapers frequently mentioned that enslaved fugitives were headed not only to Philadelphia but also to Baltimore, Norfolk, Petersburg, and Alexandria. Free African Americans who moved helped to create the upper South's first urban boom. The transfer of Virginia's state capital from Williamsburg to Richmond attracted free and enslaved Black Virginians to the town throughout the 1780s. White shopkeepers, tradesmen like John Hope, and enslaved people created the businesses that would cater to representatives and their families. Christopher McPherson, having trained as a clerk while enslaved in Fluvanna County, moved his family and his business to Richmond when he became free in the 1790s. After a Christian conversion experience, he also

---

Minutes of the Delaware Abolition Society, Acting Committee, 1802–1807, DHS; "Petition in Relation to Negroes Petitioning for Freedom," Jan. 22, 1810, Delaware Legislative Papers; Essah, *House Divided*, 36–38, 59–61.

16. Camp, *Closer to Freedom*, 7 (quotation); Katherine McKittrick, *Demonic Grounds: Black Women and the Cartographies of Struggle* (Minneapolis, Minn., 2006), xi. For interstitial spaces, see also Anthony E. Kaye, *Joining Places: Slave Neighborhoods in the Old South* (Chapel Hill, N.C., 2009), 38–41; Sylviane A. Diouf, *Slavery's Exiles: The Story of the American Maroons* (New York, 2014); Sternhell, *Routes of War*, 8; Browne, *Dark Matters*, 22.

spent time preaching millennialism in Norfolk, Williamsburg, and Portsmouth, Virginia. Free Black migrants who moved to Wilmington, Delaware, in search of wage labor made the city the center of free Black activism in the state by the Civil War. Black Marylanders also moved to Baltimore. By 1830, one-fifth of the city's residents were free African Americans, outnumbering enslaved people four to one.[17]

By moving to urban centers, enslaved and free people were sometimes able to accumulate the capital—both social and actual—to purchase themselves and their family members. In the southern Tidewater counties of Virginia, in Richmond, Petersburg, and Norfolk, and—by the early nineteenth century—in the central and southern Piedmont, free African Americans made up a significant percentage of emancipators. Some enslaved people made partial wages for self-purchase by hiring themselves out in the upper South's towns. In the 1780s, economic changes within the Tidewater region created a surplus of enslaved labor at the same time that new towns began to grow. Rural plantation owners hired out enslaved men and women in towns, where they worked as draymen, washerwomen, or canal workers. Those who were hired out had a certain amount of mobility, but their movement was not inherently liberatory. As Rashauna Johnson has shown for New Orleans, enslavers also profited from the "compulsory mobility" of the enslaved.[18]

Men like Virginian John Plenty freed themselves through self-purchase and then worked to free their families. In 1795, Petersburg residents William Shanks and John Grammer purchased Plenty from the man who enslaved

17. For fugitive ads, see, for example, advertisements for Dick in "Ran Away from Cuthbert Harrison," *Virginia Journal and Alexandria Advertiser,* May 26, 1785, [3]; for Bob in *Virginia Independent Chronicle* (Richmond, Va.), June 3, 1789; for Ben and Amherst in "Twenty Dollars Reward Will Be Given," *Virginia Gazette and General Advertiser* (Richmond, Va.), Aug. 24, 1791, [3]; or for Jedel, "Ran Away on the 23d July Last," *Virginia Gazette and General Advertiser,* Aug. 20, 1794, [3]. For Virginia towns and Black mobility, see James Sidbury, *Ploughshares into Swords: Race, Rebellion, and Identity in Gabriel's Virginia, 1730–1810* (New York, 1997), 184–219; Michael L. Nicholls, "Strangers Setting among Us: The Sources and Challenge of the Urban Free Black Population of Early Virginia," *Virginia Magazine of History and Biography,* CVIII (2000), 155–179; McPherson, *Short History of the Life of Christopher McPherson,* 5. For Delaware and Maryland, see Essah, *House Divided,* 78–80; T. Stephen Whitman, *The Price of Freedom: Slavery and Manumission in Baltimore and Early National Maryland* (Lexington, Ky., 1997), 140; Jones, *Birthright Citizens,* 22.

18. Johnson, *Slavery's Metropolis,* 2–3 (quotation, 3), 13. For emancipators, see Albert, "Protean Institution," 279; Suzanne Lebsock, *The Free Women of Petersburg: Status and Culture in a Southern Town, 1784–1860* (New York, 1984), 96. For mobility, see Sidbury, *Ploughshares into Swords,* 184–219.

him in nearby Surry County, Virginia. Within four months, Plenty had moved to Petersburg and had a deed of manumission in hand. Grammer was an Episcopal layman and held multiple positions in Petersburg's town government. He and Shanks might have served as Plenty's middlemen, agreeing to manumit him when he could raise the funds as a laborer to purchase himself. Two years later, Plenty returned to court, this time registering a deed of manumission for his wife, Polina, and their ten-year-old son, Abram. He had purchased both of them from his former enslaver in Surry County. John, Polina, and Abram Plenty all settled in Petersburg where they found work in the city—John as a laborer, Polina as a washer, and Abram as a blacksmith. The Plenty's story of family freedom was echoed across the upper South in the early Republic. John and Polina were both fifty-three by the time they had freed themselves and Abram. They spent most of their adult lives working toward freedom—an exhausting position that required constant vigilance and that diminished the capital on which they built their futures.[19]

Interstate movement was especially important in Maryland, Delaware, and Virginia because these states were perched on the edges of free states. New York and New Jersey would not take action against slavery until 1799 and 1804, when both passed gradual emancipation bills. Neighboring Pennsylvania, on the other hand, became a haven for free people within the first two decades after the American Revolution. The state was a borderland between so-called slave and free states. Philadelphia, in particular, had one of the most significant free communities in the post-Revolutionary United States in part because of its proximity to the upper South. Free African Americans from the upper South moved there for economic opportunity, finding work in the city as domestic workers and day laborers. City watchmen policed Black migrants rigorously. The majority of African Americans arrested for vagrancy in Philadelphia in the 1790s came to the city from the upper South. Philadelphia also offered free African American migrants legal rights that they did not have elsewhere. Free Black elites and white Quakers in Philadelphia shaped the city's reputation as a refuge against slavery. Black Philadelphians built independent churches, businesses, schools, and fraternal organizations beginning in the 1790s. They funneled freedom suits to

19. Registers of Free Negroes and Mulattoes in the Town of Petersburg, 1794–1819, Jan. 2, 1809, 444, May 18, 1816, 808, LVA; Petersburg County Deed Book 2, 373–374, 479, LVA. I am indebted to Michael L. Nicholls and Lenaye Howard for their transcription of deeds, wills, and registrations from Petersburg and the surrounding counties that allowed me to write about this family's story. See "Pre-1820 Virginia Manumissions," https://libguides.usu.edu/virginia-manumissions.

the Pennsylvania Abolition Society (PAS), which provided newly arrived migrants with legal aid. In 1809, members of the PAS observed that "the approving voice of the community and the liberal interpretation of the law" had encouraged them to assist hundreds of fugitives and free people to resettle in the state where they could "claim the protection of our statutes."[20]

Precisely because so many people were on the move in the late eighteenth century, legislators in the upper South considered a series of statutes that would limit Black mobility. The control of movement was rooted in the laws and customs of slavery. Early-nineteenth-century slave societies were characterized by a "geography of containment" in which enslavers attempted to control the movements of the enslaved. Slave codes required that enslaved people carry passes with them to prove they had permission to travel. In urban spaces, local codes targeted those who circulated, like peddlers or traders. Fugitive ads put white men on notice to arrest and jail runaways. The community surveillance of Black mobility was integral to upholding slave regimes in the upper South.[21]

That surveillance carried over into freedom. The states tried to strip free Black men and women of their ability to travel—one of the most basic rights of citizens—at the very moment when thousands of people newly claimed their freedom. As free people began to assert power over their mobility, upper South legislatures reacted by restricting what was considered their "legitimate 'means of movement.'" Free Black Virginians were called on to prove their free status while they were in transit. In 1793, the Virginia legislature banned any free Black person from migrating into the state and re-

20. "Pennsylvania Report to the American Convention Society," 1809, Pennsylvania Abolition Society Papers, reel 28, HSP (quotations). For Pennsylvania as a borderland, a free space, and a destination for migrants, see Gary B. Nash, *Forging Freedom: The Formation of Philadelphia's Black Community, 1720–1840* (Cambridge, Mass., 1988), 134–171; Jean R. Soderlund, "Black Importation and Migration into Southeastern Pennsylvania, 1682–1810," American Philosophical Society, *Proceedings,* CXXXIII (1989), 150; Richard S. Newman, "'Lucky to Be Born in Pennsylvania': Free Soil, Fugitive Slaves, and the Making of Pennsylvania's Anti-Slavery Borderland," *Slavery and Abolition: A Journal of Slave and Post-Slave Studies,* XXXII (2011), 413–430. See also Matthew Salafia, *Slavery's Borderland: Freedom and Bondage along the Ohio River* (Philadelphia, 2013). For African American politics in Philadelphia more broadly, see Julie Winch, *Philadelphia's Black Elite: Activism, Accommodation, and the Struggle for Autonomy, 1787–1848* (Philadelphia, 1988); Winch, *A Gentleman of Color: The Life of James Forten* (New York, 2003); Erica Armstrong Dunbar, *A Fragile Freedom: African American Women and Emancipation in the Antebellum City* (New Haven, Conn., 2008); Newman, *Freedom's Prophet: Bishop Richard Allen, the AME Church, and the Black Founding Fathers* (New York, 2008).

21. Camp, *Closer to Freedom,* 6 (quotation); Browne, *Dark Matters,* 22, 25, 31–88.

quired that free African Americans register their residency with the county clerk every three years. Free people discovered without their papers could be jailed, as was the case for Billy Johnson, who was committed to the Richmond jail in 1798 on suspicion of being a fugitive after he shipped out of Norfolk without papers. Travelers like Johnson might eventually prove their freedom by having their papers sent on from their home county, but they accrued jail fees while they waited. By the time that Hannah, jailed in Henrico County, Virginia, in 1826 as a fugitive, was able to prove her free status, she owed nearly forty-five dollars in jail fees. She was hired out by the county to work as an indentured servant until she could pay them back.[22]

Obtaining papers was helpful, and often necessary, for those who regularly moved between employers or counties. Charlotte Gilchrist applied to the clerk in Surry County, Virginia, in 1807 at age twenty-two. Because she was "about to leave this neibourhood *in search of a better* [one]," she approached the court for her free papers. In 1810, twelve years after the passage of the registration act, eighteen-year-old craftsman Carter Jackson applied to the Surry County clerk for the first time because "his Father Jessie Chatman is conscious that Carter should have a free pass the better to enable him to follow his avocation." Virginia newspapers were filled with scattered advertisements for lost free papers, attesting to their importance to their bearers. Robert Morse carried his free papers for safekeeping in a cigar box; David Poindexter tucked his into a leather pocketbook; John Stewart kept them close in his coat pocket, and when his coat went overboard into the James River, he lost the papers along with it. Papers were important for those who occupied particular trades or who wanted some claim on the state's protection from kidnapping or reenslavement.[23]

22. Torpey, "Coming and Going," *Sociological Theory*, XVI (1998), 239–259; Barbara Young Welke, *Law and the Borders of Belonging in the Long Nineteenth Century United States* (New York, 2010), 3. For the 1793 statute, see "An Act for Regulating the Police of Towns in This Commonwealth, and to Refrain the Practice of Negroes Going at Large," Dec. 10, 1793, *Acts Passed at a General Assembly of the Commonwealth of Virginia Begun and Held at the Capitol, in the City of Richmond, on Monday, the Twenty-First Day of October, One Thousand Seven Hundred and Ninety-Three* (Richmond, Va., 1794), 27–28. The 1793 statute was not dissimilar to a proposal made in the Virginia senate in 1782 to require free African Americans "going abroad" to travel with a copy of their free papers. See Parrish, "Notes on a Journey to Virginia," [1782], Parrish Family Papers, folder 6, [13] (quotation). For Johnson, see "Runaways in Richmond Jail," *Virginia Gazette, and General Advertiser* (Richmond, Va.), Dec. 4, 1798, [1]. For Hannah, see Case of Hannah, Jan. 13, 1826, Henrico Hustings Court, Henrico County Free Negro and Slave Records, LVA.

23. Charlotte Gilchrist, Letter, Apr. 7 1807, Surry County Clerk Records, 1778–1868, VMHC ("about"), Carter Jackson, Letter, Jan. 2, 1810 ("his Father"); Robert

Registration laws were not enforced with any regularity. It was rare for an individual to follow the 1793 law to the letter and register more than once, although many did obtain free papers at some point during their lifetimes. Most free Black Virginians treated the registration law as optional. Wright Walden resided in Surry County, Virginia, for fifty years before he applied for free papers. County clerks rarely expressed surprise that registrants like Walden had waited so long to be put on the books. In Amherst County, Virginia, fewer than a third of free Black men and women registered under the 1793 law. At moments of conflict, some free African Americans felt compelled to follow the letter of the law, as after Nat Turner's rebellion or in response to new restrictive travel legislation passed in 1851, when the number of Amherst County registrants spiked. There is little evidence that free African Americans were regularly prosecuted for failing to register. That such a law existed, however, shows the state's aspirations to control movement.[24]

Movement was always contested and politicized in the early Republic—for Black and Indigenous people, especially, it was posed as a problem to

---

Morse, Lost free papers, 1859, Henrico County Free Negro and Slave Records; John Stewart, Lost free papers, 1857, Petersburg Free Negro and Slave Records, LVA, David Poindexter, Lost free papers, n.d., Albemarle County Free Negro and Slave Records. For cases of jailed sailors and travelers, see, for example, "Runaway in the City Jail," *Virginia Gazette, and General Advertiser,* Mar. 9, 1805, [4]; "Was Committed to the Jail . . . ," *Enquirer* (Richmond, Va.), Oct. 20, 1814, [1]; "Committed to Norfolk Borough Jail, a Negro Man Named Tony Meredith," *Norfolk and Portsmouth Herald,* June 30, 1819, [4]. See also "To the Humane," *American Beacon and Commercial Diary* (Norfolk, Va.), Aug. 30, 1817, [4]; Advertisement for John Robertson, "Was Committed to the Jail of Henrico County," *Richmond Enquirer,* May 14, 1824, [4]; Advertisement for Jeremiah Powell, "Was Committed to the Jail at King William Courthouse," *Richmond Enquirer,* Aug. 10, 1824, [4]; Tommy L. Bogger, *Free Blacks in Norfolk Virginia, 1790–1860: The Darker Side of Freedom* (Charlottesville, Va., 1997), 97–98.

24. Ellen D. Katz, "African-American Freedom in Antebellum Cumberland County, Virginia," *Chicago-Kent Law Review,* LXX (1995), 952; Douglas R. Egerton, *Gabriel's Rebellion: The Virginia Slave Conspiracies of 1800 and 1802* (Chapel Hill, N. C., 1993), 29; Wolf, *Race and Liberty in the New Nation,* 117; Eva Sheppard Wolf, *Almost Free: A Story about Family and Race in Antebellum Virginia* (Athens, Ga., 2012), 45–48, 74; Ted Maris-Wolf, *Family Bonds: Free Blacks and Re-enslavement Law in Antebellum Virginia* (Chapel Hill, N. C., 2015), 26. Sherrie S. McLeRoy and William R. McLeRoy, for example, show that almost 75 percent of people who registered in Amherst County never reregistered. See McLeRoy and McLeRoy, *Strangers in Their Midst: The Free Black Population of Amherst County, Virginia* (Bowie, Md., 1993), 19. In the Surry County records, less than half the free people who registered there reregistered. If they did reregister, they did not do so every three years. Many only first registered years after their manumission and the passage of the 1793 act. See Dennis Hudgins, *Surry County, Virginia Register of Free Negroes* (Richmond, Va., 1995); Surry County Clerk Records, 1778–1868, VMHC.

be managed rather than a given. Federal officials kept watch over Shawnee movements across the Great Lakes in the early nineteenth century. They passed Trade and Intercourse Acts to define Native and white mobility in the trans-Appalachian West. They tried to contain white migrants who went west claiming the right to move freely. In all of these cases, state and federal officials struggled to give statutes on the books the force of law. In the upper South, states simply did not have the power to enforce registration laws, although they continued to add to them well into the nineteenth century. It was not the state but local communities that determined how to police migration and registration. At the local level, white neighbors or justices decided what kind of movement challenged the stability of white supremacy or bondage in their communities. Generally, they used the statutes on the books selectively, or they did not use them at all.[25]

Observing the hard-won successes of free people at the beginning of the nineteenth century, upper South elites began to fill the halls of state legislatures with petitions demanding strict control over Black mobility. They reinvigorated these calls after word of the Haitian Revolution reached American newspapers in 1791. The news of the burning of Le Cap in 1793 and the arrival of Caribbean planters in Maryland and Virginia prompted a backlash against abolitionism from proslavery elites. In Alexandria, proslavery legislator Elisha C. Dick burst into a meeting of the Alexandria Abolition Society and gave the group "a lengthy harangue on the impropriety of our association, and the dangerous consequences which might result from the establishment of such a society by infusing into the slaves a spirit of insurrection and rebellion which might eventually destroy the tranquillity of the state." Three years later, Dick shepherded into law a bill levying heavy fines for abolitionists who supported unsuccessful freedom suits.[26]

25. Laura F. Edwards, *The People and Their Peace: Legal Culture and the Transformation of Inequality in the Post-Revolutionary South* (Chapel Hill, N.C., 2009).

26. Archibald McClean to Wm Rogers, Feb. 15, 1796, Pennsylvania Abolition Society Papers, reel 12 (quotation); "An Act to Amend an Act, Intitled, an Act to Reduce into One the Several Acts concerning Slaves, Free Negroes, and Mulattoes, and for Other Purposes," Dec. 25, 1795, *Acts Passed at a General Assembly of the Commonwealth of Virginia; Begun and Held at the Capitol, in the City of Richmond, on Tuesday, the Tenth Day of November, One Thousand Seven Hundred and Ninety-Five* (Richmond, Va., 1796), 16; *Journal of the House of Delegates of the Commonwealth of Virginia, Begun and Held at the Capitol, in the City of Richmond, on Tuesday, the Tenth Day of November, One Thousand Seven Hundred and Ninety-Five* (Richmond, Va., 1795), 118. Two years later, the legislature restricted members of abolition societies from serving as jurors on freedom suits as well. See "An Act to Amend the Act, Intitled an Act to Amend the Act,

In Virginia, white fears of Black revolutionary politics prompted the General Assembly to restrict one of the most basic principles of interstate comity: the right to free movement between the states. Virginia's legislators believed that it was the circulation of people carrying dangerous ideas that promoted rebellion, and particularly so in urban spaces. New state laws required every free Black person living or working in cities and towns to register with the county clerk. Legislators forbid free people who were not Virginia residents from migrating into the state. Virginia's was the first law passed in the nation to restrict Black migration between the states.[27]

When the rumor of revolution arrived in Virginia once again in 1800, legislators reacted by more firmly controlling African American mobility in the legal code. On August 30, Virginia governor James Monroe and the mayors of Richmond and Petersburg received word of a rebellion organized by an enslaved man named Gabriel Prosser. Prosser planned to lead more than two thousand enslaved men from neighboring counties to take the capitol, the armory, and the governor's house in Richmond. The specter of rebellion set off a flurry of arrests and trials that lasted two months. From early September to the end of October, nearly seventy men were imprisoned in the two-story jail in Richmond, awaiting trial next door at the courthouse. Like all enslaved Virginians accused of capital crimes, the alleged conspirators were tried without a jury by a special court of oyer and terminer. At least five justices presided over these courts, and their unanimous decision could send an enslaved person to the gallows. Of the seventy men tried for insurrection, forty-four were found guilty, and twenty-seven were hanged for their purported role in the plan.[28]

That winter, when the Virginia General Assembly gathered for the year's

---

Intitled, an Act to Reduce into One, the Several Acts concerning Slaves, Free Negroes, and Mulattoes," Jan. 25, 1798, *Acts Passed at a General Assembly of the Commonweatlh [sic] of Virginia: Begun and Held at the Capitol, in the City of Richmond, on Monday, the Fourth Day of December, One Thousand Seven Hundred and Ninety-Seven* (Richmond, Va., 1798), 5–6. For the reception of news of the Haitian Revolution in the United States, see Gary B. Nash, "Reverberations of Haiti in the American North: Black Saint Dominguans in Philadelphia," *Pennsylvania History: A Journal of Mid-Atlantic Studies,* special issue, *Explorations in Early American Culture,* LXV (1998), 61; Ashli White, *Encountering Revolution: Haiti and the Making of the Early Republic* (Baltimore, Md., 2010), 124–165.

27. "An Act for Regulating the Police of Towns in This Commonwealth," Dec. 10, 1793, *Acts Passed at a General Assembly of the Commonwealth of Virginia . . . One Thousand Seven Hundred and Ninety-Three,* 27–28.

28. Governor's Communication to Speakers of the General Assembly, Dec. 5, 1800, OSEC, box 8, folder 7; Egerton, *Gabriel's Rebellion,* 80; Sidbury, *Ploughshares into Swords,* 8.

legislative session, they more firmly established removal and control over mobility in the legal code. From the state capitol building on top of the high plane of Richmond's central plateau, legislators could see down the sloping hillside southeast to Shockoe Bottom, the swampy riverbed of Shockoe Creek that emptied into the James River. They might have looked carefully for the low-lying spot just at the creek's embankment designated as a "Negro Burying Ground," where Gabriel and most of his compatriots had been hung for insurrection two months prior. From that perch, Monroe asked them to take action to prevent another rebellion.[29]

The legislature addressed Monroe's call, increasing urban policing, curtailing mobility, and embracing exile as emancipation's corollary. As Richmond's population expanded, the city's residents met, regardless of status, in the city's streets, taverns, and shops. The Richmond Common Council perceived the city's fluidity as turmoil, and they reorganized what had been sporadic city patrols after 1797. Magistrates in charge of Richmond's wards were encouraged to make monthly accountings of those who appeared "disorderly." After Gabriel's Rebellion, new policing laws moved from the general to the specific, targeting the movements of free Black Richmonders. Legislators established a regular guard in the city, armed militias in Virginia's most populous towns, and instituted new patrols in Petersburg and Fredericksburg. These changes in policing were an explicit reaction to Monroe's address and to two petitions that demanded legislative action to discourage manumission.[30]

Legislators also proposed prohibiting free Black residency in Virginia's towns altogether. Governor Monroe similarly believed that Richmond city officials should "expel" free and enslaved Black Richmonders from the city, while only permitting those who came in from the surrounding countryside to visit the city during daylight hours. Meanwhile, a new law passed in

29. Governor's Communication to Speakers of the General Assembly, Dec. 5, 1800, OSEC, box 8, folder 7.

30. Richmond Common Council Minutes, 1796–1807, 31 (quotation), 33, LVA; "An Act to Empower the Governor to Transport Slaves Condemned, When It Should Be Deemed Expedient," Jan. 15, 1801, *Acts Passed at a General Assembly of the Commonwealth of Virginia; Begun and Held at the Capitol, in the City of Richmond, on Monday, the First Day of December One Thousand Eight Hundred* (Richmond, Va., [1801]), 24, "An Act to Establish a Guard in the City of Richmond," Jan. 22, 1801, 34–35; *Journal of the House of Delegates of the Commonwealth of Virginia Begun and Held at the Capitol, in the City of Richmond, on Monday the First Day of December One Thousand Eight Hundred* (Richmond, Va., 1800), 47; James Monroe to Legislature, Dec. 7, 1801, OSEC, box 8, folder 17; Petition of Inhabitants of Petersburg, Dec. 22, 1800, VLP, box 360, folder 5, Petition of Citizens of King and Queen County, Dec. 2, 1800, box 132, folder 21.

1801 required county commissioners of revenue to maintain accurate annual registers of all free Black Virginians living in their districts. Those lists were to be posted on the door of the county courthouse so that community members could judge the legality of any Black person's presence in the county. Magistrates could lawfully arrest and jail as "vagrant[s]" Black migrants from out of state and those who moved between counties without employment. The law revealed that white legislators saw movement as transgressive when free people left their homes where they were well-known by their neighbors, thereby breeching informal community surveillance.[31]

In the 1780s and 1790s, white Virginians had published pamphlets and opinion pieces that promoted the colonization of freed people outside of the nation as a solution to what they saw as the problem of emancipation in the upper South. After Gabriel's Rebellion, legislators opened a secret correspondence with President Thomas Jefferson about creating a Black colony "without the limits of this State." Jefferson wrote back, imagining a program of mandatory removal for all newly freed people. Jefferson's colonization plan, which he included in his *Notes on the State of Virginia,* often stands alone as a symbol for colonization thought in the early Republic. The secret correspondence demonstrates the wider popularity of colonization among elite white Virginians. The Virginia House of Delegates continued to request Jefferson's opinions on colonization for years after Gabriel's Rebellion. Jefferson's ideas were periodically embraced and endorsed by state legislative committees. The General Assembly even took action, applying to Congress for "a portion of the late acquisition beyond the Mississippi" to create a Black colony in 1805. These efforts make it clear that many white Virginians hoped that emancipation would ultimately be an exclusionary project.[32]

31. James Monroe to Mayor of the City of Richmond, Dec. 27, 1800, Executive Letter book, 1800–1803, LVA ("expel"); "An Act to Amend the Act, Intitled, 'An Act, to Reduce into One the Several Acts, concerning Slaves, Free Negroes, and Mulattoes,'" Jan. 21, 1801, *Acts Passed at a General Assembly of the Commonwealth of Virginia; Begun and . . . on Monday the First Day of December One Thousand Eight Hundred,* 38 ("vagrant[s]"). Most of these resolutions were passed except for the bill prohibiting free Black people from residing in the towns. Discussion on that resolution was put off, but the session never occurred. See *Journal of the House of Delegates of the Commonwealth of Virginia . . . One Thousand Eight Hundred,* 43, 47–48, 70.

32. *Journal of the House of Delegates . . . One Thousand Eight Hundred,* 48 ("without"); John Page to Speaker of the House of Delegates, Jan. 12, 1805, OSEC, box 9, folder 24 ("portion"), Resolution of the House, Dec. 31, 1800, box 8, folder 19, James Monroe to Speaker of the House of Delegates, Dec. 9, 1802, box 8, folder 32, "Extract of a Letter from the President of the United States to the Governor," Dec. 23, 1803,

The idea of a Louisiana colony had little purchase on a national level. The state's congressmen working one hundred miles away in Washington, D. C., saw only "insurmountable difficulties" in the idea of continental colonization. They knew that other states would never agree to set aside Louisiana land, which federal officials had already envisioned as a space for white migration. Louisiana, Virginia's congressmen suggested, was "a secure and reserved Inheritance for unborn millions of our own Posterity." Their vision for Louisiana presumed that Native American dispossession would secure the land for white migrants. On the one hand, it was empty space that they had written Native peoples out of already. On the other hand, they objected to a free Black colony in Louisiana on the grounds that Indigenous people were "uncommonly hostile" to African Americans. They also disapproved of it on more universal grounds of proximity and protection. Any site for the settlement would challenge U.S. aspirations for sovereignty in the trans-Appalachian West. The Virginia delegation imagined that a colony too close to frontier settlements might eventually become "a powerful People" that would rival the United States.[33]

As a regional obsession, however, exile continued to resonate in Virginia's statehouse and in the halls of local courthouses. Undaunted by the rejection of Virginia's Louisiana colony by Congress, Monroe's successor, Governor John Page, continued to press the state legislature to sponsor it. He wished to place a tax on Virginia enslavers to fund a Louisiana removal project. Page believed that, with his plan, "but few blacks would be found in these states after a half century." In effect, Page's ideas amounted to gradual emancipation, but with removal and the erasure of blackness as its end. If his idea failed, Page suggested that Virginia might alternatively offer free people "some inducement to leave the country."[34]

At the same time, a group of Petersburg councilmen also petitioned the Virginia General Assembly to ask for various measures that would curtail

---

box 9, folder 12, Page to the Speaker of the House of Delegates, Jan. 23, 1804, box 9, folder 12; Page to Thomas Jefferson, Oct. 29, 1804, John Page Executive Papers, LVA; Jefferson to Page, Dec. 27, 1804, OSEC, box 9, folder 24, "Committee to Whom It Was Referred the Correspondence between the Governor of This State and the President of the United States . . . ," Jan. 28, 1803, box 8, folder 40; Monroe to Jefferson, June 15, 1801, in Julian P. Boyd et al., eds., *The Papers of Thomas Jefferson,* 43 vols. (Princeton, N.J., 1950—), XXXIV, 345–347, Jefferson to Monroe, Nov. 24, 1801, XXXV, 718–722.

33. "Enclosure B: Letter of Virginia Delegation," Mar. 2, 1805, in John Page to the Speaker of the House of Delegates, Dec. 10, 1805, OSEC, box 9, folder 34.

34. John Page to the Speaker of the House of Delegates, Dec. 10, 1805, OSEC, box 9, folder 34.

Black mobility. At the local level, the Petersburg Common Council had already agreed that year to bring the state's laws aimed at free Black people "into more Energetick effect into this town" by counting everyone in their wards likely to become chargeable as well as recording "their mode of living." The Petersburg councilmen now asked the state legislature to bind emancipated Virginians to the counties where they were freed, prohibiting travel and residency in other locales. The petitioners also wanted Virginia to purchase and then deport enslaved people (in the ratio of two women for each man) outside of the state or nation to serve as indentured servants elsewhere. Otherwise, they wrote that Black residents of Petersburg would "eventually claim priviledges which they enjoy not, and which our laws we hope will forever prohibit them the exercise of." Unwilling to expand the rights and privileges of freed people, the Petersburg petitioners instead wished to exile them from the state. They exposed emancipation as an exclusionary project in which freedom did not align with citizenship.[35]

In the post-Revolutionary period, hundreds of free African Americans from outlying counties moved to Petersburg in search of work and community. Freed men and women created separate churches and institutions in an autonomous neighborhood called Pocahontas Island. Of all the Virginia towns, Petersburg had the most predominant Black community in the state: one-sixth of Petersburg residents were free Black men and women by the early nineteenth century, or about one-third of the town's free population. The Petersburg petitioners couched their proposal in stark terms as a response to free Black migrants who "flock[ed] from the country to the towns." Their policies were a direct attack on the growth of a community like Pocahontas Island.[36]

Although historians think of colonization as a solely intellectual movement in the United States in this period, the Petersburg councilmen succeeded in their campaign to make removal a condition of emancipation. Because there were property requirements for voting, petitioning was the only avenue to direct political participation for many people in the early Republic. It was also the way that most legislation was introduced into Virginia's General Assembly. Addressing the Petersburg petition and Governor Page's instructions in 1806, legislators passed a law that included a provision exiling any enslaved person freed after May 1, 1806, from the state. If newly freed

35. Petersburg Common Council Minutes, II, 1, Petersburg County Courthouse, Petersburg, Va. ("into more Energetick"); Mayor, Recorder, Aldermen, and Commonalty, Petition, Dec. 11, 1805, VLP, box 360, folder 9 ("eventually").

36. Mayor, Recorder, Aldermen, and Commonalty, Petition, Dec. 11, 1805, VLP, box 360, folder 9 (quotation); Lebsock, *Free Women of Petersburg*, 91.

people did not leave within one year of manumission, they risked reenslavement and sale to the overseers of the poor for the benefit of the parish. After Gabriel's Rebellion, several attempts had been made to ban manumission in Virginia entirely. Unable to overcome the antislavery position, legislators instead mandated that removal would accompany freedom.[37]

The new legislation worked in tandem to refashion free African Americans into exiles. The policy was not a reversal of Virginia's post-Revolutionary antislavery feeling. Rather, it reflected the colonizationist thinking of the state's most ardent emancipationists. In 1796, jurist St. George Tucker wrote that, although he did not advocate the "banishment" of free African Americans from the state, "I wish not to encourage their future residence among us. By denying them the most valuable privileges which civil government affords, I wished to render it their inclination and their interest to seek those privileges in some other climate." Indeed, the 1806 law did just that, depriving free Black men and women of freedom of movement and the right to remain. It was intended to force people to leave through coercion.[38]

White fear of slave insurrections lasted long after Gabriel's Rebellion was tried in the courts. In the two years after the trials, white Virginians arrested thirty other people whom they suspected as leaders of revolts. In 1801, officials detained a man named Lewis on suspicion of planning an uprising in Richmond, Petersburg, and Norfolk to overturn slavery. They tortured him until he confirmed the rumors. Lewis told them he and the other leaders of the rebellion would "take the country of Virginia" because "the white people have had the country long enough." Lewis's testimony, forced from him by violence, was evidence of the routine terror of slavery. The content of Lewis's testimony is more difficult to parse. Lewis said that he would

37. "An Act to Amend the Several Laws concerning Slaves," Jan. 25, 1806, *Acts Passed at a General Assembly of the Commonwealth of Virginia; Begun and Held at the Capitol, in the City of Richmond, on Monday the Second Day of December, One Thousand Eight Hundred and Five* (Richmond, Va., [1806]), 36. For discussion of the bill, see *Journal of the House of Delegates of the Commonwealth of Virginia; Begun and Held at the Capitol, in the City of Richmond, on Monday the Second Day of December, One Thousand Eight Hundred and Five* (Richmond, Va., [1806]), 22, 66, 77–78, 87. In 1785, 1803, 1804, and 1805, there were serious attempts in the legislature to outlaw manumission. In 1805, the ban on manumission was barely defeated with a vote of seventy-three to seventy-five. Most support for the bill came from the Tidewater and Southside counties closer to the North Carolina border.

38. St. George Tucker, *A Dissertation on Slavery: With a Proposal for the Gradual Abolition of It, in the State of Virginia* (Philadelphia, 1796), 94 (quotations). K-Sue Park calls this "self-deportation." See Park, "Self-Deportation Nation," *Harvard Law Review*, CXXXII (2019), 1878–1941.

"set the whole Country free of the White people" and create a free Black republic in the Chesapeake. Given that white Virginians repeatedly proposed African American removal in the early Republic, Lewis might have used the language of removal because it was legible to his torturers and their expectations of his politics. On the other hand, he might just as well have imagined a future moment, brought into being by a revolution, when Virginia would be free of white Americans and white supremacy with them.[39]

The 1806 law rested on precedents stretching back to the colonial period. In the early Republic, states rather than the federal government had the right to control immigration and internal migration. Vagrancy laws and poor laws carried over from before the Revolution. These laws had defined the meaning of *residency* and *settlement* for more than a century. They enabled states to discriminate against particular groups of migrants. Under the Articles of Confederation, states could bar the entry of "paupers, vagabonds, and fugitives from justice." In Massachusetts and New York, state legislatures built on poor laws to deport poor immigrants—legislation that was clearly anti-Irish. Restrictive migration statutes that targeted free African Americans also relied on the legal architecture of poor laws. In the Virginia provision of 1806, that connection was made explicit: the overseers of the poor stood to benefit from the sale of those who remained in the state illegally. Migration restrictions targeting African Americans were unique, however, in that they did not apply to social and legal categories—"paupers, vagabonds, and fugitives from justice"—but to racial categories.[40]

Removal spread outward from Virginia, and the rest of the middle states passed laws barring or restricting free African American migration as well. These new statutes also derived from the poor laws. State legislatures defended them by invoking their ability to police migration within and across their borders. The mobility of free African Americans between the states with varied emancipation statutes on the books prompted significant discussions about interstate comity. The right of free movement between the states gave meaning to the union itself, but it was the very power of locomo-

39. Executive Papers, May 5, 1802, quoted in James Hugo Johnston, *Race Relations in Virginia and Miscegenation in the South, 1776–1860* (Amherst, Mass., 1970), 36, cited in Philip J. Schwarz, *Twice Condemned: Slaves and the Criminal Laws of Virginia, 1705–1865* (Baton Rouge, La., 1988), 270 ("take the country"); Executive Papers, box 120, quoted in Sidbury, *Ploughshares into Swords,* 143–144 ("set the whole Country," 143).

40. Articles of Confederation, 1777, art. IV (quotation); Hirota, *Expelling the Poor;* Parker, *Making Foreigners,* 53, 73–77; O'Brassill-Kulfan, *Vagrants and Vagabonds,* 84–111.

tion and settlement that the states began to restrict in the first decade of the nineteenth century.

As free Black men and women grappled with Virginia's new exile law in 1806, Maryland and Delaware immediately passed restrictive acts forbidding them from entering. The Maryland General Assembly approved its statute directly on the heels of Virginia's in 1806, fining free Black migrants for each week that they remained in the state. Maryland's reaction to Virginia's 1806 exile law was informed by the state's stark regional divide. Over the course of the nineteenth century, the epicenter of free Black life for Marylanders moved up to the northern counties, while the southern counties remained committed to slavery. Manumission had the greatest effect on Maryland's grain-growing Eastern Shore, where planters preferred to hire free laborers to meet their seasonal labor needs. The number of free people living on the Eastern Shore rose markedly after 1790.[41]

When Eastern Shore enslavers complained about a labor shortage in their counties, they might have been referring to the power of Black Marylanders to use mobility to their advantage. If they were unsatisfied with the terms of a contract, free laborers could leave plantations without workers at critical harvest time, travel to find better working conditions, or even demand higher wages. It is not surprising then, that, in 1796, the state legislature attempted to curb Black mobility by imposing fines on free African Americans who traveled through the state without employment. When the Maryland General Assembly banned free Black migrants from entering the state, the few legislators to oppose the bill hailed largely from the Eastern Shore counties. Given complaints about labor shortages, enslavers on the peninsula welcomed free Black Virginia migrants who moved into the state across Maryland's eastern border.[42]

Neighboring Delaware also took issue with Virginia's exile law. In Governor Nathaniel Mitchell's address to the Delaware legislature in 1807, he argued that it created a problem of migration and federalism. Southern free people had long traveled through the peninsula on their way to northern cities. Mitchell predicted that free Black men and women who were exiled

41. Barbara Jeanne Fields, *Slavery and Freedom on the Middle Ground: Maryland during the Nineteenth Century* (New Haven, Conn., 1985), 9–12; David Skillen Bogen, "The Maryland Context of *Dred Scott:* The Decline in the Legal Status of Maryland Free Blacks, 1776–1810," *American Journal of Legal History,* XXXIV (1990), 406.

42. "An Act relating to Negroes, and to Repeal the Acts of Assembly Therein Mentioned," 1796, in Virgil Maxcy, *The Laws of Maryland . . . ,* 3 vols. (Baltimore, 1811), II, 351; Bogen, "Maryland Context of *Dred Scott,*" *American Journal of Legal History,* XXXIV (1990), 392–395; Wright, *Free Negro in Maryland,* 81.

from Virginia would now "come into the middle, or go into the northern States" in greater numbers than before. Mitchell explained his objections to Black emigration by outlining a limited definition of who was entitled to the protection of the state. Free people who migrated into Delaware were, according to Mitchell, "utter strangers to us, and have no claims of indulgence or protection from us." On Mitchell's instructions, Delaware passed its own restrictive emigration bill on the heels of Virginia in 1807. Free Black men and women would be "warned and notified"—a reference to the warning out mechanism in state poor laws—within ten days of crossing into Delaware. The Delaware statute went further than the poor law, however. Those who refused to leave the state could be arrested, fined, and sold into indentured servitude if they could not pay. Repealed in 1808, Delaware's restrictive emigration law was reinstated in 1811. New provisions also required newly freed Delawareans to leave the state within ten days of receiving manumission papers, thus combining restrictive emigration laws with exile.[43]

Support for Delaware's measure was informed by the way that Black migration had shifted the geography of freedom in the state to create a middle ground that cut across the Mason-Dixon Line encompassing northern Delaware and southeastern Pennsylvania. White abolitionists were disproportionately centered in Delaware's two northern counties with the closest ties to Pennsylvania. Even as the two northern counties remade themselves in the image of gradualist free state Pennsylvania, southernmost Sussex County, only a day's ride from Pennsylvania, recommitted to slavery. It was Sussex County that pushed through Delaware's restrictive emigration law in reaction to Virginia in 1807. Sussex County whites had long agitated for greater restrictions around free Black mobility. In 1786, a group of Sussex residents had complained that "under the name and Character of Free Negroes many idle and evil-disposed slaves throughout this County stroll

43. "Governor's Address in the House of Representatives," Jan. 8, 1807, Delaware Legislative Papers, 14 ("come"); "An Act to Prohibit the Emigration of Free Negroes or Mulattoes into This State, and for Other Purposes," Jan. 28, 1811, *Laws of the State of Delaware, from the Seventh Day of January, One Thousand Eight Hundred and Six, to the Third Day of February, One Thousand Eight Hundred and Thirteen,* IV (Wilmington, Del., 1816), 400–404 ("warned," 401), "An Act for the Better Regulation of Free Negroes and Free Mulattoes," Feb. 6, 1807, 108–113; *Journal of the House of Representatives of the State of Delaware, at a Session of the General Assembly, Commenced and Holden at Dover, on Tuesday the Fifth Day of January, in the Year of Our Lord, One Thousand Eight Hundred and Eight*... ([Dover, Del.], [1808]), 88, 89. For more connections between poor laws and the policing of belonging, see O'Brassil-Kulfan, *Vagrants and Vagabonds;* Parker, *Making Foreigners.*

thro" the state while "Stragglers and vagabonds From the neighbouring counties . . . come and go." In the legislature, those who supported the Sussex petitioners also charged fugitives from slavery with "corrupting the minds of many both free and slaves by their examples of theft indolence and other knavish practices." The petitioners hoped to restrict mobility because they believed that it threatened slavery—they argued that running away, like rebellion, could be contagious.[44]

It was precisely because free Black Delawareans carved out significant communities for themselves that the legislature pursued a restrictive emigration bill in 1807. By 1810, free Black people in Delaware made up 18 percent of the total population—a striking difference in comparison to the 9 percent of Marylanders, 3 percent of Virginians, 3 percent of Pennsylvanians, 2 percent of New Yorkers, and 1 percent of Massachusetts residents who were free African Americans. White petitioners made it clear that they saw emancipation as a problem of population and politics. In 1810, one group of petitioners complained that state laws encouraged fugitives to see Delaware as a "refuge," thereby "daily increasing the number of those, of whom experience has proven we have already too many for the good of society." Governor Mitchell himself believed that Black tenants were taking away opportunities from white farmers by buying and renting lands in part of the state. He supported restrictive emigration laws, insisting that "we have already a great sufficiency of this description of persons." He complained that free Black men would "soon make a large proportion of the renters of land."[45]

Restrictive emigration laws were not limited to the upper South. The other middle states that bordered the Ohio River—Ohio, Kentucky, Indiana, and Illinois—soon adoped them too. In each of these states, elites tried to make free states for white migrants through Indigenous dispossession and restrictive migration laws. In the early Republic, thousands of white Virginians left the state for the western territories, bringing their legal traditions with them. The Northwest Ordinance had prohibited slavery north of the Ohio River, but challenges to African American citizenship and belonging abounded nonetheless. The new Midwestern states all restricted the rights of free African Americans. In Ohio, where white Virginians were one

44. "Petition of Sundry Inhabitants of Sussex County," June 1786, Delaware Legislative Papers ("under"), Bill for Authorising the Emancipation of Slaves, January–February 1786 ("corrupting"); Essah, *House Divided,* 81.

45. "Petition in Relation to Negroes Petitioning for Freedom," Jan. 22, 1810, Delaware Legislative Papers ("refuge"), "Governor's Address in the House of Representatives," Jan. 8, 1807 ("we have already").

of the most significant groups of migrants in the decades after the Revolution, the state constitution denied African Americans the vote. In 1804, Ohio's legislature further required that Black Ohioans register their certificates of freedom with the counties and prohibited Ohioans from aiding, sheltering, or employing those who did not carry free papers.[46]

When Virginia passed its exile law in 1806, the backlash in the new states of Ohio, Indiana, and Illinois was immediate. One Ohio editorialist remarked that Ohio "will suffer seriously, from the iniquitous policy pursued by the states of Virginia and Kentucky driving all their free negroes upon us. The people of Ohio are bound in justice to themselves to adopt some counteracting measure." The Ohio legislature did just that, taking up a new restrictive bill in their very next session. The 1807 law required Black migrants to post a five-hundred-dollar surety bond with the local court when they crossed the border. Observers at the time described Ohio's efforts to restrict free African Americans from settling in the state as a reaction to Virginia's exile measure and to a similar law passed in Kentucky the same year. In 1813, Illinois Territory prohibited free Black settlement entirely and gave migrants fifteen days to depart. After statehood, Illinois followed with a restrictive settlement law in 1819 and Indiana in 1831. Indiana governor James Brown Ray called explicitly for "corresponding measures" that would counter African American travelers from other states with new restrictions on the books.[47]

46. "An Act, to Regulate Black and Mulatto Persons," Jan. 5, 1804, *Acts of the State of Ohio Second Session of the General Assembly Held under the Constitution of the State, A.D. One Thousand Eight Hundred and Three . . . ,* II ([1804]; rpt. Norwalk, Ohio, 1901), 63–66; R. Douglas Hurt, *The Ohio Frontier: Crucible of the Old Northwest, 1720–1830* (Bloomington, Ind., 1996), 249; Joshua D. Rothman, *Notorious in the Neighborhood: Sex and Families across the Color Line in Virginia, 1787–1861* (Chapel Hill, N.C., 2003), 7. The ordinance of 1787 required that new western territories adapt their laws from those on the books in the eastern states before their legislature was organized, presumably beginning a tradition of adaptation and borrowing from the East. See Robert M. Taylor, Jr., ed., *The Northwest Ordinance, 1787: A Bicentennial Handbook* (Indianapolis, Ind., 1987), 36–38.

47. "By the Following Letter from a Gentleman on a Tour through Virginia," *The Supporter* (Chillicothe, Ohio), June 16, 1819, [3] ("will suffer"), also quoted in Frank U. Quillin, *The Color Line in Ohio: A History of Race Prejudice in a Typical Northern State* (Ann Arbor, Mich., 1913), 28; James B. Ray, "Message to the General Assembly," Dec. 8, 1829, in Dorothy Riker and Gayle Thornbrough, eds., *Messages and Papers relating to the Administration of James Brown Ray Governor of Indiana, 1825–1831* (Indianapolis, Ind., 1954), 471 ("corresponding"); William P. Quigley, "The Quicksands of the Poor Law: Poor Relief Legislation in a Growing Nation, 1790–1820," *Northern Illinois University Law Review,* XVIII (1997), 79–81; Stephen Middleton, *The Black Laws: Race and the Legal Process in Early Ohio* (Athens, Ohio, 2005); Nikki M. Taylor, *Frontiers of*

In 1815, white Quaker abolitionist Benjamin Ladd protested migration restrictions in a letter to Ohio governor Thomas Worthington by attempting a comparison. Neighboring Pennsylvania, he wrote, had "adopted no such law. And yet we do not hear her complaining of the inconveniencies which the law of this state was calculated to guard against." Ladd was not quite right, however. Even in the antislavery refuge of Pennsylvania, lawmakers reacted to Black migration by considering restrictive bills that would ban migrants from the state. Economic dislocations in the 1810s hit Black Philadelphians the hardest. They increasingly occupied low-wage jobs. Working on the docks and as mariners, Black men lost their positions when Philadelphia's Atlantic-oriented economy suffered disproportionately from Jefferson's 1807 embargo, which prohibited American ships from trading in foreign ports. In the first decade of the nineteenth century, the city became more and more spatially segregated, with Black communities on the outskirts of Philadelphia and white neighborhoods in the center. White Philadelphians began to blame their Black neighbors for segregation and accuse them of dependency on the eve of the War of 1812, rather than understanding these changes as a result of racial discrimination.[48]

Between 1804 and 1813, the Pennsylvania state legislature debated various measures to exclude Black migrants from the state—from restricting immigration to requiring all African Americans to carry freedom papers. In 1813, legislators debated one of the most restrictive of these bills considered in any state. Under the proposed bill, constables could arrest any Black person in Pennsylvania who was without free papers. If they were unable to

---

Freedom: Cincinnati's Black Community, 1802–1868 (Athens, Ohio, 2005), 32–37; Ellen Eslinger, "The Evolution of Racial Politics in Early Ohio," in Andrew R. L. Cayton and Stuart D. Hobbs, *The Center of a Great Empire: The Ohio Country in the Early American Republic* (Athens, Ohio, 2005), 81–104. For the text of the laws, see "An Act to Amend the Act, Entitled 'An Act Regulating Black and Mulatto Persons,'" Jan. 25, 1807, *Acts Passed at the First Session of the Fifth General Assembly of the State of Ohio Begun and Held at the Town of Chillicothe, December 1st, 1806, and in the Fifth Year of the Said State . . .*, V (1807; rpt. Norwalk, Ohio, 1901), 53–55; "An Act to Prevent the Migration of Free Negroes and Mullattoes into This Territory and for Other Purposes," Dec. 8, 1813, in Francis S. Philbrick, *The Laws of Illinois Territory, 1809–1818* (Springfield, Ill., 1950), 91–92; "An Act Respecting Free Negroes, Mulattoes, Servants, and Slaves," Mar. 30, 1819, *The Revised Laws of Illinois . . .* (Vandalia, Ill., 1833), 457–462; *Journal of the Senate of the State of Indiana; during the Fifteenth Session of the General Assembly; Commenced at Indianapolis, on Monday the Sixth of December, 1830* (Indianapolis, Ind., 1830), 460.

48. Benjamin Ladd to Thomas Worthington, Sept. 20, 1815, Benjamin Ladd Letter book, HQC (quotation); Nash, *Forging Freedom*, 172–183; Winch, *Gentleman of Color*, 160–163.

prove their freedom, they would be liable to sale after six months of imprisonment or seven years of hard labor for the benefit of the state. Free Black Philadelphians and their allies in the PAS submitted petitions of their own to counter the bill. Meanwhile, the house committee appointed to consider the restrictive bill found support in petitions from white Philadelphians who complained about their free African American neighbors and asked for special taxes on free people to pay for poor support, or for the indenture of those who committed crimes.[49]

Free Black sailmaker and businessman James Forten wrote by far the most detailed argument against the proposed bill in his pamphlet *Letters from a Man of Colour,* which he published anonymously in 1813. Forten published *Letters* after the bill had already failed in the Senate and before it was scheduled to be debated once more. Where Pennsylvania was once a haven, Forten contended, the law would completely dismantle the city's benevolent reputation. "Where shall the poor African look for protection, should the people of Pennsylvania consent to oppress him?" Forten turned to the term *protection* to explain the meaning of place for Black Philadelphians. If Pennsylvania joined the other states in passing an exile law, "Where shall he go? Shut every state against him . . . . Is there no spot on earth that will protect him!" Forten drew attention to the way in which the law effectively cast all free African Americans outside the bounds of state citizenship. He argued that the process of registering and monitoring the movements of all free people and their children extended the mechanisms of slavery into free life. The bill that Forten protested did not pass, but anti-Black petitions from white Philadelphians continued to be sent to the legislature the following year.[50]

The transmission of restrictive migration laws from state to state was one manifestation of a general desire by legislators to force free African Americans out of public space. Such ideas were not uncontested—they prompted debate in the legislatures and in the press—but they were a marker of how exclusion could win even in states where legislatures had already endorsed antislavery measures. Racism and antislavery were not mutually exclusive.

49. Nash, *Forging Freedom,* 180–182; Winch, *Gentleman of Color,* 168–174.

50. [James Forten], *Letters from a Man of Colour, on a Late Bill before the Senate of Pennsylvania* (n.p., [Pa., 1813]), 2, 10–11 ("Where shall the poor African," 2, "Where shall he go," 10–11); Richard S. Newman, *The Transformation of American Abolitionism: Fighting Slavery in the Early Republic* (Chapel Hill, N.C., 2002), 43; Winch, *Gentleman of Color,* 168–174; Nicholas P. Wood, "A 'Class of Citizens': The Earliest Black Petitioners to Congress and Their Quaker Allies," *William and Mary Quarterly,* 3d Ser., LXXIV (2017), 143.

Historians have documented the rise of racism in the North that was a backlash to the growth of free Black communities in the first few decades of the nineteenth century. Northern mobs targeted free African Americans in the 1820s and 1830s, while overseers of the poor warned out free Black men and women at a rate that grew exponentially over the same period. Open clashes about who had the right to occupy public space inspired Prince Hall's 1797 *Charge, Delivered to the African Lodge,* in which he asked Black Masons to exercise patience and "bear up under the daily insults you meet with in the streets of Boston . . . at such a degree, that you may truly be said to carry your lives in your hands." The growth of restrictive migration laws across the middle states demonstrates that a backlash to Black freedom was a national phenomenon that went beyond the urban north. When the Massachusetts legislature formed a committee in 1821 to consider a restrictive migration law of its own, they echoed the actions of the middle states.[51]

Debates about who had the right to travel made their way to the federal level. In 1803, Congress prohibited the immigration of foreigners of African descent into states that forbid their entry. During the debate over the bill, a committee of five southern Republicans proposed and supported it, while a group of northern Republicans immediately objected. John Bacon of Massachusetts took the lead, arguing that free African Americans were federal citizens of the United States. If the southern states restricted the rights of some citizens, he suggested, they might soon restrict them for all citizens. Bacon sounded the alarm of disunion: the proposed bill would appear to the public as "proof of the sovereign and despotic sway of the 'Ancient Dominion,'" meaning Virginia, "over most of the other States in the Union."[52]

Bacon objected that the bill violated the privileges and immunities clause of the Constitution, which guaranteed that "the citizens of each state shall be entitled to all privileges and immunities of citizens in the several states."

51. Prince Hall, *A Charge, Delivered to the African Lodge, June 24, 1797, at Menotomy* ([Boston], 1797), 10 (quotation). For northern racism and public space in the first two decades of the nineteenth century, see Horton and Horton, *In Hope of Liberty,* 101–102, 163–166; Joanne Pope Melish, *Disowning Slavery: Gradual Emancipation and "Race" in New England, 1780–1860* (Ithaca, N.Y., 1998), 190–209; Patrick Rael, *Black Identity and Black Protest in the Antebellum North* (Chapel Hill, N.C., 2002), 159–173.

52. *The Debates and Proceedings in the Congress of the United States . . . Seventh Congress—Second Session; Comprising the Period from December 6, 1802, to March 3, 1803, Inclusive* (Washington, D.C., 1851), 469 (quotations); Daniel Kanstroom, *Deportation Nation: Outsiders in American History* (Cambridge, Mass., 2007), 74–77; Padraig Griffin Riley, "Northern Republicans and Southern Slavery: Democracy in the Age of Jefferson, 1800–1819" (Ph.D. diss., University of California, Berkeley, 2007), 365–368; Wood, "'Class of Citizens,'" *William and Mary Quarterly,* 3d Ser., LXXIV (2017), 139–141.

The clause had its roots in the colonial period, when all Englishmen had the right to travel, to use the courts, and to engage in commerce with the same legal protections and obligations across the colonies. When the Articles of Confederation created a union of states, it included a privileges and immunities clause. Delegates who debated the Articles in 1778 explicitly voted not to limit the privileges and immunities clause by race, although they did exclude "paupers, vagabonds and fugitives" from its provisions. Paupers, vagabonds, and fugitives did not have the right of "free ingress and regress" between the states, but free African Americans clearly did. As Douglas Bradburn has noted, free African American citizenship was less contested in 1778 than it would be several decades later.[53]

In the midst of the 1803 debate, Bacon and his colleagues vilified immigrants of African descent, but in the resulting statute, they protected the rights of a person of African descent who was "a native, a citizen, or registered seaman of the United States." They exempted Indigenous travelers from the provision as well, although they agreed that Native Americans were not citizens. They did not, however, resolve the character of Black citizenship at the federal level. As the states chipped away at the ability of Black men and women to move across their borders, they also challenged the notion that Black Americans could be citizens of their states, too. The states used restrictive migration laws as a proxy to work out the status of free African Americans on the ground. The free passage of people between the states gave meaning to the union as a common political community. By passing restrictive migration laws, the middle states issued a stark challenge to the concept of the union and of citizenship. Over the first few decades of the nineteenth century, free African Americans increasingly lost access to the right to travel. By the War of 1812, African American migration had already emerged as a battleground in the negotiation of the meaning of freedom and citizenship in the United States.[54]

Congress reprised arguments about free African Americans and the right to travel in 1820. Amid the Missouri Crisis, Congress passed an act authoriz-

53. U.S. Constitution, art. IV, sect. 2 ("citizens"); Articles of Confederation, 1777, art. IV ("paupers"); Bradburn, *Citizenship Revolution,* 256.

54. "An Act to Prevent the Importation of Certain Persons into Certain States, Where, by the Laws Thereof, Their Admission Is Prohibited," Feb. 28, 1803, in *The Public Statutes at Large of the United States of America, from the Organization of the Government in 1789, to March 3, 1845 . . . ,* II (Boston, 1845), 205–206 (quotation, 205). For the bill's original text, see *Debates and Proceedings in the Congress of the United States . . . Seventh Congress—Second Session,* 467.

ing the Missouri Territory to form a government and create a constitution. The Missouri state constitutional convention that met in St. Louis three months later was made up of an overwhelming proslavery majority. From the beginning of the convention, the delegates included a provision called Section 26 in the draft constitution mandating that the newly constituted Missouri legislature pass a law "to prevent free negroes [a]nd mulattoes from coming to and settling in this State, under any pretext whatsoever." Missouri's state constitution had to be approved by Congress. The inclusion of Section 26 forced a national debate about the constitutionality of laws that excluded free African Americans from residency and travel within particular states.[55]

The debate over Section 26 broke down along sectional lines. Restrictionists who argued that slavery should not be allowed in Missouri saw Section 26 as a serious assault on Black citizenship. In the House, Representatives James Strong of New York and John Sergeant of Pennsylvania argued that Section 26 violated some of the most basic rights of citizens—"the humble simple privilege of locomotion" and its mirror, the power of settlement. Strong saw "the right of passing, freely and unmolested, from town to town, and place to place, within the State, and the right of residing" as fundamental to federal citizenship. "Indeed, vastly the greatest proportion of the citizens of a State have no other external mark of their citizenship," he explained. Women and children, though denied many of the rights of citizens, still had access to free passage. The only free people to whom these rights were denied were, in the language of the period, "lunatics, vagabonds, and criminals." To rescind that power to travel was to challenge the very basis of U.S. citizenship.[56]

Southern congressmen countered by arguing that African Americans were not citizens, nor had they ever been. Virginian Alexander Smith compared the status of Native Americans with that of African Americans, protesting that both were "aliens." According to Delaware Federalist Louis McLane, free Black people had some rights, but these were only at the state level. On a federal level, free African Americans were merely "inhabitants."

55. "Constitution of Missouri," 1820, in Francis Newton Thorpe, ed., *The Federal and State Constitutions, Colonial Charters, and Other Organic Laws of the States, Territories, and Colonies Now or Heretofore Forming the United States of America,* IV (Washington, D.C., 1909), art. III, sect. 26, 2154 (quotation).

56. *The Debates and Proceedings in the Congress of the United States . . . Sixteenth Congress—Second Session: Comprising the Period from November 13, 1820, to March 3, 1821, Inclusive* (Washington, D.C., 1855), 530 ("humble"), 570–572 ("right," 570, "Indeed," 571, "lunatics," 570).

Southern congressmen defended the ability of their states to pass laws for their "self-preservation" and to police their borders on behalf of the peace. Self-preservation to them meant upholding white supremacy and slavery, for which they required the "right of exclusion." The Virginia delegation made it clear that they viewed free African Americans as destructive to the welfare of a state committed to slavery. Virginia representative Philip Pendleton Barbour contended that free African Americans lived "between two societies." They were thus "perpetual monuments of discontent, and firebrands to the other class of their own color." Ultimately, the second Missouri debate ended with a compromise that did little to resolve the disagreement about Black citizenship and the right to travel. Congress eventually approved Missouri's Constitution, as long as Section 26 did not authorize any law that would infringe on the privileges and immunities of citizens from any of the other states in the Union. Left unresolved by Congress was the question of Black citizenship.[57]

In 1811, James Forten wondered of free African Americans in Pennsylvania, "Where shall he go? Shut every state against him . . . . Is there no spot on earth that will protect him!" In the wake of the Missouri debates, free African Americans sought to end the disagreement that Congress would not settle. They began to argue for birthright citizenship. By the 1830s, they invoked it in pamphlets, petitions, sermons, and speeches to protect their right to travel and to remain. In Forten's time a decade earlier, free African Americans answered his question in ways that are less visible in the archives but that were no less persistent. As Martha S. Jones has written, at a time when lawmakers began to question their citizenship, they proved they had access to particular rights by exercising them. They organized as families and communities to protect people when the state was an agent of removal, and they put their ideas in print. The ability to remain just as much as the power to move became one of the defining ideas of African American political movements in the early nineteenth century.[58]

Free African Americans also began to quietly resist state removal laws. They did so in the upper South, a region not known for a wealth of overt Black political activism in the early Republic. The passage of laws about Black mobility in the middle states shifted the legal rights of Black mi-

57. *Debates and Proceedings in the Congress of the United States . . . Sixteenth Congress—Second Session,* 549 ("between," "perpetual"), 556–557 ("aliens," 556, "self-preservation," "right," 557), 615 ("inhabitants").

58. Jones, *Birthright Citizens,* esp. 11; Robert Pierce Forbes, *The Missouri Compromise and Its Aftermath: Slavery and the Meaning of America* (Chapel Hill, N.C., 2007), 119.

grants to remain, regardless of whether those laws were uniformly or frequently enforced. For someone like John Hope, those laws had real effects that made his family's future feel precarious. By the end of his life, John Hope could not afford to purchase and free his daughter, Judith. His hard-earned wealth had gone toward the emancipation of his wife, Tenah. Could he have purchased his daughter's freedom as well, he might not have dared do so for fear that she would be banished from Virginia under the 1806 law. When Judith's mother finally purchased her freedom after John Hope's death, Judith Hope petitioned the state legislature three times between 1819 and 1821 for permission to remain with her family. John Hope was granted his freedom amid Revolutionary fervor only to see his daughter's future threatened thirty years later. Across Virginia, free Black men and women protested that migration restrictions treated them as a separate, moveable population, just as under slavery.[59]

59. Petition of Judith Hope, Dec. 21, 1819, VLP, box 278, folder 18, Petition of Judith Hope, Dec. 11, 1820, box 278, folder 20, Petition of Judith Hope, Dec. 14, 1821, box 285, folder 70.

CHAPTER 7

"TO SUNDER EVERY TIE"

Pursuing the Right to Remain in the Upper South

In January 1821, Judith Hope closed the door of her Shockoe Hill home against the stiff winter cold and traveled a short distance up a steep embankment to the Virginia state capitol building. The legislature was discussing her petition that day—the third she had submitted to request the right to remain in her home in three years. Judith's father, John Hope, had spent years laboring as a barber, first in Yorktown, then Williamsburg, and then Richmond, to save enough money to purchase and emancipate his family. Before his death in 1810, he had emancipated his son, Aberdeen, and his wife, Tenah. Tenah freed their daughter Judith after John passed away. To set his family at liberty, Judith explained, was "a principal object of her father's exertions" during his lifetime. Now, nearly three decades after John Hope was freed, his daughter's right to stay in their home was called into question. Her petition, crisp and succinct, argued that "to be driven to a separation from every friend and natural connexion upon Earth; to sunder every tie and association which years have created and matured" made "a cruel mockery" of freedom.[1]

Hope was technically an exile of Virginia. In 1806, the state legislature had passed a bill including a provision restricting the residency rights of free Black Virginians. The statute required newly manumitted people to leave the state within one year of obtaining their freedom. If they remained, they could be arrested and sold back into slavery. The proceeds of their sale would be added to the coffers of the overseers of the poor. The law was part of a wave of restrictions placed on free African Americans across the individual states. As African Americans pursued their freedom under new gradual emancipation and manumission laws beginning in the 1780s, state

1. Petition of Judith Hope, Dec. 14, 1821, VLP, box 285, folder 70 (quotations). For Hope's previous two petitions, see Petition of Judith Hope, Dec. 21, 1819, VLP, box 278, folder 18, Petition of Judith Hope, Dec. 11, 1820, box 278, folder 20. For the decision on Hope's petition, see *Journal of the House of Delegates of the Commonwealth of Virginia, Begun and Held at the Capitol, in the City of Richmond, on Monday the Fourth Day of December, One Thousand Eight Hundred and Twenty* (Richmond, Va., 1820), 32, 58, 88, 93.

FIGURE 11. *"The City of Richmond Metropolis of Virginia." Detail from James Madison,* A Map of Virginia: Formed from Actual Surveys, and the Latest as Well as Most Accurate Observations. *1807. Lionel Pincus and Princess Firyal Map Division. Lawrence H. Slaughter Collection of English Maps, Charts, Globes, Books, and Atlases. Courtesy New York Public Library. In this view of Richmond from the James River, the state capitol sits at the highest point in the center, with Shockoe Hill sloping down into Shockoe Bottom to the right.*

legislatures reacted by restricting their mobility, voting rights, and ability to pursue certain occupations. They put early colonization ideas into effect. Arguing that full freedom was not possible for free Black men and women in Virginia, legislators ordered their removal after 1806. They cleared the path for the continuing appropriation of Black labor without the example of Black freedom. By curtailing the right to remain, legislators policed what Barbara Young Welke has called the "borders of belonging."[2]

2. Barbara Young Welke, *Law and the Borders of Belonging in the Long Nineteenth Century United States* (New York, 2010); "An Act to Amend the Several Laws concerning Slaves," Jan. 25, 1806, in Samuel Shepherd, *The Statutes at Large of Virginia, from October Session 1792, to December Session 1806, Inclusive . . . ,* New Ser., 3 vols. (Richmond, Va., 1835–1836), III, 252. A 1691 Virginia colonial statute also required that manumitted people be transported outside the bounds of Virginia. See "An Act for Suppressing Outlying Slaves," April 1691, in William Waller Hening, *Statutes at Large; Being a Collection of All the Laws of Virginia, from the First Session of the Legislature, in the Year 1619,* III (Philadelphia, 1823), 87–88.

The Virginia law, however, left room for exceptions. Free people could, and did by the hundreds, petition the legislature and the county courts for the right to remain. No matter the content of state statutes, it was local courts that actually made and administered public law—law that was specific to the "peace" of local communities, as Laura Edwards has argued. Most free people lived in counties and towns that did not abide by the anti-Black statutes on the books. The threat of removal or desire for stability was nonetheless enough to bring many newly freed men and women to court and to the halls of the legislature again and again to petition for their legal residency. Though the 1806 law was not frequently enforced, it was a presence in Hope's life, as she folded and refolded her free papers. The exile law legally bound the experience of freedom to the loss of family and community, a condition that free people in Virginia protested by employing their right to petition the legislature and, after the law was amended in 1816, the county courts.[3]

In hundreds of petitions submitted in the early nineteenth century, free men and women made rich and sometimes unorthodox descriptions of the meaning of freedom, belonging, and the right to remain. The archive they produced under duress demonstrates the daily work of everyday people who had to carefully guard their right to stay in their homes and advocate for access to the state's protection. Free people knew the law well, and they approached both the courts and the state legislature (sometimes repeatedly) to protect their right to remain. Petitioners to the state legislature demonstrated that understanding by working with the 1806 law's prejudices. By seeking to prove their exceptional merit, skill, and experience, they challenged the colonizationist ideas embedded within the law that deemed all

3. Laura F. Edwards, *The People and Their Peace: Legal Culture and the Transformation of Inequality in the Post-Revolutionary South* (Chapel Hill, N.C., 2009). For the 1806 exile provision, see Melvin Patrick Ely, *Israel on the Appomattox: A Southern Experiment in Black Freedom from the 1790s through the Civil War* (New York, 2004), 8, 37–38, 46, 135, 218, 257, 379–380, 437; Eva Sheppard Wolf, *Race and Liberty in the New Nation: Emancipation in Virginia from the Revolution to Nat Turner's Rebellion* (Baton Rouge, La., 2006), 121–127, 131–147; Kirt von Daacke, *Freedom Has a Face: Race, Identity, and Community in Jefferson's Virginia* (Charlottesville, Va., 2012), 75–112; Eva Sheppard Wolf, *Almost Free: A Story about Family and Race in Antebellum Virginia* (Athens, Ga., 2012); Emily West, "'Between Slavery and Freedom': The Expulsion and Enslavement of Free Women of Colour in the US South before the Civil War," *Women's History Review,* XXII (2013), 460–477; West, "Free People of Color, Expulsion, and Enslavement in the Antebellum South," in William A. Link et al., eds., *Creating Citizenship in the Nineteenth-Century South* (Gainesville, Fla., 2013), 64–83; Ted Maris-Wolf, *Family Bonds: Free Blacks and Re-enslavement Law in Antebellum Virginia* (Chapel Hill, N.C., 2015).

free African Americans dangerous or dependent. Petitioners to the legislature easily inverted the law's terms because removal was so frequently proposed as freedom's accompaniment in the early Republic. Free African Americans in Virginia had heard the language of colonization repeatedly since the 1780s.[4]

Petitioners' appeals also defied the demographic ideas of colonizationists. They presented themselves as firmly a part of Virginia families and communities. Going to the legislature could have been an affirmative gesture for some petitioners—an assertion of their belonging. By the 1830s, Black activists would defend birthright citizenship to claim the full bundle of rights available to white men. In these early Republic petitions, however, free Black men and women appealed, not to citizenship more broadly, but to the specific right to remain. Again and again, they imagined their relationship to the state in terms of domicile—meaning the permanence of home and family—with both women and men drawing on this idea equally. Petitioners expressed the incalculability of the freedom they imagined, moving beyond its formal qualities—self-ownership and bodily autonomy—to include social feelings. In an era in which some white Americans suggested that Black Americans lacked the capacity for sentiment, petitioners attested to the suffering caused by the 1806 law. They put forward an idea about their right to remain that was centered on their collective ties to family and neighborhood. Read together, these petitions are an indictment of the way that colonizationists handily imagined separating free Black men and women from their communities. These were opening salvos in the colonization debates that historians commonly associate with the antebellum period. They emerged from the upper South, a region that is not recognized for producing a wealth of Black literary activism in the early Republic.[5]

4. For free and enslaved African Americans using and shaping the law before the Civil War, see Ariela J. Gross, *Double Character: Slavery and Mastery in the Antebellum Southern Courtroom* (Athens, Ga., 2006); Maris-Wolf, *Family Bonds;* Anne Twitty, *Before Dred Scott: Slavery and Legal Culture in the American Confluence, 1787–1857* (New York, 2016); Kelly M. Kennington, *In the Shadow of Dred Scott: St. Louis Freedom Suits and the Legal Culture of Slavery in Antebellum America* (Athens, Ga., 2017); Martha S. Jones, *Birthright Citizens: A History of Race and Rights in Antebellum America* (Cambridge, 2018); Kimberly M. Welch, *Black Litigants in the Antebellum American South* (Chapel Hill, N.C., 2018). Laura F. Edwards reviews much of this scholarship in Edwards, "Sarah Allingham's Sheet and Other Lessons from Legal History," *Journal of the Early Republic,* XXXVIII (2018), 121–147.

5. For freedom's relationship to family, see Edlie L. Wong, *Neither Fugitive nor Free: Atlantic Slavery, Freedom Suits, and the Legal Culture of Travel* (New York, 2009), 18. Barbara Young Welke decouples rights and citizenship in Welke, *Law and the Borders*

The Virginia petitions also demonstrate the importance of the local for those whose citizenship was unclear. Petitioners to the state legislature elaborately recreated their patronage networks on the page by securing testimonials and signatures from white men in their communities. After 1816, the state legislature allowed petitioners to approach the county courts to secure the right to remain. Those who did were comparatively brief in their appeals. They knew they would present them in front of neighbors who already understood their "credit" or reputation. Although petitions to the state legislature were usually rejected or ordered to be set aside, those submitted to county courts were nearly always accepted. At the state level, legislators viewed free Black petitioners as part of a demographic challenge to white supremacy. At the local level, justices of the peace did not want to see their neighbors, employees, or relations go. They did not necessarily see the removal of free Black men and women they knew as instrumental to keeping the "peace"—indeed they likely believed the opposite. That starkly different set of beliefs at the local and state levels also explains why petitioners were so loathe to leave their communities in the first place. West of the Appalachians, Indigenous people built a landscape of local and regional trade and political alliances to secure their futures amid or on the edges of colonialism. Local connections also mattered deeply in Virginia, where free African Americans' rights were so contested at the state level. Personal connections could guarantee customary, ad hoc protection that state statutes technically did not allow. In other words, when state law did not protect free Black women and men, they created protection themselves.[6]

Their appeals were part of a wider emphasis on the right to remain that characterized Black and white antislavery politics across the United States in the early Republic. From Massachusetts to Pennsylvania to Delaware, antislavery men and women mounted an increasingly vocal and visible campaign against the forced and coerced movement of free people. They peti-

of Belonging. On regional differences in the archives of Black activism, see Maris-Wolf, *Family Bonds*, 46.

6. Edwards, *People and Their Peace*, 120 (quotation). On free Black women and men creating protection for themselves, see, for example, Richard S. Newman, "'Lucky to Be Born in Pennsylvania': Free Soil, Fugitive Slaves, and the Making of Pennsylvania's Anti-Slavery Borderland," *Slavery and Abolition: A Journal of Slave and Post-Slave Studies*, XXXII (2011), 413–430; Sarah L. H. Gronningsater, "'On Behalf of His Race and the Lemmon Slaves': Louis Napoleon, Northern Black Legal Culture, and the Politics of Sectional Crisis," *Journal of the Civil War Era*, VII (2017), 206–241. For scholarship on reputation and legal culture, see Edwards, *People and Their Peace*, 100–132; Von Daacke, *Freedom Has a Face*, 41–112; Welch, *Black Litigants in the Antebellum American South*, 60–81.

tioned Congress against anti-Black laws; they assisted kidnapped people and those who ran from slavery; they created benevolent societies that affirmed their right to remain. Their claims to domicile were reflected in the language of others whose lives were marked by removal. Native people called on the right to remain to insist on their sovereignty vis-à-vis the United States. White migrants pushed west by economic and demographic change removed Native Americans in the name of their own claims to a permanent home. The twin forces of revolution and expansion put people on the move in the early Republic. As they traveled paths, roads, and rivers across eastern North America, the pursuit of a permanent home mattered deeply to many people.[7]

Struggles over the right to remain in the early Republic were clearest in Virginia, where thousands of people became free in the two decades after manumission reform in 1782. Virginia's 1806 exile law stretched the control of movement across the boundaries between slavery and freedom. By dictating that freed people had to leave the state, it codified into law the interest of many white Virginians in linking emancipation and removal. The 1806 law tried to put removal into practice. Those who remained past their date of exile could be sold for the benefit of the overseers of the poor. The law built on long-standing legal traditions rooted in the poor laws about state control over the mobility and settlement of people who were presumed to be dependents. As a product of a call for colonization that came out of white reactions to Gabriel's Rebellion, it laid bare white assumptions that free African Americans were potentially dependent, criminal, or an anomaly within a slave state.[8]

Legislators policed the "borders of belonging," but, in practice, those borders were actually more flexible than the statute books suggest. Rights were not simply determined by state legislatures—they were produced through the struggles of ordinary people. Free Black Virginians could not testify against whites in court, but they regularly sued people and won their cases nonetheless. They could not vote or serve on juries or in the militia,

7. On the right to remain for free African Americans, see Adrienne Monteith Petty, *Standing Their Ground: Small Farmers in North Carolina since the Civil War* (New York, 2013); Sydney Nathans, *A Mind to Stay: White Plantation, Black Homeland* (Cambridge, Mass., 2017); Jones, *Birthright Citizens,* 4.

8. For connections between poor laws, dependency, and the 1806 law, see Kunal M. Parker, *Making Foreigners: Immigration and Citizenship Law in America, 1600–2000* (New York, 2015); Kristin O'Brassil-Kulfan, *Vagrants and Vagabonds: Poverty and Mobility in the Early American Republic* (New York, 2019).

yet they worked at the same jobs as their white neighbors. Despite restrictive legislation, free Black men and women in early national Virginia created prosperous lives for themselves. They purchased land or rented it from their neighbors; they invested in the tools of their trade; and they worked as artisans, agricultural laborers, boatmen, and domestic workers. They accumulated property and protected it successfully in court. Access to courts was one of many important distinctions between free and enslaved life. Freedom was substantive and meaningful to the small proportion of African American Virginians who grasped it in the decades after the war.[9]

Free Black men and women built up businesses, social connections, and livelihoods in the post-Revolutionary period. At Israel Hill in Prince Edward County, Virginia, ninety people emancipated and bequeathed land by Richard Randolph founded a church, worked at trades, and farmed beside their white neighbors. Another group of enslaved people who had been emancipated by Robert Pleasants during the Revolution formed a small 250-acre community called Gravelly Hills just outside of Richmond on land owned by the Pleasants family. When Pleasants died, he gave land to some members of the Gravelly Hills community, while requiring that the Society of Friends invest the profits from his estate in a Gravelly Hills school. Freed people Scotland Green, Joseph Daves, James Buford, Samuel Flathead, Samuel Creek, and Wopping Davis also received "small legacys" from Pleasants after his death. Over time, they built homes and accumulated property and livestock of their own as well as established a school. Although white Virginians challenged the settlement soon after it was founded—neighbors "killed and destroyed [residents'] Hogs and other property" and did not hesitate to "beat" them "without cause"—the freed Black men and women of Gravelly Hills persisted.[10]

Free African Americans successfully asserted their rights at the local level, but it was harder to challenge restrictive statutes on a wider scale. After Christopher McPherson was manumitted in 1792, he moved to Richmond where he served as a clerk with the High Court of Chancery. McPherson's position advanced his social status in his community. He noted that

9. Ely, *Israel on the Appomattox,* 8, 11, 13, esp. 83–94 (for the use of the courts); Von Daacke, *Freedom Has a Face,* 11–41; Edwards, "Sarah Allingham's Sheet and Other Lessons from Legal History," *Journal of the Early Republic,* XXXVIII (2018), 125–126.

10. Robert Crew to Micajah Crew, Aug. 25, 1802, Micajah Crew Papers, box 43, HL ("small"), Micajah Crew to William Davis, May 15, 1804, box 43; Memorial of Robert Pleasants to the Governor and Council of Virginia, Pleasants Family Papers, box 13, folder 12, HL ("killed"), Will of Robert Pleasants, Sept. 3, 1800, box 13, folder 31; Ely, *Israel on the Appomattox.*

his testimony was accepted by a jury over that of two white witnesses. Still, he was not able to overcome regulations that limited the rights of free African Americans. In 1810, the Richmond Common Council forbid all Black Richmonders from riding in carriages. McPherson asked for an exception, but he received no hearing from the Common Council or the General Assembly. In the meantime, he was accused of disrupting the peace and briefly imprisoned. McPherson wrote in his 1811 memoir that "under existing circumstances, in the State of Virginia, a man of color *at present,* had but a slender chance of success, in going to law with weighty officers of the land."[11]

Free Black Virginians often resisted regulations and statutes that impinged on their rights by ignoring them. This was true for the registration law that required free African Americans to register their freedom with their county. Many people registered once in order to receive free papers, but others never did. They chose to rely on their reputations. In 1817, one Henrico County clerk who was asked to confirm the free status of a man named Jesse Paulson, for example, could not produce any papers for Paulson or for his mother because they had never come to the county court to register their freedom. Nonetheless, the clerk expressed little surprise at the situation, and he was quick to vouch for Paulson's reputation. "The said Jesse Paulson was principally raised in this county, and always passed and believed to be free," he wrote to the inquirer.[12]

Historians have argued that the 1806 law was rarely enforced, and, indeed, actual cases of reenslavement were very rare. Free people responded to the law in very different ways. Many ignored it, just as they had prior statutes that required them to register their status with the town clerk. Some left the state of their own volition or fought to remain through legal means. Others might have escaped notice by continually moving from county to county, using mobility to avoid brushes with the law. A Loudon County district attorney complained in 1836 that free people who remained in the state in violation of the law "elude the officers of justice, by flying from neighbourhood to neighbourhood, and county to county." He still succeeded, however, in prosecuting thirty-six residents of Loudon County under the 1806 law.[13]

Exile was employed more in theory than in practice. Free people were so firmly a part of their communities that their white neighbors chose not

11. Christopher McPherson, *A Short History of the Life of Christopher McPherson, Alias, Pherson, Son of Christ, King of Kings and Lord of Lords: Containing a Collection of Letters etc. Written by Himself,* 2d ed. (Lynchburg, Va., 1855), 7.

12. Jesse Paulson, Letter, Nov. 12, 1817, Runaway Slave Cases, Henrico County Free Negro and Slave Records, LVA.

13. Loudon County Court Petition, Dec. 17, 1836, VLP, box 144, folder 62.

to enforce the law. At the local level, county courts recorded manumissions after 1806 without requiring manumitted people to leave the state. That was not surprising. At the state level, there was no official capacity for enforcing the law, just as there had been no real capacity for enforcing registration laws passed in 1793 requiring free Black Virginians to record their residency with their county clerk every three years. Administration and governance in matters of public law (as opposed to civil or property law) fell to localities. In the case of the 1806 law, enforcement presumably lay with the county judges and overseers of the poor. As Laura F. Edwards has shown for North and South Carolina, the "collective interests" and "situated knowledge" of local communities—the "peace"—took precedence over state law long after lawmakers attempted to impose a rights-based legal order at the state level. Counties clearly exercised their discretion when they determined not to use the 1806 law at all. So did ordinary white men and women, who were also implicitly responsible for surveilling Black mobility and residency. As one Fauquier County delegate declared in 1832, the exile law went unenforced because "its provisions were in violation of the feelings of the people." In Virginia, as in the Carolinas, state laws do not fully capture how restrictions on Black freedom actually functioned.[14]

Still, the threat of enforcement of the 1806 law by their neighbors or the desire for stability was enough to send hundreds of free Black Virginians to the state legislature, sometimes repeatedly. They had to maintain an "anticipatory posture"—in this case an awareness of the politics of reputation that structured the possibilities of freedom. They used their only avenue of recourse to pursue the right to remain, which was to petition the legislature for a special act to be passed on their behalf. The continued importance of petitioning from 1806 through the Civil War suggests that exile was a significant fear for free people. Indeed, even Thomas Jefferson felt that he needed to include a provision in his will asking the legislature of Virginia to confirm the right to remain for the five men he freed in his will—Burwell, John Hemings, Joe Fosset, and his sons Madison and Eston Hemings. It is difficult to know what brought free people to petition the state legislature. More petitions were sent to the legislature in the immediate postwar period after 1815, and their numbers steadily rose through the 1820s. A few individuals referenced legal proceedings initiated against them for remaining

14. Edwards, *People and Their Peace*, 7–10 ("collective," 7); "Virginia Legislature; House of Delegates; Monday, Feb. 6; Removal of Free Negroes," *Richmond Enquirer*, Feb. 14, 1832, [3] ("provisions"), also cited in Wolf, *Almost Free*, 55; Ellen D. Katz, "African-American Freedom in Antebellum Cumberland County, Virginia," *Chicago-Kent Law Review*, LXX (1995), 934, 949.

in their homes after emancipation. That is what happened to Lucinda, who stayed in King George County after her emancipation only to be informed of "the forfeiture of her freedom" as a result. Other petitioners sought legal residency as a precaution against reenslavement or colonization.[15]

Lunsford Lane, an enslaved carriage driver in Raleigh, North Carolina, who became a well-known tobacconist in the city after he purchased his own freedom, left one of the most complete published accounts of his exile from North Carolina under a similar law. By 1835, Lane had earned the one thousand dollars he needed to buy his own freedom. However, because North Carolina had restricted manumission in 1796 to those who had committed "meritorious services," the state would not recognize his emancipation. Lane was married to an enslaved woman named Martha Curtis. He finally journeyed with his wife's enslaver to New York where he declared his freedom and then returned to North Carolina to purchase Martha and their six children. Lane and his family were reunited under their own roof while he labored to purchase them from slavery, and, "in this new and joyful situation, we found ourselves getting along very well," he wrote, "until September, 1840, when to my surprise, as I was passing the street one day, engaged in my business, [a] note was handed me. 'Read it,' said the officer, 'or if you cannot read, get some white man to read it to you.'" The note informed Lane that he was required to remove from the state within twenty days as he was "a free negro from another state who has migrated into this state contrary to the provisions of the act of assembly concerning free negroes and mulattoes." Lane was targeted by the officer for little reason other than his presence in the street and for having the gall to be "engaged in my business."[16]

15. Antoinette Burton, "Introduction: Travelling Criticism? On the Dynamic Histories of Indigenous Modernity," *Cultural and Social History*, IX (2012), 492 ("anticipatory"); Petition of Lucinda, Dec. 20, 1815, VLP, box 133, folder 44 ("forfeiture"); "An Act Allowing Certain Persons of Colour, Emancipated by the Will of Thomas Jefferson, to Remain in the Commonwealth," Feb. 14, 1827, *Acts Passed at a General Assembly of the Commonwealth of Virginia, Begun and Held at the Capitol, in the City of Richmond, on Monday, the Fourth Day of December, in the Year of Our Lord One Thousand Eight Hundred and Twenty-Six, and of the Commonwealth the Fifty-First*... (Richmond, Va., 1827), 127.

16. "An Act to Amend, Strengthen, and Confirm the Several Acts of Assembly of This State, against the Emancipation of Slaves," 1796, *Laws of North-Carolina; at a General Assembly, Begun and Held at the City of Raleigh, on the Twenty-First Day of November, in the Year of Our Lord One Thousand Seven Hundred and Ninety-Six, and in the Twenty-First Year of the Independence of the Said State: Being the First Session of the Said Assembly* [Halifax, N.C., 1797], 3 ("meritorious"); Lunsford Lane, *The Narrative of Lunsford Lane, Formerly of Raleigh, N.C. Embracing an Account of His Early Life, the*

Whether they were told to remove by a local official or a neighbor, or whether they chose to approach the state legislature as a precautionary measure, free Black men and women needed a detailed understanding of the law and likely the help of a lawyer to press their cases. In Virginia, petitioners reproduced their patronage networks on the page. They collected dozens of signatures from white patrons to support their applications. When free Black Virginian Samuel Johnson petitioned the legislature for his daughter's right to remain, he pinned the petition to the county courthouse door for his neighbors to sign. White neighbors also supported applications with notes of "good Character," assuaging the racist fears that had prompted the passage of the 1806 law by dubbing a petitioner "industrious" and or "peaceable." In a period in which states restricted the basic freedoms of emancipated people—the power to move, to vote, to practice particular professions—patronage was important to preserving one's livelihood and family. Petitions made those connections visible.[17]

Some particularly well-connected petitioners might have gone even further and lobbied members of the House of Delegates to support their applications to remain. Lane, for example, was a public figure in Raleigh. He wrote that he "went round to the members [of the Legislature], many of whom were known to me, calling upon them at their rooms, and urging them for my sake, for humanity's sake, for the sake of my wife and little ones, whose hopes had been excited by the idea that they were even now free; I appealed to them as husbands, fathers, brothers, sons, to vote in favor of my petition, and allow me to remain in the State long enough to purchase my family." Lane gathered support from those he knew and did not know to give weight to his petition. Increasingly, free Black men and women did not have access to the protection of the laws across the middle states. As a result, they had to work to create communities of protection for themselves.[18]

Once free Black Virginians had gathered their signatures, they presented them to the General Assembly. The legislature met during the winter, from

---

Redemption by Purchase of Himself and Family from Slavery, and His Banishment from the Place of His Birth for the Crime of Wearing a Colored Skin; Published by Himself, 2d ed. (Boston, 1842), 16, 24–25 ("meritorious," 16, "in this new," "until," 24, "free," 24–25); Wong, *Neither Fugitive nor Free,* 168–172.

17. Petition of James M. Morris, Oct. 21, 1814, VLP, box 106, folder 7 ("good"), Petition of Betty, Franky, Billy, John and Henry Dean, Dec. 4, 1811, box 12, folder 33 ("industrious"), Petition of Adam Barber, Jan. 10, 1811, box 81, folder 94 ("peaceable"); Wolf, *Almost Free,* 71.

18. Lane, *Narrative of Lunsford Lane,* 29 (quotation); "Governor's Address in the House of Representatives," Jan. 8, 1807, Delaware Legislative Petitions, 14, DPA.

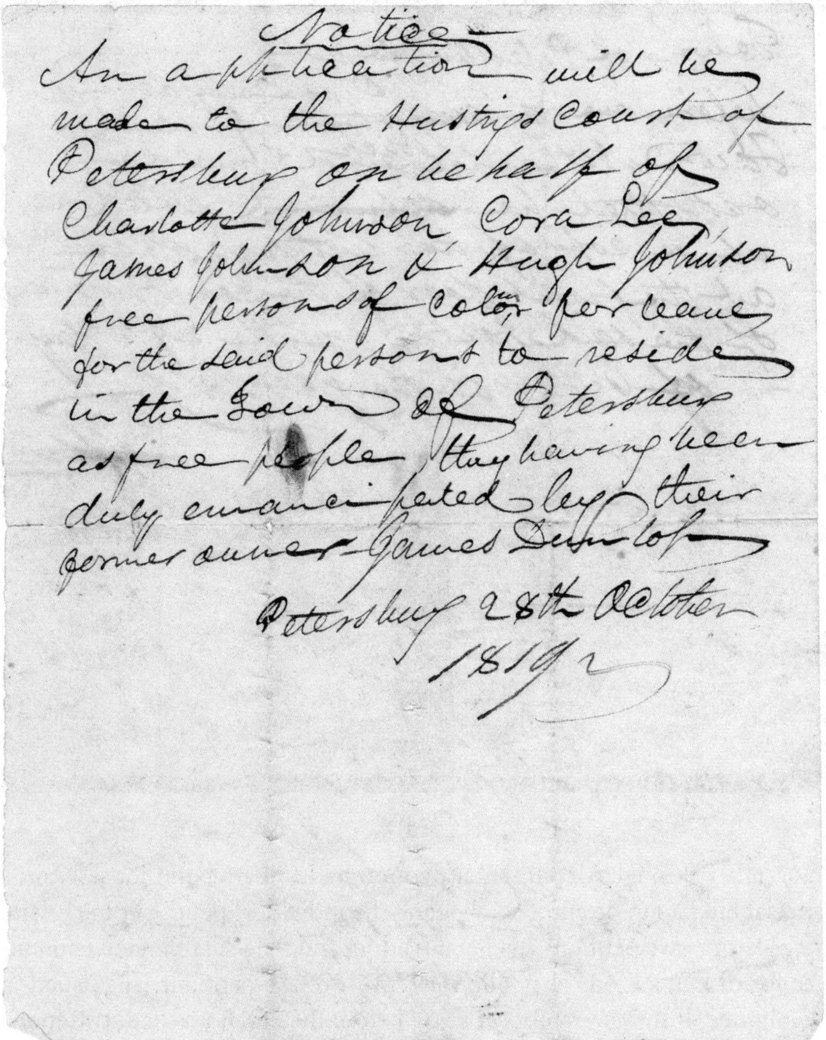

Notice
An application will be
made to the Hustings Court of
Petersburg on behalf of
Charlotte Johnson Cora Lee
James Johnson & Hugh Johnson
free persons of Colour for leave
for the said persons to reside
in the Town of Petersburg
as free people they having been
duly emancipated by their
former owner James Dunlop
Petersburg 28th October
1819

FIGURE 12. *Notice on Behalf of Charlotte Johnson, Cora Lee, James Johnson, and Hugh Johnson. Oct. 28, 1819. City of Petersburg, Free Negro and Slave Records, box 1, Barcode 1152180. Courtesy Library of Virginia, Richmond. Notices like these informed the public of an applicant's intention to petition the court or the legislature to remain.*

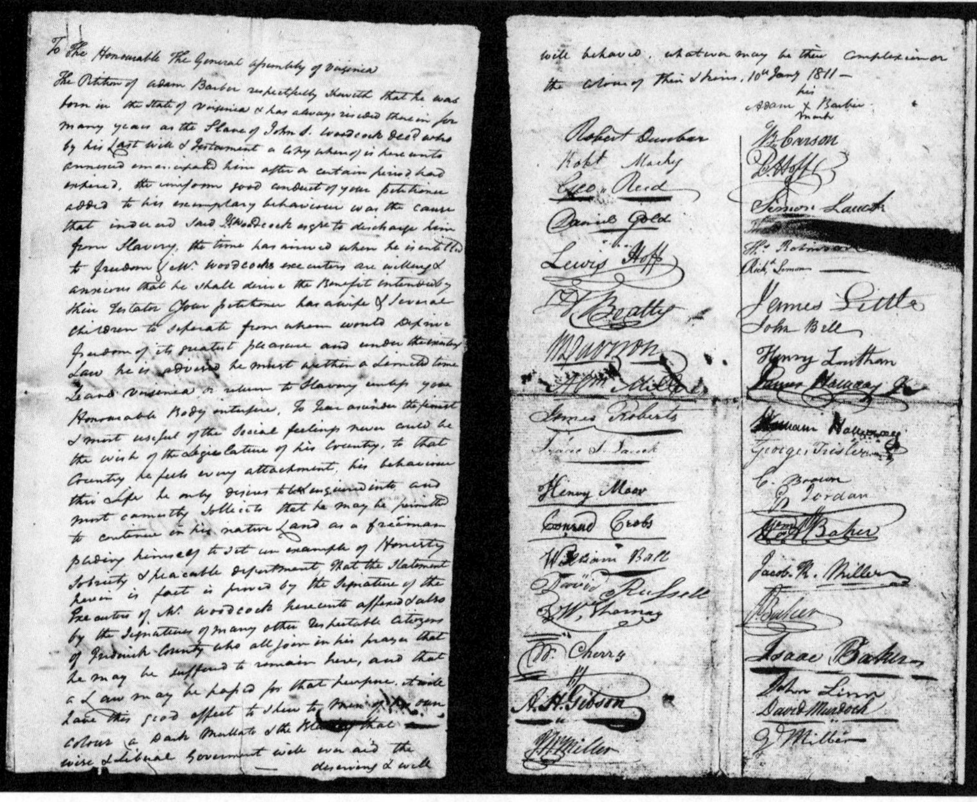
To The Honourable The General Assembly of Virginia

The Petition of Adam Barber respectfully sheweth that he was born in the State of Virginia & has always resided therein for many years as the Slave of John S. Woodcock Decd who by his Last Will & Testament a Copy whereof is here unto annexed emancipated him after a certain period had expired, the uniform good conduct of your petitioner added to his exemplary behaviour was the cause that induced said J. Woodcock agree to discharge him from Slavery, the time has arrived when he is entitled to freedom & Mr. Woodcocks executors are willing & anxious that he shall derive the Benefit intended by their Testator. Your petitioner has a wife & several children to separate from whom would deprive freedom of its greatest pleasure and under the existing Law he is advised he must within a limited time leave Virginia or return to Slavery unless your Honourable Body interfere. To tear asunder the finest & most useful of the Social feelings never could be the wish of the Legislature of his Country, to that Country he feels every attachment, his behaviour thro' Life he only desires to be enquired into and most earnestly sollicits that he may be permitted to continue in his native Land as a freeman pledging himself to set an example of Honesty Sobriety & peaceable deportment. That the Statement herein is fact is proved by the Signature of the Executors of Mr. Woodcock hereunto affixed & also by the Signatures of many other respectable Citizens of Frederick County who all join in his prayer that he may be suffered to remain here, and that a Law may be passed for that purpose. It will have this good effect to shew to men of his own colour a dark Mullatto & the [illegible] that a wise & liberal Government will ever aid the deserving & well behaved, whatever may be their Complexion or the colour of their skins. 10th Jany 1811 —

his
Adam X Barber
mark

Robert Dunbar
Robt Macky
Geo. Reed
Daniel Gold
Lewis Hoff
D. W. Beatty
[illegible]
[illegible]
James Roberts
Isaac S. Lauck
Henry [illegible]
Conrad Crebs
William Ball
David Russell
J. W. Thomas
[illegible] Cherry
A. H. Gibson
J. Miller

W. Carson
D. Hoff
Simon Lauck
Th. Robinson
Richd. Simon
James Little
John Bell
Henry [illegible]
[illegible]
[illegible]
George [illegible]
C. Brown
J. Jordan
[illegible] Baker
Jacob R. Miller
[illegible]
Isaac Baker
John Linn
David Murdoch
J. Miller

November through March. Each petition had to pass both houses, and a special bill had to be enrolled allowing the individual petitioner to remain. Legislators gave petitions a general reading and then sent them to committee for discussion out of public view. Most of the petitions languished in committee, if they were not set aside before they even reached it. Reporting on his similar experience in North Carolina, Lane wrote that "I knew when the committee was to report, and watched about the State House that I might receive the earliest news of the fate of my petition." For Lane, having his petition left to sit was a tragedy. "I had done all I could do, had said all I could say, laboring night and day, to obtain a favorable reception to my petition; but all in vain." Lane's petition did not result in a special exemption. He would be forced to leave his family enslaved in North Carolina and return North.[19]

It is likely that most petitions were not written by the petitioners them-

19. Lane, *Narrative of Lunsford Lane,* 30 ("knew"), 31 ("done").

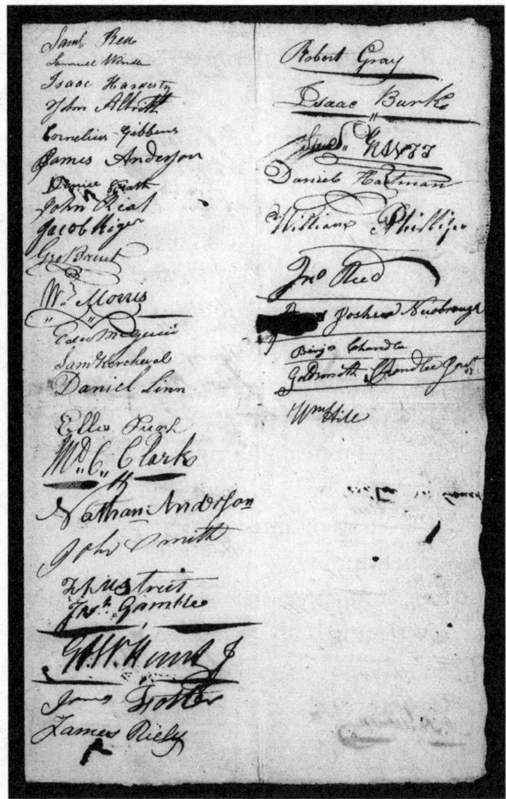

FIGURE 13. *Petition of Adam Barber. 1811. Legislative Petitions of the General Assembly, 1776–1865, box 81, folder 94. Library of Virginia, Richmond.*

Adam Barber collected rows of neat signatures to support his petition to the legislature.

selves but by local lawyers, patrons, or friends. Some concluded with a signature while others were signed with an "X," suggesting a lack of literacy. Most free Black men and women and many white Virginians had only uneven access to schooling. Moreover, the petitions were written in a neat scribal hand—a sure sign of formal education that would have been difficult for the majority of both Black and white Virginians to obtain. It is likely that most petitions were not self-authored, or that they were dictated to lawyers. The petitions demand a reading that expands the terms of literacy, to imagine oral communication passing through a scribal hand as a limited, mediated mode of authorship.[20]

20. For petitions signed with an "X," see, for example, Petition of Starke, Dec. 4, 1811, VLP, box 110, folder 38, Petition of Jerry and Susannah, Dec. 9, 1811, box 27, folder 19, Petition of Charles Ruffin, Dec. 16, 1811, box 234, folder 49, Petition of Peter Burwell, Dec. 12, 1812, box 89, folder 39, Petition of Elly, Dec. 14, 1812, box 295, folder 90, Petition of James, Dec. 9, 1813, box 101, folder 7, Petition of Nelly McIntosh, Dec. 23, 1813, box 59, folder 21. For Virginia lawyers' account books that mention work per-

Petitioning was not merely or inherently a weak right but one that had been fiercely guarded through the Revolutionary period. Petitioning was rooted in Magna Carta, and it emerged as a vital part of English governance by the seventeenth century. In the colonies, the first colonial charters included the right of petition. Petitioning did not guarantee that a request would be granted, but British legal tradition enshrined the idea that petitions should all be given a hearing, no matter their content, the status of their authors, or the number of signatures. During the American Revolution, colonists justified the outbreak of war by pointing to George III's refusal to accept the Olive Branch petition and to give it a hearing. It is no surprise, then, that the first amendment to the Constitution protected the right "to petition the Government for a redress of grievances." Even when petitions concerned the most controversial topics, the right of a petitioner to be heard was still protected by Congress, albeit narrowly. In 1790, a bitter debate erupted in Congress over the reading of antislavery petitions, with the final vote protecting the power of petitioning.[21]

Petitioning was available to anyone, no matter their status. In the early Republic, petitions ran the gamut, addressing both private, individual concerns and public matters. Even those who had access to the franchise used petitioning to recommend legislation and regulation of public and private

---

formed for African American clients, see Charles William Dabney, Account Book, 1832–1865, VMHC, Thomas Stanhope McClelland, Account Book, 1813–1827. For scholarship on lawyers who worked with enslaved and free Black plaintiffs and petitioners, see Maris-Wolf, *Family Bonds,* 45–62; Kennington, *In the Shadow of Dred Scott,* 44–45, 69–78; Twitty, *Before Dred Scott,* 96–125. Even in freedom, Black Virginians faced barriers to accessing education. Some might have attended schools run by individuals or by subscription. Because literacy was spotty for both white and Black Virginians, as Melvin Patrick Ely writes, illiteracy "did not brand them as inferior in the way it would have in a later era." See Ely, *Israel on the Appomattox,* 288–290 (quotation, 289); Heather Andrea Williams, *Self-Taught: African American Education in Slavery and Freedom* (Chapel Hill, N.C., 2005); Antonio T. Bly, "Breaking with Tradition: Slave Literacy in Early Virginia, 1680–1780" (Ph.D. diss., College of William and Mary, 2006); Christopher Hager, *Word by Word: Emancipation and the Act of Writing* (Cambridge, Mass., 2013), 40–47.

21. U.S. Const., amend. I (quotation); Christine Daniels, "'Liberty to Complaine': Servant Petitions in Maryland, 1652–1797," in Christopher L. Tomlins and Bruce H. Mann, eds., *The Many Legalities of Early America* (Williamsburg, Va., and Chapel Hill, N.C., 2001), 219–249; Maggie McKinley, "Lobbying and the Petition Clause," *Stanford Law Review,* LXVIII (2016), 1131–1205; Nicholas P. Wood, "A 'Class of Citizens': The Earliest Black Petitioners to Congress and Their Quaker Allies," *William and Mary Quarterly,* 3d Ser., LXXIV (2017), 109–144. For the 1790 debate, see Richard S. Newman, "Prelude to the Gag Rule: Southern Reaction to Antislavery Petitions in the First Federal Congress," *Journal of the Early Republic,* XVI (1996), 588–591.

matters alongside women, free African Americans, and Native Americans. Petitioning was the preserve of everyone.[22]

U.S. historians have documented a shift in petitioning practices after the Revolution in which disenfranchised people used it as a form of collective political action to wield political power in larger national debates about policy in the early Republic. Yet throughout the antebellum period, it served individuals whose citizenship was contested as they sought redress for personal grievances. It also remained an important means of creating legislation at the state level.[23]

The 1806 law included a petition loophole in recognition of the right of free Black men and women to legal recourse. Petitions were not instructions—legislators did not have to respond positively—but they did have to hear grievances and incorporate them into the legislative record at the very least. Although the language used by free Black Virginians in their petitions cast them as supplicants, their words were heard on an equal footing with those of any other petitioner to the legislature. In practice, their language called on the duty of elected officials to provide for their welfare, and the expectation of a hearing gave their petitions power.

The petition loophole also granted white neighbors control over the right to remain. Although petitioning gave newly freed people space to articulate rights fundamental to freedom, it was the circumscription of those rights that led them to petition in the first place. Petitioners had to appeal to the structure of the law in order to protest it. The Virginia petitioners by necessity framed their desires as responses to the logic of colonization written into the 1806 law. They understood well the racist presumptions behind the law because colonization ideas had been popular in Virginia for decades. The petitions were composed for the consumption of white state legislators, and thus influenced by their ideas about freedom and belonging. Petition-

22. Welke, *Law and the Borders of Belonging,* 63; McKinley "Lobbying and the Petition Clause," *Stanford Law Review,* LXVIII (2016), 1131, 1137.

23. This argument about a shift in petitioning practices as an expression of collective political action has been particularly important to historians of women. See Nancy F. Cott, "Divorce and the Changing Status of Women in Eighteenth-Century Massachusetts," *William and Mary Quarterly,* 3d Ser., XXXIII (1976), 586–614; Cynthia A. Kierner, ed., *Southern Women in Revolution, 1776–1800: Personal and Political Narratives* (Columbia, S.C., 1998), xix–xxviii, 231–232; Mary Hershberger, "Mobilizing Women, Anticipating Abolition: The Struggle against Indian Removal in the 1830s," *Journal of American History,* LXXXVI (1999), 15–40; Susan Zaeske, *Signatures of Citizenship: Petitioning, Antislavery, and Women's Political Identity* (Chapel Hill, N.C., 2003). For a rejoinder to Hershberger, see Tiya Miles, "'Circular Reasoning': Recentering Cherokee Women in the Antiremoval Campaigns," *American Quarterly,* LXI (2009), 221–243.

ers assured the legislature of their economic independence, their meritorious service, or their childlessness. Many of their appeals called on common tropes—old age, productive labor, or the knowledge of a valuable trade. The archive they produced under duress underscored the colonizationist ideas foundational to the 1806 law, which labeled freed people as dependents or political subversives in a slave state.[24]

The 1806 law was intended as a solution for what legislators perceived to be a demographic crisis of dependency. It was based in part on white assumptions that free Black Virginians would not be able to support themselves without slavery. Petitioners responded by explaining that they should be allowed to remain because they had property of their own or that they were unlikely to become "chargeable." Some listed their personal property within their petitions. Mary of Stafford County wrote in 1813 that she had been freed by will and had been given a house and garden along with the promise of annual payments of "Twenty Dollars cash, three hundred pounds of Pork, and three Barrells of Indian Corn." Her white patron attested to the exact amount of those annual payments. Married couple Julius and Lucinda who petitioned in 1811 hoped that the legislature would allow them to exercise their "right of acquiring property." Pompey Branch, who had purchased his own freedom, explained that he had a "small plantation" in Isle of Wight County where he resided with his family. Petitioners called on one of the rights that was perhaps most respected by the Virginia legislature, and one that was still guaranteed to them—the right of property.[25]

24. For petitions mentioning old age, see, for example, Petition of Toney, Phyllis, and Phebe, Dec. 6, 1810, VLP, box 295, folder 46, Petition of Samuel Harris, Dec. 6, 1811, box 67, folder 64, Petition of Joe Booth, Dec. 10, 1811, box 234, folder 48, Petition of Daniel Webster, Dec. 11, 1812, box 210, folder 96, Petition of George Butler, Dec. 9, 1813, box 249, folder 88, Petition of Jenny Parker, Dec. 10, 1813, box 240, folder 32, Petition of Richard Williams and Evan, Dec. 12, 1815, box 143, folder 48, Petition of Samuel K. Jennings, Dec. 18, 1815, box 46, folder 78, Petition of Justice Mims, Dec. 26, 1815, box 296, folder 28. For petitions mentioning labor or a trade, see, for example, Petition of Gloucester Stewart, Dec. 4, 1811, VLP, box 295, folder 67, Petition of Sam, Dec. 13, 1811, box 72, folder 88, Petition of Joseph Sport, Dec. 3, 1812, box 260, folder 37, Petition of Harry Minor, Dec. 13, 1815, box 238, folder 100. For a similar point about appealing to the law to protest it, see Edwards, "Sarah Allingham's Sheet and Other Lessons from Legal History," *Journal of the Early Republic*, XXXVIII (2018), 144.

25. Petition of John and Lucy Ann Dungie, Dec. 19, 1825, VLP, box 134, folder 71 ("chargeable"), Petition of Mary, Dec. 9, 1813, box 238, folder 93 ("Twenty"), Petition of Julius and Lucinda, Dec. 10, 1811, box 295, folder 72 ("right"), Petition of Pompey Branch, Dec. 10, 1810, box 122, folder 35 ("small"), Petition of Toney, Phyllis, and Phebe, Dec. 6, 1810, box 295, folder 46, Petition of Joe Booth, Dec. 10, 1811, box 234, folder 48, Petition of Jenny Parker, Dec. 10, 1813, box 240, folder 32.

Similarly, white patrons sometimes noted that the petitioner had no children, referencing the demographic impetus behind the exile law. In the case of Gloucester Stewart, a forty year old farmer, and his wife, Nancy, a note on the back of the petition from John Clarke, who had enslaved them until his death, explained that the couple "have no Children neither do I Expect they Ever will have any." Just as slaveholders figured an enslaved woman's reproductive capabilities into their calculations of projected profits, petitions continued that logic into freedom, but with the opposite aims.[26]

Petitioners appealed to the prejudices of the law, exposing its logic in their attempt to avoid its consequences. Nowhere was this clearer than in an 1811 petition submitted by Fincastle Sterrett of Washington County. Sterrett invoked the specter of slave rebellion to set his appeal apart. The petition was addressed to legislators who might view free people on the level of population rather than as members of a community. Sterrett assured the legislature that the county where he lived had a very small enslaved population, and he was thus unlike other freed people who were "from that part of the country thickly peopled with dissatisfyd Slaves." In the words of Barbara Young Welke, though petitioners like Sterrett managed to "escape from their subject identity," their "escape came at the cost of reinforcing the subject status of others, advantaged men over women, and reinforced the abled, racialized, and gendered borders of belonging more generally." Prescribed by the racial conventions of white Virginians, free Black petitioners translated their claims to belonging in terms that would be comprehensible to legislators—an act that by necessity reinforced the idea that free Black men and women were racialized others.[27]

In the midst of the War of 1812, for example, Burke of Washington County hoped that he was a "security rather than a dangerous injury to the country," and he argued he was worthy of the "patronage of all good men." Burke had purchased his freedom for four hundred dollars in 1811. His wife and children, who had already once been threatened with sale and separation, remained enslaved nearby. When his 1812 petition was cast aside, Burke

26. Petition of Gloucester Stewart, Dec. 4, 1811, VLP, box 295, folder 67 (quotation). For reproduction and slavery, see Jennifer L. Morgan, *Laboring Women: Reproduction and Gender in New World Slavery* (Philadelphia, 2004); Sasha Turner, *Contested Bodies: Pregnancy, Childrearing, and Slavery in Jamaica* (Philadelphia, 2017).

27. Petition of Fincastle Sterrett, Dec. 10, 1811, VLP, box 249, folder 80 ("from that part of the country"); Welke, *Law and the Borders of Belonging*, 63–64 ("escape from," 63, "escape came," 63–64); Kimberly Welch, "Black Litigiousness and White Accountability: Free Blacks and the Rhetoric of Reputation in the Antebellum Natchez District," *Journal of the Civil War Era*, V (2015), 382.

petitioned again after the war ended, stressing that he would not challenge white supremacy or bondage. "Your petitioner feels confident that all those who know him, wish him to continue his residence in this State, that they apprehend no mischief from his residence amongst them, and that however dangerous or inconvenient a population of the class to which he belongs, may be in the Eastern Section of this State where that population is abundant; the Same Causes of apprehension do not exist in the western part of this state, where the black population is verry small and where labour is scarce and difficult to be procured." Most free people lived in the older Tidewater region of the state, where enslavers had moved away from labor-intensive tobacco in the 1760s. Burke called on the prejudices of the law by pointing out the geography of freedom in Virginia.[28]

Petitioners worked within the law to testify to their usefulness to their county and state as well as to their white neighbors. They attested to their value to their communities, drawing on their history of "meritorious" service or acts of "valor," for example. Sterrett told the legislature in 1811 that he had been involved in "extensive Merchantile pursuits, extending from Baltimore to Orleans." Sterrett further argued that, although he was a slave, he "has been raised the companion of freemen and tho a man of colour possesses Character, Integrity and Sensibility." Sterrett elevated himself above the prejudices enshrined in the exile law by testifying to his supposed exceptionalism. White patrons similarly referenced a man who was "second to no man white or black," argued that a petitioner was "nearly white," or wrote that she was not "addicted as far as I know to any of those practices which render free negroes dangerous and troublesome neighbours." Patrons and petitioners appealed to the structure of the law in order to seek an exception to it.[29]

The idea that enslaved people needed to be prepared for freedom and deemed worthy of emancipation tempered the radical promise of natural rights in the early Republic. When petitioners pronounced themselves particularly deserving of the right to remain, they acknowledged the law was predicated on the idea that one could be worthy or unworthy of freedom. Indeed, the petitioning provision was included in the law in the first place

28. Petition of Burk[e], Dec. 3, 1812, VLP, box 249, folder 83 ("security"), Petition of Burke, Dec. 9, 1815, box 250, folder 6 ("Your").

29. Petition of Sam, Dec. 13, 1811, VLP, box 72, folder 88 ("meritorious," "second"), Petition of Swan Hambleton, Dec. 12, 1821, box 137, folder 29 ("valor"), Petition of Fincastle Sterrett, Dec. 10, 1811, box 249, folder 80 ("extensive," "raised"), Petition of Betty, Franky, Billy, John and Henry Dean, Dec. 4, 1811, box 12, folder 33 ("nearly"), Petition of Samuel K. Jennings, Dec. 18, 1815, box 46, folder 78 ("addicted").

so that petitioners could prove, by appeal, their exceptional preparedness for freedom. When William Yancey of Richmond applied to the legislature for the right to remain, he began with a preamble that commended a policy that limited emancipators from exercising "an indiscriminate Emancipation of the unworthy." And yet, he suggested that he was set apart by his own "uniform good and orderly conduct in every Situation" and should be an exception to the "ordinary cases of Emancipation." Petitioners like Yancey and Sterrett made individual assertions of belonging by referencing their singularity. Their appeals set them apart as individuals, despite the tendency of white legislators to think about them as a demographic problem. Their petitions attempted to overcome a law that treated all free Black people as dangerous or dependent.[30]

Petitioners also made appeals that exceeded colonizationist rhetoric by presenting themselves as part of Virginia families and communities. They wrote that they were loath to leave their "native state" because they would be strangers elsewhere. Tanner Abraham Britton confessed that "from having spent all his life in this Commonwealth," he "feels an attachment for his native state which he believes he could not be brought to feel for any other." Others wrote that they had never left the limits of their county. To do so would cast them among strangers. To describe their condition, petitioners often used the word *banishment,* a punishment and term usually reserved in this period for enslaved people who were convicted of crimes. In 1800, ten enslaved people implicated in Gabriel's Rebellion were banished from the state and sold into slavery in Louisiana. Petitions pushed against the "borders of belonging" in Virginia by reframing the 1806 law as unjust banishment.[31]

Almost all of the petitioners to the legislature made appeals to social bonds, describing their attachment to the state of Virginia or the county they called home by connecting their right to dwell with poignant appeals for their personal or familial relationships. When Nansy, enslaved in Cumberland County, was freed by her enslaver's will at his death in 1810 along with

30. Petition of William Yancey, Dec. 13, 1815, VLP, box 277, folder 52 (quotations), Petition of Fincastle Sterrett, Dec. 10, 1811, box 249, folder 80.

31. Petition of Abraham Britton, Dec. 5, 1811, VLP, box 125, folder 20 (quotations). Jenny Parker wrote that she did not wish to leave for an "unknown quarter of our country." See Petition of Jenny Parker, Dec. 10, 1813, VLP, box 240, folder 32. Charity wrote that she did not want to live "among strangers, in some other state." See Petition of Charity, Dec. 20, 1815, VLP, box 224, folder 63. See also Petition of Jacob Prosser, Dec. 19, 1815, VLP, box 296, folder 26, Petition of Burke, Dec. 9, 1815, box 250, folder 6, Petition of Burk[e], Dec. 3, 1812, box 249, folder 83.

her daughter Sophia, for example, she petitioned three years later for the right to remain in Virginia. She argued without success that "the attempt to seek those blessings to which they are entitled in an unknown Land, in the midst of strangers, cut off from the society and aid of relations and friends, as almost to shut out from their view the prospect of freedom which is held up to them." Nansy was "compelled either to renounce the greatest possible of all human blessings, or to burst asunder forever all those bonds which connect us to friends, Kindred and Country." Nansy's sense of home was inseparable from her connections; to be cast into "an unknown Land" was also to be "in the midst of strangers." She listed "friends, Kindred and Country" together, expressing her attachment to her native state through the prism of personal relationships.[32]

For free people in the upper South, banishment did not just mean the loss of family—it also meant the loss of the power of patronage. Many people in the early Republic had never left the state where they were born. When Nansy wrote that immigration was "fraught with peril," she might have been referring to the dangers of travel, especially for free Black people, who had to be prepared to prove and defend their free status. She also might have been referring to the dangers of leaving behind the personal connections who provided protection when the state failed to do so. Fifty-eight-year-old Daniel Webster of Prince William County wrote in 1812 on behalf of himself and his wife, Lucy. They were, as Webster remarked, "in the decline of life." He suggested that by remaining "where they are known and have made some Patrons they are able to live in comfort but to be turned out into another and Strange State where they are unknown" would surely render them dependent in their old age. As petitioners lined up neat rows of signatures from white patrons on their petitions, they recorded the networks that allowed them to use formal law to their advantage.[33]

Petitioners routinely turned upside down the idea of dependency embedded in the 1806 law to show how exile would make them dependent by tearing apart their families. Jingo had been enslaved by an Accomack

32. Petition of Nansy, Dec. 7, 1813, VLP, box 61, folder 78 (quotations). See also, for example, Petition of Mary, Dec. 20, 1810, VLP, box 238, folder 87, Petition of Jacob, Dec. 17, 1813, box 241, folder 31, Petition of Fincastle Sterrett, Dec. 10, 1811, box 249, folder 80, Petition of Joe Booth, Dec. 10, 1811, box 234, folder 48, Petition of Burk[e], Dec. 3, 1812, box 249, folder 83.

33. Petition of Nansy, Dec. 7, 1813, VLP, box 61, folder 78 ("fraught"), Petition of Daniel Webster, Dec. 11, 1812, box 210, folder 96 ("decline"), Petition of Edward Woodson, Dec. 8, 1813, box 202, folder 67. On the dangers of travel, see Elizabeth Stordeur Pryor, *Colored Travelers: Mobility and the Fight for Citizenship before the Civil War* (Chapel Hill, N.C., 2016).

County merchant named William Barclay. In 1798, Barclay went to England leaving Jingo behind to live as a free man but without legally manumitting him. When Barclay returned to Virginia in 1810, Jingo sought him out and secured his manumission, but he was too late to avoid falling under the 1806 law. In 1810, he was "advised" that he would have to leave the state. One of Jingo's patrons attested that he and his wife had five children, "several of whom are yet young and helpless" and were in need of his support. Jemima Hunt of Southampton County purchased her husband Stephen after six years of making annual payments to the man who owned him. When she petitioned in 1811, she owned her husband but could not free him for fear that he would be banished. The couple had "a numerous family of Children" who would be rendered dependent on the county without Stephen's income. These arguments were strategic, of course, but there was also a wider truth to them. The nineteenth-century family was fragile. It was an economic as well as a social and legal institution. The loss of a parent or spouse threatened children with apprenticeships and husbands and wives with dependency.[34]

Still others married across the bounds of slavery and freedom, and their families were constantly under threat from slaveholders. Enslaved people were not legally allowed to marry—a denial of their legal personhood at the root of slavery. As one Black soldier remarked at the end of the Civil War when former bondsmen and women rushed to legalize their marriages, "The Marriage Covenant is at the foundation of all our rights." Marriages between free and enslaved people in early-nineteenth-century Virginia were routinely destroyed by enslavers who sold hundreds of thousands of enslaved Virginians to the lower South in the domestic slave trade in the nineteenth century. The trade tore apart one-third of first marriages in the Chesapeake, while the hiring out system disrupted still others.[35]

34. Petition of Jingo, Dec. 8, 1810, VLP, box 1, folder 42 ("advised"), Petition of Jemima Hunt, Dec. 9, 1811, box 234, folder 47 ("numerous"). See also Petition of Richard Williams and Evan, Dec. 12, 1815, VLP, box 143, folder 48, Petition of Willis, Oct. 20, 1814, box 175, folder 68.

35. J. R. Johnson, "A Freedman's Bureau Agent at Alexandria, Virginia," June 1, 1866, in Ira Berlin, ed., *Freedom: A Documentary History of Emancipation, 1861–1867*, Ser. 2, The Black Military Experience (New York, 1982), 672 ("Marriage Covenant"), quoted in Tera W. Hunter, *Bound in Wedlock: Slave and Free Black Marriage in the Nineteenth Century* (Cambridge, Mass., 2017), 7. For mixed-status marriages, see Erica Armstrong Dunbar, *A Fragile Freedom: African American Women and Emancipation in the Antebellum City* (New Haven, Conn., 2008), 31–32; Terri L. Snyder, "Marriage on the Margins: Free Wives, Enslaved Husbands, and the Law in Early Virginia," *Law and History Review*, XXX (2012), 141–171; Wolf, *Almost Free*, 32–33; Hunter, *Bound in Wedlock*, 91–101. For family separation and the legal standing of enslaved marriages,

The exile law was a reminder that in freedom, as in slavery, family separation remained a threat that diminished the meaning of liberty. Like Jemima Hunt, other Black Virginians owned their spouses but were unable to free them because of the 1806 law. John Charleston owned his wife and five children; Jenny's two children were owned by their sibling; Daniel Webster owned his wife, Lucy, and was "unwilling to hold in bondage one thus [connected] with him and the mother of his children" but could not free her. Some petitioners were in the process of purchasing enslaved spouses and children, and they worried they would be exiled before they could complete the arrangements. After the man who enslaved him left the state, Jacob purchased himself in order to stay with his family only to be threatened with banishment. Another enslaved man named Will was married to his wife for twenty years, despite that they lived twenty-five miles apart. As Will grew older, he worried that he would no longer be able to travel such a great distance to see her. Will paid for her freedom instead, so that they could live together. Now with his wife on the verge of emancipation, it was freedom under the 1806 law that threatened to tear them apart.[36]

Free men and women sometimes had little control over the futures of their children either. Married couple Jerry and Susannah were freed in 1811 by the will of their enslaver John B. Craighill, but Craighill's will did not emancipate their four children, who were to be sold away from them in the dispersal of Craighill's estate. They had been caring for Jerry's elderly mother for several years past, and they feared that the exile law would require them to leave behind what little family they had left. Most manumissions only liberated individuals. Historians often describe emancipation in the early Republic as a long process extending from the American Revolution to the Civil War. For Jerry and Susannah, that long process put their children at risk, bringing the logic of slavery into the experience of freedom.[37]

This was true for Lucinda of King George County, who petitioned the

---

see Anthony E. Kaye, *Joining Places: Slave Neighborhoods in the Old South* (Chapel Hill, N.C., 2007), 53–54, 63–64; Scott Nesbit, "Scales Intimate and Sprawling: Slavery, Emancipation, and the Geography of Marriage in Virginia," *Southern Spaces* (2011), 1–23, https://southernspaces.org/2011/scales-intimate-and-sprawling-slavery-emancipation-and-geography-marriage-virginia/; Hunter, *Bound in Wedlock*, 25–26, 67, 87, 91–92.

36. Petition of Daniel Webster, Dec. 11, 1812, VLP, box 210, folder 96 (quotation), Petition of John Charleston, Oct. 13, 1814, box 12, folder 39, Petition of Jenny Parker, Dec. 10, 1813, box 240, folder 32, Petition of Jemima Hunt, Dec. 9, 1811, box 234, folder 47, Petition of Jacob, Oct. 29, 1814, box 69, folder 97, Petition of Samuel K. Jennings, Dec. 18, 1815, box 46, folder 78.

37. Petition of Jerry and Susannah, Dec. 9, 1811, VLP, box 27, folder 19, Petition of Citizens, Dec. 2, 1812, box 27, folder 23; Hunter, *Bound in Wedlock*, 87.

legislature in 1813 with an exceptional request after she had been brought to court to answer for the charge of staying in the state past the date of her legal exile. Lucinda had been freed by the will of Mary Mathews, who had emancipated all of her slaves and "directed that they should be removed by her executor to someplace where they could enjoy their freedom by the laws there in force." Her language suggests that a neighbor or sheriff watched the freed people emancipated by Mathews carefully and brought the suit to Lucinda's doorstep. Although the group was forcibly taken to Tennessee that year, Lucinda chose to remain with her husband, who was enslaved in the same county, from whom freedom "could not induce her to be separated." Now subject to be sold to the overseers of the poor for the crime of remaining in her home, Lucinda could no longer petition the courts or the legislature for the right to remain. Instead, she asked to be sold to the man who owned her husband, wishing to "guard against such a heartrending circumstance" that she might be made to live apart from her husband.[38]

Petitioners called on family feelings in their petitions for good reason. Enslavers justified bondage by insisting that enslaved people did not have the capacity for sentiment, which was, as Nicole Eustace has written, "tied explicitly to the capacity to make moral judgments and lay somewhere between the realms of thought and feeling." Sentiment, in the parlance of the eighteenth century, meant the ability to temper one's emotions through reason, bringing the two into balance. Sentiment was a quality that white writers deemed essential to civility, and it was precisely that capacity they insisted Black men and women lacked. When Jefferson determined in his 1785 *Notes on the State of Virginia* that Black men and women were more likely to employ "sensation" rather than "reflection," he was making a judgment about who had the capacity to express reasoned emotion. In one of his most infamous and virulent statements on race—one on which he was challenged by his liberal peers at the time—Jefferson insisted that "their griefs are transient. Those numberless afflictions, which render it doubtful whether heaven has given life to us in mercy or in wrath, are less felt, and sooner forgotten with them." By the antebellum period, proslavery writers would use this particular line of thinking to justify family separation in the domestic slave trade, arguing that African American families were not rooted in the bonds of affection and thus could be broken up at will.[39]

38. Petition of Lucinda, Dec. 20, 1815, VLP, box 133, folder 44 (quotations). For reenslavement, see Emily West, *Family or Freedom: People of Color in the Antebellum South* (Lexington, Ky., 2012); Maris-Wolf, *Family Bonds,* esp. 165–177.

39. Nicole Eustace, *Passion Is the Gale: Emotion, Power, and the Coming of the American Revolution* (Williamsburg, Va., and Chapel Hill, N.C., 2008), 70–79, 484

After the Revolution, white and Black activists used grief as a rhetorical strategy to promote antislavery. It was in this vein that the free Black Philadelphia minister and activist Absalom Jones asked Congress in 1797 to consider that "black people" also "have natural affections, social and domestic attachments and sensibilities." Northern antislavery activists condemned enslavers for profiting from an institution that challenged the stability of the family. They attempted to elicit the sympathy of white people by making moral appeals to domestic life. The Virginia petitioners did the same. Jacob suspected that the legislators who heard his petition believed that "a black man cannot have the tender affection of a husband and a father," and he set out to convince them otherwise. Meanwhile, Burke, who had petitioned the legislature in the 1810s, exclaimed that, "although he is a person of Colour, he has attachments and affections, perhaps as Strong as if it had pleased heaven to give him a whiter skin."[40]

Petitioners who challenged the 1806 law took part in this transatlantic conversation about sentiment. Because white legislatures imagined Black men and women's "griefs" to be "transient," the appropriate display of emotional suffering could be a powerful strategy to challenge white supremacy. But the display of grief was also a tool of the supplicant that, as Eustace writes, "signaled weakness and subservience" while making a "claim to the mercy" of white legislators. Grief could be wielded by Black men and women much like the petition—as a claim on the duties owed to those whose rights were called into question.[41]

The overwhelming catalog of grief produced by petitioners was at once strategic and also a measure of the meaning of their freedom. Petitioners went beyond the logic of the law. In his 1811 petition, for example, Adam Barber of Frederick County explained that to leave his wife and children "would Deprive freedom of its greatest pleasure." Barber's attachment to his "Country" (Virginia) was mediated by what he called "Social feelings." The kind of collective politics that petitioners brought to bear in their peti-

("tied"); Jefferson, *Notes on the State of Virginia,* ed. Peden, 139 ("sensation"); Hunter, *Bound in Wedlock,* 17, 37–38. For more on how presumed capacities justified legal inequality in early America, see Welke, *Law and the Borders of Belonging,* 11; Holly Brewer, *By Birth or Consent: Children, Law, and the Anglo-American Revolution in Authority* (Williamsburg, Va., and Chapel Hill, N.C., 2005).

40. "To the President, Senate, and House of Representatives," January 1797, in Herbert Aptheker, ed., *A Documentary History of the Negro People in the United States,* I, *From Colonial Times through the Civil War* (New York, 1951), 40–44 ("black people," 43); Petition of Jacob, Dec. 17, 1813, VLP, box 69, folder 96 ("black man"), Petition of Burke, Dec. 9. 1815, box 250, folder 6 ("although"); Eustace, *Passion Is the Gale,* 265.

41. Eustace, *Passion Is the Gale,* 299–300 (quotations, 299).

tions represented freedom as a set of social formations that had value in relation to family, "Country," and community. This was very different from the ideas of individual freedom so central to freedom suits that consumed Black and white abolitionists in the same period. As Edlie Wong writes, freedom was often intertwined with loss. If forced displacement was common under slavery, then what she calls a "profound yearning for stasis" might have defined freedom for many petitioners.[42]

Judith Hope's appeals to the legislature, in particular, encapsulate both the limits imposed by colonizationist thought and the possibilities for expressing collective visions of freedom opened up by the petition. In 1819 and 1820, Hope presented multiple petitions for the right to remain in Virginia. Hope insisted that her "longest life of humble utility and quiet good conduct" should not be "rewarded with banishment." She cast her actions in terms of the 1806 law, writing that "she trusts that from the documents presented herewith, she will not be regarded as a vicious or even as an unprofitable member of the community." Hope worked within the law's terms to assuage colonizationist fears about her position in Virginia, but she also continued by making a larger claim about the value of her freedom: "Dear as freedom is to your petitioner, and she thinks she does not undervalue it," Hope wrote, "she can hardly say with truth, that it is prized in her estimation 'above all price.'" Hope reasoned that her freedom *did* come at a price, "for to go into eternal banishment from a kind mother, to sever every connexion and every habit and partiality of her life, does seem to her to be purchasing even this great possession at a rate which as a female perhaps she may be pardoned for considering as too dear." Hope argued against the idea that liberty was an individual condition that did not have a relative value. As Hope noted, she knew exactly the price of her freedom. Her father had labored painstakingly to emancipate her—an object that her mother, Tenah, was able to achieve only after John's death in 1810. Yet she persisted in valuing her "connexion[s]" more highly than her liberty. Between 1819 and 1821, Judith Hope petitioned the Virginia legislature three times for the right to remain. Her final petition in 1821 was endorsed by the legislature—one of the few that was accepted and enrolled.[43]

42. Petition of Adam Barber, Jan. 10, 1811, VLP, box 81, folder 94 ("Deprive"); Wong, *Neither Fugitive nor Free,* 10 ("profound"). For collective politics and localism as crucial to the Revolutionary era, see Terry Bouton, *Taming Democracy: "The People," the Founders, and the Troubled Ending of the American Revolution* (New York, 2007).

43. Petition of Judith Hope, Dec. 21, 1819, VLP, box 278, folder 18 ("longest," "rewarded," "Dear," "hardly," "eternal"), Petition of Judith Hope, Dec. 11, 1820, box 278, folder 20 ("trusts"). A few other petitioners talked about the price or value of freedom.

Moreover, Hope made space for her critique by suggesting that her gender caused her to value the bonds of sentiment above her own liberty. Gender masked the radical notion of freedom that she presented in her petition. A formerly enslaved woman whose body and labor had been commodified from birth, Hope now named family and friends and "every habit and partiality of her life" as being without value, over and above the freedom which her father had labored to secure. Her petition countered the 1806 law, which denied that newly freed people were already part of social and familial networks, enslaved and free. Her arguments for belonging were pitted against colonizationist assumptions that free Black petitioners could be transplanted at will. She and many of her copetitioners also challenged normative ideas about formal equality to put forward unorthodox ideas about the meaning of freedom itself. In judging what freedom meant to her, Hope went beyond its formal qualities—self-ownership and bodily autonomy—to highlight social feelings.[44]

The Virginia petitioners used their petitions to renegotiate the bounds of their everyday lives, but they did so from a place of marginality. The right to remain was critical to legal personhood in the early Republic, and it was the assault on their right to remain that brought them to petition in the first place. In 1819–1821, the discussion of the admission of Missouri into the Union brought national attention to the clash between the idea of federal citizenship and the anti-Black statutes on the books in many states. The Missouri Constitution provoked a debate in Congress over whether or not free Black men and women were citizens. As a result, by the 1830s, Black writers and reformers would claim birthright citizenship to secure their rights. In a period in which the relationship between citizenship and rights was ill-defined, claiming one could be a bid for the other.[45]

In the early Republic, however, the Virginia petitioners did not frame their desires in relationship to the state with the language of citizenship. It is likely that they might have described their desires very differently outside the halls of the legislature and within the bounds of their own home. Or perhaps petitioners spoke strategically of their relationship to the state in terms

---

See Samuel Harris, who declared freedom "too dearly purchased," or Fincastle Sterrett, who called family separation the "price of this best of all Gifts" (Petition of Samuel Harris, Dec. 6, 1811, VLP, box 67, folder 64, Petition of Fincastle Sterrett, Dec. 10, 1811, box 249, folder 80).

44. Petition of Judith Hope, Dec. 21, 1819, box 278, folder 18; David Kazanjian, *The Brink of Freedom: Improvising Life in the Nineteenth-Century Atlantic World* (Durham, N.C., 2016), 10, 18, 26.

45. Jones, *Birthright Citizens*, 11.

of their right to domicile—meaning here the permanence of state, county, and family. Rather than envisioning themselves as autonomous individual citizens, petitioners argued for the right to remain on the basis of community ties. They called on an old and deeply rooted localism that had also been central to the Revolutionary era and to localized legal culture, which treated people as part of a web of relationships. In the terms that they used before the legislature, petitioners presented the right to remain as a collective rather than an individual claim for the good of their communities.[46]

The Virginia petitioners who forged their own language about their right to remain did so in the context of mounting challenges to African American rights across the new nation, particularly in the middle states. Black and white antislavery activists worked to thwart kidnappers, aid fugitives and migrants, and organize petition campaigns against removal and restrictive migration laws. Like Indigenous leaders, Black activists were aware of the way that their rights could shift across borders. They claimed the protection of the laws through their legal work, and they created networks of protection themselves when property rights in people reached northward. In each of these cases, claiming the protection of the laws meant, in essence, the right to remain.

Reformers and activists embraced the right to remain as they worked to thwart a crisis of kidnapping in the early Republic—a crisis that found its clearest expression in the abolitionist community of Philadelphia before rippling outward to the national level. After the passage of the state's Gradual Emancipation Act in 1780, in Philadelphia alone, the free Black population rose exponentially, from 241 in 1780 to more than 6,000 in 1800, making it one of the most significant free communities in the United States in the early Republic. Sitting at the edges of multiple slave states and separating the upper South from the mid-Atlantic, Pennsylvania also functioned as a borderland between slavery and freedom. The proximity of the state's

46. For the desire to stay, see Sydney Nathans, *A Mind to Stay: White Plantation, Black Homeland* (Cambridge, Mass., 2017). Martha S. Jones writes that "in the fabric of everyday disputes were the threads of a story about rights and citizenship." Laura F. Edwards shows that local law was concerned with the "collective order of the peace, not the rights of individuals." See Jones, "Leave of Court: African American Claims-Making in the Era of Dred Scott v. Sandford," in Manisha Sinha and Penny Von Eschen, eds., *Contested Democracy: Freedom, Race, and Power in American History* (New York, 2007), 55 ("fabric"); Edwards, *People and Their Peace,* 11 ("collective"), 12–13. For the relationship between citizenship and rights, see also Jones, *Birthright Citizens;* Welke, *Law and the Borders of Belonging;* Edwards, "Sarah Allingham's Sheet and Other Lessons from Legal History," *Journal of the Early Republic,* XXXVIII (2018), 144.

borders to Maryland and Delaware made it a locus for fugitives, free Black migrants, slave catchers, and kidnappers.[47]

Philadelphia's Black leaders used independent churches, schools, and benevolent associations to support newly arrived migrants and to organize on behalf of their freedom claims. The problem of protection from kidnapping that they identified created a unity of purpose between Black and white organizations that performed emancipation work. Ministers Richard Allen and Absalom Jones who had organized the Free African Society (FAS) collaborated with white abolitionists of the Pennsylvania Abolition Society (PAS). The PAS worked to protect people from illegal enslavement. Free Black leaders like Allen and Jones linked the goals of the FAS and the PAS, referring cases to white lawyers on behalf of Black clients. The PAS was a secular society, but many of its members were Quakers. Quaker members of the Philadelphia Meeting for Sufferings (PMS), which supported the antislavery testimony of Friends, and the PAS connected Black leaders to Quaker networks in other states, and they supported their petitions to Congress. Because of this depth of antislavery activism, Philadelphia became a bulwark against the northward reach of property rights in people.[48]

By the early 1790s, Philadelphia's antislavery leaders identified one piece of legislation that particularly undermined their mission to protect free Philadelphians and new migrants. The Fugitive Slave Act, passed in 1793, allowed enslavers to reclaim fugitives across state lines and confirmed that slave status could follow migrants between states. Enslavers or their agents were required to bring fugitives before a federal, state, or county judge before removing the individual across state borders. To be granted a certificate of removal, the slaveowner or agent was required to submit "proof to the satisfaction of such judge or magistrate" of a fugitive's legal status. The kind of proof required was not detailed by the law itself, however, leaving

47. Gary B. Nash, *Forging Freedom: The Formation of Philadelphia's Black Community, 1720–1840* (Cambridge, Mass., 1988), 134–171; Newman, "'Lucky to Be Born in Pennsylvania,'" *Slavery and Abolition: A Journal of Slave and Post-Slave Studies,* XXXII, no. 3 (2011), 413–430.

48. Nash, *Forging Freedom,* 100, 108; Julie Winch, *Philadelphia's Black Elite: Activism, Accommodation, and the Struggle for Autonomy, 1787–1848* (Philadelphia, 1988), 4–8; Bruce Dorsey, *Reforming Men and Women: Gender in the Antebellum City* (Ithaca, N.Y., 2002), 23–25; Richard S. Newman, *Freedom's Prophet: Bishop Richard Allen, the AME Church, and the Black Founding Fathers* (New York, 2008), 55; Manisha Sinha, *The Slave's Cause: A History of Abolition* (New Haven, Conn., 2016), 113–122; Wood, "'Class of Citizens,'" *William and Mary Quarterly,* 3d Ser., LXXIV (2017), 109–144; Paul J. Polgar, *Standard-Bearers of Equality: America's First Abolition Movement* (Williamsburg, Va., and Chapel Hill, N.C., 2019).

it to the discretion of judges to determine what constituted evidence of enslavement.[49]

Because the burden of proof required for the recovery of fugitive slaves remained vague, the 1793 act left Black men and women, free and slave, across the nation subject to illegal arrest. In Pennsylvania, the protection of free people was coordinated by multiple people—PAS representatives, Black leaders, and the parents and family members of fugitives of those who had been kidnapped. Free people who had been illegally imprisoned frequently sent word to the PAS by their jailors asking that they relay proof of an indenture or manumission recorded in the society's books. Those requests, communicated via third parties, appear as short notes dashed off in the PAS minute books. In 1805, for example, Charles Shiply was arrested in New Jersey "on suspicion of being a slave" because he was going about without his free papers. Shiply's case reached the attention of white abolitionists because he insisted to his jailor that his indenture papers on file in Philadelphia would prove that he was a free man.[50]

African American women asked the PAS for assistance in recovering husbands and children who had been illegally trafficked south. Their requests to the PAS kept the society's team of lawyers and network of Quakers traveling between states in search of affidavits and free papers that would serve as crucial evidence in freedom suits. Through the early nineteenth century, free Black indentured children were at particular risk of being sold illegally into slavery in neighboring states. "Transferrd out of the government" of Pennsylvania, they would also "Loose the benefit of the Law." In one particularly dramatic case, a ten-year-old boy named Wagelmoy was bound to a Frenchman who then determined to return to France with him. Without consulting Wagelmoy's mother, the man and his wife stole him away on a stage boat bound for New Castle. The boat had already departed when PAS lawyer Isaac Hopper received word of Wagelmoy's kidnapping. Hopper followed the stage boat as far as the Jersey shore, where he intercepted it, found Wagelmoy, and brought him back to his mother.[51]

49. "An Act Respecting Fugitives from Justice and Persons Escaping from the Service of Their Masters," Feb. 12, 1793, in Theodore Calvin Pease, ed., *The Laws of the Northwest Territory, 1788–1800* (Springfield, Ill., 1925), 546–548 (quotation, 547); Paul Finkleman, "The Kidnapping of John Davis and the Adoption of the Fugitive Slave Law of 1793," *Journal of Southern History,* LVI (1990), 415.

50. Pennsylvania Abolition Society Minute Book, 1798–1810, Dec. 31, 1804, 275, Pennsylvania Abolition Society Papers, HSP.

51. Quarterly Meeting, Aug. 28, 1786, Pennsylvania Abolition Society General Meeting Minute Book, 1775, 1784–1787, Pennsylvania Abolition Society Papers, HSP (quotations), Pennsylvania Abolition Society Acting Committee Meeting Book, 1798–

The right of reclamation across state borders guaranteed by the 1793 Fugitive Slave Act exposed all African Americans, regardless of their individual legal status, to forced removal and sale. As one observer noted, the act was clearly "calculated with very unfavourable intentions towards free people" in general. In response, white and Black antislavery activists highlighted the right of free people to remain as one of the most important political crises of their time. The idea of protection from reenslavement became an essential function of all early manumission societies. The white physician Elihu Hubbard Smith reported that antislavery men had formed the New York Manumission Society (NYMS) after they "noticed the violent attempts which had been made to deprive" people of their freedom by removing them into slave states illegally. Like the PAS, the NYMS was formed in response to requests for protection, and that term appeared in the society's full name: the New-York Society for Promoting the Manumission of Slaves, and Protecting Such of Them as Have Been, or May Be Liberated. The Delaware Abolition Society called meetings to attend to kidnapping cases, and they petitioned the legislature asking for the protection of free people.[52]

Beyond legal efforts at the local level to stop the forced removal of free people into slavery, Black and white antislavery leaders also began a national conversation about the "right of residence" in the late 1790s. In 1797, Jacob and Jupiter Nicholson, Job Albert, and Thomas Pritchet approached Quaker members of the PMS. The four men had been emancipated by Quakers in North Carolina contrary to the laws of the state, which did not allow private manumissions without proof of "meritorious services." After each of the men had been threatened with reenslavement, they fled north

---

1810, III, Aug. 19, 1801, 142. For kidnapping, see Julie Winch, "Philadelphia and the Other Underground Railroad," *Pennsylvania Magazine of History and Biography,* CXI (1987), 3–25; Gary B. Nash and Jean R. Soderlund, *Freedom by Degrees: Emancipation in Pennsylvania and Its Aftermath* (New York, 1991), 196–201; Carol Wilson, *Freedom at Risk: The Kidnapping of Free Blacks in America, 1780–1865* (Louisville, Ky., 1994); Thomas D. Morris, *Free Men All: The Personal Liberty Laws of the North, 1780–1861* (Union, N.J., 2001), 1–41; Richard Bell, *Stolen: Five Free Boys Kidnapped into Slavery and Their Astonishing Odyssey Home* (New York, 2019).

52. J. P. to undisclosed recipient, Aug. 12, 1793, Pennsylvania Abolition Society Committee of Correspondence Letter book, I, 1789–1794, Pennsylvania Abolition Society Papers, 104 ("calculated"), E. H. Smith, "History of the New York Manumission Society, 1794," American Convention of 1795, Miscellaneous Materials ("noticed"); Abolition Society of Delaware Minute Book, 1801–1819, Nov. 16, 1803, 21–22, Dec. 17, 1808, 69–70, Nov. 22, 1816, 100, Feb. 3, 1817, 113; Winch, "Philadelphia and the Other Underground Railroad," *Pennsylvania Magazine of History and Biography,* CXI (1987), 4–5.

to Virginia. Because of the Fugitive Slave Act, they were still subject to reenslavement, despite their journeys. The men were compelled to "leave the State wherein we had a right of residence" at the risk of reenslavement. The men attested that they had "been hunted day and night" by slave catchers on their way out of the state.[53]

Laws that pushed free African American migrants out of the upper South brought slavery's legal entanglements northward. Having been compelled to leave "the State from whence we are exiles," the four North Carolina men were galvanized to act after another North Carolina fugitive, Moses Gordon, was arrested in Philadelphia and threatened with reenslavement. Quaker members of the PMS were already concerned by the treatment of North Carolina freed people, and they assisted in producing the petition, likely with help from Allen and Jones as well. A Pennsylvania representative presented their final petition to Congress on January 30, 1797. It demanded the aid of Congress for those who had been deemed "unentitled to that public justice and protection which is the great object of Government." Although the petition detailed the cases of the four migrants, the bulk of the text excoriated the illegal interstate traffic in free people and lack of protection for them from kidnapping. The petition was ultimately dismissed in the House because Southern representatives prevailed in convincing some Northern representatives that North Carolina's laws were beyond the jurisdiction of Congress.[54]

Only two years later in 1799, a group of Black Philadelphians, "members of the African Church, and of diverse other religious Societies of the People of Colour" likely led by Jones and Allen, worked with representatives from the PMS and the PAS to petition Congress once again. This time they approached Congress on behalf of "our afflicted and suffering Brethren under various circumstances in different parts of these states." They petitioned because they were a "class of citizens," a statement of belonging that justified their claim for a hearing. The petitioners began by celebrating Philadel-

53. *The Debates and Proceedings in the Congress of the United States . . . Fourth Congress—Second Session; Comprising the Period from December 5, 1796, to March 3, 1797, Inclusive* (Washington, D.C., 1849), 2015–2018 ("right," "leave," 2015, "hunted," 2016); "An Act to Amend, Strengthen and Confirm the Several Acts of Assembly of This State, against the Emancipation of Slaves," 1796, *Laws of North-Carolina,* 3 ("meritorious"); Wood, "'Class of Citizens,'" *William and Mary Quarterly,* 3d Ser., LXXIV (2017), 112.

54. *Debates and Proceedings in the Congress of the United States . . . Fourth Congress—Second Session,* 2015–2018 ("State," 2018, "unentitled," 2017). Debates about the authorship and presentation of this petition are in Winch, *Philadelphia's Black Elite,* 73; Nash, *Forging Freedom,* 186–187; Wood, "'Class of Citizens,'" *William and Mary Quarterly,* 3d Ser., LXXIV (2017), 125–131.

phia, where they received "the protection of our persons and property, from the oppression and violence which so great a number of like colour and national descent are subject to." And yet, the petitioners reminded legislators that Congress was responsible for protecting free African Americans across the nation. Nonetheless, slave traders, they wrote, kidnapped free men and women and purchased others legally from owners who "claim a property in them," taking both "upon the waters of Maryland and Delaware" and into slavery. Black men and women were every day hunted "by armed men, under colour of this law, cruelly treated, or brought back in chains to those that have no claim upon them." They demanded that Congress take action against the illegal slave trade, address the impact of the 1793 Fugitive Slave Act on free people, and consider a plan for emancipation. They condemned both the legal domestic slave trade and kidnapping as "wicked" movements.[55]

Both the 1797 petition and the 1799 petition had afterlives beyond their presentation to Congress. The 1797 petition was reprinted pseudonymously in William Lee's *American Universal Magazine.* The 1799 petition was reprinted in its entirety in the appendix of Quaker John Parrish's 1806 pamphlet *Remarks on the Slavery of the Black People.* Parrish, who had likely helped to draft the 1799 petition, lamented that the internal trade separated families, and he linked the increase of that forced movement with the kidnapping of free individuals. He wrote that free and enslaved people were continually spirited off to southern jails in "the dead of night" to conceal those who had been kidnapped. Those who were taken from mid-Atlantic states were secreted overland and by boat to slave markets in Virginia. As Parrish noted, the 1793 Fugitive Slave Act allowed enslavers free reign, "even where slavery is not tolerated."[56]

Although their concerns were different, Native peoples used similar

55. J[oh]n Drinker and JP [John Parrish?], "The Petition . . . of the People of Colour, Free Men within the City and Suburbs of Philadelphia," [1799], Cox-Parrish-Wharton Papers, box 15, folder 52, HSP ("members"); "The Petition of the People of Colour, Free Men, within the City and Suburbs of Philadelphia," in John Parrish, *Remarks on the Slavery of the Black People; Addressed to the Citizens of the United States, Particularly to Those Who Are in Legislative or Executive Stations in the General or State Governments; and Also to Such Individuals as Hold Them in Bondage* (Philadelphia, 1806), 49–51 ("our afflicted," "class," "protection," "claim," "upon," 49, "armed," 50, "wicked," 49); Wood, "'Class of Citizens,'" *William and Mary Quarterly,* 3d Ser., LXXIV (2017), 134–139.

56. Parrish, *Remarks on the Slavery of the Black People,* 10 ("dead") 12 ("even where"), "The Petition of the People of Colour, Free Men, within the City and Suburbs of Philadelphia," ibid., 49–51; Nash, *Forging Freedom,* 187.

strategies to pursue the right to remain. They collaborated with their neighbors. They claimed the protection of the federal government. Like white and Black abolitionists, they also watched their borders. Native Americans had to have an understanding of how treaty lines and international borders shifted their right to remain. Just so, free African Americans across the eastern seaboard watched the borders. They mobilized the power of petitioning against the Fugitive Slave Act that allowed slaveholders' property rights to cross into free states. They were vigilant and aware of how their rights changed as they crossed state and local borders. They knew that some claims might be well received in Pennsylvania and not across the border in Maryland or Delaware.

Long before the dramatic expansion of the domestic slave trade, the popularization of the American Colonization Society (ACS), or the passage of the Fugitive Slave Act of 1850 sparked protest against removal, white and Black activism centered on the ability of free people to remain in their homes. The right to remain was important to the formation of abolition societies across the states in the late eighteenth century. The trafficking of free people demonstrates that even those who were legally allowed to remain still experienced removal. In a period in which many states were slowly restricting African American rights, Black abolitionists argued that states owed them the protection of the laws. The Virginia petitions were part of a wider movement of Black activists who insisted that freedom also meant belonging. Decades before an anticolonization movement gained wide recognition, free African Americans across the states were making arguments about their right to remain.

The Virginia petitioners wrote of the meaning of liberty and the costs of exile. The exile law treated free Black men and women as a separate, moveable population, just as under slavery. To protest the law, some worked within its bounds to detail their individual merit. Others used their petitions to explain their place in a wider circle of friends, family, and community. Free Black applicants translated their ideas about the meaning of freedom into language that would be comprehensible to white legislatures and judges. Yet, when one petitioner stated that she was "desirous to remain where she has lived so long," she also exceeded the language employed by the Virginia law that presumed she was merely one of many people who did not have the right to remain in Virginia. Her petition was a statement of belonging.[57]

57. Petition of Patty Daniel, Dec. 14, 1842, VLP, box 99, folder 33 (quotation). Loren Schweninger has painstakingly reconstructed Daniel's case. See Schweninger, "The

In 1832, in response to Nat Turner's Rebellion, the Virginia House of Delegates attempted to mandate compulsory, state-funded deportation for newly free people once again. Unsuccessful in their efforts, the Virginia General Assembly instead set aside an annual appropriation of eighteen thousand dollars to support the voluntary deportation of free African Americans to Liberia under the auspices of the ACS. A newly formed board of commissioners tasked county commissioners of revenue with submitting annual lists of all free African Americans to the court of each county. In partnership with the overseers of the poor, they went door to door, asking each free person if they would emigrate. The records the commissioners kept were akin to a census, listing the age, gender, occupation, and residence of the free people in each county. They sent those records back to a central Board of Commissioners for the Transportation of Free Negroes who would allocate state funds and funnel them through the ACS.[58]

In 1833, Armistead and Rachel Hughes opened their door to a Pittsylvania County commissioner carrying a blank census. The Hughes had settled in Pittsylvania County on the North Carolina border nine months prior with their two daughters and one son. They were approached at the same time as Thea Burnell and Sandy Edwill, who had both been born in the county and had lived there their entire lives. This time, the commissioner asked the Hughes, Burnell, and Edwill whether they would emigrate to Liberia. In all three cases, the answer was a resounding "no." The commissioner moved on, leaving his census sheet blank. At household after household, free Black men and women were once more called on to protect their right to remain. Their responses to the census takers amount to a protest against removal, neatly arrayed in ledger form.[59]

Vass Slaves: County Courts, State Laws, and Slavery in Virginia, 1831–1861," *Virginia Magazine of History and Biography,* CXIV (2006), 464–497.

58. "An Act Making Appropriations for the Removal of Free Persons of Colour," Mar. 4, 1833, *Acts Passed at a General Assembly of the Commonwealth of Virginia, Begun and Held at the Capitol, in the City of Richmond, on Monday, the Third Day of December, in the Year of Our Lord, One Thousand Eight Hundred and Thirty-Two, and of the Commonwealth the Fifty-Seventh* (Richmond, Va., 1833), 14–15; John Floyd et al., Letter, Apr. 11, 1833, Board of Commissioners Correspondence, LVA; Alison Goodyear Freehling, *Drift toward Dissolution: The Virginia Slavery Debate of 1831–1832* (Baton Rouge, La., 1982), 177–188; Wolf, *Race and Liberty in the New Nation,* 196–234.

59. "A List of Free Persons of Color Residing in the County of Pittslvania This 1st Day of March 1833 including Their Descendants since That Time," Registers of Those Willing to Emigrate, Board of Commissioners for the Transportation of Free Negroes Correspondence, LVA. On the experience of census taking in a different context, see Martha Hodes, "Fractions and Fictions in the United States Census of 1890," in Ann

As the commissioners went door to door in 1833, free Black Virginians repeatedly and nearly universally declared their intention to remain. In some counties, commissioners personally urged particular families to consider emigration, or they advertised the new state appropriation in the local newspaper. In Amelia County, the court clerk used every argument he could think of to persuade people to consider emigration, but "not one will consent," he lamented. In Middlesex, one commissioner explained that "there is not a person of Color in the County of Middlesex that is willing to be removed to the Colony of Liberia on any terms." Another commissioner in Fluvanna attested that "I could find not one that seem to have the most distant idea of leaving their native land to go to Liberia or elsewhere unless compeld." James Foster summed up the answers in Petersburg pithily: "The unvarying and unhesitating answer has been 'NO' . . . I would sooner be a Slave here than a free man in Africa or Liberia."[60]

Commissioners who fanned out across nineteen Virginia counties in 1833 only added a handful of names to the list of free people willing to emigrate. By 1834, the board of commissioners complained that two-thirds of Virginia's counties had still failed to follow through with their lists. That year, only thirty people left Virginia for Liberia through the board's efforts at a total cost of $830—a tiny fraction of the free people who lived in the state and of the annual appropriation. The great majority of those who did leave were largely from three Petersburg and Norfolk families. Called on once again to protect their right to remain, free people rejected the idea that they did not belong in their "native state," where they had sought the protection of patrons, built their homes, purchased property, and raised their families.[61]

Laura Stoler, ed., *Haunted by Empire: Geographies of Intimacy in North American History* (Durham, N.C., 2006), 251–258.

60. Report of J. T. Leigh, Oct. 23, 1833, Board of Commissioners for the Transportation of Free Negroes Correspondence, LVA ("not one"), George Healy, Report of Middlesex County Court, Sept. 23, 1833 ("there"), R. Creedson, Report of Fluvanna County Court, June 19, 1833 ("I could find not one"), Report of James Foster to Prince William County Court, Aug. 28, 1833 ("unvarying").

61. Report of William Crane, Simon Frayser, Clement White, George Woodfin, Richard C. Wortham, Benjamin Brand to Richmond Hustings Court, July 26, 1833, Board of Commissioners for the Transportation of Free Negroes Correspondence, LVA, Report of John Grammar to Petersburg Hustings Court, Sep. 21, 1833, Report of Jonathan A. Cash, Oct. 21, 1833, Report of Joseph Jackson, Mar. 21, 1834, Joseph Gales to Board of Commissioners, Mar. 13, 1834.

CHAPTER 8
THE AGE OF REMOVAL

In 1816, a path leading west opened up to free Black Methodist preacher John Stewart. Stewart had journeyed from Virginia to Ohio in 1811, where he experienced conversion at a camp meeting in Marietta. In 1816, he followed the western path, traveling to Ohio on a mission to preach at Upper Sandusky, a Wyandot town just south of Lake Erie. He was assisted by Jonathan Pointer, a Black interpreter who had been raised by the Wyandots after being taken captive in the 1780s. Pointer's experience was not unusual. Wyandots routinely adopted Native, Black, and white captives in the eighteenth century. "Negro Point" in Wyandot country was supposedly named for a settlement of enslaved people who had escaped from slavery in the late eighteenth century. On the one hand, Stewart's journey evidences the increasing "boundlessness" of North American life in the decades after the American Revolution. His western path opened as the Second Great Awakening transformed religion and as geographic and political barriers to travel were swept away with the conclusion of the War of 1812. On the other hand, Stewart arrived at Upper Sandusky when white Ohioans were increasingly using removal to establish the borders that would define Ohio as a "free state." In 1816, that term was still in flux.[1]

Historians who have read nineteenth-century African American and Native American histories of removal side by side most often look South. In Georgia, Alabama, and Mississippi, the dispossession of Cherokees, Choctaws, Creeks, and Chickasaws led to the expansion of chattel slavery. Between the 1790s and the Civil War, thousands of enslaved people were marched overland in chains or carried away on ships each year to trans-

1. Helen Hornbeck Tanner, ed., *Atlas of Great Lakes Indian History* (Norman, Okla., 1987), 99 ("Negro Point"); James H. Merrell, "American Nations, Old and New: Reflections on Indians and the Early Republic," in Frederick E. Hoxie, Ronald Hoffman, and Peter J. Albert, eds., *Native Americans and the Early Republic* (Charlottesville, Va., 1999), 350 ("boundlessness"); Joseph Mitchell, *The Missionary Pioneer; or, A Brief Memoir of the Life, Labours, and Death of John Stewart, (Man of Colour) Founder, under God of the Mission among the Wyandotts at Upper Sandusky, Ohio* (1827; rpt. New York, 1918), 15; John P. Bowes, *Exiles and Pioneers: Eastern Indians in the Trans-Mississippi West* (New York, 2007), 161–163.

form Native homelands into cotton plantations. The domestic slave trade and Indian removal were indelibly linked. The story looked different in the North, where Indian removal created a series of free states that prohibited slavery.[2]

Those who built free states, however, had a narrow definition of who belonged there. Long before the sectional crisis, speculators, policymakers, and white migrants hoped that the free states would serve white freedom only. They imagined that white families would purchase Native homelands north of the Ohio River. Free labor rather than slavery would power small family farms. Native peoples were the impediment to their plans, and African American migrants were not part of them. To a large extent, their visions came true. In Ohio, Indiana, and Illinois, federal treaties made Native Americans into migrants; federal preemption laws encouraged the mobility of white men and women; new state laws limited Black movement and residency. Together, these provisions structured migration to speed removal. Continuous demand for lands by purchasers in Ohio, Indiana, and Illinois made those states the fastest growing in the country.[3]

Yet free African Americans and Native Americans challenged this limited vision of who free states were for. They competed to determine the states' racial geography through their individual choices to stay or to go. Wyandots and Miamis remained on their lands, and free African Americans from the upper South followed Stewart's northwestern path, but as migrants not missionaries. For Black migrants, the fragile freedom they found in Ohio, Indiana, and Illinois was also built on the heels of Native dispossession. Their experiences expose the limits of the dichotomy between settler and Indigenous. Black Americans like Stewart who went to Indian country were participating in settler-colonial projects, though not on terms of their own making. They settled, but not always by choice. They themselves were exiles who had left their homes under threat of expulsion or violence in the eastern states.[4]

2. Adam Rothman, *Slave Country: American Expansion and the Origins of the Deep South* (Cambridge, Mass., 2007); Walter Johnson, *River of Dark Dreams: Slavery and Empire in the Cotton Kingdom* (Cambridge, Mass., 2013); Sven Beckert, *Empire of Cotton: A Global History* (New York, 2014), 120–121.

3. For explorations of slavery and freedom north of the Ohio River, see Matthew Salafia, *Slavery's Borderland: Freedom and Bondage along the Ohio River* (Philadelphia, 2017); Tiya Miles, *The Dawn of Detroit: A Chronicle of Slavery and Freedom in the City of the Straits* (New York, 2017); M. Scott Heerman, *The Alchemy of Slavery: Human Bondage and Emancipation in the Illinois Country, 1730–1865* (Philadelphia, 2018).

4. Tiya Miles interrogates the "settler-native" divide in Miles, "Beyond a Boundary: Black Lives and the Settler-Native Divide," *William and Mary Quarterly*, 3d Ser.,

Stewart might have thought of himself as a "civilizer" or perhaps even as part of U.S. expansion. At the same time, he might well have thought of himself as an exile, struggling for a more secure future in a nation committed to bondage. Stewart's right to live in the free state of Ohio was contested by both white Americans and Indigenous people alike. During his journey, he was mistaken for an enslaved fugitive. A group of white traders heard Stewart preach, and they "advised the Indians to drive him out the country; stating that he was not a licensed preacher; but a runaway slave, a villain, etc. and that he had only come among them for protection." Once there, he was welcomed by some Wyandots, who found Methodist teachings about salvation appealing, or who perhaps hoped that a Methodist mission might help them remain on their lands. Others like Wyandot chief Bloody Eyes read him as a racial subject and questioned conversion as a strategy for securing the right to remain. Bloody Eyes objected to Stewart's insistence that Wyandots give up aspects of their culture to accept salvation; he also believed that because Stewart was Black, the missionary would hurt the Wyandot's social position and perhaps their own chances to remain on their lands. He suggested that it was "derogatory to their character, to have it said, *that they had a Negro for their preacher,* as that race of people was always considered inferior to Indians." The exchange between Bloody Eyes and Stewart represents the tension at the heart of new free states in the nineteenth century. What did free states mean on the ground, and who had a claim to them? Bloody Eyes and Stewart confronted these questions amid the age of removal, a period of nationalism after the War of 1812 in which white Americans reconciled their own anxieties about the place of African Americans and Native Americans in the nation by embracing colonization and Indian removal with new urgency.[5]

LXXVI (2019), 417–426. Jodi A. Byrd suggests that immigrants of African descent were "arrivants" who had different experiences of settler colonialism than white migrants. See Byrd, *The Transit of Empire: Indigenous Critiques of Colonialism* (Minneapolis, Minn., 2011), xix.

5. Mitchell, *Missionary Pioneer,* 24 ("advised"), 52, 68 ("derogatory"). By 1821, Stewart's post had been taken over by the white minister James Finley, although Stewart remained at Upper Sandusky until his death in 1823. Pointer lost his pay as an interpreter after he began working with Stewart. See To the Bishops and Members of the Annual Conference Assembled at Lebanon, Sept. 4, 1821, Methodist Episcopal Church Papers, folder 9, OHC; Bowes, *Exiles and Pioneers,* 161–162; James Buss, "The Politics of Indian Removal on the Wyandot Reserve, 1817–1843," in Charles Beatty-Medina and Melissa Rinehart, eds., *Contested Territories: Native Americans and Non-Natives in the Lower Great Lakes, 1700–1850* (East Lansing, Mich., 2012), 176.

After the War of 1812, Americans rushed to create new states. President James Monroe used the occasion of his 1817 annual address to Congress to tout western lands as the source of future riches for the United States. He predicted "progress" for the country in its expansion west of the Appalachian Mountains, "which the rights of nature demand, and nothing can prevent." He envisioned white western settlements linked to each other and extending from Ohio to Michigan Territory and through Indiana and Illinois to the Mississippi River. In the South, U.S. settlements would reach the Mississippi River, too. Emigration to western spaces from the eastern states would increase, the value of land rising alongside it, and new states and territorial governments would follow in migrants' wake, "happily organized, established over every other portion in which there is vacant land for sale." Because territories achieved statehood through population growth, migrants created new states as they moved. In 1817, when Monroe imagined this vast empire, "progress" had already created the state of Ohio in 1803 and Indiana in 1816. Illinois became a state in 1818. By 1820, migrants and federal officials would carve most of the land east of the Mississippi River into a series of free and slave states.[6]

The meaning of "free" and "slave" states was more ambiguous than it sounds. Maps depicting the early-nineteenth-century United States present a clear dividing line between those categories. That geographic imagination developed after the American Revolution as northern states slowly ended slavery through immediate and gradual abolition. In reality, the idea of a free state was more complex. In some supposed free states, like New Jersey, gradual emancipation left small numbers of people to labor in bondage through the 1840s. North of the Ohio River, slavery was prohibited in the Northwest Territory when it was first organized, but its status as a free territory was just as complicated. Thomas Jefferson's 1784 plan for laying out the federal government's western territories recommended banning slavery and servitude west of the Appalachians entirely after 1800. Southern delegates managed to defeat the proposal, but Jefferson's restriction clause was nonetheless included in the third of the western ordinances in 1787. Article VI of the Northwest Ordinance prohibited slavery in the Northwest Territory north of the Ohio River, while it implicitly allowed slavery in the Southwest Territory on the other side of the river.[7]

6. "First Annual Message," Dec. 2, 1817, in Stanislaus Murray Hamilton, ed., *The Writings of James Monroe . . .*, VI, *1817–1823* (New York, 1902), 38–41 ("progress," 40, "happily," 41).

7. Thomas Jefferson, Draft Report of the *"COMMITTEE Appointed to Prepare a PLAN for the Temporary Government of the WESTERN TERRITORY,"* March 1784,

Long after 1787, slavery's advocates continued to press for the institution's expansion in the free space of the Northwest Territory. The constitutional ambiguity of the Northwest Ordinance made it an easy target. Those who wished to reinstate slavery in the Northwest Territory argued that the ordinance was a piece of legislation and therefore could not place binding limits on the new states it created. Ohio outlawed slaveholding when it became a state in 1803, but Indiana and Illinois debated bondage for much longer. In 1805, the Indiana territorial legislature allowed enslaved people to enter the territory "voluntarily." Proslavery measures had powerful supporters—Indiana territorial governor William Henry Harrison for one—but Indianans decisively repealed the act only a few years later. When Indiana became a state in 1816, the Indiana constitution banned slavery but allowed indentured servitude, a provision that was not repealed for another five years. In the Illinois Territory, French slaveholders and their descendants, whose property rights had been guaranteed to them by the Treaty of Paris in 1763, kept enslaved people in bondage despite the ordinance. Their right to own enslaved people was protected even after Illinois statehood in 1818. Proslavery advocates argued that the Northwest Territory would never attract large numbers of migrants without slavery. They argued over who the Northwest Territory would be for: Enslavers or those who did not own slaves? Enslaved laborers or free laborers?[8]

Federal policymakers believed that the free states of the Northwest Territory would support white families, and they facilitated their movement west. War delayed the surveying, advertisement, and auctioning off of lands by local land offices, but eastern migrants nonetheless settled illegally on public and private lands. At the same time that federal officials warned out squatters and President James Madison weighed in with a proclamation against illegal settlement in 1815, Congress contradicted federal policy

---

Manuscript Division, LOC; Paul Finkelman, "Slavery and the Northwest Ordinance: A Study in Ambiguity," *Journal of the Early Republic,* VI (1986), 345; James J. Gigantino, II, *The Ragged Road to Abolition: Slavery and Freedom in New Jersey, 1775–1865* (Philadelphia, 2015), 214.

8. Andrew R. L. Cayton, *Frontier Indiana* (Bloomington, Ind., 1996), 187–193 (quotation, 190); Finkelman, "Slavery and the Northwest Ordinance," *Journal of the Early Republic,* VI (1986), 346–348; Peter S. Onuf, *Statehood and Union: A History of the Northwest Ordinance* (Bloomington, Ind., 1987), 14–21, 122; James Oliver Horton, "Race and Region: Ohio, America's Middle Ground," in Geoffrey Parker, Richard Sisson, and William Russell Coil, eds., *Ohio and the World, 1753–2053: Essays toward a New History of Ohio* (Columbus, Ohio, 2005), 49–50; Stephen Middleton, *The Black Laws: Race and the Legal Process in Early Ohio* (Athens, Ohio, 2005), 14; Heerman, *Alchemy of Slavery,* 87–88.

by passing twenty-four different measures that gave migrants preemption rights when the land they occupied came to market. Preemption converted vast Native homelands into private property before any treaties were signed or land was surveyed. In essence, it transformed "settlers into speculators." Indiana and Illinois congressmen advocated for preemption in the capital. Beginning in 1813, a series of laws promised preemption rights in both states. In the Ohio Valley and lower Great Lakes, preemption was a boon to migrants who poured into the region in anticipation of further laws legitimizing their claims. Local land offices spent the postwar years sorting through these claims, making for a brisk business selling Native homelands.[9]

Economic failure pushed people past the Appalachians, too. In 1815, the eruption of Mount Tambora on Sumbawa Island in the East Indies caused a climate emergency in the coastal United States. A series of cold fronts swept the Atlantic coast from Canada to New England to Virginia in the summer of 1816. The volcano's effects spared the Ohio Valley and the lower Great Lakes, which produced bumper crops to supply Atlantic markets. Fleeing widespread crop failures, migrants went west. Once they reached federal lands, they did not necessarily stop in one location. The great majority of newcomers moved again within a decade. Between 1812 and 1821, Ohio land offices sold 3,750,000 acres of Native lands at auction, more than any other state or territory. Sales in Indiana were close behind. By the end of the war, migrants coveting the 3,000,000 acres of Delaware, Shawnee, Potawatomi, Miami, and Kickapoo territory ceded at the controversial 1809 Treaty of Fort Wayne crowded the local land office in Vincennes. The year after the land came to market in 1816, the land office in Vincennes sold more acres than any other land office in the country. Despite the ban on slaveholding, white migrants proved proslavery advocates wrong by moving to the former Northwest Territory in large numbers.[10]

9. Jessica Intrator, "From Squatter to Settler: Applying the Lessons of Nineteenth Century U. S. Public Land Policy to Twenty-First Century Land Struggles in Brazil," *Ecology Law Quarterly,* XXXVIII (2011), 207 (quotation); Malcolm J. Rohrbough, *The Land Office Business: The Settlement and Administration of American Public Lands, 1789–1837* (New York, 1968), 61–62, 75–77, 84; Paul W. Gates, *History of Public Land Law Development* (Washington D.C., 1968), 219–247; Stuart Banner, *How the Indians Lost Their Land: Law and Power on the Frontier* (Cambridge, Mass., 2005), 135–139, 160–168; James Joseph Buss, *Winning the West with Words: Language and Conquest in the Lower Great Lakes* (Norman, Okla., 2011), 42–70.

10. Rohrbough, *Land Office Business,* 86, 103–107; Allan Kulikoff, *The Agrarian Origins of American Capitalism* (Charlottesville, Va., 1992), 218; Daniel Walker Howe, *What Hath God Wrought: The Transformation of America, 1815–1848* (New York, 2007),

Understandings of what a free state was and who would be allowed to settle there, however, were circumscribed. The free states excluded slaveholding, but they also supposedly excluded free Black migrants. To create free states for white migrants, territorial and state governments made migration more difficult for African Americans. Each of the new free states formed directly before and after the War of 1812 followed the eastern states in discouraging Black migration. Ohio barred the settlement of enslaved people who ran from slavery. The state's 1804 law required new migrants to register certificates of freedom with the counties and punished Ohioans for aiding or employing those who did not have free papers. By 1807, the Ohio legislature raised the bar even higher for free African Americans who wished to live in the state, requiring a surety bond for settlement. Indiana would not approve a restrictive settlement law until 1831, but the Illinois Territory prohibited free Black settlement in 1813 and passed another particularly punitive law restricting settlement after it became a state in 1819.[11]

The formation of new free states in the West was not only designed to exclude free African Americans, it also depended on Indian removal. By the end of the War of 1812, Native people held reserves across the Ohio River valley and lower Great Lakes. Federal policymakers saw the reserves as a major hindrance to the development of free states. Michigan territorial governor Lewis Cass, for example, believed that reserves around the Black Swamp on the Ohio-Indiana-Michigan territorial borders hampered Michigan's connections to neighboring states. Wyandot, Seneca, Delaware, Shawnee, Potawatomi, Odawa, and Ojibwe territory along the Maumee River watershed encompassed the Black Swamp. The swamp stretched across the cor-

---

42, 140–142; Gillen D'Arcy Wood, *Tambora: The Eruption That Changed the World* (Princeton, N.J., 2014), 199–228.

11. "An Act, to Regulate Black and Mulatto Persons," Jan. 5, 1804, *Acts of the State of Ohio Second Session of the General Assembly Held under the Constitution of the State, A.D. One Thousand Eight Hundred and Three . . .*, II ([1804]; rpt. Norwalk, Ohio, 1901), 63–66; "An Act to Amend the Act, Entitled 'An Act Regulating Black and Mulatto Persons,'" Jan. 25, 1807, *Acts Passed at the First Session of the Fifth General Assembly of the State of Ohio Begun and Held at the Town of Chillicothe, December 1st, 1806, and in the Fifth Year of the Said State . . .*, V (1807; rpt. Norwalk, Ohio, 1901), 53–54; "An Act to Prevent the Migration of Free Negroes and Mullattoes into This Territory and for Other Purposes," Dec. 8, 1813, in Francis S. Philbrick, *The Laws of Illinois Territory, 1809–1818* (Springfield, Ill., 1950), 91–92; "An Act Respecting Free Negroes, Mulattoes, Servants, and Slaves," Mar. 30, 1819, *The Revised Laws of Illinois . . .* (Vandalia, Ill., 1833), 457–462; *Journal of the Senate of the State of Indiana; during the Fifteenth Session of the General Assembly; Commenced at Indianapolis, on Monday the Sixth of December, 1830* (Indianapolis, Ind., 1830), 460.

ner of northwest Ohio and was notoriously difficult to traverse. During the War of 1812, American general William Hull and his troops had cut a military trail through the Black Swamp—a demanding process that impeded American defensive efforts. Drawing on wartime experience, Cass believed that the Maumee River reserves "render[ed] the Territory of Michigan an insulated point upon the map of the nation" and thus undesirable to migrants from the East. Better "approximat[ing]" Michigan Territory to the rest of the United States would ensure "a speedy settlement and an active and enterprising population," he contended.[12]

Michigan would not become a state until 1837, and even when it did, Native peoples retained sovereignty and power and remained on their homelands. In Ohio, Indiana, and Illinois, statehood produced different effects. Statehood proceeded rapidly because federal officials systematically targeted Native reserves for appropriation. The War Department instructed its agents to pursue lands near existing American settlements to make them "more compact." Federal officials argued that new purchases of Native land would rationalize the borders of the states. For the most part, they were effective at crafting the free states they imagined. Ohio, Indiana, and Illinois were largely dependent on white families for their development.[13]

Federal treaties and federal and state law removed Native peoples in the service of a narrow definition of freedom. Ultimately, however, both free African Americans and Native Americans contested and stretched this limited idea of who free states were for. To make the free states of Ohio, Indiana, and Illinois, federal officials first tried to acquire Native homelands within their bounds. They wanted to achieve what the Monroe administration understood to be regular borders by eliminating the competing sovereignties of Native nations. Before the War of 1812, federal policymakers did not have the military or political power to direct Native migration in treaty

12. Lewis Cass and Duncan McArthur to George Graham, Sept. 29, 1817, in *ASPIA,* II, 137–138 (quotations, 137), Graham to Cass, Mar. 23, 1817, 136; Cass to Elkanah Watson, Nov. 3, 1815, Lewis Cass Papers, box 2, BHC, Cass to William H. Crawford, Aug. 31, 1816, box 2; William Carl Klunder, *Lewis Cass and the Politics of Moderation* (Kent, Ohio, 1996), 25–28.

13. William H. Crawford to [William] Clark, [Ninian] Edwards, and [Auguste] Chouteau, May 7, 1816, in *ASPIA,* II, 97 (quotation); "First Annual Message," Dec. 2, 1817, in Hamilton, ed., *Writings of James Monroe,* VI, 38–40; Francis Paul Prucha, *American Indian Treaties: The History of a Political Anomaly* (Berkeley, Calif., 1994), 146; Michael Witgen, "Seeing Red: Race, Citizenship, and Indigeneity in the Old Northwest," *Journal of the Early Republic,* XXXVIII (2018), 581–611.

language. Instead, they hoped that Indigenous people would remove voluntarily over time when confronted with white migrants. After the War of 1812, the federal and state governments began to write removal into treaties more explicitly. They used several provisions: land exchange, allotments, and payments to federal contractors who would take Native peoples to specific locations. Yet, at the same time that treaty commissioners more boldly asserted their power to determine who free states were for, Native peoples did the same. They pushed back against these new provisions or used them to their advantage.[14]

Land exchange and allotments were not wholly new. Trading eastern for western lands became common in federal treaties after the War of 1812, but the policy had roots in the early Republic. Jefferson had proposed land exchange in a constitutional amendment that he drafted in 1803 in the wake of the Louisiana Purchase. In 1808, he brought the idea to the Cherokees, urging them to replace their eastern lands with those west of the Mississippi. After the War of 1812, federal officials routinely proposed the Mississippi River as a natural barrier between Indian country and U.S. settlements. In an 1817 report, the congressional Committee on Public Land expressed their hope that all Native people would agree to exchange their "right of possession" in lands east of the Mississippi for lands west of the river.[15]

Treaty commissioners brought land exchange to southern Native nations first. Cherokee chiefs fought to retain tribal lands claimed by North Carolina, Tennessee, and Georgia by adopting the trappings of U.S. government and "civilization plans"—a bicameral legislature, a constitutional government, plow agriculture, and even the enslavement of African Americans. Three thousand separatist Cherokees charted a different course by agreeing to move to federally designated reserves beyond the Mississippi River. Eastern Cherokees who remained fended off federal treaty commissioners who insisted they should give a portion of their homelands equal to what their "emigrant brethren" took out West. They eventually traded two tracts in Georgia and North Carolina for land on the Arkansas and White Rivers in 1817. The agreement paid for the transportation of those who wished to

14. "Exchange of Lands with the Indians; Communicated to the Senate," Jan. 9, 1817, in *ASPIA,* II, 124.

15. Ibid., II, 124 (quotation); Prucha, *American Indian Treaties,* 146; James P. Ronda, "'We Have a Country': Race, Geography, and the Invention of Indian Territory," *Journal of the Early Republic,* XIX (1999), 739–755, esp. 741–742; Nicholas Guyatt, "'The Outskirts of Our Happiness': Race and the Lure of Colonization in the Early Republic," *Journal of American History,* XCV (2009), 995; John P. Bowes, *Land Too Good for Indians: Northern Indian Removal* (Norman, Okla., 2016), 57.

emigrate, the first treaty to write transportation explicitly into its provisions, rather than assuming that people would leave on their own.[16]

Federal commissioners approached Delaware leaders about land exchange the following year in 1818. Most eastern Delawares lived on the White River in nearly a dozen villages. The White River lands fell within the state of Indiana, where land sales increased exponentially in the 1810s. At the time of statehood in 1816, the non-Native population of Indiana was 65,000; it more than doubled over the next four years. By 1820, it had risen to 147,000. Given persistent migration in the neighborhood of Delaware towns, land exchange might have seemed like the best among many bad options. Hundreds of Delaware migrants had already opened up paths from the White River lands to Louisiana, Texas, Missouri, and Canada in the preceding decades. For some Delawares, removal preserved their autonomy away from migrants from the East. They would follow the path of earlier Delaware relocations dating back to the 1770s. Others might have felt compelled by area traders, to whom they were indebted, to agree to land exchange. Merchants and traders who attended the 1818 treaty with their account books open made sure their debts were settled. Federal negotiators promised to pay Delaware debts—$13,312.25 in total—to facilitate their departure. Commissioners also secretly gained support for the treaty from special annuities granted to Delaware chiefs William Anderson and Lapanihilie.[17]

When the White River Delawares ceded all of their lands in Indiana in exchange for a four-thousand-dollar annuity, federal commissioners wrote removal directly into the agreement. The treaty compensated Delawares for the expense of migration—the full value of their improvements in the region as well as horses, boats, and provisions to support their journey. Federal Indian agent John Johnston hired an interpreter to "conduc[t]" the Delawares west of the Mississippi. They had three years to depart. By 1821, most White River Delawares had left for Missouri. Those who could not emigrate

16. "Exchange of Lands with the Indians," Jan. 9, 1817, in *ASPIA,* II, 124–126 (quotation, 126), William H. Crawford to William Clark, Ninian Edwards, and Auguste Chouteau, May 27, 1816, 97–98, Return J. Meigs to Crawford, Aug. 19, 1816, 114; Anthony F. C. Wallace, *The Long, Bitter Trail: Andrew Jackson and the Indians* (New York, 1993), 52, 62; Theda Perdue, "The Conflict Within: Cherokees and Removal," in William L. Anderson, ed., *Cherokee Removal: Before and After* (Athens, Ga., 1991), 61; William G. McLoughlin, *Cherokee Renascence in the New Republic* (Princeton, N.J., 1986), 228–230; Banner, *How the Indians Lost Their Land,* 194; Prucha, *American Indian Treaties,* 146.

17. Melissa Rinehart, "Miami Resistance and Resilience during the Removal Era," in Beatty-Medina and Rinehart, eds., *Contested Territories,* 139; Bowes, *Exiles and Pioneers,* 40; Bowes, *Land Too Good for Indians,* 75, 84, 104.

remained behind in Indiana, including "two aged and decrepid men utterly unable to commence new improvements in the Country West of the Mississippi." Those two men watched as Delaware parties left them behind. Both "exiles and pioneers," in the words of John P. Bowes, Delawares weighed complicated factors of kinship ties and autonomy when making the decision to leave.[18]

Allotments—breaking up Native land into parcels of private property—also had deep roots in the eighteenth century. Native communities made decisions about how people would use common lands. Families might hold rights to farm particular plots of land or to use hunting grounds, and they often passed those rights down to their children. The Mashpees, for example, explained that "we are tenants in common, all our lands being undivided, but our improvements are in allotments." Native land tenure was not unchanging, either. By the late eighteenth century, many New England Natives had already begun to move from communal fields to far-flung individual farms in response to dispossession. Nonetheless, federal plans for allotments threatened Native sovereignty. Late-eighteenth-century civilization plans encouraged private property in order to incorporate Native peoples into the United States by eliminating tribal governments and their control over communal land. William Henry Harrison tried something similar in 1803, when he allotted the Kaskaskia's treaty annuity by dividing it into a separate payment for each family, bypassing the chiefs who usually made those divisions.[19]

The Monroe administration picked up allotments after the War of 1812 as a tool of removal, but Native peoples intervened to use them to their advantage when they could. The Monroe administration believed that Native proprietors needed to be prepared for landholding. They wanted to

18. "Johnston's Appointment of James Wilson," John Johnston Account Book, Beinecke Library, Yale University, New Haven, Conn. ("conduc[t]"); Lewis Cass to John Calhoun, Jan. 13, 1819, Lewis Cass Papers, box 4, BHC ("two aged"); Bowes, *Exiles and Pioneers;* "Treaty with the Delawares," Oct. 3, 1818, in *ASPIA,* II, 169; Rinehart, "Miami Resistance and Resilience during the Removal Era," in Beatty-Medina and Rinehart, eds., *Contested Territories,* 139.

19. Mashpee petition, Massachusetts, Documents relating to Unpassed Senate Legislation, Massachusetts Archives, no. 1643 (1792), quoted in Daniel R. Mandell, *Tribe, Race, History: Native Americans in Southern New England, 1780–1880* (Baltimore, Md., 2008), 10–12 ("we are tenants," 10); Nancy Shoemaker, *A Strange Likeness: Becoming Red and White in Eighteenth-Century North America* (New York, 2004), 19–20. For the Kaskaskia Treaty, see "Treaty with the Kaskaskia Made in Vincennes," Aug. 13, 1803, WHH, reel 1, 632–636; "The Kaskaskia and Other Tribes; Communicated to the Senate," Oct. 31, 1803, in *ASPIA,* I, 687.

separate remaining Native reserves into allotments held as "life estate[s]" that could not be sold by the original owners. Life estates would be inherited by children or widows in fee simple, owned completely without any conditions. Life estates were similar to the "preparation state" imagined by colonizationists who argued that free African Americans needed to be prepared for freedom. In the case of Native Americans, Cass argued that life estates would prohibit Native proprietors from selling lands until "time and experience should give them a proper knowledge of the value of the property." Cass's ideas were paternalistic. They were also indicative of changes in how white Americans saw Native peoples—as occupants rather than owners of their homelands who did not have the right to decide how to manage them.[20]

The wars of the 1780s and 1790s convinced federal officials that Native land needed to be purchased rather than appropriated. At the same time, a blossoming trade in preemption rights—the right to purchase land in the future when it had been ceded by Native nations—also undermined Native proprietorship. Courts began to support the claims of thousands of western migrants who had purchased preemption rights, shifting legal rights along the way. In *Johnson v. McIntosh* (1823), Chief Justice John Marshall bolstered the property rights of American speculators and migrants by denying that British or U.S. officials had ever understood Native Americans to be landowners in fee simple. As Stuart Banner has written, "When Indian land could be bought and sold with the Indians still on it, the Indians' right to the land started to feel, to the buyers and sellers, less like fee simple ownership."[21]

Once again, the Monroe administration first pursued allotments in the South. Cherokees who wished to remain in Georgia, North Carolina, Tennessee, and Alabama had to apply for a 640-acre individual reserve on their southeastern lands, and they had to become U.S. citizens. The policy encountered objections from all sides. White Georgians protested against the extension of U.S. citizenship to Cherokees. Meanwhile, the Cherokee National Council resisted the new policy by denying tribal citizenship to anyone who left Cherokee country or applied for allotments. Ultimately, 300

20. George Graham to Lewis Cass, Mar. 23, 1817, in *ASPIA*, II, 136 ("life estate[s]"); [Moses Fisk], *Tyrannical Libertymen; A Discourse upon Negro-Slavery in the United States: Composed at——, in Newhampshire; on the Late Federal Thanksgiving-Day* (Hanover, N.H., 1795), 10 ("preparation"); Lewis Cass to John Johnston, Apr. 11, 1818, Johnston Papers, box 1, folder 5, OHC ("time").

21. Banner, *How the Indians Lost Their Land*, 159–164, 163 (quotation), 178–190, 182–183.

out of 3,200 Cherokee heads of families did apply for U.S. citizenship and private allotments. Some quickly lost them, as Georgia surveyed and sold the allotments to white buyers before federal surveyors arrived, and Tennessee and North Carolina refused to recognize them. Others used them to remain in Cherokee homelands after removal in the 1830s. Deeming allotments a failure, federal agents spent the late 1810s and early 1820s buying out Cherokee allotment holders.[22]

Federal officials brought allotments north as they sought to eliminate Native sovereignty and create free states in Ohio, Indiana, and Illinois. They used allotments in 1817 at the Treaty of the Maumee Rapids, where they hoped to achieve border regularity in Ohio and Indiana by grasping Native lands in northern Ohio on the Michigan border. According to Cass, who was charged with the negotiations alongside military officer Duncan McArthur, the acquisition would connect American settlements and "present an iron frontier" during a future war. Cass particularly coveted Wyandot lands at Brownstown on the west side of the Detroit River, which had been the location of the council fire of the United Indian Confederacy. At the treaty, the Wyandots, alongside Senecas, Delawares, Shawnees, Potawatomis, Odawas, and Ojibwes ceded nearly four million acres of land to the United States. For the Wyandots, the cession constituted the majority of their remaining lands in Ohio. The Wyandots would remain on smaller reserves at Upper Sandusky and Broken Sword Creek; the Senecas maintained thirty thousand acres between the Sandusky River and the mouth of Wolf Creek; the Shawnees concentrated their lands at Wapakoneta and Hog Creek; and the Senecas and Shawnees kept reserves at Lewiston. Cass and McArthur hoped to divide the reserves into allotments encumbered with legal limitations.[23]

Wyandot leaders tried to turn allotments to their own advantage. In Washington, they lobbied successfully for larger reserves. They recognized that a flood of eastern migrants into the Ohio country made their land valuable, and they demanded a substantial annuity paid, not in goods, but in

22. See Jos. McMinn to William H. Crawford, Oct. 25, 1816, in *ASPIA,* II, 115, George Graham to Andrew Jackson, May 16, 1817, 142; William G. McLoughlin, "Experiment in Cherokee Citizenship, 1817–1829," *American Quarterly*, XXXIII (1981), 7, 9–10, 15–25; Julie L. Reed, *Serving the Nation: Cherokee Sovereignty and Social Welfare, 1800–1907* (Norman, Okla., 2016), 47–50.

23. Lewis Cass to James Monroe, Sept. 30, 1817, Lewis Cass Papers, box 3, BHC (quotation), Cass to William H. Crawford, July 30, 1816, box 2; "Treaty with the Wyandots, Senecas, Delawares, Shawanees, Pattawatamies, Ottawas, and Chippewas," Sept. 29, 1817, in *ASPIA,* II, 131–135, Graham to Cass, Mar. 23, 1817, 136.

specie, along with gristmills, sawmills, and a blacksmith. Moreover, they insisted that the allotments on their remaining reserves be "conveyed absolutely." They agreed to sell their lands only if they were given clear title to the allotments in fee simple. Wyandot leaders were convinced of "the importance of securing the land, upon which they must make valuable improvements, to their descendants." The treaty included articles listing dozens of private allotments. It also gave Wyandot proprietors the ability to sell allotments to anyone, as long as they had permission from the president or a federal agent.[24]

Wyandot leaders further upended the removal plans of federal negotiators by designating the recipients of allotments themselves. In the seventeenth and eighteenth centuries, French men and Anglo-American captives married Wyandot women, with the implication that their children would have clan ties to the Wyandots given the Wyandots' matrilineal society. Wyandot politics were organized around the clans—the Wyandot council was composed of the male chiefs and female councils of each. Wyandots wanted to keep adoptees and those with clan ties to their Upper Sandusky community close by securing allotments for them. It was particularly important to the Wyandots to cement these ties in the case of politically powerful adoptees and their children. The Wyandot tribal council, for example, wanted William Walker, Sr., to be included in the list of allotment holders. Walker had been taken captive in Virginia in the 1770s and had lived with the Wyandots ever since. Walker's wife, Catherine Walker (née Rankin), was a biracial Wyandot woman and a supporter of the Methodist mission at Upper Sandusky. His son William Walker, Jr., would become a leader of Wyandot resistance to removal. All three were interpreters for the Wyandots. Warfare and dislocation between the 1770s and 1815 had fractured the Wyandot clan structure and diminished the role of the female councils, cre-

24. Extract of a Letter from Lewis Cass to John C. Calhoun, May 28, 1818, Johnston Papers, box 1, folder 5 ("conveyed"), Cass to John Johnston, Jan. 22, 1818, box 1, folder 5; Cass to William H. Crawford, July 30, 1816, Lewis Cass Papers, box 2, BHC ("importance"), Cass to Calhoun, Nov. 21, 1818, box 4; "Treaty with the Wyandots, Senecas, Delawares, Shawanees, Pattawatamies, Ottawas, and Chippewas," Sept. 29, 1817, in *ASPIA,* II, 132–133, Cass and Duncan McArthur to George Graham, Sept. 30, 1817, 138–139, Graham to Cass and McArthur, Oct. 17, 1817, 140, "Amendments Proposed to the Treaty with the Wyandots, Senecas, Delawares, Shawanees, Pattawatamies, Ottowas, and Chippewas; Communicated to the Senate," Dec. 29, 1817, 148–149; *Journal of the Executive Proceedings of the Senate of the United States of America, from the Commencement of the First, to the Termination of the Nineteenth Congress,* III (Washington, D.C), Dec. 11, 1817, 94–95.

ating new openings for biracial men like Walker, Jr., to take on prominent roles in Upper Sandusky politics.[25]

Federal commissioners tried to keep biracial descendants and adoptees like the Walkers from the allotments because they saw them as politically troublesome. In the case of Walker, Sr., Cass and McArthur believed he might lead resistance to removal in the future. Ultimately, they were unsuccessful at drawing these limits on allotments. The Wyandots skirted federal commissioners by securing an allotment for Catherine Walker, instead. They also extended allotments to adopted kin. John Vanmeter, who was taken captive by the Wyandots, received land for himself, his Seneca wife, and his wife's three brothers. The Wyandots insisted on their right to determine access to landholding, thereby affirming their own vision of kinship and tribal membership. They shaped who in their political community would be able to remain in the free states.[26]

Wyandot maneuvers around the allotment system caused dissension in Congress, and the Senate refused to ratify the treaty. The War Department, meanwhile, used the Wyandot's fee simple allotments as an example of what not to do when they dispatched instructions to other treaty commissioners. When William Clark received directives from the War Department to hold a treaty with the Quapaws shortly thereafter, he was instructed not to allow a repeat of the Wyandot negotiations. By September 1818, the Wyandot tribal council at Upper Sandusky met with Cass and McArthur again at St. Mary's in Ohio to sweep away the allotments. The Wyandot reserve would be held as all of their previous reserves had been: in common. They would maintain their reserves in the midst of the free state of Ohio, frustrating federal plans to establish border regularity.[27]

Miami negotiators tried to use allotments strategically to secure their right to remain in Indiana as well. Secretary of War John C. Calhoun believed that Miami reserves that overlapped with Indiana left the state in "an inconvenient form," and he wanted to "render it more convenient and compact." In 1818, Miami negotiators were forced to sell most of their lands in cen-

25. Buss, "Politics of Indian Removal," in Beatty-Medina and Rinehart, eds., *Contested Territories,* 169–179, n12, 171; Bowes, *Exiles and Pioneers,* 162–164.

26. "Treaty with the Wyandots, Senecas, Delawares, Shawanees, Pattawatamies, Ottawas, and Chippewas," Sept. 29, 1817, in *ASPIA,* II, 132–133.

27. "Amendments Proposed to the Treaty with the Wyandots, Senecas, Delawares, Shawanees, Pattawatamies, Ottowas, and Chippewas," Dec. 29, 1817, in *ASPIA,* II, 148–150. For Senate discussion, see *Journal of the Executive Proceedings of the Senate of the United States of America,* III, Dec. 11, 1817, 94–95, Jan. 9, 1818, 110–111, Jan. 13, 1818, 111–113, Jan. 15, 1818, 113, Jan. 30, 1818, 116–118, Feb. 3, 1818, 118, Feb. 5, 1818, 121, Dec. 18, 1818, 158–159, Dec. 23, 1818, 160–161; Prucha, *American Indian Treaties,* 138.

tral Indiana at the Treaty of St. Mary's. Miami leaders held back allotments for a few powerful elites. The most prominent of these men, Miami civil chief and trader Jean Baptiste de Richardville, secured fee simple reserves for himself. Richardville was the son of Joseph de Richerville, a trader at the Miami village of Kekionga, and Tecumwah, Miami chief Little Turtle's sister. De Richerville's relationship with Tecumwah gave him access and power within the Miami community. Richardville's ability to secure property for his family was a sign of his power and of his personal interest in a successful treaty. The private allotments allowed some Miamis to remain in Indiana after most were forced to remove west.[28]

Federal efforts to design free states for white migrants sent treaty commissioners to Native councils again and again after the War of 1812. Free states required the removal of Native peoples. Federal treaty proposals included blatant removal schemes—land exchange, allotments, and federally contracted migration—that signaled a shift in federal policy to an era of rapid removal in Ohio, Indiana, and Illinois. Native leaders did not accept these innovations passively—they made the best out of a bad set of choices. They also sometimes rejected them entirely. When federal commissioners suggested that the Wyandots should exchange their eastern lands for those in the Missouri Territory, they knew that the tribal council would likely reject the proposal in the strongest possible terms.[29]

The most effective tool federal officials believed they had to wield against Native negotiators was population growth. Cass assured his superiors back in the federal capital that they only needed to be patient. "As our settlements gradually surround them, their minds will be better prepared to receive this proposition," he wrote. The Treaty of the Maumee Rapids did indeed create a land rush in northwest Ohio. Migrants with preemption rights who had followed the Senate conversation with impatience immediately moved into the new cession. Federal troops built a road connecting the new purchase between Sandusky and Detroit to facilitate white migration. Between 1820 and 1830, the non-Native population of newly formed Sandusky County tripled. After the War of 1812, the notion that Native Americans would leave voluntarily persisted, but it was accompanied by aggressive techniques of

28. John C. Calhoun to Johnathan Jennings, Lewis Cass, and Benjamin Parke, May 2, 1818, in *ASPIA,* II, 174 (quotations, 174), "Treaties with the Miamies," Oct. 6, 1818, 169–170; Jennings to John Johnston, July 28, 1818, Johnston Papers, box 1, folder 5; Donald Chaput, "The Family of Drouet de Richerville: Merchants, Soldiers, and Chiefs of Indiana," *Indiana Magazine of History,* LXXIV(1978), 103–116; Bowes, *Land Too Good for Indians,* 70–77.

29. Lewis Cass to William Clarke, July 24, 1818, Johnston Papers, box 1, folder 6.

removal as federal officials prioritized the making of new free states. Native resistance continued to shape the meaning of free states as Indigenous people thwarted federal plans to eliminate competing sovereignties.[30]

Despite the efforts of state officials to keep them out, Black men and women likewise disrupted limitations on who was welcome in the new free states as they moved into Ohio and Indiana on the heels of Indian removal. They laid out spaces of Black freedom atop Native lands north of the Ohio River with great rapidity in the first three decades of the nineteenth century. These journeys were nonetheless not always freely chosen. Black migrants left under conditions that were not of their own making. Sometimes they moved to avoid migration restrictions on the books in the southern states. Sometimes they were forced to go. Southern enslavers surprisingly provided the impetus for some Black migration. Virginians and North Carolinians manumitted hundreds of free Black Virginians to Pennsylvania, Ohio, Indiana, and Illinois, complying with exile laws on the books in their states by assisting—or compelling—people to settle out of the state as a condition of their freedom. They defied or narrowly complied with migration restrictions in the Midwest to satisfy those in South. As a result, Black migrants might have thought of themselves as settlers, but they might just as well have thought of themselves as exiles.

Enslavers who sought to emancipate people by following restrictive migration laws in Virginia and North Carolina often relied on western Friends to do so. After the War of 1812, Ohio became the destination for those whom Philip J. Schwartz has termed "migrants against slavery"—those who left slave states in the upper South to relocate to the former Northwest Territory in the early Republic. In the decade after statehood, most of Ohio's white migrants came from New England, western New York, Pennsylvania, and Virginia. Ohio's population doubled between 1817 and 1820. The state also became a place of refuge for white evangelicals and Quakers, who saw an apocalyptic destiny for slaveholding communities on the Atlantic seaboard. As states in the upper South moved to restrict antislavery activism, Baptist radicals moved west to Kentucky and then into Ohio. Prominent white abolitionists and ministers traveled west to Ohio in the 1790s. Hundreds of white Quaker families from the upper South left for Ohio after

30. Lewis Cass and Duncan McArthur to John Calhoun, Sept. 18, 1818, University of Wisconsin-Madison Digital Collections, http://digital.library.wisc.edu/1711.dl/History.IT1818n097, accessed Apr. 3, 2018 (quotation); Extract of a Letter from Cass to Calhoun, May 28, 1818, Johnston Papers, box 1, folder 5; Bowes, *Land Too Good for Indians*, 123–124.

1800. By the 1810s and 1820s, Indiana also attracted Quaker migrants from Guilford and Randolph Counties in North Carolina, where many Friends lived. They made settlements in southern Indiana and along the Ohio-Indiana border.[31]

It is likely that in the first two decades of the nineteenth century, Quaker networks laid the path for many Black migrants who left, or were forced to leave, the upper South for Ohio and Indiana. In 1803, for example, a North Carolina justice of the peace enlisted one Quaker to accompany a Black family, replacing the man they had hired to "conduct them out" to Ohio. Quaker towns in Ohio welcomed new free people who had migrated north. In Indiana, Quakers assisted the Cabin Creek settlement in building and staffing a school, purchasing books, and assisting individuals and families who first arrived at the settlement.[32]

The experience of Virginia Quaker Benjamin Ladd is a case in point. The problem of Virginia slavery so vexed Ladd that he finally left the state in 1815. After moving to Ohio, Ladd assisted Virginians who wished to manumit enslaved people by sending them west. In 1820, Ladd solicited donations from "Christians of various denominations" for a group of manumitted people who "have fallen under the force of laws which have reduced them to a state of extreme suffering." Ladd maintained contact with Friends in the Virginia Piedmont and Tidewater regions who likely connected him

31. Philip J. Schwartz, *Migrants against Slavery: Virginians and the Nation* (Charlottesville, Va., 2001), 1, 11; Horton, "Race and Region," in Parker, Sisson, and Coil, eds., *Ohio and the World,* 47–49; Monica Najar, "'Meddling with Emancipation': Baptists, Authority, and the Rift over Slavery in the Upper South," *Journal of the Early Republic,* XXV (2005), 157–186; James D. Essig, *The Bonds of Wickedness: American Evangelicals against Slavery, 1770–1808* (Philadelphia, 1982), 143. For Quakers, see Amos Neal Henry, "Early Friends Settlements in Ohio" (M.A. thesis, John Carroll University, 1954), 12–18; Xenia E. Cord, "Free Black Rural Communities in Indiana: A Selected Annotated Bibliography," submitted in partial fulfillment of the requirements for A500 (Dec. 7, 1982), iii–iv.

32. Gottlieb Shober to William Hodgins, Apr. 19, 1803, Black History Collection, box 5, folder 10, LOC (quotation); Short Creek Quarterly Meeting Minutes, Aug. 16, 1828, Ohio Society of Friends Records, box 2, folder 1, 68, OHC; James L. Burke and Donald E. Bensch, *Mount Pleasant and the Early Quakers of Ohio* (1975; rpt. Columbus, Ohio, 1994). For Cabin Creek, see, for example, New Garden Quarterly Meeting, Aug. 24, 1828, Committee on the Concerns of the People of Colour, ECQA. For other Indiana meetings and settlements assisting migrants, see West Branch Quarterly Meeting Committee on the Concerns of the People of Colour, ECQA, Dunkirk Monthly Meeting of Antislavery Friends; Indiana Early African American Settlements Heritage Project, Fountain County, box 2, folder 25, IHS, Grant County, box 3, folder 3; Claude A. Clegg, III, *The Price of Liberty: African Americans and the Making of Liberia* (Chapel Hill, N.C., 2004), 43–44.

with enslavers looking to send manumitted men and women outside of the state. In 1820, he helped to purchase Ohio land for 350 to 500 Black Virginians who had been freed by the will of British banker and absentee planter Samuel Gist. Gist had entrusted the purchase of land for them in Ohio to his lawyer, William Fanning Wickham. Wickham and Ladd bought more than two thousand acres for the group in two settlements in Hillsboro, Ohio. Ladd was "one of a committee to superintend the business" that likely included other appointees from his quarterly meeting. The Gist group was not the only group of freed people that he assisted. In 1825, for example, Ladd facilitated the migration of a group of people freed by Thomas Beaufort—Nathaniel Benford, Ben Messenburg, Collier Christian, Lee Carter, Paige Benford, David Cooper, William Toney, Fielding Christian, Fitzhugh Washington and their families—from Charles City County, which neighbored Ladd's former home in Henrico County, to Smithfield, Ohio.[33]

By 1819, 270 of the men and women who had been owned by Gist had already settled on the land, and another 100 to 200 would be resettled there in the 1820s. Gist's estate paid for the carts, provisions, and men to accompany the migrants on their journey. It is clear from Wickham's papers that many people did not wish to go. Wickham noted in 1828 that "several of the Slaves who were removed to Ohio have returned to the land in Hanover." The Richmond Court of Chancery would not allow them to remain there, however, and Wickham determined that they could legally "be carried back to Ohio at the expence of the estate" when the next group of migrants left. British traveler Edward Abdy, who visited the settlement in 1834, was told by residents that "when they quitted the plantation, they were accompanied by three armed men, and two of them were hand-cuffed with irons, because they were unwilling to go." Enforcement of restrictive migration laws was left to to enslavers and local communities.[34]

When slaveholders bought land for freed people in the state of Ohio,

33. Benjamin Ladd to Oladiah Jennings, Mar. 27, 1820, Benjamin Ladd Letter book, HQC (quotations); C. A. Powell, B. T. Kavanaugh, and David Christy, "Transplanting Free Negroes to Ohio from 1815 to 1858," *Journal of Negro History,* I (1916), 302–306.

34. William Wickham to Creed Taylor, Mar. 10, 1828, Wickham Family Papers, folder 4, VMHC ("several"); E[dward] S. Abdy, *Journal of a Residence and Tour in the United States of North America, from April, 1833, to October, 1834,* 3 vols. (London, 1835), 75 ("when they quitted"); Henry Howe, *Historical Collections of Ohio . . .* (Cincinnati, Ohio, 1851), 71; Schwartz, *Migrants against Slavery,* 122–148; Michael Trotti, "Freedmen and Enslaved Soil: A Case Study of Manumission, Migration, and Land," *Virginia Magazine of History and Biography,* CIV (1996), 455–480.

the deeds were often shrouded in legal entanglements that made it impossible for formerly enslaved people to stake a claim to their own property or to deed that property to others. This was so for the Gist settlers, whose lands were entrusted to the lawyer who made the purchase on their behalf. By the 1830s, the Gist migrants were clearly dissatisfied with their relocation. The land that had been purchased for them was not sufficient for farming. Solemon Hudson, one member of the group, wrote to Wickham, "Allthough I am black I have sence enough to know that we have Been Badley treated by our agents here." Similarly, Beaufort purchased two hundred acres of land for the freed people he sent to Smithfield, laid out in five-acre plots. It is likely that Ladd acted as purchaser in the transaction, as he was also named the trustee of the 200-acre Beaufort plot. Trusteeships such as these put Black migrants in a precarious position. Landownership was important to freedom and political autonomy. Denied the power to fully control their property, the Gist and Beaufort groups experienced freedom as dependency. They were required to leave the southern states as a result of emancipation. Yet, even in the free states, they did not have full control over the terms of their settlement.[35]

The pull for former enslaved people to return home was strong. In 1828, North Carolinian James Roberts moved to Henry County, Indiana, and his cousin, Willis Roberts, who accompanied him, split off for neighboring Rush County. Not long after, Willis Roberts told his cousin that he planned to return home. James Roberts wrote and warned him that "I would not this night if I had Children take them to Such a place . . . to Bringe them to See trobble and not enjoy ther Selves as A free man." James Roberts emphasized the dangers of pursuing a free life amid slavery in North Carolina. Willis Roberts had left family and friends behind in North Carolina, however, and while he ultimately stayed in Indiana, his homesickness did not dissipate so easily.[36]

Still others were deeply committed to making a new home for themselves in the western states, despite the upheaval of leaving friends and relations behind. In 1819, Virginian Edward Coles traveled westward with the seven-

35. Solemon Hudson to William Wickham, Nov. 19, 1849, Wickham Family Papers, folder 2 (quotation); C. A. Powell to ?, n.d., in Powell, Kavanaugh, and Christy, "Transplanting Free Negroes to Ohio," *Journal of Negro History,* I (1916), 304–305; Trotti, "Freedmen and Enslaved Soil," *Virginia Magazine of History and Biography,* CIV (1996), 454–480.

36. James Roberts to Willis Roberts, 1831, Roberts Family Papers, 299, LOC (quotation); Stephen A. Vincent, *Southern Seed, Northern Soil: African-American Farm Communities in the Midwest, 1765–1900* (Bloomington, Ind., 1999), 1, 12, 32, 172n.

teen enslaved people he had inherited from his father on the pretense they were bound for a slave state. He freed them on reaching Illinois and gave 160 acres of land to each head of family. Coles lamented in 1814 that his decision not to hold slaves had "forced me to leave my native state, and with it all my relations and friends." He took for granted that his decision to leave Virginia also compelled the people he freed to leave their "relations and friends" behind in the state, too. Nonetheless, when Coles repeatedly encouraged his former slaves to emigrate to Liberia, they refused to go. Robert Crawford, a minister formerly enslaved by Coles, explained that he was determined to remain where he was. According to Coles, Crawford was "fully engrossed and happily occupied in attending to his Family, his Farm, and his Congregation," and he had no intention of leaving.[37]

African Americans who left for Ohio, Indiana, and Illinois ended up redefining the states as battlegrounds in a national conflict over slave and free territory. Large manumissions to Ohio and Indiana drew the ire of local observers who wrote derisively about free Black colonies to be "planted in our adjoining county." One writer imagined that white Ohioans would not "quietly submit to have their farms and hard earnings of the best portion of their lives to be rendered worthless by the settling down amongst them of a colony of manumitted slaves." Another could not see "these rapid accessions without some degree of alarm." Their words were evidence of a wider racist backlash against free African Americans who moved across state borders in the early national period.[38]

Some groups were met with violence in Ohio. Ladd related how one Virginia Quaker deeded Ohio land to two of his former slaves. But when the two men reached their land, a neighbor used the state's restrictive migration laws to bar their settlement until they were "hunted out of the state." In July 1846, four hundred enslaved people liberated by Virginia legislator John Randolph journeyed at the direction of his executors via canal boats to New Bremen, Ohio, where they disembarked and traveled overland to

37. Edward Coles to Thomas Jefferson, July 31, 1814, in J. Jefferson Looney et al., ed., *The Papers of Thomas Jefferson: Retirement Series,* 15 vols. (Princeton, N.J., 2004—), VII, 503–504 ("forced, " 504); Edward Coles, Unfinished letter, 1844, Coles Family Papers, box 2, folder 11, HSP ("fully").

38. A. T. to the Editor, May 10, 1819, quoted in Powell, Kavanaugh, and Christy, "Transplanting Free Negroes to Ohio from 1815 to 1858," *Journal of Negro History,* I (1916), 309 ("planted"); St. Mary's Ohio, *Sentinel,* n.d., as copied by *The Liberator,* Aug. 7, 1846, quoted in William H. Pease and Jane H. Pease, *Black Utopia: Negro Communal Experiments in America* (Madison, Wis., 1963), 27 ("quietly"); *Ohio State Journal,* May 3, 1827, quoted in Frank U. Quillin, *The Color Line in Ohio: A History of Race Prejudice in a Typical Northern State* (Ann Arbor, Mich., 1913), 26 ("rapid").

3,200 acres of land in Mercer County that had been purchased for them from his estate. The next day, a group of white men gathered and, in the words of Ohio abolitionist Augustus Wattles, used "misrepresentation and whiskey" passed around in buckets and tin cups to incite a riot against the group. They had the support of influential white men, including the commander of the local militia, who published a notice calling for the group to be driven from their lands. White mobs forced them to leave the county.[39]

Despite violence and vitriol, African Americans fashioned free states into antislavery preserves by choosing to stay or to go. Federal land policy that promoted brisk land sales as well as the position of Ohio, Indiana, and Illinois on the border of slave states made them a destination for enslaved people escaping slavery or free people looking for opportunity beyond the upper South. Ohio's and Indiana's surviving county record books show that some free African Americans who migrated to these states did comply with registration laws, recording their names and places of emancipation at the county court on their arrival. Together, they made at least forty independent settlements in Ohio and thirty rural settlements in Indiana before the Civil War, with dozens more Black landowners scattered across Ohio, Indiana, and Illinois.[40]

There were significant ties between African Americans in the Midwest that likely predated their moves out of the South. County registration books show that many people migrated in family groups rather than as individuals. Virginian Godfroy Brown, for example, moved to Ohio in 1822 with nine family members after he was emancipated. Thornton Alexander and his wife and four children also left Virginia as a family for Indiana in the 1810s.

39. Benjamin Ladd to Thomas Worthington, Sept. 20, 1815, Benjamin Ladd Letter book ("hunted"); Augustus Wattles to Mordecai Bartley, Aug. 16, 1846, Mordecai Bartley Papers, box 3, folder 3, OHC ("misrepresentation"); Howe, *Historical Collections of Ohio,* 355–356, 465–466; William Buckner McGroarty, "Exploration in Mass Emancipation," *William and Mary Quarterly,* 3d Ser., XXI (1941), 208–226.

40. For the Ohio River as a boundary between slavery and freedom, see Salafia, *Slavery's Borderland.* On independent settlements, see Mary Ann Brown, "Vanished Black Rural Communities in Western Ohio," *Perspectives in Vernacular Architecture,* I (1982), 97–113, 115–116; Vincent, *Southern Seed, Northern Soil;* Cheryl Janifer LaRoche, *Free Black Communities and the Underground Railroad: The Geography of Resistance* (Urbana, Ill., 2014); Anna-Lisa Cox, *The Bone and Sinew of the Land: America's Forgotten Black Pioneers and the Struggle for Equality* (New York, 2018). For estimates of the number of settlements, see United States Department of the Interior, National Park Service, "Clemens, James and Sophia Farmstead," National Register of Historic Places Multiple Property Documentation Form, Mar. 15, 2001, (NPS Form 10-900), sect. no. 7–8, 3; Cord, "Free Black Rural Communities in Indiana," iv; Cox, *Bone and Sinew of the Land,* viii–ix.

Neighbors from the same counties in Virginia and North Carolina migrated to the same counties in Ohio and Indiana to register their emancipation. In Logan County, Indiana, nearly all of those who registered migrated from Charlotte County, Virginia, between 1836 and 1852. Rural settlements maintained ties to each other as well. The Longtown settlement in Ohio was connected to Snow Hill and Cabin Creek—Black settlements located just across the Indiana border. In the 1820s, the Roberts family founded the Beech Settlement in central Indiana. They later moved with several Beech Settlement families to found the Roberts Settlement and other communities in Vigo County, Indiana.[41]

African American migrants expanded the definition of free states through their actions. Darke County on the Indiana-Ohio border was home to one of Ohio's first Black communities, and it was a frequent destination for families escaping Virginia's exile laws. Greenville Settlement in Darke County, later renamed Longtown, was founded by James Clemens, a free Black settler from Rockingham County, Virginia. Clemens purchased land at Longtown in 1818 and married Sophia Sellers. The Clemenses eventually amassed 790 acres of farmland and orchards. They started the first school in the settlement in the 1820s, and they later established a manual labor boarding school called the Union Literary Institute that educated Native, Black, and white students. Longtown became a stop on the Underground Railroad and remained a center for abolitionism. African American migrants protected fugitives against fugitive slave provisions that gave enslavers and their agents the power to cross the Ohio River to reclaim enslaved people. In so doing, they made Ohio a free state.[42]

Rural Black settlements created a web of antislavery activity that stretched north from the Ohio River toward the Canadian border. Along the Ohio River, prominent Black and white abolitionist communities cemented the reputation of these states as free spaces. Ripley, Ohio, was founded in 1819 by Virginians who were freed and brought to Ohio. The town became an

41. Logan County Emancipation Index, Special Collections and Archives, Wright State University Libraries, Dayton, Ohio, Greene County Emancipation Index, 8–13; John Otis Wattles, undated notes, Wattles Family Papers, box 1, folder 22, WRHS. For the Beech and Roberts Settlements, see the Elijah Roberts Collection and the Mount Pleasant Library Collection at IHS and the Roberts Family Papers at LOC; Vincent, *Southern Seed, Northern Soil.*

42. John Otis Wattles, Undated notes, Wattles Family Papers, box 1, folder 22; United States Department of the Interior, National Park Service, "Clemens, James and Sophia Farmstead," National Register of Historic Places Multiple Property Documentation Form, Mar. 15, 2001, (NPS Form 10-900), sect. no. 7–8, 3.

abolitionist center. In Fountain County, Indiana, men and women who had absconded from slavery settled in several dozen cabins at the edge of the county's swamps and ponds. They arranged their settlement near an antislavery community of local Quakers who had emigrated from North Carolina. In one free community in Madison, Indiana, a British traveler met six men and women who had escaped slavery and were taking shelter in the cottage of an African American settler as they made their way further north. Although legislators hoped to make free states for white families, Black migrants reimagined the definition of free states in their own towns in concert with white abolitionists.[43]

Although dispossession in the Southeast led to the expansion of slavery, the theft of Native lands in the Ohio Valley and the lower Great Lakes instead led to the creation of free states. The new free states drew the boundaries of belonging tightly. In Ohio, Indiana, and Illinois, a series of early-nineteenth-century treaties dispossessed Indigenous people in the service of expanded white landed autonomy and a truly limited and qualified idea about Black freedom. It is worth considering then, whose idea of freedom was at work in what is now called the Midwest. After the War of 1812, Black migrants formed communities in what became Ohio's Van Wert, Paulding, Shelby, and Mercer Counties, all above the Greenville Treaty line, much of which was still Indian country. At Longtown, free Black migrants built homes and farms only thirty miles from Fort Recovery, the site of the United Indian Confederacy's victory against federal forces in 1791. Ohioans still purportedly discovered the bones of men who had died in that battle into the nineteenth century. The Longtown settlement demonstrates the ways in which Ohio functioned as a new space of freedom carved from Indian country and laid out amid memories of regenerative violence encompassed by Arthur St. Clair's defeat. Black migrants settled there, but they did not always control the terms of settlement. Activists and writers seldom linked Indian removal and Black colonization in their pamphlets, articles, speeches, and books before the late 1820s. Yet, for those who lived north of the Ohio River, those coerced movements existed side by side.[44]

43. Horton, "Race and Region," in Parker, Sisson, and Russell Coil, eds., *Ohio and the World,* 59; Abdy, *Journal of a Residence and Tour in the United States,* II, 370–373; J. Wesley Whicker, *Historical Sketches of the Wabash Valley* (Attica, Ind., 1916), 93. Steven Hahn argues that communities like these were "maroon communities." See Hahn, *The Political Worlds of Slavery and Freedom* (Cambridge, Mass., 2009), 24.

44. George Wood Wolfe, *A Pictorial Outline History of Darke County, Ohio, with Portraits and Biography of Prominent Citizens of the County, County and Ex-County Officials, Attorneys at Law, City Officials, Bankers, Capitalists, Business Men, Teachers, Min-*

Removal was ubiquitous after the War of 1812 because life in the United States came unbound in the postwar years. Some Americans lauded unfettered economic opportunity; others competed for converts in an expanding religious marketplace; many embraced the ideal of free migration by moving west; still others celebrated expanded suffrage for white men. "Boundlessness," however, came at a cost to Indigenous people and African Americans. Land sales hemmed in Native communities. African Americans lost voting rights in many states just as white Americans gained them. Removal resolved a larger anxiety about the place of Native Americans and African Americans in a nation devoted to opportunity and equality for white men. In the wake of the War of 1812, some white Americans embraced a new nationalism devoted to the myth of a "singular national ethnos" and a more rigid biological racism.[45]

Plans to incorporate territories into the nation through removal went beyond the free states. Removal was a national project. Native homelands east of the Mississippi River were carved into new states with brutal swiftness after 1815. In 1800, three hundred thousand non-Native people lived west of the Appalachians. By 1820, that number had increased to more than two million. Six new states were added to the union in the six years after the end of the War of 1812.[46]

As the pace of state making quickened, removal's proponents made their plans palatable to the public by repackaging them as supposedly benevolent projects that would secure the future of eastern North America's many peoples. Benevolence took on greater meaning after 1815 as a salve for the violence of removal's rapid pace. Americans navigated many postwar changes—the expansion of wage labor, the decline of slavery in the North,

---

isters, Agriculturalists and Notable Citizens of the County (Newark, Ohio, 1889), 10–11; Richard Slotkin, *Regeneration through Violence: The Mythology of the American Frontier, 1600–1860* (Norman, Okla., 2000).

45. Merrell, "American Nations, Old and New," in Hoxie, Hoffman, and Albert, eds., *Native Americans and the Early Republic,* 350 ("boundlessness"); Arjun Appadurai, *Fear of Small Numbers: An Essay on the Geography of Anger* (Durham, N.C., 2006), 4 ("singular"); Steven Watts, *The Republic Reborn: War and the Making of Liberal America, 1790–1820* (Baltimore, Md., 1987), 275–321; Sean Wilentz, *The Rise of American Democracy: Jefferson to Lincoln* (New York, 2005), 155, 167, 177–202; Howe, *What Hath God Wrought,* 79–89; Donald Ratcliffe, "The Right to Vote and the Rise of Democracy, 1787–1828," *Journal of the Early Republic,* XXXIII (2013), 219–254, esp. 229–230, 237; Sarah L. H. Gronningsater, "'Expressly Recognized by Our Election Laws': Certificates of Freedom and Multiple Fates of Black Citizenship in the Early Republic," *William and Mary Quarterly,* 3d Ser., LXXIV (2018), 465–506.

46. Howe, *What Hath God Wrought,* 140.

the growth of immigration—by turning to benevolence. They poured their energies into forming nonsectarian benevolent societies with religious missions. By the postwar period, removal as benevolence similarly justified two national movements—one for colonization in Liberia and the other for Indian removal beyond the Mississippi River. Proponents of removal argued that it would protect Native Americans and African Americans from the rapaciousness of market capitalism, racial discrimination, and territorial expansion. Benevolence ushered in an age of removal. It made removal acceptable to a broad cross section of white Americans in the United States, and it worked just as well if one looked east as if one looked west.[47]

Not only state and federal officials but also white ministers, missionaries, and Quakers embraced removal. Philadelphia Quaker Ann Mifflin fueled a revival of interest in colonization in the United States by traveling to Virginia with Friend Sarah Zane in 1810 to promote it. The pair gained the support of former Virginia governor James Wood and the mild endorsement of Thomas Jefferson. Mifflin also turned to Paul Cuffe, a Quaker ship captain of Wampanoag and African descent, whom she and Philadelphia Quaker James Pemberton hoped would take up missionary work to Sierra Leone. Cuffe threw himself into the work, too, casting aside his initial hesitation that he was "Very febel . . . and uncapabel of doing much for my Brethren the afferican Race." He spent the next decade attempting to promote trade and migration between the United States and Sierra Leone. Cuffe did not advocate colonization as a spur to gradual abolition. He endorsed limited, voluntary migration as a path to racial equality. By moving to Sierra Leone, he wrote, African American migrants would "place our children in the contry of their origian upon a level with our neighbours the white Brother." In Sierra Leone, Black migrants would "become their national Representatives their merchants and their navigators" for themselves.[48]

47. Bruce Dorsey, *Reforming Men and Women: Gender in the Antebellum City* (Ithaca, N.Y., 2002), 7–8; Susan M. Ryan, *The Grammar of Good Intentions: Race and the Antebellum Culture of Benevolence* (Ithaca, N.Y., 2003), 14–16; Guyatt, "'Outskirts of Our Happiness,'" *Journal of American History,* XCV (2009), 988.

48. Paul Cuffe to James Pemberton, Sept. 14, 1808, Paul Cuffe Manuscript Papers, Part I, microfilm, New Bedford Whaling Museum, New Bedford, Mass. ("febel"); Cuffe to Cato Sawyer, Feb. 17, 1814, in Rosalind Cobb Wiggins, *Captain Paul Cuffe's Logs and Letters, 1808–1819: A Black Quaker's "Voice from within the Veil"* (Washington, D.C., 1996), 271 ("place"), Cuffe to John James and Alexander Wilson, June 10, 1809, 80. For Mifflin, see John Lynch to Thomas Jefferson, Dec. 25, 1810, in Looney, ed., *Papers of Thomas Jefferson, Retirement Series,* III, 267–270; Gary B. Nash, *Warner Mifflin: Unflinching Quaker Abolitionist* (Philadelphia, 2017), 317n. For Cuffe, see Lamont D. Thomas, *Rise to Be a People: A Biography of Paul Cuffe* (Urbana, Ill., 1986), 34–36;

Cuffe's project was popular with Black and white reformers in the United States, and he ended up knitting together a transatlantic network of colonizationists and emigrationists. On his first voyage to Sierra Leone, he founded an association there to support trade with the United States. He visited with the London African Institution and corresponded with its members. Once back in the United States, Cuffe petitioned Congress and received President Madison's approval for his voyages. The War of 1812 scuttled his plans for another journey to Sierra Leone. Instead, Cuffe traveled to Baltimore, New York, and Philadelphia to meet with white Quakers and African American leaders. Black leaders James Forten, Richard Allen, Russell Parrot, Peter Williams, Jr., and Daniel Coker all formed auxiliary African Institutions in their respective cities in response. By 1815, Cuffe made a return voyage to Sierra Leone with thirty-eight people of African descent from Boston, Philadelphia, Newport, and New York.[49]

While Cuffe was on his second journey to Sierra Leone, white writers who saw removal as a nation-building project began proposing a variety of plans of their own for colonization. Evangelicals who read about Cuffe's voyages and his petition to Congress thought of colonization as a missionary venture. Missionaries who had once confined their work to North America were just beginning to identify new fields for their labors beyond North America. They believed they were uniquely positioned to lead the world toward the millennium because of the superiority of Anglo-American culture and evangelical Protestantism. In 1810, a group of white students at Andover Theological Seminary led by Samuel Mills successfully pushed the General Association of Congregational Ministers of Massachusetts to create a missionary board called the American Board of Commissioners for Foreign Missions (ABCFM). The students published a seven-part story on Cuffe in the *Boston Weekly Messenger.* As the agent of a missionary training school in Cornwall, Connecticut, for Indigenous and white students, Mills also urged the Pres-

---

Nicholas Guyatt, *Bind Us Apart: How Enlightened Americans Invented Racial Segregation* (New York, 2016), 259–262; Nash, *Warner Mifflin,* 229.

49. Paul Cuffe, Logbook, in Wiggins, *Captain Paul Cuffe's Logs and Letters,* 215–216, Cuffe to William Allen, June 12, 1812, 224, Cuffe to Elisha Tyson, Apr. 25, 1813, 246, Cuffe to Hannah Little, June 16, 1813, 251, Cuffe to Tyson, June 18, 1813, 251, [Memorial Petition], June 1813, 252–253, Cuffe to Allen, Sept. 23, 1813, 255, Cuffe to Respected friends of the Friendly Society, Sept. 29, 1813, 261, W[illia]m Rotch, Jr., to Christopher Gore, Dec. 10, 1813, 266, W[illia]m Dean to Timothy Pickering, Dec. 12, 1813, 266, Cuffe to Cato Sawyer, Feb. 17, 1814, 271, Cuffe to William Allen, Mar. 6, 1814, 274; Thomas, *Rise to Be a People,* 83, 88–90; Richard S. Newman, *Freedom's Prophet: Bishop Richard Allen, the AME Church, and the Black Founding Fathers* (New York, 2008), 189–191; Julie Winch, *A Gentleman of Color: The Life of James Forten* (New York, 2003), 177–206.

byterian synod of New York and New Jersey to fund a separate school that would train African American missionaries to work in Africa or the southern states. He wrote Cuffe about the mission, and he pitched the idea of a Black colony in North America. Meanwhile, Connecticut Congregational minister Jedidiah Morse, who served on the ABCFM, gathered the names of potential emigrants who wished to board Cuffe's ships.[50]

White southerners were also interested in colonization as a national project. In Virginia, Federalist Charles Fenton Mercer learned of Jefferson's 1801 correspondence with the Virginia legislature about colonization, and he introduced a resolution in the Virginia House of Delegates seeking federal support for colonization. From Mercer, the idea passed to lawyer Francis Scott Key and Elias Boudinot Caldwell, clerk of the Supreme Court, to Caldwell's cousin Robert Finley, a New Jersey Presbyterian minister and director of Princeton's Theological Seminary. Finley likewise embraced African colonization as a missionary venture. Meanwhile, the American Convention of Abolition Societies petitioned Congress for a colony on the "unappropriated land of the South or West" in response to letters from enslavers in North Carolina, Virginia, Kentucky, and Tennessee who asked for their advice about manumission. Cuffe would eventually call for a western land grant for a free Black colony, too.[51]

By the time he returned to the United States from Sierra Leone in 1816, Cuffe was surprised by the outpouring of support for colonization from across the country. Mills, Morse, Mercer, Key, Caldwell, and Finley were all mulling over the idea, and most of them had corresponded with him about it. "The Slumbering would Seem much awakened and making many Enquiries warethe [whether] people of Coular may be Colonized were A gen-

50. Paul Cuffe to Samuel J. Mills, Mar. 15, 1814, in Wiggins, *Captain Paul Cuffe's Logs and Letters,* 279, Mills to [Cuffe], July 15, 1816, 422–424, Jed[idia]h Morse to Cuffe, July 27, 1816, 429; Gardiner Spring, *Memoir of Samuel John Milles,* 2d ed. (Boston, 1829), 120, 129–130; Thomas, *Rise to Be a People,* 89, 91, 106; Howe, *What Hath God Wrought,* 287–289; Emily Conroy-Krutz, *Christian Imperialism: Converting the World in the Early American Republic* (Ithaca, N.Y., 2015), 22–24, 108.

51. Extract of a Letter from Mr. Evan Lewis [or Lewes] of Wilmington, State of Delaware, June 12, 1816, Thomas Clarkson Papers, HL (quotation); Paul Cuffe to [James Brian], Jan. 16, 1817, in Wiggins, *Captain Paul Cuffe's Logs and Letters,* 498, Cuffe to James Forten, Mar. 1, 1817, 509; Douglas R. Egerton, "'Its Origin Is Not a Little Curious': A New Look at the American Colonization Society," *Journal of the Early Republic,* V (1985), 463–480; Beverly C. Tomek, *Colonization and Its Discontents: Emancipation, Emigration, and Antislavery in Antebellum Pennsylvania* (New York, 2011), 37–38; Marie Tyler-McGraw, *An African Republic: Black and White Virginians in the Making of Liberia* (Chapel Hill, N.C., 2014), 19–20; Guyatt, *Bind Us Apart,* 263–266.

eral manimission to take place," Cuffe observed. These awakenings culminated in December 1816, when Finley, Key, Caldwell, and Mills joined with Washington's political elites to constitute the American Colonization Society (ACS). Their goal was "ameliorating the condition of the Free people of Colour in the United States" through colonization in North America or Africa. Cuffe's project had widespread appeal, particularly among white Americans for whom it was a nation-building project of exclusion.[52]

From the outset, the ACS accommodated the varied interests of the white enslavers, ministers, reformers, and antislavery men who made up its founding members. ACS board members differed in the degree to which they embraced emancipation. Mercer expressed his desire to manumit and colonize those he enslaved, for example, while ACS vice president and Kentucky congressman Henry Clay remained committed to slaveholding. Colonizationists promoted the ACS as a missionary venture that would send African Americans to Christianize West Africans as a way to encourage gradual emancipation in the United States, as a solution to what they saw as dependency and poverty, and as a means of suppressing what they called the illegitimate commerce of the Atlantic slave trade by fostering a legitimate trade in palm oil, camwood, and rice from West Africa. At the same time, in a bid to attract Southerners, ACS officials promised not to interfere with southern slavery, even going so far as to argue that it would prop up the institution. ACS board members were only united by their belief that emancipation required the removal of free African Americans. ACS materials used racist ideas about Black criminality and poverty to explain that emancipation could not proceed without "manifest injury" to the United States.[53]

52. Paul Cuffe to W[illia]m Gibbons, Jan. 16, 1817, in Wiggins, *Captain Paul Cuffe's Logs and Letters,* 495 ("Slumbering"), [Cuffe] to Robert Finley, Jan. 8, 1817, 492; "Origin, Constitution, and Proceedings of the American Society for Colonising the Free People of Colour of the United States," American Colonization Society Papers, reel 289, 4, LOC ("ameliorating"); Guyatt, *Bind Us Apart,* 263–267.

53. *The First Annual Report of the American Society for Colonizing the Free People of Color, of the United States; and the Proceedings of the Society at Their Annual Meeting in the City of Washington, on the First Day of January, 1818* (Washington, D.C., 1818), 15 (quotation). For the debate about the ACS and its goals and implications, see Egerton, "'Its Origin Is Not a Little Curious,'" *Journal of the Early Republic,* V (1985), 463–480; Matthew Spooner, "'I Know This Scheme Is from God': Toward a Reconsideration of the Origins of the American Colonization Society," *Slavery and Abolition: A Journal of Slave and Post-Slave Studies,* XXXV (2014), 559–575; Samantha Seeley, "Beyond the American Colonization Society," *History Compass,* XIV (2016), 95–96; Guyatt, *Bind Us Apart,* 267–272. For proslavery arguments, see *The Second Annual Report of the American Society for Colonizing the Free People of Colour of the United States; with an Appendix* (Washington, D.C., 1819), 9; Thomas, *Rise to Be a People,* 111.

The ACS had widespread appeal because its leaders clothed removal in the language of benevolence. ACS materials called colonization a matter of both "patriotism" and "the public good." It purported to offer free African Americans subject to racism and inequality full citizenship and economic opportunity in West Africa, where they would serve as missionaries. At an ACS meeting in 1818, the organization's president and Supreme Court justice Bushrod Washington explained that it would connect "the political emancipation and future comfort of an unfortunate class of men, with the civilization and happiness of an afflicted, oppressed, and degraded quarter of our globe." Others argued that colonization would protect free African Americans from an epidemic of kidnapping in the North. Northern abolition societies made kidnapping a focal point for their work. The Delaware Abolition Society began a campaign against it in 1816, and the American Convention of Abolition Societies condemned the practice at their annual meetings. When Caldwell and Key's associate, Philadelphia doctor Jesse Torrey published a book excoriating the domestic slave trade and kidnapping in 1817, he appended reports about the newly formed ACS in the back pages. Given the stakes, Henry Clay asked, "Why should they not go? Look at the earliest history of man . . . and you find him continually migrating."[54]

Black Americans who worried over colonization's sudden resurgence across the country argued that removal was not benevolence. ACS founders acted at the very moment when Black Americans were expanding their efforts to secure the right to remain. Black Philadelphians expressed uneasiness with African colonization publicly beginning in 1816 in reaction to Cuffe's voyage—Cuffe himself was called to Philadelphia to help assuage those fears. They inaugurated protest over colonization only a few weeks after the ACS's founding. In January 1817, nearly three thousand Black Philadelphians—including elites such as sailmaker James Forten and ministers Richard Allen, Absalom Jones, and John Gloucester—organized a

54. "Origin, Constitution, and Proceedings of the American Society for Colonising the Free People of Colour of the United States," American Colonization Society Papers, reel 289, 14 ("patriotism"); *First Annual Report of the American Society for Colonizing the Free People of Color,* 6 ("political"), 17 ("Why should"); Guyatt, "'Outskirts of Our Happiness,'" *Journal of American History,* XCV (2009), 997–1000. For kidnapping, see Abolition Society of Delaware Minute Book, 1801–1819, 87, 100, 113, Pennsylvania Abolition Society Papers, HSP; Jesse Torrey, *A Portraiture of Domestic Slavery, in the United States: With Reflections on the Practicability of Restoring the Moral Rights of the Slave, without Impairing the Legal Privileges of the Possessor; and a Project of a Colonial Asylum for Free Persons of Colour: Including Memoirs of Facts on the Interior Traffic in Slaves, and on KIDNAPPING* (Philadelphia, 1817), 29–30; Tomek, *Colonization and Its Discontents,* 38.

meeting at Mother Bethel Church in Philadelphia to discuss their position on colonization. Despite the private interest of Forten and Allen in the idea of Black-led emigration schemes, the meeting unanimously denounced the plans of the ACS. They tore apart the reasoning of white colonizationists. They resolved "that we view with deep abhorrence the unmerited stigma attempted to be cast upon the reputation of the free people of color, by the promoters of this measure, 'that they are a dangerous and useless part of the community.'" The group declared that "whereas our ancestors (not of choice) were the first successful cultivators of the wilds of America, we their descendants feel ourselves entitled to participate in the blessings of her luxuriant soil, which their blood and sweat manured." The ACS was attempting nothing less than the deportation of free Black people to prop up the institution of slavery. As Forten reported, "There was not one sole that was in favor of going to Africa."[55]

That summer, twelve influential Black Philadelphians crafted a longer statement against colonization, throwing their support behind the anticolonization sentiments of the larger public meeting. Rejecting Finley's insistence that free people would be eager to leave, they pronounced that "we have no wish to separate from our present homes." The 1817 meetings were a crucial turning point. The growth of white colonization ideas as well as the death of Cuffe in September of that year turned Black Philadelphians, and eventually Black elites like Forten and Allen, against West African colonization.[56]

Despite mounting hostility to the ACS among Black Americans, colonization became one of the most popular voluntary movements in the United States among white Americans. Across the United States, colonization agents set up local auxiliaries that would work as the fundraising arms for the parent society as early as 1818. Meanwhile, Mercer and Clay, who served in the House of Representatives, successfully tied federal funding for colonization to the suppression of the slave trade. After the abolition of the slave trade in

55. "A Voice from Philadelphia," January 1817, in W[illia]m Lloyd Garrison, *Thoughts on African Colonization: or, An Impartial Exhibition of the Doctrines, Principles, and Purposes of the American Colonization Society; Together with the Resolutions, Addresses, and Remonstrances of the Free People of Color* (Boston, 1832), II, 9 ("that we view"); James Forten to Paul Cuffe, Jan. 25, 1817, in Wiggins, *Captain Paul Cuffe's Logs and Letters,* 502 ("not one sole"), Cuffe to Peter Williams, Jr., June 14, 1816, 414–415, John James to Cuffe, June 7, 1816, 416.

56. Garrison, *Thoughts on Colonization,* II, 10 (quotation); Forten to [Cuffe], Jan. 25, 1817, in Wiggins, *Captain Paul Cuffe's Logs and Letters,* 501–502; Winch, *Gentleman of Color,* 195–197.

1808, transatlantic slave trade captives whose ships were intercepted by the U. S. Navy were placed under federal jurisdiction and could not be sold in the United States. In 1819, with President Monroe's support, funds for the suppression of the slave trade were allocated for the creation of a West African colony called Liberia. Both free African Americans and refugees of the slave trade would be resettled there.[57]

Liberia was the first overseas colonial venture undertaken by the United States and jointly funded and administered by the federal government and a private organization. The first group of eighty-six colonists, missionaries, and ACS agents sailed for the west coast of Africa aboard a federally chartered ship in 1820. In 1821, ACS agent Eli Ayres and U.S. Navy lieutenant Robert Field Stockton used federal funds to purchase land at gunpoint from Dei King Peter in the Cape Mesurado region on the west coast of Africa. Within two years, 150 people lived in the capital of Monrovia in Liberia, overseen by Jehudi Ashmun, who held dual posts as a U.S. agent and an ACS agent.[58]

While members of Congress advocated for federal funding for the ACS, they also discussed allocations for an Indian school fund. Maryland Quaker and Superintendent of Indian Trade Thomas McKenney led the effort. In 1818, he sent a confidential circular to missionary organizations asking them to petition Congress to fund Native schools. By the end of February 1819, Congress had received more than a dozen petitions from an array of churches requesting an Indian school fund "to promote the security, the preservation, and the improvement of the Indians." In response, Congress set aside ten thousand dollars of federal funds each year to support schools teaching Native students agricultural skills, reading, writing, and arithmetic. The slave trade bill and the Indian schools bill were debated simultaneously in Congress; President Monroe signed them both into law on March 3, 1819. It is no surprise that they were funded at the same time. Both were the product of lobbying by supposedly benevolent men who saw

57. For the building of local auxiliaries, see, for example, American Colonization Society Papers, reel 1, Ser. 1, I. For federal funds for colonization, see Eric Burin, "The Slave Trade Act of 1819: A New Look at Colonization and the Politics of Slavery," *American Nineteenth Century History,* XIII (2012), 1–14; Nicholas P. Wood, "The Missouri Crisis and the '*Changed* Object' of the American Colonization Society," in Beverly C. Tomek and Matthew J. Hetrick, eds., *New Directions in the Study of African American Recolonization* (Gainesville, Fla., 2017), 149–151, 153–154, David F. Ericson, "The American Colonization Society's Not-So-Private Colonization Project," 111.

58. Ericson, "American Colonization Society's Not-So-Private Colonization Project," in Tomek and Hetrick, eds., *New Directions,* 114–115.

an expanded field for their labors after the War of 1812. Between 1819 and 1824, the federal government oversaw a significant expansion in the number of Indian schools, from four to twenty-one.[59]

McKenney's plans, however, only went so far. At the same time that colonization became a national movement, a wide cross section of Americans—ministers and missionaries as well as state and federal officials—from across the United States began to argue that Indian removal was benevolent as well. In the 1790s, policymakers contended that civilization programs would support U.S. expansion by diminishing Native sovereignty. After the War of 1812, demand for Native lands was so great that policymakers abandoned those programs altogether. Secretary of War Calhoun who had supported the Indian school fund reversed course and suggested that federally funded reform efforts were doomed. Calhoun contended that the federal government would have to extend the laws of the states over Indian country or watch Natives "waste away in vice and misery." Predictions of the disappearance of Native people justified removal by the 1820s. Indeed, the language of benevolence shifted over the course of the 1820s to accommodate more strident demands for removal. Federal officials like Cass, for example, wrote that it would protect Native Americans "from the exterminating pressure of our progressive settlements."[60]

Protection had not always meant removal. Early federal treaties, particularly those of the 1780s, offered Native nations "protection" in return for ceded lands—an attempt to undermine Native sovereignty through paternalistic benevolence. Protection was supposed to entail swift justice meted out to white intruders by federal agents, military alliances, and hospitality at federal forts in return for land cessions. After the War of 1812, as the British

59. For the petitions, see *Journal of the House of Representatives of the United States, at the Second Session of the Fifteenth Congress, in the Forty-Third Year of the Independence of the United States* (Washington, D.C., 1818), Dec. 15, 1818, 95, Dec. 23, 1818, 125–126, Jan. 12, 1819, 172, Jan. 20, 1819, 199 (quotation), Feb. 1, 1819, 222, Feb. 6, 1819, 235, Feb. 15, 1819, 268; "An Act Making Provision for the Civilization of the Indian Tribes Adjoining the Frontier Settlements," Mar. 3, 1819, in *The Public Statutes at Large of the United States of America, from the Organization of the Government in 1789, to March 3, 1845 . . .*, III (Boston, 1846), 516–517; Herman J. Viola, *Thomas L. McKenney: Architect of America's Early Indian Policy, 1816–1830* (Chicago, 1974), 33–43; David Andrew Nichols, *Engines of Diplomacy: Indian Trading Factories and the Negotiation of American Empire* (Chapel Hill, N.C., 2016), 156–157; Bowes, *Land Too Good for Indians*, 56–57; Guyatt, *Bind Us Apart*, 281–282.

60. J. C. Calhoun to H[enry] Clay, Jan. 15, 1820, in *ASPIA*, II, 201 ("waste"); Lewis Cass to John Johnston, Jan. 30, 1818, John Johnston Papers ("exterminating"); Jean M. O'Brien, *Firsting and Lasting: Writing Indians out of Existence in New England* (Minneapolis, Minn., 2010).

threat receded, American negotiators were less inclined to make these reciprocal agreements, for they felt they no longer served U.S. interests. In an 1814 War Department report, federal officials reflected on Native power, predicting that "a few years will so diminish their numbers as to render their hostility harmless and their friendship useless." Treaties that confirmed the boundaries between Native nations and the United States at the end of the War of 1812 largely abandoned the pretense of protection.[61]

Those who had previously defended civilization programs embraced removal instead. McKenney, a self-professed "frien[d] of the Indian[s]" who had ardently supported trading factories and schools as the tools of civilization, advocated for removal after 1822. Fort Wayne Indian agent Johnston hoped that the Wyandots would leave Ohio for new lands, without which they "cannot be saved from destruction." Baptist missionary Isaac McCoy, who had also previously advocated for civilization plans, hoped to create an Indian colony west of the Mississippi River. Johnston and McCoy proposed that a colony should progress through the territorial model to become a state. McCoy and Connecticut Congregationalist minister and geographer Jedidiah Morse both received federal support for promoting removal. In 1827, McCoy was granted a large appropriation to oversee a tour west of the Mississippi to look for land for a Choctaw, Chickasaw, and Cherokee colony—"a home for a homeless people," in his words. Morse went on his own tour to take stock of Indian country with funds from missionary groups and the federal government. At the beginning of his tour, Morse believed that civilization plans leading to citizenship were the only antidote to "misery and extirpation." By 1822, however, when he published a report of his travels, he had changed his mind. He called for removal as a benevolent measure. Morse simultaneously founded a short-lived private voluntary organization called the American Society for Promoting the Civilization and General Improvement of the Indian Tribes that encouraged private citizens to aid the work of removal.[62]

61. "Treaty with the Winnebagoes," June 3, 1816, in *ASPIA,* II, 95 ("protection"); "An Estimate of the Annual Expenditure of the Indian Department at Detroit," Lewis Cass Papers, box 1, BHC ("few years"). For an example that dropped the promise of protection versus one that included it, see "Treaty with the Choctaws," Oct. 24, 1816, and "Treaty with the Winnebagoes," June 3, 1816, in *ASPIA,* II, 95.

62. Thomas L. McKenney, *Memoirs, Official and Personal; with Sketches of Travels among the Northern and Southern Indians; Embracing a War Excursion, and Descriptions of Scenes along the Western Borders* (New York, 1846), 240 ("frien[d]"); John Johnston to James B. Finley, June 26, 1823, Finley Papers, United Methodist Archives Center, Ohio Wesleyan University Library, Delaware, Ohio ("cannot be saved"), quoted in Charles C. Cole, Jr., *Lion of the Forest: James B. Finley, Frontier Reformer* (Lexington,

Indigenous people and their allies pushed back against the idea that removal was benevolence. In the South, Cherokees and their missionary allies became the staunchest defenders of Cherokee rights. The ABCFM, which had benefitted from federal missionary funds for the Cherokees, actively opposed removal. The dispossession of Cherokees, in the eyes of many white Americans, was egregious because Cherokee elites had already folded the central tenets of federal civilization plans into existing labor and gender relations, and they had consolidated Cherokee nationhood while centralizing political and legal power in a National Council beginning in 1809 and culminating in a new constitution ratified in 1827. Although missionaries deemed Cherokees worthy of the right to remain, there was no comparable debate among white missionaries and reformers in the East about Wyandot, Miami, or Shawnee rights to the north. American missionaries saw northern Native societies as smaller, more diffuse, and less likely to adopt the civilization project. When Morse visited the Great Lakes region, for example, he incorrectly painted a picture of northern Native societies in decline. In Michigan at L'Arbre Croche, Morse and his son met with the Odawa chief Ceitaw. Ceitaw tried to disabuse Morse of these notions, and he declined Morses's suggestion that they take up civilization plans. "If other tribes wished for the institutions of the whites, he and his tribe were glad and wished them well," Ceitaw observed, "but for themselves they did not feel poor, did not intend to leave their lands."[63]

Northern Native peoples did not have the weight of a powerful national organization like the ABCFM on their side in the eastern United States, but they used similar strategies to counter the age of removal. At Upper

---

Ky., 1994), 82; Isaac McCoy, Journal, July 6, 1828, Isaac McCoy Collection, Kansas State Historical Society Library, Topeka, quoted in George A. Schultz, *An Indian Canaan: Isaac McCoy and the Vision of an Indian State* (Norman, Okla., 1972), 103 ("home"); Jedidiah Morse to Lucretia B. Morse, Feb. 5, 1820, Morse Family Papers, YUA ("misery"); Schultz, *Indian Canaan,* 94–97, 99; R. Pierce Beaver, "Church, State, and the Indian: Indian Missions in the New Nation," *Journal of Church and State,* IV (1962), 25; *The First Annual Report of the American Society for Promoting the Civilization and General Improvement of the Indian Tribes in the United States* (New Haven, Conn., 1824). Nicholas Guyatt illuminates the intellectual world of these men in Guyatt, *Bind Us Apart,* 282–286, 288–293.

63. Richard Morse to Lucretia B. Morse, July 20, 1820, Morse Family Papers, box 8 (quotations); Jedidiah Morse, *A Report to the Secretary of War of the United States, on Indian Affairs*... (New Haven, Conn., 1822), 24–30; Wallace, *Long, Bitter Trail,* 60–61; Theda Perdue, *Cherokee Women: Gender and Culture Change, 1700–1835* (Lincoln, Neb., 1998), 143–145; Guyatt, "'Outskirts of Our Happiness,'" *Journal of American History,* XCV (2009), 996. For Cherokees as worthy of the right to remain, see Conroy-Krutz, *Christian Imperialism,* 131–132; Banner, *How the Indians Lost Their Land,* 208, 210–211.

Sandusky, Methodism drove a wedge through the Wyandots after James Stewart's arrival there in 1816. For centuries, Wyandots had used conversion to accrue social power. Beginning in the 1600s, Wyandots had strengthened their ties to Jesuit missionaries and the French by practicing Catholicism. Some Wyandots objected to Stewart's mission and to the cultural changes Methodist converts demanded. Bloody Eyes rejected conversion, telling Stewart, "I do not believe the Great Spirit will punish his red children for dancing, feasting, etc." A significant number of Wyandots took to Stewart's message, however. They asked the Methodist Quarterly Meeting in Urbana, Ohio, to open an official Grand River Mission in 1819. They found Methodism's promise of salvation appealing, and they also likely hoped that a Methodist mission might help them remain on their lands at a moment when white Ohioans were calling for new land cessions. The Wyandots built a church, a mill, a blacksmith shop, and a school that brought missionaries and resources to Upper Sandusky. By the time they left their Ohio lands in 1843, they had also adopted a set of written laws and turned to yearly elections to determine their next chief, removing political power from female councils in the process. James Finley, a white Methodist minister who joined the Wyandot mission in 1821, used these changes to argue against Wyandot removal. He explained that many Sandusky Wyandots were descended from white Americans and thus should not be removed. "Their fathers were citizens," he wrote. "Why not their children?"[64]

Colonization and Indian removal betrayed a larger anxiety among white Americans about race and belonging in the nation. Nationalist exclusions ushered in the age of removal—a moment of cultural, social, and political change in the United States that sanctified expanded suffrage and economic opportunity for white men and the exile of African Americans and Native Americans. Those who supported Indian removal saw similarities between their ideas and colonization—indeed, many of them *were* colonizationists. McCoy's plan for an Indian "colony," for example, was inspired by his support for the ACS. At a mission school that he ran on the Vermillion River in Indiana, McCoy taught Wea and Piankeshaw students and one African American student, whom he hoped to send to Liberia with the ACS. Be-

64. Mitchell, *Missionary Pioneer,* 66–67 ("I do not believe"); James B. Finley, *History of the Wyandott Mission, at Upper Sandusky, Ohio, under the Direction of the Methodist Episcopal Church* (Cincinnati, Ohio, 1840), 301 ("fathers"); To the Bishops and Members of the Annual Conference Assembled at Lebanon, Sept. 4, 1821, Methodist Episcopal Church Papers, folder 9; Bowes, *Exiles and Pioneers,* 162–164; Buss, "Politics of Indian Removal," in Beatty-Medina and Rinehart, eds., *Contested Territories,* 176.

nevolence offered people like McCoy an opportunity to repackage removal just as it was deployed with a new ferocity as a national project. Moreover, they discovered that benevolent removal worked just as well when they deployed it in Washington, D.C., or Ohio, or Indiana, or Georgia—no matter how different the histories and circumstances of African Americans and Native Americans were.[65]

Over time, extensive Native homelands in Ohio, Indiana, and Illinois were transformed into places of white freedom premised on the exclusion of African Americans. Missionary John Stewart and Bloody Eyes died within a few years of each other in 1823 and 1827. By that time, many white Ohioans did not see a place for either of them in the state. Native homelands and the free states changed around them. Though white writers and policymakers tried to write Native peoples and African Americans out of the history of the free states, they remained. Both men died on the precipice of the age of removal's most devastating effects. At the same time, a community of activists emerged to protest against removal on the national stage. By the late 1820s, in newspapers, petitions, pamphlets, and speeches, Native, white, and Black leaders opposed removal and colonization as racist projects to whiten the nation and destroy Native sovereignty. They argued that removal was not new. Americans carried out removal projects with greater rapidity after the War of 1812, and at great cost. But while the scale of those projects and the suffering they caused was anomalous, they built on ideas that had been implemented and debated for much longer.

65. Schultz, *An Indian Canaan,* 33; Guyatt, *Bind Us Apart,* 288–293. It made sense that McCoy linked these ideas—as Emily Conroy-Krutz has argued, missionaries saw the world as one field of labor and a "Christian empire." See Conroy-Krutz, *Christian Imperialism,* 30, 135–136, 207–208 (quotation).

CONCLUSION
The Power of Figuring

Let no man of us budge one step, and let slave-holders come to beat us from our country. America is more our country, than it is the whites—we have enriched it with our blood and tears. *The greatest riches in all America have arisen from our blood and tears:—and will they drive us from our property and homes, which we have earned with our* blood?
—*David Walker,* Walker's Appeal, in Four Articles, *1829*

I know it is easy to make calculations. I know it is an old maxim, that 'figures cannot lie': and I very well know, too, that our philanthropic arithmeticians are prodigiously fond of FIGURING, *but of doing nothing else. Give them a slate and pencil, and in fifteen minutes they will clear the continent of every black skin; and, if desired, throw in the Indians to boot. . . . O, the surpassing utility of the arithmetic! it is more potent than the stone of the philosopher, which,* when discovered, *is to transmute, at a touch, base metal into pure gold!*
— *William Lloyd Garrison,* Thoughts on African Colonization, *1832*

Assemble all nations together in your imagination, and then let the whites be seated among them. . . . Now suppose these skins were put together, and each skin had its national crimes written upon it—which skin do you think would have the greatest? I will ask one question more. Can you charge the Indians with robbing a nation almost of their whole continent, and murdering their women and children, and then depriving the remainder of their lawful rights, that nature and God require them to have? And to cap the climax, rob another nation to till their grounds and welter out their days under the lash with hunger and fatigue under the scorching rays of a burning sun? I should look at all the skins, and I know that when I cast my eye upon that white skin, and if I saw those crimes written upon it, I should enter my protest against it immediately and cleave to that which is more honorable."
— *William Apess, "An Indian's Looking Glass for the White Man," [1833]*

In his 1832 *Thoughts on Colonization,* white abolitionist William Lloyd Garrison considered the power of "FIGURING." Garrison asked his readers to picture the "philanthropic arithmeticians" with their slates and pencils. "In fifteen minutes they will clear the continent of every black skin; and, if desired, throw in the Indians to boot." This was "the surpassing utility of the arithmetic," he fiercely declared. Philanthropic arithmeticians proposed clearing the continent of Native Americans and African Americans, and they masked it as benevolence. The power of their "FIGURING" was dangerous no matter how unlikely it was that they might succeed. It had a profound effect on everyday life. Removal was an integral part of state law and national diplomacy. These calculations and schemes—what Black abolitionist David Walker called "the colonizing trick"—cast particular groups of people as living outside the body politic. They became a measure of belonging in a nation in which the rights of African Americans and Indigenous people were up for debate. Armed with new ideas about race and emboldened by manifest destiny, white Americans across all regions and religious and political persuasions questioned Indigenous sovereignty and Black citizenship. The schemes of philanthropic arithmeticians were calculations about the place of African Americans and Native Americans in the United States and in relationship to it.[1]

Observing these transformations in 1833, Pequot Methodist preacher and writer William Apess imagined arraying before him the nations of the world and writing their "national crimes" on their skins. Apess used writing as a metaphor to turn the figuring of philanthropic arithmeticians back on itself. The crimes of white Americans—dispossession and slavery—would be the figures in his account book. "I know that when I cast my eye upon that white skin, and if I saw those crimes written upon it, I should enter my protest against it immediately," he wrote.[2]

1. W[illia]m Lloyd Garrison, *Thoughts on African Colonization; or, An Impartial Exhibition of the Doctrines, Principles, and Purposes of the American Colonization Society; Together with the Resolutions, Addresses, and Remonstrances of the Free People of Color,* Part 1 (Boston, 1832), 155 ("FIGURING"); David Walker, *Walker's Appeal, in Four Articles, Together with a Preamble to the Colored Citizens of the World, but in Particular and Very Expressly to Those of the United States of America . . .* (Boston, 1829), 66 ("colonizing"); Susan M. Ryan, *The Grammar of Good Intentions: Race and the Antebellum Culture of Benevolence* (Ithaca, N. Y., 2003).

2. William Apess, "An Indian's Looking Glass for the White Man," [1833], in Barry O'Connell, ed., *On Our Own Ground: The Complete Writings of William Apess, a Pequot* (Amherst, Mass., 1992), 157 (quotations); Maureen Konkle, *Writing Indian Nations: Native Intellectuals and the Politics of Historiography, 1827–1863* (Chapel Hill, N.C., 2004), 115–119.

When Apess published his essay, removal had already begun to shape new political and reform movements across the United States. Removal was a long process that began in the early Republic, rather than a single moment in the 1830s. In important respects, however, the antebellum period did represent a decisive shift. African American and Native American activists used writing, petitioning, lobbying, and public meetings to protest colonization and Indian removal in ways that increasingly captured the attention of white Americans in the eastern United States. On the eve of the 1830s, Black abolitionists castigated colonization while claiming birthright citizenship. Their public fight against colonization galvanized activists from David Walker to New Haven minister Hosea Easton to New York's Reverend Peter Williams, Jr., and it fueled the Black convention movement. Cherokee leaders turned the subject of removal into a national debate by petitioning and lobbying the federal government, working with influential missionaries, and hiring lawyers to argue their cause before the Supreme Court. By the time that Garrison, Walker, and Apess wrote about removal in the early 1830s, it was already one of the most pressing problems of the era.[3]

Activists began to see removal as uniquely American in the 1830s because of the simultaneous rise of Indian removal and colonization. In 1824, President James Monroe had drawn up a plan to create a separate Indian territory west of the Mississippi River as a colony for all eastern Native peoples. He created the Office of Indian Affairs, which would oversee Indian removal at its peak in the 1830s. What James P. Ronda has called "the invention of Indian Territory" coincided with efforts by the states to support colonization as a national project. That same year, the American Colonization Society (ACS) asked the states to lobby the federal government on their behalf. The Ohio General Assembly obliged, proposing a constitutional amendment requiring both gradual emancipation and colonization. Eight northern and midwestern states submitted resolutions supporting Ohio's plan, while the southern states denounced it as an abolitionist cause. The ACS had become a sectional organization, but it nonetheless remained one of the most popular private associations in the United States.[4]

3. For the 1830s as an amplification of earlier policies, see Stuart Banner, *How the Indians Lost Their Land: Law and Power on the Frontier* (Cambridge, Mass., 2005), 191–192. For birthright citizenship, see Martha S. Jones, *Birthright Citizens: A History of Race and Rights in Antebellum America* (Cambridge, 2018); Christopher James Bonner, *Remaking the Republic: Black Politics and the Creation of American Citizenship* (Philadelphia, 2020).

4. James P. Ronda, "'We Have a Country': Race, Geography, and the Invention of

Removal garnered national attention by the 1830s because the Cherokee Nation was so effective in publicizing their fight to retain their tribal homelands against the incursions of the state of Georgia. In 1827, the Cherokees created a new constitution, an action to which Georgia responded by extending its sovereignty over the Cherokee Nation. When Andrew Jackson was elected president in 1828, southerners expected that he would expel the Cherokees from their territory, and Jackson did indeed move swiftly to propose a removal bill that gave him the power to move all eastern Native peoples beyond the Mississippi River. The lobbying of Cherokee leaders against Georgia's actions and the debate over Jackson's proposed bill made removal a national conversation.[5]

Jackson's proposal was not a wholly new idea, but it was a sweeping one, and it caused a public uproar largely along sectional lines. On one side were southerners and westerners who hid their own self-interest by arguing, like Jackson, that expulsion was actually a benevolent project of protection. Lewis Cass best represented this argument in a series of essays in the *North American Review* in which he explained that removal would protect Natives from their "utter recklessness of the future." On the other side were Cherokee leaders and their allies, particularly in the North, who touted Cherokee exceptionalism to argue for their right to remain. Principal chief John Ross emphasized his "civilized habits and feelings" and his work to "cement the interests of the Cherokee Nation with those of the U. States." Cherokee delegations lobbied federal officials to uphold their treaty obligations, as William Shorey Coodey, Ross's nephew, did in 1830. Coodey observed that Georgia persisted in trying to take Cherokee lands because of Jackson's encouragement. "Because we love our country they treat us with contempt and call us savages," he wrote of Georgians. The Cherokee cause was championed by the American Board of Commissioners for Foreign Missions secretary Jeremiah Evarts, Catherine Beecher, and the members of other religious and benevolent societies, particularly women, who waged a public opinion campaign across the Northeast on their behalf.

Indian Territory," *Journal of the Early Republic,* XIX (1999), 742–743, 755; James Monroe, "Extinguishment of Indian Title to Lands in Georgia; Communicated to the House of Representatives, April 2, 1824," Mar. 30, 1824, in *ASPIA,* II, 460; Daniel Walker Howe, *What Hath God Wrought: The Transformation of America, 1815–1848* (Oxford, 2007), 265; Lacy K. Ford, *Deliver Us from Evil: The Slavery Question in the Old South* (Oxford, 2009), 302–328; Nicholas Guyatt, "'The Outskirts of Our Happiness': Race and the Lure of Colonization in the Early Republic," *Journal of American History,* XCV (2009), 997–998.

5. Theda Perdue and Michael D. Green, *The Cherokee Nation and the Trail of Tears* (New York, 2008), 42–68; Banner, *How the Indians Lost Their Land,* 201.

In 1829, Evarts published a series of articles in the *National Intelligencer* under the name of William Penn that defended Cherokee sovereignty. The essays fueled congressional debates over Jackson's removal bill. At Evarts's prompting, Beecher and other activists in Hartford, Connecticut, organized a public petition campaign in 1829 that reached seven northern states and sent hundreds of petitions to Congress against the Indian removal bill.[6]

Activists mounted a strong defense of Indian rights—a catchall term that described Cherokee rights to self-government and sovereignty as well as the civil rights they might lose under Georgia's jurisdiction. If Cherokee leaders needed an example of how Georgia's actions would take away their rights, they needed to look no further than to their free African American neighbors. As one writer argued, "The jurisdiction of Georgia is one thing to the whites; but another and an opposite thing to all of a different complexion." For white men, Georgia's law secured them equality and freedom, but for Indigenous people, Georgia's law "degrades him, from the rank of a freeman, to the level of a disfranchised mulatto and negro." To be under Georgia's jurisdiction also meant being subject to the state's racialized citizenship, which already denied rights to free African Americans.[7]

The Indian Removal Act, passed on May 28, 1830, provided the impetus for the eventual exile of forty-six thousand eastern Indigenous people from their lands over the next decade. Meanwhile, in *Worcester v. Georgia* (1832), the Supreme Court confirmed Cherokee sovereignty. Georgia refused to follow the ruling and carried out a land lottery that distributed

6. [Lewis Cass], "Documents and Proceedings relating to the Formation and Progress of a Board in the City of New York, for the Emigration, Preservation, and Improvement of the Aborigines of America, July 22, 1829," *North American Review* [Boston], January 1830, 65 ("utter"); John Ross to Jeremiah Evarts, Apr. 6, 1830, Jeremiah Evarts Family Papers, YUA ("civilized"), William S. Coodey to Evarts, Oct. 23, 1830 ("Because"); William G. McLoughlin, *Cherokee Renascence in the New Republic* (Princeton, N.J., 1986), 434–436; Ronda, "'We Have a Country,'" *Journal of the Early Republic*, XIX (1999), 744; Banner, *How the Indians Lost Their Land*, 198–214. On the petition campaign, see [Catherine E. Beecher et al.], "Circular: Addressed to Benevolent Ladies of the U. States," *Christian Advocate and Journal and Zion's Herald* (New York), Dec. 25, 1829, 65–66; Mary Hershberger, "Mobilizing Women, Anticipating Abolition: The Struggle against Indian Removal in the 1830s," *Journal of American History*, LXXXVI (1999), 15–40; Alisse Theodore, "'A Right to Speak on the Subject': The U.S. Women's Antiremoval Petition Campaign, 1829–1831," *Rhetoric and Public Affairs*, V (2002), 601–623. For an important rejoinder, see Tiya Miles, "'Circular Reasoning': Recentering Cherokee Women in the Antiremoval Campaigns," *American Quarterly*, LXI (2009), 221–243.

7. *Relations between the Cherokees and the Government of the United States* (n.p., [1829]), 13.

Cherokee lands. Facing such brazen theft, one group of dissenters split off from the Cherokee national council and agreed to removal. At the Treaty of New Echota in Georgia in 1835, the dissenters sold Cherokee homelands in exchange for five million dollars and the promise to move West. In summer 1838, U.S. soldiers gathered Cherokee families into stockades at gunpoint. In a series of forced marches, federal contractors forced fourteen thousand people to leave Cherokee lands for Oklahoma. Four thousand people died during the journey of disease, malnutrition, and a lack of supplies.[8]

African American leaders who pressed for Black citizenship and emancipation increasingly saw their criticisms of colonization as parallel to the debate over Cherokee removal. Black abolitionist societies like the Baltimore Society to Protect Free People and Boston's General Colored Association formed strong political coalitions in the fight to abolish slavery and protect free Black rights. Black leaders had access to new outlets for putting their objections to colonization into print. *Freedom's Journal,* the first African American newspaper, published by editor Samuel Cornish in 1827, became a forum for anticolonization ideas, as did his subsequent newspaper *Rights of All.* Cornish's coeditor John Russworm cast his support behind the ACS, but he faced widespread condemnation for that position—a sign of how uncommon it was at the time. Richard Allen used the pages of *Freedom's Journal* to decry the idea that African Americans, who had "*tilled* the ground and made fortunes for thousands," were yet labeled as outsiders. Allen wrote that "this land which we have watered with our *tears* and *our blood,* is now our *mother country.*" He was joined by Philadelphian James Forten, Baltimorean William Watkins, and a range of pseudonymous writers who denounced the idea that the ACS was a benevolent organization. Rather, as Easton proclaimed to a Providence meeting, "the *Colonizing Craft*" was "a diabolical pursuit."[9]

8. Francis Paul Prucha, *The Great Father: The United States Government and the American Indians,* abridged ed. (Lincoln, Nebr., 1984), 77; McLoughlin, *Cherokee Renascence,* 436–451; Perdue and Green, *Cherokee Nation and the Trail of Tears,* 86–89, 91–115, 123–140.

9. "Letter from Bishop Allen," *Freedom's Journal* (New York), Nov. 2, 1827, 134, quoted in Walker, *Walker's Appeal,* 57 *("tilled");* Hosea Easton, "An Address: Delivered before the Coloured Population, of Providence, Rhode Island, on Thanksgiving Day, Nov. 27, 1828," in George R. Price and James Brewer Stewart, eds., *To Heal the Scourge of Prejudice: The Life and Writings of Hosea Easton* (Amherst, Mass., 1999), 58 *("Colonizing");* Stephen Kantrowitz, *More Than Freedom: Fighting for Black Citizenship in a White Republic, 1829–1889* (New York, 2012), 24; Manisha Sinha, *The Slave's Cause: A History of Abolition* (New Haven, Conn., 2016), 201–205.

Allen's claim to the power to remain *because* of the theft of slavery rather than *despite* it became a trope of anticolonization writing. Reverend Williams, rector of New York's St. Philip's Church, for example, argued in his 1830 Fourth of July speech that "we are natives of this country. . . . We have toiled to cultivate it, and to raise it to its present prosperous condition." Like Allen and Williams, anticolonization writers made a claim to the United States as their "native country" and protested their "banishment" from it. By 1829, when free Black Bostonian and abolitionist Walker sat down to pen his *Appeal . . . to the Coloured Citizens of the World,* he might have seen the pamphlet as a culmination of anticolonization protest. Walker declared that "America is more our country, than it is the whites—we have enriched it with our *blood and tears* . . . will they drive us from our property and homes, which we have earned with our *blood?*" His appeal to "coloured citizens" was part of a new emphasis on birthright citizenship among Black abolitionists. The term called attention to the tension inherent in the idea that citizenship could be qualified.[10]

African American protest against colonization took on such urgency because of the extralegal violence of white mobs—and anti-Black riots in Cincinnati, Ohio, in 1829, in particular. The riots began with removal policy. In Cincinnati in March 1829, the overseers of the poor announced their intention to uphold the letter of Ohio's 1807 restrictive migration law. In August, white rioters burned Black homes and businesses, forcing as many as fifteen hundred Black Cincinnatians to flee the city. Several hundred of the émigrés went to Canada that fall, where they founded the upper Canadian colony of Wilberforce in 1830. Black-led alternatives to Liberian emigration abounded in the 1820s. Many Black writers championed Haitian emigration in the mid-1820s after Haitian president Jean Pierre Boyer promised American émigrés tools, land grants, and civil rights if they settled there. Six thousand people went to Haiti after Reverend Loring D. Dewy of New York and Jonathas Granville toured the Northeast and mid-Atlantic to sell the plan in 1824. Within two years, one-third of the emigrants returned dis-

10. Peter Williams, *A Discourse Delivered in St. Philip's Church, for the Benefit of the Coloured Community of Wilberforce, in Upper Canada, on the Fourth of July, 1830* (New York, 1830), reprinted in Dorothy B. Porter, ed., *Early Negro Writing, 1760–1837* (Boston, 1971), 297 ("we are natives"); "Speech of Nathaniel Paul Delivered at the Anti-Colonization Meeting: London, 1833," in Porter, *Early Negro Writing,* 288 ("native"); Henry Foster and Paul Drayton, "A Voice from Hartford," July 14, 1831, in Garrison, *Thoughts on African Colonization,* part 2, 29 ("banishment"); Walker, *Walker's Appeal,* 64 ("America"); Kantrowitz, *More Than Freedom,* 14, 33–40; Sinha, *Slave's Cause,* 205–207; Jones, *Birthright Citizens.*

enchanted. Altogether, far more émigrés went to Canada than ever traveled to Liberia under the auspices of the ACS or to Haiti.[11]

Anticolonization organizing and Canadian emigration fueled the Black convention movement. A call for a national Black political convention was first printed in *Freedom's Journal* in 1827, and it was repeated by Baltimorian Hezekiah Grice after the Cincinnati riots. In September 1830, Philadelphia hosted the first annual meeting of a national convention of free Black delegates from across the nation. The conventions, which met continuously until 1835 and then sporadically through the Civil War, embraced Canadian emigration while denouncing the ACS. African American commentators saw the Wilberforce colony and other Black-led emigration schemes as categorically different from Liberian colonization. Peter Williams, for example, judged Liberia to be a settler-colonial project that would cause the "ruin" of West Africans just as settler colonialism had done to Natives in North America.[12]

Williams's comparison of Liberian colonization to dispossession in Native North America was purposeful. African Americans who had long opposed the ACS hoped that the popularity of the Cherokee cause would also convince white antislavery activists to abandon colonization. In the conventions and in the press, they explicitly connected Indian removal and colonization to critique white supremacy. Activists at New York's 1831 convention urged white northeasterners aligned against Jackson's Indian policy to consider both causes as one and the same. "Finally, we hope that those who have so eloquently pleaded the cause of the Indian, will at least endeavor to preserve consistency in their conduct," they wrote. Anticolonization activists found an ally in white abolitionist William Lloyd Garrison. Black abolitionists William Watkins and Jacob Greener had begun working with Garrison while he was editing the antislavery newspaper the *Genius of Universal Emancipation* in Baltimore in 1829. Watkins and Greener convinced Garrison to take a definitive stance against the ACS. Garrison's subsequent

11. Nikki M. Taylor, *Frontiers of Freedom: Cincinnati's Black Community, 1802–1868* (Athens, Ohio, 2005), 51–79; Howe, *What Hath God Wrought*, 266; Ada Ferrer, "Haiti, Free Soil, and Antislavery in the Revolutionary Atlantic," *American Historical Review*, CXVII (2012), 40–66; Sara Fanning, *Caribbean Crossing: African Americans and the Haitian Emigration Movement* (New York, 2015); Sinha, *Slave's Cause*, 207–208.

12. Williams, *A Discourse Delivered in St. Philip's Church*, reprinted in Porter, ed., *Early Negro Writing*, 297 (quotation); Garrison, *Thoughts on African Colonization*, part 2, 5; Sinha, *Slave's Cause*, 208–210.

Thoughts on African Colonization denounced both Cherokee removal and Liberian colonization in fiery terms.[13]

White activists influenced by Garrison's *Thoughts on African Colonization* soon joined him in taking up these connections between the expulsion of Indigenous people and African Americans. By the 1830s, some white abolitionists who had thrown themselves into the campaign for Cherokee rights believed they could no longer justify their support for African colonization. Elizur Wright read *Thoughts on African Colonization* and realized that he had been mistaken in citing white prejudice as a reason for supporting colonization rather than attacking racism itself. He and James Birney abandoned the ACS after the Cherokee debates. Kentucky activist Daniel Parker worked for the ACS until he had a revelation that it was a proslavery organization aimed at "getting rid of colored people merely." Arthur and Lewis Tappan, Gerrit Smith, Samuel J. May, Theodore Weld, and Joshua Leavitt all supported the ACS in the 1820s before abandoning it in the 1830s. Ohio Quaker Benjamin Ladd became convinced restrictive migration laws were just as pernicious in forcing free African Americans out of individual states as "the gradual steps which have led to this result in the case of the poor Indians." African American activists, however, were never able to generate the same sea change of white opposition to colonization that the Cherokees had to Indian removal. Most white activists who spoke out against the expulsion of Indigenous people did not abandon colonization. Abolitionists grew frustrated by the staying power of anti-Black racism. Many of the fiercest defenders of Indian rights—Daniel Webster, Lydia Sigourney, Henry Clay, Theodore Frelinghuysen, and Edward Everett—remained committed to the ACS, to the great condemnation of their abolitionist peers.[14]

Conversations about removal in the eastern press foregrounded the Cherokee Nation and the ACS, masking how removal was carried out throughout the rest of the United States, particularly in the middle states. Although the

13. *Resolutions of the People of Color, at a Meeting Held on the 25th of January, 1831; With an Address to the Citizens of New-York, in Answer to Those of the New-York Colonization Society* (New York, 1831), 8 (quotation); Sinha, *Slave's Cause,* 215–216.

14. "Daniel Parker's Autobiography," Daniel Parker Papers, 50, OHC ("getting rid"); Benjamin Ladd to Nathaniel Crenshaw, Mar. 15, 1832, Brock Collection, box 15, folder 6, HL ("gradual"); Elizur Wright to Henry Cowles, Feb. 5, 1833, OHC; Natalie Joy, "The Indian's Cause: Abolitionists and Native American Rights," *Journal of the Civil War Era,* special issue, *The Future of Abolition Studies,* VIII (2018), 216–226.

Cherokees started a national debate about their rights, northern Indian removal received comparatively little widespread attention. The 1830s were also a removal era for Native peoples north of the Ohio River. Georgia's actions ignited a flurry of activity across midwestern governments. After Georgia extended state sovereignty over the Cherokee Nation, other state governors and legislators did likewise, or considered doing the same. Governor James Brown Ray of Indiana recommended that Indiana divide the "national property" of Native people "into individual rights" and extend Indiana law over their lands. Ray and the Indiana General Assembly aggressively pursued Miami and Potawatomi lands. In 1826 and 1828, Miamis and Potawatomis had agreed to sell three hundred million acres of land and to run the Wabash canal through Miami territory. Still unsatisfied, the Indiana Assembly petitioned Congress six times from 1829 to 1831 for Miami and Potawatomi expulsion.[15]

Ohio also took action to dissolve Shawnee, Seneca, and Wyandot reserves. Although Ohio's governor and the Ohio Supreme Court determined that the legislature did not have the authority to follow Georgia in abrogating Native sovereignty, Ohioans threatened to do so nonetheless. Shawnees and Senecas remained on reserves at Lewiston, Hog Creek, and Wapakoneta until 1831, when they agreed to exchange their Ohio lands for those in Kansas. Black Hoof, who had so steadfastly defended Shawnee lands at Wapakoneta, refused to sign the treaty, and he died on the eve of Shawnee expulsion. Wyandots on the Grand Reserve, a 150,000-acre portion of their homelands in central Ohio, strategized to remain by subdividing their common lands into private plots. They employed missionaries as a defense against Ohioans, who began to insist that state laws applied in Wyandot country and confiscated their property and cattle as payment for debts. The Wyandots held onto the Grand Reserve until 1843, when they were forced to leave.[16]

15. James B. Ray, "Message to the General Assembly," Dec. 8, 1829, in Dorothy Riker and Gayle Thornbrough, eds., *Messages and Papers relating to the Administration of James Brown Ray Governor of Indiana, 1825–1831* (Indianapolis, Ind., 1954), 473 (quotations), Ray to [John Quincy Adams], Nov. 25, 1825, 57, Ray, "Message to the General Assembly," Dec. 7, 1830, 570–571; "Indian Affairs—Miamis," Jan. 14, 1830, in Logan Esarey, ed., *Governors Messages and Letters: Messages and Papers of Jonathan Jennings, Ratliff Boon, William Hendricks,* III, *1816–1825* (Indianapolis, Ind., 1924), 406–407; Stewart Rafert, *The Miami Indians of Indiana: A Persistent People, 1654–1994* ([Indianapolis, Ind.], 1996), 95. For northern removal, see John P. Bowes, *Land Too Good for Indians: Northern Indian Removal* (Norman, Okla., 2016).

16. James B. Finley, *History of the Wyandott Mission, at Upper Sandusky, Ohio, under the Direction of the Methodist Episcopal Church* (Cincinnati, Ohio, 1840), 274, 299, 300–301; R. David Edmunds, "Forgotten Allies: The Loyal Shawnees and the War

Wyandot, Miami, and Potawatomi leaders were able to control some of the terms of expulsion by sending exploring parties out to visit western lands. Several groups traveled west with federal funds to examine lands chosen by Indian agents. They were roundly disappointed by what they found. Wyandot William Walker, Jr., took charge of one of these parties in the 1830s. After his return, he led efforts to protest removal over the next ten years. Miami leaders sent small exploring parties to visit western lands in 1838 and 1845. The six chiefs who went returned even more determined not to be dispossessed of their eastern lands. Others migrated on their own terms. When Potawatomi leaders agreed to go to the Missouri River, some left their Indiana, Michigan, Wisconsin, and Illinois lands between 1834 and 1840 in more than a dozen separate journeys overseen by federal contractors. Other Potawatomis moved to upper Canada, Kansas, Michigan, and Wisconsin outside of federally controlled forced marches. They left in the family and clan groups that had long structured Potawatomi migration.[17]

Those who failed to appear at federal collection points were arrested by traders or the military. Potawatomi headman Menominee refused to leave after his reserve was sold from under his feet in 1836. Local militia arrested Menominee at gunpoint and forced the inhabitants of his reserve to prepare to march overland to Kansas. They formed a long line that stretched for several miles. Forty people died on Menominee's forced march west. Miamis in Indiana similarly refused to leave, holding on to private reserves that allowed them to keep a foothold in their homelands. The Miamis were expelled in 1846–1847, after they were forced to a collection point by a small military unit and the Miami subagent threatened to take away their government annuities if they did not leave. Federal officials hired a local trader to track down those who had eluded the government contractor.[18]

Those who were expelled west by federal contractors suffered greatly on their journeys, beset by poor weather, disease, and federal mismanagement.

---

of 1812," in David Curtis Skaggs and Larry L. Nelson, eds., *The Sixty Years' War for the Great Lakes, 1754–1814* (East Lansing, Mich., 2001), 347; Sami Lakomäki, *Gathering Together: The Shawnee People through Diaspora and Nationhood, 1600–1870* (New Haven, Conn., 2014), 163.

17. R. David Edmunds, *The Potawatomis: Keepers of the Fire* (Norman, Okla., 1978), 268; Bert Anson, *The Miami Indians* (Norman, Okla., 1970), 200; Rafert, *Miami Indians of Indiana,* 108–110; James A. Clifton, *The Prairie People: Continuity and Change in Potawatomi Indian Culture, 1665–1965,* expanded ed. (Iowa City, Iowa, 1998), 290–294; James Joseph Buss, *Winning the West with Words: Language and Conquest in the Lower Great Lakes* (Norman, Okla., 2011), 74–92.

18. Edmunds, *Potawatomis,* 265–268; Rafert, *Miami Indians of Indiana,* 111–112; Clifton, *Prairie People,* 298–300; Bowes, *Land Too Good for Indians,* 76, 169–170.

William Polke conducted a party of 859 Potawatomis to Missouri in 1838. When the group arrived at the Osage River that winter, the houses that were supposed to be prepared for them were not yet completed. They were shocked by the "desert" they found there. Meanwhile, traders and contractors capitalized on their suffering. Expulsion was a lucrative business, and federal removal contracts often passed between multiple hands. Traders provided goods to the federal government to supply removal treaties at inflated prices. They speculated on those treaties, selling goods on credit to Indigenous people with the understanding that the federal government's purchase price for Native land would include the assumption of their debts. Debts served as currency north of the Ohio River, backed by the federal government with all the certainty of the state's desire for Indigenous dispossession.[19]

Other Ohioans and Indianans celebrated these journeys, alternately mourning the end of a frontier era and lauding the so-called progress that expulsion represented to them. Despite the supposed erasure of a Native presence in the North, however, Indigenous people remained there long after the 1840s. Some Wyandots stayed at Upper Sandusky. Others left for Kansas only to return years later. Upward of one thousand Potawatomis in Michigan and Wisconsin never left, and they were joined by Potawatomi émigrés who moved from the Indiana-Michigan border and returnees who journeyed back from Kansas and Iowa. Potawatomi Leopold Pokagon secured his town in southern Michigan by cultivating ties to Baptist missionary Isaac McCoy and local Catholic priests. In Indiana, Potawatomi chief Stephen Benack capitalized on his relationships with white traders and neighbors. They intervened with Indian agent John Tipton to secure Benack's right to remain on his family's allotment in Indiana even after the rest of his settlement was expelled. Miami elites Francis Godfroy and Jean Baptiste de Richardville also used the treaties of the 1830s to secure private reserves in their names that allowed them to remain in Indiana even after most Miamis were forced to leave in 1846–1847. When the Miamis signed a removal treaty in 1838, one-third were exempted from removal, including members of the Meshingomesia, Slocum, Godfroy, and Richardville-Lafontaine families. Richardville and Godfroy's reserves became refuges for those who stayed.[20]

19. William Polke to unnamed recipient, Nov. 14, 1838, William Polke Papers, folder 4, ISL (quotation), George W. Proffit, Journal of Emigration of Potawatomis, 1837. For examples of debt trading like currency, see Daniel Bearss Collection, ISL.

20. Anson, *Miami Indians,* 207–209, 226; John J. Vogel, *Indians of Ohio and Wyandot County* (New York, 1975), 67; Clifton, *Prairie People,* 280–282, 301; Rafert, *Miami*

Colonization had a more diffuse history in the middle states beyond the ACS as well. The ACS never became the national organization its founders had imagined, in part because fundraising fell to state auxiliaries. Jackson ended federal funding for the ACS in 1830. Still, support for colonization persisted in different forms in the various states. In Virginia, after Nat Turner's Rebellion in Southampton County in August 1831, slavery and colonization became, in the words of one observer, "the principal topic of fireside discussion." Virginia governor John Floyd blamed free African Americans for the rebellion, and he hoped "absolutely to drive from this State all free negroes." In the Virginia General Assembly, moderates and conservatives united to pass a colonization bill that appropriated eighteen thousand dollars annually to send free Black Virginians to Liberia.[21]

Across the middle states, white Americans reacted to Nat Turner's Rebellion by turning to colonization and exclusion. In Delaware, petitioners wrote to the legislature demanding more legislation to limit Black migration into the state. Colonization thrived in Kentucky, where white Kentuckians formed thirty-one ACS auxiliaries by 1831. The Maryland legislature was inundated with petitions asking for colonization. In response, the legislature set aside two hundred thousand dollars over twenty years to pay for it. Most of the funds were channeled through the Maryland Colonization Society, founded in 1831, which began its own colony just south of Liberia. In Pennsylvania, colonization found supporters among the Quaker Pennsylvania Yearly Meeting and the newly formed Pennsylvania Colonization Society. In Ohio, Indiana, and Illinois, anti-Black racism and colonization also went hand in hand. The Ohio Assembly endorsed a virulently racist report on colonization in 1832 in the wake of the Cincinnati riots. In Indiana,

Indians of Indiana, 99–100; Mark R. Shurr, "Archaeological Indices of Resistance: Diversity in the Removal Period Potawatomi of the Western Great Lakes," *American Antiquity,* LXXV (2010), 45–48; Bowes, *Land Too Good for Indians,* 72–75; "Township No. 27 N, Range No. 4 E 2nd Mer.," Miami National Reserve Maps, ISL. For the fiction of erasure, see Jean M. O'Brien, *Firsting and Lasting: Writing Indians out of Existence in New England* (Minneapolis, Minn., 2010).

21. John S. Brooks to Alexander St. C. Boys, Mar. 5, 1832, Alexander S. Boys Papers, box 1, folder 1, OHC ("principal"); John Floyd to James Hamilton, Jr., Nov. 19, 1831, in Henry Irving Tragle, *The Southampton Slave Revolt of 1831: A Compilation of Source Material* (Amherst, Mass., 1971), 275–276 ("absolutely," 276); Alison Goodyear Freehling, *Drift toward Dissolution: The Virginia Slavery Debate of 1831–1832* (Baton Rouge, La., 1982), 177–189; Ford, *Deliver Us from Evil,* 361–378; David F. Ericson, "The American Colonization Society's Not-So-Private Colonization Project," in Beverly C. Tomek and Matthew J. Hetrick, eds., *New Directions in the Study of African American Recolonization* (Gainesville, Fla., 2017), 113–116.

both the governor and the legislature publicly supported federal aid for the ACS. Meanwhile, a flurry of new measures limited free Black settlement in Indiana in 1831 and in Illinois in 1848. Indiana followed with a provision in the state's 1851 constitution that fined Black migrants for crossing state borders and put the funds raised toward colonization.[22]

Although restrictive migration and settlement laws were rarely enforced by individual states, extralegal violence and community pressure took their place. In the 1850s, anti-Black rioters expelled the Snelling settlement, begun by free Black Kentuckian Joseph Snelling in 1822 in Decatur County, Indiana. In Madison, Indiana, one Black family reported that they were "pestered and plagued by the whites with offers, and all sorts of inducement" to leave their farms for Liberia. One woman exclaimed that she and her husband "were almost tired out, and the poor man could not sleep of a night for thinking of his family, and what was to become of them." Despite the persistence of African American and Native communities, removal shaped Ohio, Indiana, and Illinois into places that were devoted to white freedom—nineteenth-century exclusions that had remarkable staying power.[23]

The removal era continued long after the 1830s. White migrants pressed for the right to settle on and to purchase Native lands. To facilitate expulsion, Congress rescinded Native American treaty rights in 1871. A decade later, the 1887 General Allotment Act parceled out plots of reserved tribal lands to individuals, appropriating millions of acres of "'surplus' lands" for white

22. For Kentucky, see Ford, *Deliver Us from Evil,* 384–389. For Maryland, see Penelope Campbell, *Maryland in Africa: The Maryland State Colonization Society, 1831–1857* (Urbana, Ill., 1971). For Pennsylvania, see Beverly C. Tomek, *Colonization and Its Discontents: Emancipation, Emigration, and Antislavery in Antebellum Pennsylvania* (New York, 2011), 43–62. For Ohio, see Frank U. Quillin, *The Color Line in Ohio: A History of Race Prejudice in a Typical Northern State* (Ann Arbor, Mich., 1913), 30. For Indiana and Illinois, see Emma Lou Thornbrough, *The Negro in Indiana before 1900: A Study of a Minority* (Bloomington, Ind., 1993), 57–58, 75; Ray, "Message to the General Assembly," Dec. 8, 1829, in Riker and Thornbrough, eds., *Messages and Papers,* 469–471; Illinois Const. of 1848, art. XIV; Jerome B. Meites, "The 1847 Illinois Constitutional Convention and Persons of Color," *Journal of the Illinois State Historical Society,* CVIII (2015–2016), 284; Indiana Const. of 1851, art. XIII.

23. E[dward] S. Abdy, *Journal of a Residence and Tour in the United States of North America, from April, 1833, to October, 1834,* II (London, 1835), 365 (quotations); Decatur County, box 12, folder 17, Indiana Early African American Settlement Heritage Initiative Collection, IHS; Xenia E. Cord, "Free Black Rural Communities in Indiana: A Selected Annotated Bibliography, 1982," submitted in partial fulfillment of the requirements for A500 (Dec. 7, 1982), iv–v.

purchasers in the process. These policies were not inevitable, but the dismissal of alternative proposals demonstrates the persistence of removal well beyond the early national period.[24]

Colonization continued to be emancipation's corollary. In the midst of the Civil War, President Abraham Lincoln was a ready advocate. He championed federally compensated emancipation accompanied by colonization in December 1861 as he tried to keep slaveholding border states in the union. Washington, D.C., passed legislation setting aside funds for colonization. The Second Confiscation Act of 1862 authorized the president to do the same. Through 1862, Lincoln explored possible colonies in the Chiriqui region of New Grenada, Haiti, Texas, and Florida. His preliminary Emancipation Proclamation of 1862 confirmed his support for voluntary colonization, and the day before he signed the Emancipation Proclamation into law in 1863, he endorsed a federally funded contract to colonize five thousand freed people on Île-à-Vache off the coast of Haiti. Lincoln eventually abandoned colonization, but the ACS outlasted the Civil War. African Americans left for Liberia under its auspices throughout the 1890s.[25]

During the Civil War and Reconstruction, southern legislatures echoed earlier restrictive emigration laws as they sought to reinstate white supremacy after emancipation. The Union Army imposed restrictions on the labor mobility of freed people across the occupied South, from Mississippi Valley cotton fields to Louisiana sugar plantations. Immediately after the Civil War, the southern states passed a series of Black codes that made any Black person liable to arrest if they could not produce a labor contract. Southern Republicans eventually repealed coercive labor codes, but northern states simultaneously passed their own vagrancy laws to punish dependency and restrict mobility.[26]

State-level immigration regulations were built on early national precedents as well. Before the Civil War, states had the ability to control the entry of immigrants, and Northern states had used the poor laws as models for deporting and restricting the entry of foreign paupers into their states just as

24. C. Joseph Genetin-Pilawa, *Crooked Paths to Allotment: The Fight over Federal Indian Policy after the Civil War* (Chapel Hill, N.C., 2012), 150.

25. Daniel Kanstroom, *Deportation Nation: Outsiders in American History* (Cambridge, Mass., 2007), 87–90; Eric Burin, *Slavery and the Peculiar Solution: A History of the American Colonization Society* (Gainesville, Fla., 2008) 163–166.

26. Eric Foner, *Reconstruction: America's Unfinished Revolution, 1863–1877* (New York, 1988), 50–60, 198–205, 372, 519; Amy Dru Stanley, *From Bondage to Contract: Wage Labor, Marriage, and the Market in the Era of Slave Emancipation* (Cambridge, 1998), 98–137.

they did African Americans. Western states used these tactics against Chinese immigrants who arrived during the 1849 California Gold Rush and after the Civil War, copying restrictive laws that the middle states used to target free African Americans and applying them to Chinese immigrants. In 1879, the new California Constitution authorized the state and local governments to remove Chinese immigrants at their discretion.[27]

The late-nineteenth-century deportation regime in the United States originated from very different legal precedents, but it resonated with older histories of removal. After the Civil War, the courts turned decisively toward federal rather than state control over immigration. With the 1882 Chinese Exclusion Act, Congress prohibited the entry of Chinese laborers into the United States for ten years and extended that prohibition in 1888. When the Supreme Court ruled on exclusion in *Chae Chan Ping v. United States* (1889), the justices laid out the "plenary power" doctrine that still guides immigration policy today: that, in the absence of specific directives in the Constitution, full and absolute power to regulate immigration extends de facto to Congress and the executive branch as a matter of national security. Armed with the plenary power doctrine, Congress also asserted its right to deport those who entered in contradiction to these restrictions. Daniel Kanstroom argues that colonization and earlier fugitive slave laws served as the "conceptual matrices" for deportation after the Civil War. During the debate over the 1892 Geary Act, for example, which required Chinese immigrants to carry registration certificates or face deportation, one senator held up Indian removal as a precedent. There were clear differences between deportation in the late nineteenth century and removal efforts in the early Republic, but that did not stop congressmen from looking to earlier histories to understand their present.[28]

Removal was rooted in the early days of the U.S. Republic. It drew what Barbara Welke has called the "borders of belonging" as the state sought to identify and name its citizens. Indigenous people and African Ameri-

27. Kanstroom, *Deportation Nation,* 95–108. See also Kunal M. Parker, *Making Foreigners: Immigration and Citizenship Law in America, 1600–2000* (New York, 2015), 81–115; Hidetaka Hirota, *Expelling the Poor: Atlantic Seaboard States and the Nineteenth-Century Origins of American Immigration Policy* (New York, 2017).

28. Chae Chan Ping v. United States, 130 U.S. 581 (1889); Natsu Taylor Saito, "The Enduring Effect of the Chinese Exclusion Cases: The 'Plenary Power' Justification for On-Going Abuses of Human Rights," *Asian Law Journal,* X (2003), 13–16; Kanstroom, *Deportation Nation,* 90 ("conceptual"), 93, 113–122; Beth Lew-Williams, *The Chinese Must Go: Violence, Exclusion, and the Making of the Alien in America* (Cambridge, Mass., 2018), 188–193; George Anthony Peffer, *If They Don't Bring Their Women Here: Chinese Female Immigration before Exclusion* (Urbana, Ill., 1999), 32–37, 115–117.

cans were subject to removal while white male citizenship took shape in the shadow of their experiences. Black abolitionist Sarah Forten Purvis wrote in 1837 that African American colonization was motivated by "the longing desire of a separation" on the part of white Americans. She believed that for African Americans, "The spirit of 'this is not your Country' is made manifest by the many obstacles it throws in the way of their advancement mentally and morally. No doubt but there has always existed the same amount of prejudice in the minds of Americans towards the descendants of Africa; it wanted only the spirit of colonization to call it into action." Removal was and continues to be, in Purvis's words, "the offspring of Prejudice." Today, exclusion is still used as a thinly veiled tool of prejudice, wanting only the law to call it into action. Central to state making long before the United States existed, removal has been part of the fabric of the nation since its inception.[29]

29. Barbara Young Welke, *Law and the Borders of Belonging in the Long Nineteenth Century United States* (New York, 2010); Sarah Forten to Angelina Grimké, Apr. 15, 1837, in Gilbert H. Barnes and Dwight L. Dumond, eds., *Letters of Theodore Dwight Weld, Angelina Grimké Weld, and Sarah Grimké, 1822–1844,* I (Gloucester, Mass., 1965), 380 ("longing"); Linda K. Kerber, "The Stateless as the Citizen's Other: A View from the United States," *American Historical Review,* CXII (2007), 15–18.

ACKNOWLEDGMENTS

I am glad to finally be able to acknowledge the many people who have made this book possible. I first began this project as a dissertation with guidance from the extraordinary faculty in the Department of History at New York University. I was lucky to be able to work with Martha Hodes, who encouraged me to choose my own path but was ready with precise feedback and criticism when I needed it. I am deeply grateful for her advice, and I am a better writer for her efforts. Nicole Eustace and Jennifer Morgan have been the most generous mentors. I am still striving to emulate their integrity and meticulous scholarship. Maria Montoya's support and wisdom got me through graduate school. Karen Kupperman, Andrew Needham, and David Waldstreicher stepped in to provide feedback on the dissertation along the way. At Brown University, Michael Vorenberg, Seth Rockman, Jim Egan, and Elliott Gorn showed me how to be a scholar while I was just starting out. How privileged I am to have learned from each one of them.

At New York University, friends and colleagues shaped my understanding of the past and present more than they know. The members of my graduate school writing group, Laura Helton, Justin Leroy, Max Mishler, and Shauna Sweeney, read pieces of this book over the years. They continue to stretch my thinking on this project and on many other things. Their example is all over these pages. Thank you to Natalie Blum-Ross, Eric Owens, Peter Wirzbicki, Meg Rooney, Mairin Odle, Ebony Jones, David Klassen, Boyda Johnstone, Christy Thornton, Stuart Schrader, Daniel Rodriguez, Susan Rohwer, Reynolds Richter, Alex Manevitz, Tyesha Maddox, Kate Mulry, Larissa Kopytoff, Greg Childs, Tom Fleischman, Beatrice Wayne, Aaron Jakes, Anelise Shrout, Gabriel de Avilez Rocha, Katy Walker, Devin Jacob, Hayley Negrin, and the members of the Atlantic History Workshop for their wisdom. Their commitment to the world beyond themselves continues to inspire me.

I have been fortunate to work with Catherine Kelly at the Omohundro Institute. She helped shape this book with a firm guiding hand and brilliant advice. I am grateful to her and to Nadine Zimmerli for seeing promise in the manuscript early on. Kaylan Stevenson provided patient, expert copy editing that improved my prose. Kathleen DuVal and an anonymous reader for the press gave critical feedback on the whole manuscript that pushed the book forward. Maggie Taft stepped in with editorial support when I needed it most. Rebecca Wrenn drew the maps, Kristina Poznan completed the index, and Alexis Hills and Joanna Hejl were skillful research assistants at the end of the process.

Many people kindly gave their time to help me improve this work in its multiple iterations. Peter Wirzbicki agreed to read the manuscript cover to cover, perhaps before he understood how long it was. Mairin Odle has been my intellectual sounding board for the past decade. Finishing this book would have been much more difficult without her clear-eyed comments on various chapters. Drew Cayton, Nicholas Guyatt, Rob Harper, Adam Lewis, James Merrell, Chris Parsons, Dan Richter, and Cameron Strang provided important feedback on manuscript chapters that changed how I imagined the project's bounds. Eleventh-hour comments and sources from Justin Leroy, Alex Manevitz, Max Mishler, Robert Paulett, and Doug Winiarski strengthened my arguments and gave me the confidence to forge ahead.

More people than I can easily name on these pages have offered suggestions or comments on chapters at one point or another. I have benefitted from feedback on pieces of the book from the scholars who attended New York University's Atlantic Workshop, the Brown Bag Series at the McNeil Center for Early American Studies, the American Origins Dissertation Workshop at USC Dornsife, the Newberry Library Seminar, Brown University's Nineteenth Century U.S. History Workshop, the Yale Gilder Lehrman Center's Brown Bag Lecture Series, the Fred W. Smith National Library for the Study of George Washington brown bag series, the University of Virginia Early America Seminar, the Omohundro Institute Colloquium, and the Triangle Early American History Seminar. For their thoughts, conversation, and collegiality at various venues, thank you especially to Sari Altschuler, Richard Bell, Krysten Blackstone, Christopher Bonner, Mark Boonshoft, Lori Daggar, Samuel Davis, Michael Dickinson, Carolyn Eastman, Andrew Fagal, Hannah Farber, Sarah Gronningsater, Scott Heerman, Craig Hollander, Natalie Joy, Adam Malka, Elspeth Martini, Kate Masur, Michael McDonnell, Johann Neem, Brooke Newman, Kristin O'Brassill-Kulfan, K-Sue Park, Paul Polgar, Sarah Schuetze, Danielle Skeehan, Steve Smith, Matthew Spooner, Evan Taparata, and Nicholas Wood. Alda Benjamen, Tamika Galanis, Katrin Horn, Tori Langland, Lev Weitz, and Duncan Yoon kept me company at the John W. Kluge Center while I finished the manuscript.

At the University of Richmond, my colleagues have welcomed me into the Department of History. Thank you especially to Hugh West, Carol Summers, and Joanna Drell for their support and for encouraging me to take leave to work on this project. My thanks also to Terri Halperin, Sydney Watts, Nicole Sackley, Eric Yellin, Tze Loo, Manuella Meyer, David Brandenberger, Yucel Yanikdag, Chris Bischof, Michelle Kahn, Bob Kenzer, John Treadway, and Debbie Govoruhk for their kindness.

The generosity of several institutions made it possible for me to develop this book over the past ten years. The John W. Kluge Center at the Library of Congress, the Newberry Library, and the Gilder Lehrman Center for the Study of Slavery, Resistance, and Abolition at Yale University provided sabbatical support. Funding from the McNeil Center for Early American Studies and New York University gave me time to formulate the project at its beginnings. Short term grants from the University of Richmond, the Fred W. Smith National Library for the Study of George Washington, the

Huntington Library, the Newberry Library, the David Library of the American Revolution, the Virginia Museum of History and Culture, and the William L. Clements Library made this a better book.

My thanks especially to the people who make these libraries and institutions productive places to work. Dan Richter, Amy Baxter-Bellamy, Barbara Natello, Meg McSweeney, Kathy Ludwig, Brian Dunnigan, Jayne Ptolemy, Brad Hunt, Daniel Greene, David Blight, Michelle Zacks, Thomas Thurston, Melissa McGrath, and Samantha Snyder were kind and welcoming. Closer to home, Lynda Kachurek, Sam Schuth, and Jalesa Taylor kept me in books at the Boatwright Memorial Library. The staffs of the Library of Virginia, the Historical Society of Pennsylvania, the Delaware State Archives, the Library of Congress, and the Detroit Public Library made my visits there particularly fruitful.

A multitude of people have had nothing to do with this book, and I am grateful to them for that. To my dearest friends from our time in Massachusetts, Rhode Island, New York, and now Virginia: Our brush with mobility has sent us to live in all corners of the United States and beyond. No matter where we are, our phone calls, group chats, woods walks, and Chicago meet-ups have been the best distraction from this book. Thank you also to my two extended families for giving me a sense of place in the world. Our family cheerleaders Bill, Liz, and Nancy were some of the only people to voluntarily read this project when it was a dissertation. The Gilliland-Lawlers gave me a home away from home while I worked on this project in graduate school. Chris, Kathi, Hillary, Ross, Miles, Cora, and Greg are the best adopted family I could imagine. Thank you for always siding with me.

To Susan and George, my only regret about writing this book is that I missed time with you to do it. Thank you for encouraging my early attempts at authorship and for supporting me in the pursuit of this career, even when it took me away from home. I am proud to come from a family of teachers. Shastin brings such energy to her classroom, and Scott, Ben, and Reid are the only people who can match her enthusiasm and spirit. Guy arrived as I was finishing this book. That he is already reaching out to crumple up these pages as I edit them is a sign that it is time to bring it to a close. Geoff, you have made our partnership joyful. Thank you for traveling with me to places you wanted to go to and some you did not. I have loved each of our new homes because you were there with me. I am grateful for your banter and for your brilliant thoughts about the world we have inherited and the one we are creating. This book is for you.

INDEX